D0421039

How to access the supplemental online student resource

We are pleased to provide access to an online student resource that supplements your textbook, *Recreation, Event, and Tourism Businesses*. This resource includes business plan worksheets, learning activities, references, Web links, and additional information that you can use to further explore the ideas in the text. We are certain that these online resources will enhance your learning experience.

Accessing the online student resource is easy! Simply follow these steps:

1. Using your Web browser, go to the **Recreation, Event, and Tourism Businesses** product Web site at **www.HumanKinetics.com/ RecreationEventAndTourismBusinesses**.

2. Click on the **View Student Resources** button on the right side of the home page.

3. Click on the please register now link. You will create your personal profile and password at this time.

4. Write your e-mail and password down for future reference. Keep it in a safe place.

5. Once you are registered, enter the key code exactly as it is printed at the right, including all hyphens. Click **Submit**

6. Once the key code has been submitted, you will see a welcome screen. Click the **Continue** button to open your online student resource.

7. After you enter the key code the first time, you will not need to use it again to access the student resource. In the future, simply log in using your e-mail and the password you created.

For technical support, send an e-mail to:
support@hkusa.com . . . . U.S. and international customers
info@hkcanada.com . . . . Canadian customers
academic@hkeurope.com . . . . European customers
keycodesupport@hkaustralia.com . . . . Australian customers

HUMAN KINETICS
The Information Leader in Physical Activity

Product: Recreation, Event, and Tourism Business online student resource

Key code: PFISTER-8SH8QBUV-97807360063531

This unique code allows you access to the online student resource

Access is provided if you have purchased a new book. Once submitted, the code may not be entered for any other user.

Recreation, Event, and Tourism Businesses

Sta   ple

Library of Congress Cataloging-in-Publication Data

Pfister, Robert E.
  Recreation, event, and tourism businesses / Robert E. Pfister, Patrick T. Tierney.
      p. cm.
  Includes bibliographical references and index.
  ISBN-13: 978-0-7360-6353-1 (soft cover)
  ISBN-10: 0-7360-6353-6 (soft cover)
  1. Recreation industry--Management. 2. Tourism--Management. I. Tierney, Patrick T. II. Title.
  GV188.P45 2008
  790.06'9--dc22

2008020317

ISBN-10: 0-7360-6353-6
ISBN-13: 978-0-7360-6353-1

The Web addresses cited in this text were current as of July 1, 2008, unless otherwise noted.

Acquisitions Editor: Gayle Kassing, PhD; **Developmental Editor:** Melissa Feld; **Assistant Editors:** Bethany J. Bentley, Martha Gullo, and Anne Rumery; **Copyeditor:** Patricia L. MacDonald; **Proofreader:** Sarah Wiseman; **Indexer:** Betty Frizzéll; **Permission Manager:** Martha Gullo; **Graphic Designer:** Joe Buck; **Graphic Artist:** Dawn Sills; **Cover Designer**: Keith Blomberg; **Photographers (cover):** (clockwise from top right) Eyewired, courtesy of Giants Enterprises/Edgar Lee (Green Day concert), and Robb Kendrick/Aurora Photos; **Photo Asset Manager:** Laura Fitch; **Photo Office Assistant:** Jason Allen; **Art Manager:** Kelly Hendren; **Associate Art Manager:** Alan L. Wilborn; **Illustrator:** Lineworks, Inc.; **Printer:** Versa Press

Printed in the United States of America   10 9 8 7 6 5 4 3 2 1

Human Kinetics
Web site: www.HumanKinetics.com

United States: Human Kinetics
P.O. Box 5076
Champaign, IL 61825-5076
800-747-4457
e-mail: humank@hkusa.com

Canada: Human Kinetics
475 Devonshire Road Unit 100
Windsor, ON N8Y 2L5
800-465-7301 (in Canada only)
e-mail: info@hkcanada.com

Europe: Human Kinetics
107 Bradford Road
Stanningley
Leeds LS28 6AT, United Kingdom
+44 (0) 113 255 5665
e-mail: hk@hkeurope.com

Australia: Human Kinetics
57A Price Avenue
Lower Mitcham, South Australia 5062
08 8372 0999
e-mail: info@hkaustralia.com

New Zealand: Human Kinetics
Division of Sports Distributors NZ Ltd.
P.O. Box 300 226 Albany
North Shore City
Auckland
0064 9 448 1207
e-mail: info@humankinetics.co.nz

Contents

Preface

As both commercial recreation business owners and professors, we believe there is a need for a more comprehensive, advanced textbook on commercial recreation, event, and tourism businesses; how this industry works; and how companies in it are started, operated, and managed. Sales and participation in recreation, event, and tourism (RET) activities are booming, and according to the World Tourism Organization, tourist arrivals worldwide are expected to grow 20 percent in the next five years, and outdoor recreation continues to be enormously popular in the United States, with 97 percent of Americans participating. The U.S. Bureau of Labor Statistics projects that by 2016, jobs in the arts, entertainment, and recreation section will expand at three times the rate of the overall economy, and event and conference planning and management will expand at twice the rate. There are similar projections in Canada. However, students and professors interested in this growing industry have been limited to general business or basic commercial recreation texts.

We have written *Recreation, Event, and Tourism Businesses* to meet this need by focusing on small and medium enterprises (SMEs) from both entrepreneurial and operations management perspectives. SMEs are providing the fastest job growth in the U.S. and Canadian economies and make up the majority of RET companies. This book is designed to provide a comprehensive overview of the industry; offer new insights for current practitioners; and prepare students for a successful career in the dynamic recreation, event, and tourism industry. We strive to make this book serve two broad purposes. First, it is a practical guide to the start-up of RET enterprises and the writing of a business plan, with clear directions, many sample businesses, and needed forms. Numerous profiles and case studies of exemplary RET businesses give insights into how these organizations were planned, started, and funded. The second broad purpose is to be a source for modern theories and practical management applications tailored to the RET industry. Examples of four domains of particular relevance in the RET industry are leadership, service, risk management, and environmental management, and they are thoroughly discussed in this text. Special "tech application" sections describe current and future program and management applications that are or will be used in the RET industry. The RET industry is global in nature; thus we offer case studies that focus on the United States and Canada but also include China and Costa Rica. So in this book, the related student Web site, and the instructor guide, we provide detailed models, principles, methods, and global company profiles that highlight the unique operational aspects of the RET industry.

Sustainable operations are required of every business. This traditionally has meant just the ability to generate sufficient profit to propel long-term growth. Profitability still is the primary measure of business success, and this book provides detailed planning and management principles and practices to foster it. However, there is a growing international trend toward measuring business success not only by profit but also by steps the business takes to minimize its impacts on the environment and by the degree it helps the local community and society. This book builds and elaborates on this important movement by providing extensive discussion, case studies, and "green tips" to help RET businesses move toward a triple bottom line perspective and sustainable operations.

TEXTBOOK GOALS

The goals of this text are to

- prepare students for success in the recreation, event, and tourism industry by providing foundation and advanced knowledge in a comprehensive, lively, and captivating way that enhances the learning process;
- provide persons currently working in the RET industry with insights into advanced management and marketing strategies, techniques, and technical applications;

- help students learn about the diverse opportunities in the RET industry and how they can find fulfilling employment in a current organization or start their own company;
- describe the steps and methods for developing a business plan for an RET start-up;
- provide a student-oriented textbook and helpful package for instructors; and
- help the industry move forward toward a more-sustainable, environmentally friendly, and socially responsible future.

ORGANIZATION

The text has 13 chapters organized into four sections:

- **Part I Preparation:** RET overview, opportunities, and start-up planning process
- **Part II Planning Basics:** Business concept, profit centers, market analysis, and marketing
- **Part III Management Principles and Practices:** Leadership, human resources, service quality, sustainability, and environmental and risk management
- **Part IV Pulling the Plan Together:** Financial analysis and planning, implementing the business plan, and preparing for an RET career

SPECIAL FEATURES

Contained within the text and online student resource are special features that offer examples and illustrations of the concepts, techniques, and strategies presented in the text. Here is a listing of these special features:

- **Spotlight On:** Brief snapshots of RET businesses, including company background, products and services offered, and business advice

and plans, or successful entrepreneurs with their personal background and motives for starting the business. These are found throughout the chapters.
- **Case Studies:** Detailed analysis of an RET business, with discussions on start-up, services provided, marketing, revenues and costs, management challenges, and future plans. These are presented in the online student resource.
- **Tech Applications:** Descriptions of specialized technology and its application to the RET industry. This feature is often found adjacent to a technology discussion in the body of the chapter.
- **Green Tips:** Guides and examples of ways to make your business more environmentally friendly and sustainable.

ADDITIONAL STUDENT RESOURCES

A valuable source of information for students is the online student resource. Here students can find business plan worksheets, additional references, Web site links, student activities, and supplemental materials on the textbook's Web site, located at www.HumanKinetics.com/RecreationEventandTourismBusinesses.

This logo ⟨⟩ has been placed at locations in the textbook where additional helpful materials are available on the online student resource.

MATERIALS FOR INSTRUCTORS

A test package, presentation package, and instructor guide are available to instructors who adopt this book. Available at www.HumanKinetics.com/RecreationEventandTourismBusinesses.

Acknowledgments

The authors wish to acknowledge the efforts of Gayle Kassing, who encouraged and supported the writing of this new text. Melissa Feld truly deserves credit for her consistent attention to the details in all stages of development of the text and ancillaries. We wish to thank Lori Pennington-Gray for her thoughtful review of the draft document and the valuable suggestions she made for improvements. In addition, we are especially grateful for the entrepreneurs and business owners who agreed to share their personal experiences and successes in the special features which are found in the Spotlight On and Case Study sections.

Finally, we reserve special recognition to our spouses, Jeanne and Robin, who provided moral and practical support in numerous ways over an extended period of time. Their support created the atmosphere and home environment that permitted this creative endeavor to succeed among the other activities demanding attention. Thanks to Eric and Ian, whose joy of life is contagious.

Part

I

Preparation

Chapter 1

Your Commercial Recreation, Event, and Tourism Business Adventure

Learning Objectives

After reading this chapter you will be able to

- discuss how goods, services, and experiences are created and consumed as the result of decisions by the service provider and the consumer;
- identify and examine stages of the recreation or tourism experience from the point of view of the consumer;
- evaluate alternative conceptual frameworks for describing the various sectors of the recreation, event, and tourism industry;
- describe the role the commercial sector performs in the recreation, event, and tourism industry and its importance in terms of the global economy;
- apply models and typologies for classifying types of commercial recreation businesses and the range of services they provide within the RET industry; and
- describe the benefits a person finds when starting a business and why young professionals are so often attracted to the recreation, event, and tourism industry.

Key Terms

business typology

capability–commitment matrix

commercial sector

consumer experience model

consumer perspective

destination marketing organizations

event industry

nonprofit sector

on-site experience

public sector

RET business

RET industry model

service provider

service provider model

small and medium enterprises (SMEs)

supply–demand framework

tourism-recreation model

Imagine this scenario:

It's a warm Saturday during the spring softball season, so you and your friends head to the stadium to watch your favorite team play. You buy a program, get something to eat, and stop off at a pub before returning home after having a terrific time. The following weekend, you are attracted to the Atlantic coast and travel to the Outer Banks for a hang-glider lesson. You camp at a park, and in the evening, you attend a theater performance about the notorious pirate Blackbeard. Back home on Sunday evening and in your favorite chair, you reflect on another great leisure experience. The next week you attend a conference in Boston with several people from work, and besides the education sessions you are able to enjoy leisure activities before, during, and after the conference—including a show, a reception and interactive games at a museum, a dinner cruise around the harbor, and a short visit to the mountains—all as part of the conference package. Later in the month, you plan for an entire week-long holiday to Anaheim, California, as part of a great travel package that includes a Disneyland pass; a tour of Page Museum at the La Brea Tar Pits; and two days at the local beaches to enjoy the sun, surf, and water sports. As it turns out, your leisure-time choices prove to be lots of fun and result in special memories that will bring a smile for a long time as you recall the experiences with your friends. Later in the summer, your new Canadian friend sends you tourism marketing literature highlighting fun activities on Vancouver Island in British Columbia, with an invitation to join him. It involves the week-long Pacific Rim Whale Festival in Tofino, a native heritage center in Cowichan; the proposed package is highlighted by a whale-watching cruise off the coast of Victoria. You decide to accept this invitation because it is a special and thoughtful itinerary. So you pack your bags and head out for yet another memorable experience.

The basic question is *who* made it possible for you and your friends to share such a variety of recreation, event, and tourism (RET) experiences, and what was it they did? As you cast your eyes across the landscape of those people providing services to you (i.e., service providers), which of them are commercial operations, and which are something else? Without a doubt, it takes a mixture of service providers in order for each of us to engage in leisure experiences on any particular day or while traveling to distant locations while on vacation. So if asked to sort it out, can you identify which of the service providers should be categorized as public, nonprofit, or commercial? What criteria are used today to place a service provider in the commercial category? What are the basic differences between these three sectors?

An equally important question in the scenario relates to the decisions you made and the fact that those memorable experiences were, in a large part, carefully planned and managed by the service providers and not accidental. You searched in advance for these services, made plans (e.g., made reservations, bought tickets), and acted on these plans as a consumer. The result of your actions in concert with the service providers should be many shared memories of time well spent. Taking a close look at consumers and the choices they make reveals the link between specific decisions made before, during, and after they engage in a leisure activity or experience. The agencies, organizations, and businesses—referred to as the recreation, event, and tourism industry (more on this later)—that contributed to the opportunity for you and your friends to rendezvous somewhere and enjoy some quality time together need to be recognized. Chapter 1 explores answers to the preceding questions from several vantage points. There are alternative perspectives, or points of view, as to what it is that drives the recreation, event, and tourism economy. Although the following pages recognize all service providers involved in producing memorable experiences, specific attention is paid to the commercial sector because many small and medium commercial businesses are key contributors to the recreation, event, and tourism industry. Because the industry is dominated by these less visible **small and medium enterprises (SMEs)**, they are the primary focus of the entire book.

Although the beginning chapter describes where you as a consumer fit into the processes of the marketplace, the goal of the book is to carefully document in great detail how a person or team can start up and operate an SME in the RET industry. We explore core elements of organizing and managing a business but also pay particular attention to aspects that are especially important to the RET industry, such as quality service, environmental management, and risk management. But let's begin at this point by looking at you as the consumer and the expectations you may place on the service providers that make up the RET industry.

CONSUMER PERSPECTIVE

When you closely examine specific decisions you make to bring you, your friends, and special places together during your free time, ask yourself if there is anything your decisions have in common. One element could be that a set of decisions led to actions, and these actions in turn resulted in good times and memorable experiences. However, there are other common elements of the leisure experiences in the opening scenario, and they might include

- recognition that you wanted to do something and the anticipation of what you planned to do;

- travel to and from a desired location where you carried out your intentions;

- engagement in one or more recreation, event, and tourism experiences; and

- finally, reflection on the memories of the experience after returning home.

The description of a leisure or travel experience represents a combination of specific decisions and actions initiated by the consumer, and what these have in common can fit into a consumer experience model. This type of model looks at a sequence of decisions associated with consumer behavior.

CONSUMER EXPERIENCE MODEL

The **consumer experience model** displayed in figure 1.1 sets out five separate steps or actions that when taken collectively represents a leisure or travel experience. Decades ago, Clawson and Knetch (1966) sought to describe each of the stages as a means of describing the creation of an "experience." Today it can be considered a central component to what recreation, event, and tourism businesses provide to the consumer. Before this time, most writers treated only the on-site component of the experience as the relevant element deserving of close attention. The five dimensions are as follows:

- *Anticipation*: The first dimension of the experience begins with anticipation, or the planning for the activity. You begin to think about what you would like to do with your free time, ponder the choices, and then decide to do something.

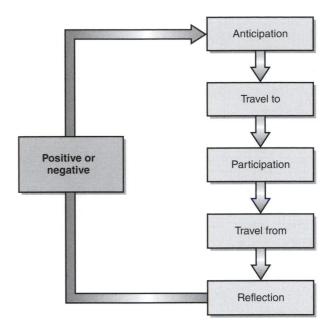

Figure 1.1 Stages of the consumer experience model.
Adapted from M. Clawson and J.L. Knetch, 1967, *Economics of outdoor recreation* (Baltimore: Johns Hopkins University Press), 33-36.

- *Travel to:* The second phase is the actual travel to the location where the experience can be realized. Whether a short walk or a long ride, there is the need to leave your home and then engage in the experience.

- *On-site experience:* The **on-site experience** (what Clawson and Knetch call *participation*) is a major phase of the total recreation experience, but this "third phase may be less than half of the total, whether measured by time involved, expense incurred, or total satisfaction gained" (p. 34). It can be said that regardless of how long, the value added to the experience at this stage might very well determine the value of the entire experience.

- *Travel from:* The fourth phase recognizes that the trip back will not likely be the same as the trip to the site. "If travel is back from a vacation, memories of the vacation and anticipation of the job are certainly different from the thoughts on the outbound trip" (p. 34).

- *Reflection:* The experience you sought and participated in is now over, but the memories remain. Your degree of satisfaction with the overall product, as you reflect upon the quality of it can be influenced by whether or not the RET business has remained in contact with you upon your return home. This contact by the RET business can very well determine whether or not a return visit is likely. Your memory of the actual experience can change over time as you selectively reflect on important elements of the experience that either exceeded or fell short of your expectation. The aspect of customer satisfaction is what a business needs to clearly understand and is addressed in depth in chapter 8.

Future business owners can reflect on any one of the different stages of decision making displayed in figure 1.1 and then pose several questions with reference to the five different experiences. What occurs in the mind of the customer at each stage? What role is played by various service providers involved with the one-day, weekend, and week-long experiences? What action can a commercial enterprise take to ensure the customer reflects positively on the experience and is likely to return at some future date? The amount of time involved in moving through each of the five stages is an important consideration in this model because it can be very short in the case of an afternoon softball experience or considerably longer for a one-week vacation.

SERVICE PROVIDER PERSPECTIVE

When you reflect on the five leisure experiences in the opening scenario, you'll see that a variety of service providers added value to each leisure experience. A **service provider** is any organization or business that provides goods or services for those seeking leisure experiences. Some were large organizations or corporations, and others were small businesses. However, each can be placed into one of three categories—public, nonprofit, or commercial—and together they produced parts of the experience enjoyed by you, the consumer. The task is to identify where the various contributors to the experience best fit among the three categories and how they interact.

So, what did the *public agency* provide? There was a facility (i.e., the baseball stadium) for the game to be played in; a public place for hang gliding at Jockey's Ridge State Park on the trip to the Atlantic coast; and, for the tour to the Los Angeles area, you had a choice of more than 15 public beaches along the California coast between San Onofre and Malibu for sun, surf, and water sports. The *nonprofit sector* would include a nonprofit sports booster club that raises money in

support of athletic programs (e.g., your softball team) and probably both printed and sold the program you purchased at the stadium. A nonprofit society sponsored and organized the theatrical production about Blackbeard (e.g., local volunteer-based theater company), and a nonprofit organization operated the Page Museum at the La Brea Tar Pits attraction (e.g., nonprofit membership-based foundation). The convention was held at the Boston Convention and Exhibition Center, which is owned and managed by the nonprofit Massachusetts Convention Center Authority. A nonprofit stakeholder society serves as a destination marketing organization (e.g., Tourism Vancouver Island) to distribute the "lure publications" (brochures and literature) to travelers which showcases the special features of the island as well as the business operators' products and services.

The *commercial sector* includes diverse enterprises or businesses of all sizes. Your experience benefited from the small enterprise holding the concessionaire contract for food services at the stadium when you watched softball, as well as the business owner that operated the sports pub visited after the game. Other commercial operations include the hang-gliding business that offered lessons and rented the equipment for you to enjoy your trip to the Outer Banks of North Carolina; the adventure tourism operator taking you offshore on a whale-watching trip; and a conference and event planning company that planned and managed the convention activities. The displays, rides, and performances enjoyed at Disneyland were provided by the Walt Disney Company—a multinational entertainment corporation renowned worldwide for its theme parks and tourism training programs. Another event planning company developed the festival program for the Pacific Rim Whale Festival, and that company contracted with a number of entertainment, recreation, and rental businesses to execute the week-long event.

SERVICE PROVIDER MODEL

In a parallel fashion to the decision making of the consumer, the service providers in the scenario also carry out a set of decisions to ensure that a range of goods and services are available to the people they serve. The basic functions that define the components of the **service provider model** involve the following:

- *Planning* that goes into assessment of demand and the creation of value-added products and programs (e.g., goods and services) for the consumer
- *Marketing* of the products, goods, services, and programs
- *Delivery* of the goods and services in a timely manner to the market
- *Monitoring* of the results once the consumer has purchased the goods or services

All service providers performing the above-noted functions have an interest in consumer satisfaction information in one form or another. The services they provide are valued by the customer to the degree they meet the consumers' expectations. This topic of consumer satisfaction will be examined in chapter 8, where the success factors related to customer loyalty

and quality service are covered in detail. In figure 1.2, two separate decision-making processes are displayed. The first process is the consumer experience model from figure 1.1, and the second process is the four functions carried out by service providers as noted in the preceding paragraph. Combining the two independent processes permits us to visually integrate images of separate decision processes and place them into the "big picture" that illustrates the production and consumption of goods and services. This interaction leads to purchases and an economic transaction between the provider and the consumer.

Seeing the RET industry from the perspective of the agency, organization, or enterprise offering products represents a general overview of a process that is followed by the two parties involved in the exchange. To understand the differences among the diverse service providers playing a role in one of three sectors,

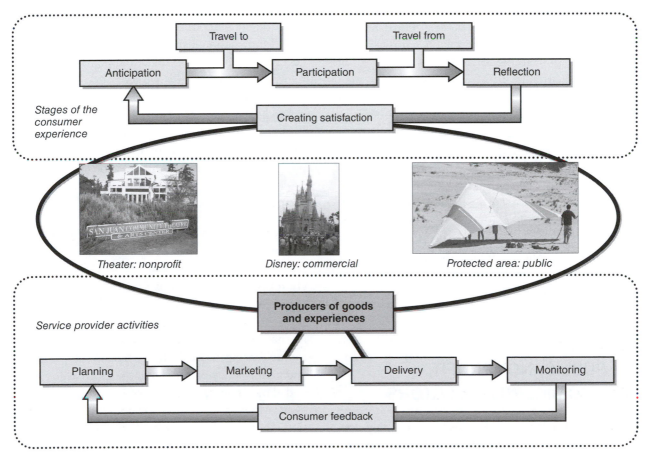

Figure 1.2 Synthesis of the consumer and service provider perspectives applied to the opening scenario.
Photos left to right: J.S. Pfister, Stephen Davies, and iStockphoto/Jill Lang

you might consider the manner by which they obtain funds to deliver their services. For example,

- public sector services rely heavily on tax revenue,
- nonprofit services rely on fees and charges obtained from their members and foundation grants, and
- commercial service providers depend on the sale of their goods and services to customers based on a fair market price.

The commercial sector remains a dynamic element in the economy, and it has expanded noticeably in recent times. Although it has not been a drastic shift, commercialization of leisure services has been a prevalent and significant pattern in many countries. Roberts (2004) points out that commercialization of leisure services " . . . is certainly a powerful trend. It developed throughout the twentieth century and it is continuing" (p. 9), often assisted by government policies reflecting the philosophy of the political right. This shift has been observed in Great Britain, Canada, and the United States. Of course, strong sentiments can be found for and against the trend of commercialization in the leisure field; however, such criticisms are ill founded. Commercial leisure services have been around a long time, and the growth of such services has not eliminated any of the offerings of the nonprofit or public sector alternatives. Roberts (2004) observes that the service provider in the commercial sector occupies a specific niche and does not have a direct impact on either the nonprofit or public service providers unless either of those service providers chooses not to deliver desired services. It appears there are important distinctions between the type of providers involved exclusively in leisure services and those involved in tourism services. These differences will be examined next.

SNAPSHOT OF PUBLIC, NONPROFIT, AND COMMERCIAL SECTORS

A three-sector framework allows us to apply and expand on criteria for describing the sectors and to further examine the type of functions they perform. The public and nonprofit sectors often appear differ-

ent depending on whether or not their primary focus is on leisure-oriented or tourism-oriented services. Some examples of the difference are depicted in table 1.1.

Public Service Providers

Land and water management agencies that have recreation mandates and that operate parks, recreation sites, and historic areas at the county, regional, or national level are important in the **public sector**. The parks, recreation and heritage sites, multiplex facilities, and public gardens serve as major tourist attractions and concurrently add to the quality of life of local residents. For these dual-purpose organizations, attendance at the parks or recreation areas is measured in terms of visitor days. Thus, there is a tendency not to differentiate between leisure and tourist markets in terms of their customer base.

Because they are tax supported, the community leisure services departments are definitely focused on local citizens. Community visitor and convention organizations are indirectly tax supported and perform roles in marketing the community as a destination. Many national agencies and state or provincial government offices also make public funds available to others in order to advance economic development initiatives and meet the workforce needs of the tourism industry. Public land management and regulatory agencies oversee organizations under their jurisdiction through regulations and permits (see chapter 2) for public safety and environmental protection.

Nonprofit Service Providers

There is a tendency for some types of nonprofit organizations to be more involved with local recreation services than with tourism services. For example, churches and civic groups are more likely to offer leisure services in the form of youth programs and summer camps and are not oriented to participate in the type of services prevalent in the **nonprofit sector** serving tourists. By contrast, entertainment and performance-oriented organizations (e.g., theater and dance companies), professional tourism trade associations, and destination marketing organizations are more likely to be evident in the commercial enterprise sector. In terms of tax code, these nonprofit organizations commonly enjoy the benefit of reduced tax liability, which is not the case for commercial

Table 1.1   Commercial Enterprise: A Common Component of the Leisure and Tourism Industry

Components of the Leisure Industry		
Public sector	**Nonprofit sector**	**Commercial enterprises**
Recreation and park programs Special park districts County parks and facilities Open spaces and public gardens	YMCA/YWCA Boys and Girls Clubs Campus recreation services Volunteer sport associations Hobby clubs, pet shows	Entertainment business Adventure and ecotourism guides Travel agencies and tour operators Restaurants, cafes, and pubs Fitness, health, and sports clubs Retail recreation equipment Resorts and time-share condos Coaches and rail travel Cruise ships and airlines Bed-and-breakfasts Sport and hunting camps Event, party, and gift services Equipment manufacturing
Components of the Tourism Industry		
Public sector	**Nonprofit sector**	**Commercial enterprises**
National tourism office State–provincial tourism agencies City convention and visitors bureaus Sports stadiums and multiplexes	Theater companies Music and arts celebrations Special events, craft fairs Tournament of Roses	Entertainment business Adventure and ecotourism guides Travel agencies and tour operators Restaurants, cafes, and pubs Fitness, health, and sports clubs Retail recreation equipment Resorts and time-share condos Coaches and rail travel Cruise ships and airlines Bed-and-breakfasts Sport and hunting camps Event, party, and gift services Equipment manufacturing

operations in the tourism industry. The **destination marketing organizations (DMO)** in Canada or convention and visitor bureaus (CVB) in the United States serve their members by promoting area attractions along with the services and products of tourism businesses seeking to serve domestic and international tourists.

Nonprofit service providers will generally pursue only those activities they were constituted to promote (e.g., YMCA, Boys and Girls Clubs). These activities or functions may include youth development, sports and athletics, leisure benefits for senior citizens, or attracting tourists. Often, they deliver services to their members. The scope of activities engaged in by nonprofit organizations is guided by their mission and is specifically identified in the bylaws of their association or society. An association or society may promote the interests of tourism professionals (e.g., Association of Tourism Professionals) and mobilize volunteers to sponsor celebrations or other special events. Associations and societies tend to be very important in the area of performing arts, heritage preservation, and historical reenactments. When a convention and visitors bureau attracts visitors, it directly benefits all the tourist-serving organizations in the region, which indirectly benefits all residents of the area.

Ron Koeberer/Aurora Photos

J.S. Pfister

Public facilities, such as a swimming pool or ice arena, provide recreational opportunities by revenues commonly raised by resident property taxes.

Commercial Service Providers

The **commercial sector** may serve local customers or tourists. Whether or not a commercial enterprise puts more emphasis on serving one or the other relates to the marketing strategy contained in the business plan, which is prepared to ensure profitability. However, the commercial sector differs from public and nonprofit organizations in at least five ways. The distinguishing characteristics include pricing of services, packaging of products, ability to be sold, responsiveness to market opportunities, and seasonality. See table 1.2 for a comparison.

• *Pricing of services:* Commercial operations need to price their goods and services competitively for their target markets. Yet, the domestic consumer (e.g., resident of the country) and international customer (e.g., inbound travel from another country) can purchase the identical product for the same price. Most public agencies are largely based on local taxes and have to consider surcharges for patrons that would like to participate in their programs but do not pay taxes to the community or taxing district because they are not residents. Although public facilities and programs can be very important assets for residents and tourists, elected officials will expect leisure service providers to have policies in place to ensure cost recovery when nonresidents of the community enroll in programs or when tax-supported facilities are used for commercial purposes.

• *Packaging of products:* Commercial operations may choose to work with other commercial operators to creatively combine goods and services, resulting in an attractive travel package that can be sold by a travel agency and the businesses that created the package. Public and nonprofit organizations are not usually inclined or experienced in creating leisure program packages that involve multiple public agencies.

• *Ability to buy or sell:* Commercial sector enterprises can be created, bought, and sold in the marketplace. Businesses have a reputation, financial records, and a customer base that allow the owners to establish a market value and sell the business when it suits their goals. Nonprofits have restrictive charters, whereas the public sector has boards or commissions that govern their actions. The option of buying or selling a public or nonprofit organization is contrary to its mandate.

• *Responsiveness to market changes:* Commercial recreation can, and often must, respond quickly to

Human Kinetics

A YMCA is an example of a nonprofit service provider in the leisure industry.

Table 1.2   Comparison of Service Sectors Based on Five Characteristics

	Commercial	Public sector	Nonprofit
Pricing of services	Single competitive price	Based on resident fees	Limited to members
Tour packaging	Commonplace	Rarely undertaken	Done for members
Can be sold	Yes	No	No
Ability to quickly respond to changes in the market	High capability	Limited capability	Some capability
Seasonal products or programs	Outdoor operators shift between geographic regions	If facility based, programs often change	Shift based upon member preferences

changes in customer preferences. If a business needs to create products to capture a new market, then it will be necessary to quickly hire the specialists needed to deliver a new product. Responsiveness is an important attribute of commercial service providers and less so for other service providers in the other sectors.

• *Seasonality:* Commercial recreation may choose to be largely seasonal operations, particularly if located in regions with distinct seasons. Ski resorts are seasonal operations dependent on snowfall; a white-water rafting operation may be dependent on changes in water flow. The cyclical nature of fish migration, or simply favorable weather, can create seasonal patterns for sport fishing guides. Event businesses are also very seasonal because of holidays, sports seasons, and the heavy-use periods in the scheduling of conferences.

The nature and attributes of the commercial sector are even more differentiated as we look at a variety of recreation, event, and tourism (RET) businesses in the context of their services to the consumer. The creation of a new RET acronym reflects the adoption of the North American Industry Classification System (NAICS) of 2002, which represents a new statistical structure jointly adopted by the United States, Canada, and Mexico to provide consistent, comparable information on an industry-by-industry basis for all three economies. In that statistical structure, NAICS 71 refers to the arts, entertainment, and recreation economic sector as an integrated data set produced from national census enumerations. The category (NAICS 71) covers all establishments primarily engaged in operating facilities or providing

J.S. Pfister

Commercial operations succeed by setting a fair market price that is acceptable to its target market.

services to meet the cultural, entertainment, and recreational interests of their customers whether they serve domestic or tourist markets. This refers to establishments that

- produce, promote, or participate in live performances, events, or exhibits intended for public viewing;

- provide the artistic, creative, and technical skills necessary for the production of artistic products and live performances;

- preserve and exhibit objects and sites of historical, cultural, or educational interest; or

- operate facilities or provide services that enable patrons to participate in sports or recreational activities or pursue amusement, hobbies, and leisure-time interests (www.ic.gc.ca/canadian_industry_statistics/cis.nsf/IDE/cis71defe.html and www.bls.gov/oco/cg/cgnaics.htm).

Thus, the opportunity now exists to examine enterprises using standard codes applicable to three partners of the North America Free Trade Agreement (NAFTA). RET describes a diverse set of businesses responsible for a wide range of commercial leisure services in urban, rural, and even remote locations that tend to attract persons to participate in leisure or a combination of business and leisure activities and travel to new destinations. Recreation enterprises vary from providing indoor batting cages in urban areas to renting outdoor equipment in remote barrier islands off the coast. Event businesses might arrange large spectator festival events in large urban venues or small family weddings in rural communities. Small tourism businesses may offer special services to large time-share resort destinations or may offer dogsled trips in the Yukon Territory. Any new term seeking to capture the diversity of commercial activities evident today is likely to experience a slow rate of adoption if for no other reason than it is a departure from previous terminology and typologies. The following section addresses the rationale for recognizing this category of businesses and provides a description of how previous models or typologies chose to group types of businesses.

RECREATION, EVENT, AND TOURISM (RET) BUSINESSES

An **RET business** featured herein refers generally to smaller business operations (1-50 employees) that provide a set of leisure-oriented goods or services with the intent of being profitable within a reasonable period of time. This definition contains elements that deserve further comment. First, a *business operation* can be differentiated from other leisure service providers in several ways. A small commercial operation has the following characteristics:

- It is unique in the context of the legal authority and can be classified either as a sole proprietorship, a partnership, or a corporation in North America. These three ways of doing business are examined more closely in chapter 2.

- It is focused on a set of recreation, event, or tourism goods and services. The term *goods and services* is a synonym for the products sold by the commercial sector, which is examined in more detail in chapters 3 and 5.

- It is established to be profitable within a reasonable period of time. A variety of measures exist to assess the competitiveness of a business (chapter 5), and the amount of time it takes to accomplish the goal of profitability will vary based on the type of business. The financial details for achieving profitability appear in the business plan (see chapter 12) of every commercial enterprise if it is to have a chance for success.

In many ways, any effort to identify the key attributes of commercial recreation, event, and tourism is a bit like listening to the dialogue of three blind individuals attempting to describe an elephant when they are touching different parts (e.g., trunk, tusk, leg, tail) of the animal. When something is as large as an elephant, it is possible to describe particular physical features within reach, but a complete image is based on more than a few select features. So it is with commercial recreation, event, and tourism. Everyone has a perceptual environment in which to operate, see things, and imagine opportunities. It is not uncommon to have blind spots when first entering a new territory, and the subject material of this chapter may very well fit that situation. The

important aspect of any exploratory journey is to be aware of your surroundings and to recognize the value of observing the recreation, event, and tourism industry from different perspectives. Next we examine RET businesses as business types and then consider how the component parts of various sectors can be linked together in a model based on a set of functions.

EARLY MODELS OF RET BUSINESSES

Businesses can be grouped according to their functions, such as travel, entertainment, food services, and recreation products. In the past, advocates for the **business typology** approach tended to group businesses into activities such as transportation, accommodation, and entertainment functions that are important to the traveler, together with some attention to the retail function. In one such typology, businesses fit into one of four sectors (Ellis and Norton, 1988), and the second effort to group businesses requires them to fit into one of five sectors (Bullaro and Edginton, 1986). An example of these two models for labeling or creating categories for businesses is shown in table 1.3.

A close look at this approach illustrates a definite structure to the RET industry, but there is also some confusion when creating labels to describe the categories of businesses. Another area of confusion can be found in contemporary texts covering the hospitality industry in that they describe the tourism–hospitality industry but the focus in this case is the predominate importance given the hosting function (e.g., lodging and food services) as the core elements of the industry. Under the "hospitality umbrella" five categories, or sectors, are generally recognized: recreation, events, travel, lodging, and food services; however, the hospitality perspective would be inclined to focus upon lodging and food services as the drivers in the travel decisions. Figure 1.3*a* reflects the importance hospitality would give to these two sectors (e.g., lodging and food) whereas figure 1.3*b* illustrates more of the "tourism perspective" when it comes to describing the tourism–hospitality industry. The difference here is that the tourism perspective would make recreation, events, and modes of travel the core drivers of travel decisions made by a group of individuals because tourism research tends to have a long history of

Table 1.3 Typology of Business Types

Ellis and Norton (1988)	Bullaro and Edginton (1986)	Types of businesses
Tourism • Services for nonresidents	Travel and tourism • Transporting individuals to points of interest, attractions, or end destinations	Tour agency Tour guide or operator Transport agency
Local commercial recreation • Businesses that offer either outdoor or indoor programs and services	Hospitality services • Those leisure service businesses involved in housing or feeding the consumer	Hotels, motels, bed-and-breakfasts Restaurants Taverns and pubs
Retail sales • Sale of equipment, clothing, vehicles, and specialty items	Entertainment services • Those leisure services involved with spectator events, night clubs, race tracks, sports clubs, fitness centers, video arcades, and so on	Facility manager Promotions director Booking agent Sales manager
Manufacturing • Production and distribution of recreation and travel equipment	Leisure services in the natural environment • Services involved with a wide variety of adventure experiences in the out-of-doors; both water- and land-oriented products	Tour guide Instructor and host Interpreters Adventure or ecotour operator
	Retail outlet • Leisure service goods and products sold in the marketplace	Salesperson Manager Wholesaler

examining consumer motivations, destination images and preferences, together with the role of attractions (e.g., recreation and events) in the decision-making process.

MODEL FOR THE RET INDUSTRY

In an effort to synthesize earlier typologies and terms, it is timely to present an organizing concept for the recreation, event, and tourism (RET) industry so that each of the tourism trade sectors and business groupings begins to appear in a logical place. Travel is said to simply require a motive for travel, information about the opportunities, destination attractions or something to do, and a place to eat and sleep. Using this idea as an organizing principle for the model, it is possible then to examine the primary function each business, agency, or organization performs within the overall industry. Figure 1.4 shows businesses of all sizes (small and medium enterprises as well as large corporations) that represent three basic functional areas of the **RET industry model**: (1) attraction, (2)

support and facilitation, and (3) the hosting function. There are also two integrated functional groups that merge elements of the attraction, support, and hosting functions.

At the top level of the figure, attraction businesses and public sector facilities provide the motive and stimulation for travel and attract people to specific destinations. In the recreation, event, and tourism (RET) industry, attractions provide the services and products that are the reasons why people travel, and they power the demand for businesses in the other two functional areas by promising and creating memorable visitor experiences. Attraction businesses consist of three subcomponents:

- *Tourist attractions*, which primarily lure nonresident tourists. They range from natural and cultural attractions to theme parks, adventure, casinos, and shopping to seeing family and friends.
- *Event* experiences, or short-term activities that generally are not repeated often and that attract

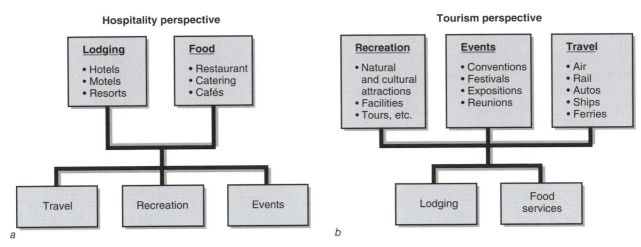

Figure 1.3 Tourism–hospitality industry typology.

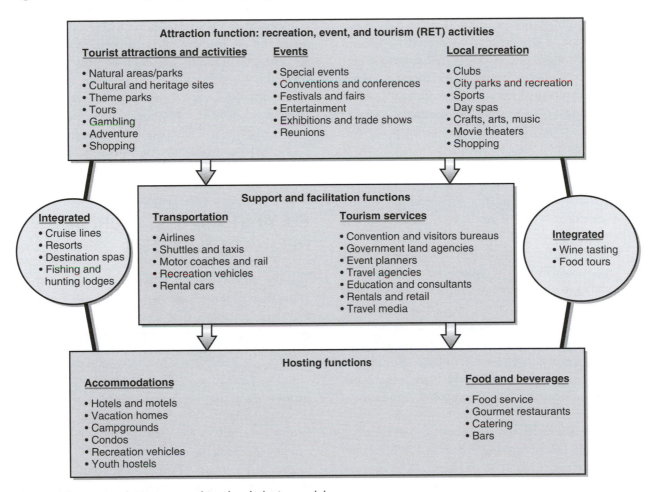

Figure 1.4 Recreation, event, and tourism industry model.

both nonresidents and visitors. They include special events, conventions and conferences, festivals, exhibitions, and reunions.

- *Local recreation*, consisting of facilities and activities that provide residents with frequently repeated leisure experiences. Examples of local

recreation organizations include clubs; city recreation departments; sports organizations; day spas; arts, craft, and music suppliers; and movie theaters.

Figure 1.4 clearly shows the importance of the RET industry because without these businesses creating the demand for travel, there would be no need for the transportation and tourism services or hospitality elements such as accommodation and food services. Length of stay at a destination is also directly related to the number and quality of attractions. The figure also shows the wide range of businesses and organizations found in the RET industry. This is a reminder that young professionals in the field have chosen a vital, essential, and valuable field to study and work within.

The support and facilitation function contains two components: transportation and tourist services. Transportation providers, such as airlines, taxis, railroads, RVs, and rental cars, deliver the tourist to the destination. Without reasonably priced and safe transportation, people would not get to the desired destination and use other elements of the system. There are countless services geared toward assisting visitors, including travel facilitators (e.g., travel agencies), convention and visitors bureaus, event planners, government land management agencies (e.g., Parks Canada), university tourism programs, research consultants, equipment rental firms, rental and retail businesses, and the travel media. Without these support services, other businesses would function less effectively, and the person might choose another destination or be less satisfied with her experience.

The hosting function consists of accommodations and food and beverage services. Overnight lodging is provided to visitors by hotels and motels, vacation homes, campgrounds, recreation vehicles, bed-and-breakfasts, and family and friends. Lodging is a basic visitor necessity, and its quality can greatly influence the visitor's experience. A variety of accommodation options are available, some of which are free (homes of friends or relatives) or low cost (hostels and campgrounds).

Food and beverage services range from restaurants, fast food, and event catering to bars and coffee shops. Like accommodations, food and beverage services are a basic necessity and vary greatly in cost and quality. They can have a large impact on visitor satisfaction. Many food and beverage businesses have an integrated function with RET by offering activities such as wine tasting, food tours, catering for events, and gourmet restaurants. Gourmet restaurants are an increasingly important element because they attract "foodies," visitors who are attracted to the destination by these

establishments and are willing to travel long distances. A wide variety of travel packages are created around wine testing tours and food experiences, such as the Taste of Chicago festival or the San Francisco Crab Festival events.

Many accommodation businesses have an integrated function with attraction and support organizations by combining lodging with elements of each at one site. Examples of integrated accommodation businesses are resorts, cruise lines, destination spas, and hunting or fishing lodges because they serve as attractions and provide accommodations and food, and some offer a wide range of tourist services.

A cruise ship is a great example of a fully integrated RET business. Clients are attracted to buy a cruise vacation because of the activities and events on board and ashore. Passengers use a variety of tourism services, stay in cabins, and eat most meals on board while the ship transports them to new destinations.

You can also use the recreation, event, and tourism model to identify and describe links within the business environment. For example, specific parts of the RET model can be reviewed separately to consider interrelationships applicable to either a tourism or event model.

ELEMENTS OF THE TOURISM-RECREATION SYSTEM

Tourism and recreation activities can be examined as a system of three basic elements—form, function, and consequences—that identify and describe the system. This **tourism-recreation model** is outlined in figure 1.5.

- The *form element* displays a **supply–demand framework** at the core of economic literature examining consumers and their purchasing activities. In this case, it is further divided into three linked components. The *demand* component is identified by the characteristics of the general population seeking opportunities or experiences to consume and participate. The *supply* component illustrates the attractions, facilities, and amenity resources that pull people to tourism destinations or desired recreation sites. The *linking* component reflects the transportation and communication infrastructure that creates the capacity to bring together the supply–demand components.

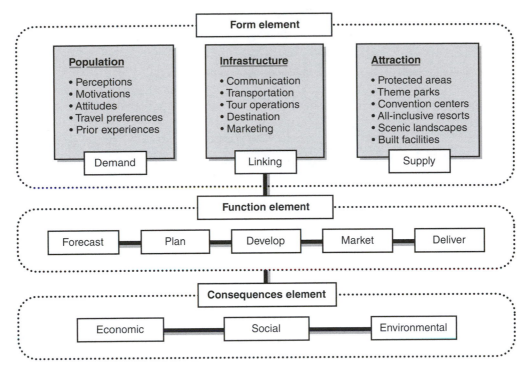

Figure 1.5 Elements of the tourism-recreation system.

• The *function element* captures the management processes—research, policy, planning, marketing, and training activities—that are carried out as part of tourism or recreation business decisions, along with their various operational practices.

• The *consequences element* refers to the economic, social, and environmental outcomes that are produced by the supply–demand components. Consumers in pursuit of their leisure interests spend money and have a direct, or indirect, impact on public resources in the course of engaging in recreation and tourism activities.

ELEMENTS OF THE EVENT INDUSTRY

The basic components of the **event industry** are displayed in figure 1.6. This industry consists of three primary components:

• *Client-side planners* that sponsor and help plan events, such as associations, corporations, and government

• *Intermediaries* that act on behalf of the client-side planners to plan the event and contract suppliers, such as independent meeting planners, destination management companies, and association management companies

• *Suppliers* that provide the basic services to make the event operate. The suppliers are split into (1) venues and facilities and (2) other suppliers, such as equipment rental, entertainment, florists, and transportation companies. Specialized occupations can be found in all three major elements of the event industry.

Now that the **consumer perspective** has been outlined and alternative approaches to examining the industry have been displayed, the final question is why you would want to pursue a career in the commercial field.

APPEAL OF RECREATION, EVENT, AND TOURISM BUSINESS OPPORTUNITIES

Perhaps the most important question to address at this point is why people get involved with this commercial sector of the economy. Without doubt, attention should be given to basic benefits that make the

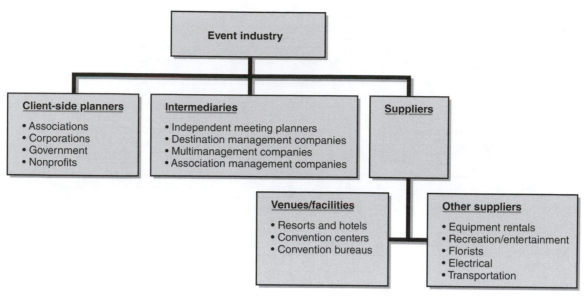

Figure 1.6 The event industry.

commercial sector so attractive to leisure, tourism, and recreation professionals of all ages. Although many professionals have probably heard or read about the National Recreation and Park Association's upbeat message that "the benefits are endless" in leisure services, it is primarily targeted to the general public. However, many business owners operating in the commercial sector have long recognized several key benefits important to professional development, industry engagement, and personal well-being.

If you explore the commercial recreation, event, and tourism (RET) industry with the aspiration of owning your own business, two benefits will likely stand out and capture your interest. First, as an independent business owner, you can tailor your work to build on your personal strengths. Essentially the opportunity exists to define your dream job: doing what you love and getting paid for it. How many career paths offer that option? In choosing an enterprise to create and operate, you can define the purpose of the enterprise and create the work setting that makes going to your business every day a pleasure. Loving what you do for a living is, at the very least, 50 percent of what is needed to achieve success. Second, regardless of being an independent businessperson, you will become part of a community of interrelated businesses that share ideas and knowledge through professional associations. You will soon discover there are many diverse and attractive characteristics of the RET business

community, and the special features make the work that much more appealing. The wide-ranging nature of the industry puts the world at your doorstep. Both of these benefits will be clarified in greater detail.

BENEFITS OF HAVING A CLEAR PATH TO SUCCESS

The key ingredients to personal satisfaction and success in earning a living today may simply be having the opportunity to focus your greatest strengths, or capabilities, on a business goal and to do it with passion. If you would like to succeed in the commercial sector of the economy, then choose a business that allows you to do what you love to do. In other fields, it is not unusual for capable people to end up employed in an organization where they are not satisfied and do not find the work fulfilling. When you are in business for yourself, having a passion for the job that needs to be performed is a real benefit, and it puts you well down the pathway to success.

Perhaps the second ingredient in this situation is ensuring that your love for the services you provide is matched by your capability to manage the business enterprise. Thus, two attributes that are cornerstones for RET business ventures are a clear personal commitment to the business purpose and a capability to do it very well. Of course, each of us often provides the first ingredient as we discover what we love to do.

As for capabilities to operate a business, the following chapters will guide you in acquiring the skills needed to operate a business of your choice. The **capability–commitment matrix** illustrates how these two ingredients come together to put a motivated person in a position to succeed as an owner of his own business.

COMBINATION OF COMMITMENT TO PURPOSE AND CAPABILITY

The two attributes most commonly associated with successful business ventures are *commitment* to the purpose of the business ("I love it") and *capability* to do it well ("my abilities match the tasks"). These two variables can be combined in four possible ways as noted in figure 1.7.

Small or medium business owners, and their employees, can follow a pathway to success if they can fit into one of the two quadrants on the right side of the matrix. These two areas are promising territory if the business is to succeed in the long run. The four quadrants can be described as follows.

High Commitment/High Capability

This is home base for the most successful RET business ventures. The potential for success is highest in this location because commitment is high ("I love it") and the persons involved are capable of doing well at it ("very capable"). This is the rich environment where promising entrepreneurs will grow, expand, and flourish. "I am passionate about what I do, and I am capable of excelling at it." The following two chapters will provide the information necessary to assess what it takes to occupy this area.

High Commitment/Low Capability

This territory is often home base to aspiring but less-prepared business owners; these people have high energy and enthusiasm but insufficient skills or experience (yet) to deliver the goods and meet the needs of their target markets. The knowledge and skills to move upward into the box described in the preceding paragraph can be acquired by the trial-and-error method, which is somewhat risky, or by following the steps outlined in the subsequent chapters. The sooner every commercial venture moves upward and out of this box, the better. Close attention to the business planning steps ensures start-up enterprises do not have to begin in this territory.

Low Commitment/High Capability

This quadrant is where the person needs to rethink what she is doing. Life is too short to invest in unfulfilling work where you are not stimulated by the job you do. As a business owner, you do not want an employee that is not committed to the mission of the business, even if capability exists to perform the assigned tasks well. Although capability may be high, accountability will be lacking, and both are necessary conditions in an entrepreneurial environment.

Low Commitment/Low Capability

This quadrant is a major energy drain for everyone—the person in it and those around him. He does not like what he does and is willing to do it poorly. The only time a business owner wants to observe someone in this position is when that individual is employed by the competition. If you find such a person in your shop, it is time to help them move on to another quadrant.

Having a passion for what you like to do is a starting point. In the case of ScubaTech, the owner pursued training in an academic area separate from her personal interest in sports diving. However, by matching commitment to a businesses purpose with personal talent, the ideal scenario for business success came together. See Spotlight On ScubaTech for the reflection of an owner that offers a combination

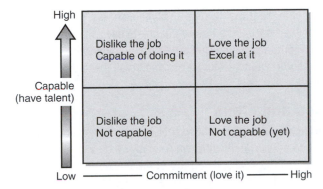

Figure 1.7 Capability-commitment matrix.

ScubaTech

Location

In Destin, Florida, Nancy Birchett and Steve Thompson started ScubaTech of Northwest Florida in 1986. Three years into the business, Steve made the decision to sell his interest in the business, and Nancy bought him out. Destin is unique in that the natural limestone reefs come within three miles of the coastline and there are a few artificial reefs (wrecks) that divers enjoy diving from. People come from all the surrounding states to dive and take scuba lessons.

Nancy Birchett

Jason Garner

Background

ScubaTech offers scuba and snorkeling charters and instruction, retail equipment, rental equipment, air, nitrox, and equipment repair. The business is open seven days a week year round; the higher-income months are June through the beginning of September. Sea Cobra, the charter boat, was added in 1987. The same year, Carla Moore began working for ScubaTech and in 1995 Nancy gave Carla 40 percent ownership in the business. Carla had become such a valuable part of the business that Nancy couldn't afford to lose her. Carla is in charge of retail store sales and accounting, and Nancy runs the boats every day and completes the purchasing and planning of all business activities. It is almost like having two separate businesses.

Products and Services

ScubaTech primarily teaches Scuba Schools International (SSI) courses, although the business is certified to teach PADI, NAUI, and other agencies' courses. Nancy reports, "One thing I've never allowed was to be branded by one teaching agency. I do what is best for my customers and my business. We teach using nitrox and fill nitrox tanks at our facility, which enables the divers longer bottom times but safer dives because of increased oxygen and less nitrogen in the mix that the divers breathe. It is not to be used for deeper dives." ScubaTech carries the best in diving equipment and specializes in Scubapro and Aqualung. Nancy believes that over the years in business, these two manufacturers offer the best quality together with the best customer and dealer support. This type of business is very time consuming and labor intensive.

Nancy says, "Like farming, everything depends on the weather. If it's raining or windy, the boats don't run. If the boats don't run, the store has no income. By far, the biggest challenge is a hurricane. In the event of a hurricane, everything ends and the season may be over. The customers are afraid to come back and the water is so murky that it takes a long time to clear up. The season is very short and we have to make hay while we can."

The liability with the business is very high, so Nancy tries to keep the best staff year round, which is a financial burden. Her yearly staff work very hard during the season; their lives are centered on the business and the payoff is a salaried winter and lots of vacation time. It is a very challenging business, but it can also be very rewarding. The business has enabled Nancy to travel to many exotic islands, ride giant manta rays and whale sharks, shoot fish, and take superb underwater photos as well as see a world unlike what others have a chance to see. Although she has the burden of running a business, her job allows her to work outdoors in the Gulf of Mexico, mingling with nature and enjoying all that goes on within it. She would like to retire and travel to exotic places and do all these things for fun and on her own schedule while she is still physically able.

Business Advice and Plans

Nancy says, "I started my own business when I was 27 years old after completing an associate's degree in veterinary medicine. One thing I would like to tell readers is that I went into a field totally different from my studies, and it was for the love of the sport. I had to work hard, and the knowledge of the sport helped to put the business together. I had no financial help from anybody, just a good business plan and a banker who believed in me. I believe to this day that if you are willing to put your heart and soul into what you want, then you have no limitations. Sometimes you just have to look for the right angles and work just a little harder to get what you want."

Photo courtesy of Nancy Birchett.

of a dive charter operation together with a retail element.

Beyond the personal benefit of being able to do what you excel at on a daily basis, there is another benefit as well: working in the vibrant and exciting RET industry as depicted in figure 1.4. Although there is an institutional benefit associated with public or nonprofit organizations, an important set of attributes helps describe the RET industry, and these attributes are highlighted next.

BENEFITS ASSOCIATED WITH THE RECREATION, EVENT, AND TOURISM INDUSTRY

When you examine commercial RET opportunities, you will discover that you are entering an exciting community of businesses that are global, diverse, committed to ethical standards, proactive for "green practices" in tourism, and open to entrepreneurs of all cultural and ethnic backgrounds. The RET industry is also a set of businesses and corporations that contribute significantly to the world economy. They are ever changing and technology dependent. What do these special features mean to a business owner? The following paragraphs offer a partial answer.

• *Global:* For the business-minded person, the opportunity exists to explore many places around the world where your idea for a commercial enterprise might exist or be a good fit. The United Nations World Tourism Organization (UNWTO) reports tourism is now the world's largest employer. Leisure accounts for 75 percent of all international travel, and domestic travel (i.e., within one's own country) is likely to be four times larger than the number of international arrivals associated with a particular country. Domestic travel and commercial recreation have been important for a very long time. Corporate, sport, and private events are held in worldwide destinations and bring together global participants, as in the case of the Olympics. Although economists began talking about the emergence of a global economy about a decade ago, leisure travel, special events, and domestic tourism have been worldwide activities for more than three centuries.

At the 2005 World Tourism Day celebration, the UNWTO secretary-general reviewed the growth in the tourism industry. He noted that in 1950, travel involved "twenty million, last year 760 million and by 2020 it is expected that the number of international travelers will exceed 1.6 billion per year. . . . Travel enables us to enrich our lives with new experiences, to enjoy and to educate ourselves, to learn respect for foreign cultures, to establish friendships, and above all to contribute to international cooperation and peace throughout the world" (Frangialli 2005).

More recently, World Tourism Day in 2007 celebrated women's achievements in the tourism sector and stimulated continuous action in support of the UN's 3rd Millennium Development Goal: Promoting Gender Equality and Women Empowerment.

• *Diverse:* Leisure interests and tourism trends are continuing to expand, and new markets are evident every year. The number of small businesses providing diverse products and services to society is vital to leisure experiences and appears almost infinite. If there is a societal demand, there is an opportunity for an entrepreneur to fill it. Although there is no perfect classification to reveal all the commercial enterprises that are encompassed by the leisure or tourism industry, figures 1.4 through 1.6 reveal components of the tourism industry. Entrepreneurship is critical to tourism and travel. Gunn and Var (2002) state the case well: "Because of the dynamics of tourism, opportunities for innovative service businesses continue to appear. . . . There needs to be a volume of business people interested in and able to see opportunity, obtain a site, gather the financial support, plan, build and operate a new business. Small business continues to offer the greatest opportunities in spite of the many risks and obstacles" (p. 68).

• *Codes of conduct and ethical standards:* The United Nations World Tourism Organization (UNWTO) initiated a multi-year process to define a set of ethical standards for global tourism, and it resulted in a 10-point Global Code of Ethics for Tourism. This document represents the culmination "of an extensive consultative process- (and) was approved unanimously by the UNWTO General Assembly meeting in Santiago in October 1999." Francesco Frangialli, Secretary-General of the UNWTO stated at the time

"With international tourism forecast to nearly triple in volume over the next 20 years, members of the World Tourism Organization believe that the

Scott Walking Adventures

Location

With its home base in Nova Scotia, Scott Walking Adventures (SWA) offers vacation experiences designed for travelers who want to see the world in a different way . . . and what better way than on foot! The company mission is to create memorable walking experiences in beautiful places of natural history and cultural heritage. Their professional management, staff, and guides ensure customer satisfaction and responsible travel that upholds ecotourism, community sustainability, and the ideals of risk management.

Background

In 1992, founder Wendy Scott had a vision of sharing her homeland with visitors; that vision encompassed two core values: integrity and responsibility. Scott Walking Adventures has been committed to offering culturally rich, low-impact, high-end walking adventures that benefit traveler and host alike with mutual respect and awareness of the regions visited. This means working with local communities, businesses, and individuals to develop sustainable tourism opportunities that help local economies while at the same time minimizing negative environmental and cultural impacts.

Products and Services

Angela Chisholm purchased the business in 2003 and continued to build on past successes. The number of scheduled trips appearing in the catalog has expanded from 30 to 45, and destinations have increased from 11 to 23. The staff at SWA believe an authentic travel experience can be a life-changing event through awareness of the culture, history, and natural environment of the region. Out of this awareness comes respect for the local people and their customs, beliefs, and economic needs, which engender a reverence for all living matter in the eco-zone visited.

All adventures are designed with the RARE principle in mind:

Respect
Awareness
Reverence
Experience

Angela Chisholm.

SWA achieves an authentic experience through the use of small, locally owned properties rather than big foreign-owned hotels. They also use local characters as guides and seek out spontaneous and authentic experiences rather than the contrived enactments of conventional tourism. They travel in small groups (a maximum of 12, with an average group size of 8) that are less intrusive on trails and in natural areas.

In a recent survey of travel adventure companies, *National Geographic* magazine rated the company as one of the best adventure companies in Canada—92 percent satisfaction in terms of customer experience. The magazine reported, "New clients should consider Scott Walking Adventures' bread-and-butter locale: eastern Canada, from the banks of Québec's lake-studded Eastern Townships to the puffin- and whale-watching waters along the Newfoundland coast. Nights are spent in the region's top hotels and lodges. Repeat guests (of which there are many) can spice it up in Iceland and Tasmania."

How do they qualify for such praise? SWA works with a code of conduct and ethics that encompass all aspects of their business . . . and they are always seeking to improve and grow. (See the online student resource for five codes of conduct applicable to the travelers, guides, the home office, sustainability, and the trail.)

Business Advice and Plans

In this type of business within the adventure travel industry, there is an increase in the number of companies introducing new customers to the world. Staying on top of technology to attract new customers to their code of conduct is a constant. As a seasonal business, cash flow in the off-season is imperative to ensuring the sustainability of the business itself. Fluctuations in fuel prices and exchange rates cause uncertainty with long-term travel planning in the North American markets, which means building strong relations with suppliers in order to adjust to last-minute travel decisions.

Angela notes, "By incorporating all aspects of being a responsible travel company, we have established a loyal client base. Our reservations each year reflect that our market appreciates what we are doing together to make a difference. Over 50 percent of our travelers each season are return guests and 20 percent are word-of-mouth customers. Our guests continue to spread the word and are amazing ambassadors for Scott Walking Adventures."

Photo courtesy of Angela Chisolm.

Global Code of Ethics for Tourism (GCET) is needed to help minimize the negative impacts of tourism on the environment and on cultural heritage while maximizing the benefits for residents of tourism destinations. The Global Code of Ethics for Tourism is intended to be a living document. Read it. Circulate it widely. Participate in its implementation. Only with your cooperation can we safeguard the future of the tourism industry and expand the sector's contribution to economic prosperity, peace and understanding among all the nations of the world." (www.unwto.org/code_ethics/eng/9.htm)

In chapter 9, a code of conduct and ethical practices are examined in more detail from the perspective of operational decisions taken by entrepreneurs to adopt a responsible travel policy and code of ethics for their business, and provide training to staff. The Spotlight On Scott Walking Adventure illustrates an award-winning business recognized for its code of conduct. Refer to figure 9.2 or the online student resource for an expanded examination of the codes they have adopted.

• *Green practices:* The New Tourism Plan prepared by the World Tourism and Travel Council (www.wttc.travel/) advocates new partnerships with public authorities to strengthen a shared commitment for growth and property in the tourism industry. One area of shared responsibility relates to minimizing tourism impact on the environment. Most RET businesses recognize that their actions can result in a negative impact on the environment and, therefore, look to joint public–private initiatives to protect the natural amenities valued by their customers. Recent attention has been on aspects of the transportation sector (e.g., air, water, and land transport) because it means consumption of fossil fuels. It is evident actions need to be taken in all transport sectors to mitigate the effects of exhaust emissions upon such things as air quality and global warming. Tourism is no exception, so there are actions being taken by the government and the RET industry to address impacts associated with travel.

Because greenhouse gases (e.g., CO_2) in the atmosphere contribute to global warming, the Carbon Tax Center (CTC) recommends a tax be placed on the use of fossil fuels. Putting an additional price on the use of carbon is viewed by CTC as a necessary mechanism for reducing the increasing amount of carbon emission released into the atmosphere, thereby mitigating the devastating effects we know are associated with climate change. It is suggested such a tax will create incentives for energy efficiencies in vehicles, promote the development of renewable sources of energy (e.g., wind and solar), advance research support creating low-carbon biofuels, and encourage conservation practices based on behavior by consumers (e.g., recycling, mass transit, etc.). See the following green tip for application of this policy to tourism.

• *Economic impact:* The economic benefits associated with commercial and tourism services are extremely important. Tourism is the fastest-growing economic sector in terms of foreign exchange and job creation. This growth can stimulate public and private investments in the economy and improve local living conditions for residents. Every year new projects are undertaken by the business council of the UNWTO

Green Tip

Greenhouse Gases and a Carbon Tax on Burning Fossil Fuels

When you are hosting an event or tour, you are indirectly responsible for generating greenhouse gases that contribute to the process of global warming. When attendees travel to a special event, they often burn fossil fuels (e.g., gasoline, diesel, propane, aviation fuel) in the course of travel. Since the carbon content of every fossil fuel is known, the amount of carbon dioxide (CO_2) released into the atmosphere when the fuel is burned is known. As you will learn in chapter 9 and elsewhere in the text, there are a number of actions a tourism operator or host can initiate to promote sustainable practices and to offset the CO_2 introduced into the atmosphere as the result of travel.

At the 2008 Tourism Industry Conference in British Columbia, the organizer had each registrant pay a supplemental $5 "carbon fee" as a partial offset of their travel to the conference. The fees were committed to a nonprofit carbon-offset society supporting installation of non–fossil fuel energy systems, specifically ground-source heat pumps, at four rural locations. At this same 2008 conference, the provincial minister responsible for tourism spoke to attendees about the policy actions the government was taking as part of their "green tourism" initiative, which includes a carbon tax on fossil fuel sold in the province. (For additional details on such a tax, see www.carbontax. org.) The provincial legislation to implement a carbon tax was the first such taxation policy by any government in North America. As noted by climate specialist Ian Bruce of the David Suzuki Foundation, "The Government has used the most powerful tool, a carbon tax, to reduce greenhouse gas emissions" (Rosenblum, 2008). In British Columbia the tourism logo is "Super, Natural British Columbia," and the natural beauty of the province has been a significant part of the attraction for tourists. Now steps have been taken to match the marketing brand with a conservation policy designed to reduce the impact of tourism on climate change.

to strengthen public–private cooperation and partnerships. The small and medium enterprises (SMEs) that dominate the commercial sector occupy a vital role in the recreation, event, and tourism industry. Small and medium enterprises are vital to a nation's economy, and the services provided by SMEs readily represent 50 to 55 percent of the private-sector jobs in North America. Canada's tourism industry is made up of more than 200,000 mostly small and medium-sized enterprises that are involved in getting travelers into and around the country. The Canadian tourism industry in 2005 generated nearly $70 billion in visitor spending and UNWTO placed it 12th in the world in receipts and 11th in visitation (www.tiac-aitc.ca/english/welcome.asp). In the United States, the National Federation of Independent Businesses (NFIB) states that nearly 16 million individuals reported operating their own business regardless of its legal form, as their principal occupation in 2005. "Ninety-nine (99) percent of employing businesses are small under prevailing definitions. Another way to look at it: 60 percent of all businesses that employ people, other than the owners, have 1 to 4 employees; another 20 percent have 5 to 9 employees" (www.411sbfacts.com/speeches.html#q1).

• *Technology dependent:* The influence of new technology is very evident in all aspects of commerce, and this influence applies particularly to the commercial sector of the recreation, event, and tourism industry. Although many recreation services are not themselves "high tech," the business of providing services frequently utilizes technology. Technology provides a means to disseminate and obtain information quickly from many sources and allows consumers to make more-informed decisions. The changes observed in information and communication systems have profound influence on reservation systems, multimedia distribution of promotional material and special programs, the educational component of events, the nature of e-commerce, and even the capacity to support highly mobile office space for travel and home-based businesses. Tourism applications and Internet sites already have a dominant position on the World Wide Web, and the small-business sector of leisure

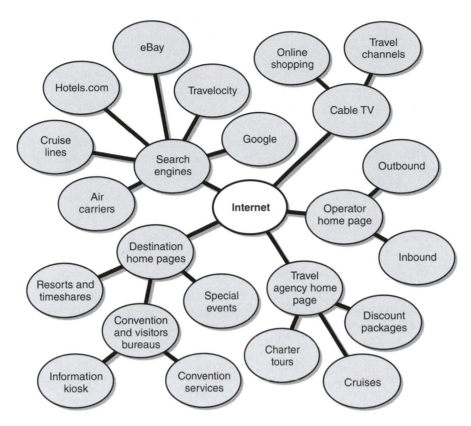

Figure 1.8 Communication technology and distribution of consumer information.

and tourism continues to occupy more sites with the creation and sale of more Internet domains (see figure 1.8). Technology means more opportunities than ever before for the consumer to carefully select among tourism products.

• *Open:* The public marketplace is open to everyone who has or is willing to acquire the knowledge and skills necessary to contribute to the leisure and tourism industry. The free enterprise system is the cornerstone of the open economy, and it is one of the reasons the commercial sector thrives in the leisure and tourism field. The global trend toward privatization of public services has also opened new opportunities for RET businesses. You may have interpersonal abilities in dealing with people based on family history, personal travel experiences, language training, recreational lifestyle preferences, or even cultural heritage that will be an asset in a particular aspect of the industry. For example, the cultural aptitude of entrepreneurs from India may explain their inclination to dominate the small- and medium-size enterprise in the U.S. lodging sector. On the AAHOA

Web site (www.aahoa.com/aboutAAHOA), the following has been posted:

Many young people immigrated to the United States from India and in 1989 participated in forming the Asian American Hotel Owners Association (AAHOA). Today the association has more than 8,000 members who together own over 20,000 hotels representing more than 37 percent of all hotel properties and 50 percent of the economy lodging properties. The membership of AAHOA is individual entrepreneurs who each have a myriad of personal success stories. The market value of hotels owned by AAHOA is around $38 billion and they create at least a million jobs.

SUMMARY

Commercial recreation and tourism can be recognized as an industry that adds value to the human experience as consumers seek goods and services that meet their leisure and recreation needs. It is an industry that is global, diverse, important, dynamic, technology dependent, and open to entrepreneurs of all backgrounds. The prospect of identifying a promising commercial venture can be substantial once the decision is made to acquire specific knowledge and the ability to prepare a business plan. Preparing a business plan is addressed in the next chapter. Everyone brings to the leisure and tourism field a blend of knowledge, experience, ability, and passion. These ingredients can be applied to a wide range of leisure or tourism opportunities. One of the first tasks involves sorting out what is important to you and then setting out to explore, in a systematic way, a business purpose, or vision, that matches it. Several practical strategies are available to help you think about a commercial idea that appeals to you and then acquire additional information about it. Chapters 2 and 3 address this subject from several points of view.

Service providers can be compartmentalized under one of three categories—public, nonprofit, and commercial. Each of the three sectors has a vital role to play in the health, growth, and diversification of leisure and tourism goods and services. This book provides both the current RET business manager and the potential entrepreneur with knowledge of the commercial recreation, event, and tourism sector together with the knowledge and skills necessary to write a plan to start your own business and sustainable practices to operate it.

 Check out the online student resource for additional material, including case studies, Web links, and more.

Chapter 2

Entrepreneurship and the Business Planning Process

Learning Objectives

After reading this chapter you will be able to

- describe opportunities for entrepreneurs within the recreation, event, and tourism industry;
- identify the most common legal forms and permits of small recreation businesses;
- explain the fatal mistakes of small recreation businesses; and
- describe the need for and steps in developing a business plan.

Key Terms

business plan	general partnership	noncompete agreement
copyright	goodwill	patent
distressed business sale	guest experience	severe acute respiratory syndrome (SARS)
doing business as	intrepreneur	
domain name	lifestyle business	sole proprietorship
entrepreneur	limited liability company (LLC)	stockholders
fixed assets	Meeting Professionals International	subchapter S corporation
franchise		trademark

Imagine this scenario: You get up early most mornings because you are truly excited about the workday ahead. You know what the day's priorities are because you've identified them in advance, run them by some key staff persons, and then made the final decision. But you also realize there will be surprises because everyone comes to you for answers to the big questions about your new RET business. Sales have jumped 25 percent in the last month, and you are interviewing two new staff persons this week. You've been thinking about other potential companies to approach for further sales. You are keeping track of progress in the development of the business by comparing it with your business plan projections, and it is coming along nicely. However, you had a big setback yesterday that really stung; a large company that had given you tentative approval for a contract backed out and went with your number one competitor. There were serious concerns about having enough money to cover the next payroll without dipping into your line of credit again. You ended up working till nine at night yesterday, unsuccessfully trying to convince the big account to go with you, responding to three other requests for quotes, and getting started on payroll. But you didn't seem tired because at the end of that day you knew the efforts you were making would have a big impact in building up your new company. Today you finish payroll and get caught up. This afternoon you plan to take off early to conduct a site inspection of a new deluxe facility for an event, then try some of the new company adventure gear. As you walk through the door you realize it is a glorious day and a great place to live. Life is busy and challenging, but so good.

Although this scenario may seem far-fetched at the moment, it is representative of "a day in the life" of a recreation, event, and tourism (RET) business entrepreneur. The challenges seem overwhelming at times, but the rewards can be there. In this chapter we help you identify untapped consumer needs, the importance of a sound business concept, the elements of a solid business plan, and the importance of incorporating the company and acquiring the necessary permits so your company can start off smoothly and grow. Even if you have no plans to start your own company, you can still carry the elements of entrepreneurship identified later into existing businesses and help them prosper.

OPPORTUNITIES FOR ENTREPRENEURS AND INTREPRENEURS

Citizens of the United States, Canada, and countries worldwide have become more concerned about—and spend more of their income on—leisure-time pursuits including recreation, events, and entertainment. As will soon be demonstrated, the demand for RET services and products is booming, and this provides opportunity for *entrepreneurs* and *intrepreneurs*. An **entrepreneur** spots an opportunity; identifies a business idea to capture it; develops a plan to amass and manage the resources to provide the service; and takes the risk by investing their time, talent, and funds to start their own venture. An **intrepreneur** (Pinchot, 1985) is also a person who sees an opportunity, but they prefer to work within and foster change to an existing organization where they are employed in order to lead it in new directions and grow the company. Are you an entrepreneur, or at this time are you satisfied with managing rather than starting and owning a commercial recreation business?

Characteristics of an Entrepreneur

- Risk taker
- Innovative
- Strong leader
- Self-disciplined
- Self-starter
- Invests personal funds

An entrepreneur, as shown in the list just given, is often characterized as an innovative and self-disciplined risk taker who is willing to invest their own funds. They must also be a self-starter to get the enterprise going and a strong leader to keep it progressing. See Spotlight On Downieville Adventure Company Bike Shop and Mountain Bike Shuttle Service for an introduction to Yuba Adventures, an independent bicycle shop and mountain biking shuttle service, and Case Study 2.1 in the online student resource for a detailed discussion of the company.

Downieville Adventure Company Bike Shop and Mountain Bike Shuttle Service

Location

Downieville Adventure Company is located in downtown Downieville, California, a town of several thousand people in a rugged part of the Sierra Nevada Mountains in the north-central part of the state. The steep, heavily forested mountains are crossed by old logging and gold-mining trails. These trails, along with more recent additions, attract serious mountain biking enthusiasts and are the site of a very challenging downhill bike race.

Background

Gregg Williams was a hard-core mountain bike enthusiast in 1990 when he discovered an amazing combination of little-used motorcycle and hiking trails that had easy automobile access to the starting point near the sleepy town of Downieville. The set of trails plunged 4,700 feet (1,433 m) down steep, rocky terrain, through tall forests and shallow creeks, eventually dumping bikers right into downtown Downieville. The trail has become nationally recognized as the Downieville Downhill. Gregg, with help from the community in 1995, started the Downieville Classic downhill mountain bike race, renowned as one of the fastest, toughest, and most grueling races in the United States. In 1996 he started Yuba Expeditions in downtown Downieville and began providing commercial shuttles to the start of the trail system and opened a mountain bike shop to support the throngs of mountain bike enthusiasts flooding the town. The business grew from a seasonal hobby to a year-round endeavor by 2005, when Gregg raised the funds to start up Downieville Adventure Company, LLC, under which Yuba Expeditions and the Downieville Classic reside. Now Gregg is able to live his dream lifestyle in a small town in the mountains.

Patrick T. Tierney

The Downieville Adventure Company shop is a successful rental and retail location as well as a great place to hang out.

Products and Services

The Downieville Adventure Company has a fleet of five diesel 15-passenger vans equipped with the latest bike racks. The vans leave every two hours to shuttle mountain bikers up to 6,800 feet (2,073 m), where the famous Downieville Downhill trails begin. They have also expanded their downtown retail store, which sells top-line bikes and related equipment. Upscale full-suspension Santa Cruz mountain bikes can be rented from the store. In the back of the store is a full-service bicycle repair shop. Their store is known as a friendly, low-key place to hang out, as well as the place with the best bike gear and mechanics in town.

Business Advice and Plans

In the near future the company hopes to purchase the building where their store and shop reside to have control over this expense. This may be done through a Small Business Administration loan. In addition, they hope to continue to expand the single-track trail system in the area through cooperating with private land owners and the U.S. Forest Service. This would open up new trails for their clients and the public to use.

LIFESTYLE BUSINESSES

The RET field offers a myriad of opportunities for motivated persons to not only operate their own profitable businesses but also follow their passion and live a desirable lifestyle. A **lifestyle business** is one in which your work requires you to be an expert in exciting or fun activities, such as skiing or wedding planning, that you are passionate about. Your work schedule allows you some flexibility, and you live in a desirable location, from a small resort community to an exciting big city. You may sacrifice some income, compared with working in an 8:00-to-5:00 job for a huge corporation that does not excite you, but the other benefits more than compensate.

MODERATE FUNDING BUT SIGNIFICANT PASSION

RET businesses can often be started with moderate amounts of funding, but they need substantial owner passion and planning. Unlike other types of businesses, such as hotels, which require extremely large capital investments for start-up and have stiff international competition from large corporate chains, or communications technology companies that require high-tech wizardry, an RET business more likely demands keen attention to what customers want, the cultivation of a guest-responsive staff, and moderate funds from personal and outside sources.

FATAL START-UP MISTAKES OF RET BUSINESSES

No two businesses have the exact same challenges, but there is a consistent pattern of problems that can be fatal to a new business. What follows is a list of the most frequently seen fatal mistakes of new RET businesses, as observed by us and the Small Business Administration (Small Business Administration, 2006). These illustrate key problems that can slow a company's growth or even lead to its demise. You should be particularly cognizant of these when planning a new RET business.

- Rushing too quickly to start up your company
- Not conducting enough prestart research
- An unclear business concept

- Too little financial backing
- Lack of clear policies on how you will control operating costs and receivables
- Inadequate and ineffective initial marketing and promotion
- Lack of understanding of need for a permit and limitations of permits
- Hiring the wrong staff
- Not protecting your ideas with trademarks and copyrights
- Lack of organization and planning

Each of these is covered within chapters in this book. We provide ways to avoid them altogether or minimize the damage caused by these problems.

ELEMENTS OF A RECREATION BUSINESS

A recreation, event, and tourism business is usually considered to be in the service industry, where you cater to consumer needs and wants by creating a memorable **guest experience** for which people will pay top dollar. An experience goes well beyond a simple product or service, as it becomes a memorable and richly satisfying engagement with your company. This engaging experience may have four basic elements:

1. A personalized service-generated *guest experience*. Moving from just a standard service, such as a lesson or a tour, to a memorable event that goes beyond your client's expectations is the heart of every RET business. This normally includes use of your facilities, equipment, and staff.

2. A *retail sales* component, consisting of souvenirs, gear, gifts, and other tangible products. This retail sales element can be an extremely profitable portion of a high-volume business. You might also sell specialized equipment the guest needs to best enjoy the recreation or event.

3. *Rentals* of specialized recreation, event, and tourism equipment, ranging from snowboards, event tents, or rafts can be a minor or major profit center for an RET business. For example,

the rental of party and event equipment (e.g., tents, chairs, crystal glasses, serving trays) is a main element of some event businesses.

4. *Small-scale manufacturing* of specialized recreation gear is the last component of some recreation firms. Manufacturing is usually undertaken by more-experienced owners, but it can provide profits as well as a steadier year-round revenue stream.

RET businesses always have an outstanding guest experience as the core of what they provide, but they also may include a retail component. Some firms conduct small-scale manufacturing of recreation equipment, normally after a number of years' experience in the industry.

GROWING DEMAND FOR RET GOODS AND SERVICES

Citizens in developed as well as developing countries are demanding more from their limited leisure time and are looking to organizations to meet their recreation and entertainment needs. The trend over the last 30 years has been clear: growing interest and demand for leisure-time activities. An article by the editors of *BusinessWeek* magazine (1994) determined that the fundamental demand for goods and services in the United States has shifted more to the entertainment and recreation economic sector and called the country the United States of Play. The article identified this sector as the "growth industry of the 1990s," with consumer spending increasing at twice the rate of the overall economy and new construction of more than $13 billion. A more recent assessment found that rising incomes, more leisure time, and growing awareness of the health benefits of stress reduction and physical fitness will greatly increase the demand for event, arts, entertainment, and recreation services. According to the U.S. Bureau of Labor Statistics, the RET industry is projected to grow 31 percent over the 2006-2016 period, compared with 11 percent for all economic sectors combined. Many of these jobs serve tourists, or visitors

from other regions and countries. If one adds to this the expected 20 percent increase in job growth for professionals planning events such as meetings and conventions, then RET spending is truly a powerful economic engine in North America (U.S. Bureau of Labor Statistics, 2007). This 10-year projection is consistent with reported growth in specific sectors in the Canadian economy as well. Western Economic Diversification Canada (2005) examined growth in the small business sector between 1999 and 2004, and they found the arts, entertainment, and recreation sector was the largest provider of new jobs for small businesses. In British Columbia, employment grew 36.9 percent during the period.

People increasingly see recreation, events, and tourism as an essential element of their lifestyles rather

Bruce Bennett/Getty Images

An indication of the demand for RET services is shown by lines at the entrance to an attraction.

than a luxury. Even during economic recessions, events and local recreation services are still popular and people still travel, although they travel in smaller numbers to closer locations and buy less-expensive services. In 2003, for example, during the difficult travel times of the U.S.–Iraq War and the worldwide **severe acute respiratory syndrome (SARS)** epidemic, domestic travel continued, and people just postponed more-exotic international travel (World Tourism Organization, 2003). But the industry can rebound quickly. For example, international travel to the United States recorded an 11.2 percent increase in 2004, one of the largest jumps ever recorded in one year (Travel Industry Association of America, 2004).

This explosion in RET demand is a global phenomenon. Workers in countries such as Germany and France have long valued three- to four-week vacations and active travel, but now developed countries in other parts of the world, such as Japan, are taking more time off and spending greater sums of money on RET. Increasingly, residents of developing countries, such as China and Brazil, have the discretionary income to afford better and more frequent leisure pursuits. Research by the World Travel and Tourism Council (2007) shows that travel and tourism has rebounded from the terrorism of September 11, 2001. It will generate US$7 trillion in economic activity worldwide in 2007 and is expected to grow 4.3 percent annually through 2017. Outdoor recreation in the United States continues to increase. The Outdoor Foundation (2005) discovered that 159 million Americans aged 16 and older (71 percent of the population) participated in at least one of 22 human-powered outdoor recreation activities, such as hiking, bicycling, and canoeing, in 2004. Since 1998, overall participation has grown 6 percent. In China there is a rapidly growing young, urban, and wealthy segment of the population that is very interested in recreation, events, and tourism activities, ranging from international destination weddings to gambling in Macau (Long, 2007).

Recreation is increasingly being viewed as "purposeful," with clear benefits identified beyond just hedonistic pursuits. Businesses employ recreation and events as a tool to build teamwork and enhance communication among staff, to nurture client relationships, and to reward outstanding employee performance. **Meeting Professionals International**

(2006), a national association of professional meeting and event planners that provides services primarily to business clients, forecasts an average 7 percent growth in meetings, and a 14 percent growth in meeting and event expenditures in 2006. Cappa and Graham, a successful event planning company, is shown in Spotlight On Cappa and Graham and described in more detail in Case Study 2.2 in the online student resource.

CHANGING CONSUMER WANTS AND USE PATTERNS

Consumer use and expenditure patterns are changing at a blistering pace. Megatrends, such as aging of the populations in Europe, Canada, and the United States; increased travel safety concerns; and the Internet revolution are just three of many factors that are having profound effects on society and RET. But these changes are also opening new opportunities for commercial recreation entrepreneurs. Older adults are much more concerned about managing their health and use outdoor recreation as their main form of exercise. Younger workers are more likely to turn to recreation and spa services to reduce stress and to escape. More people are seeking active adventure activities over passive ones. These are just a few of the trends that open up opportunities for new or expanding commercial recreation businesses. There are completely novel business opportunities that insightfully track and build on trends.

STARTING YOUR OWN BUSINESS VERSUS BUYING AN EXISTING BUSINESS

An entrepreneur has a choice in how to proceed, starting her own business from scratch or buying an existing business (including purchasing a **franchise**) and using its tested systems. A franchise is where a parent company (franchisor) develops a successful business concept and system and then sells the rights to use the franchise name and system to an individual or small company (franchisee) for a fee. Most people visualize themselves starting their own recreation company, but it is worth considering the advantages and disadvantages of buying a franchise or ongoing

SPOTLIGHT ON

Cappa and Graham, Inc.

Location

The offices of Cappa and Graham are located near the downtown financial district and the convention center in San Francisco, California. This location gives them quick access to corporate meeting planners, the convention center, hotels, and event sites in the city.

Background

Barbara Cappa and Pat Graham founded the company in 1978 and incorporated in 1979. The company began as a transportation management provider. Transportation success and the charismatic personalities of the two owners led to developing the business to include special events and tours. In 1997 Barbara's daughter and son-in-law moved to San Francisco with the express purpose of reinvigorating the company. They are now the owners and chief operating officers of the company.

Linda and Gordon Thompson, owners of Cappa and Graham event planning and management.

Products and Services

Cappa and Graham specializes in event management, planning, and production; VIP and incentive programs; meeting planning; team building; custom group tours; and group transportation in the San Francisco Bay region. Cappa and Graham has managed, planned, and produced private events for up to 5,000 guests; orchestrated VIP programs attended by California Governor Arnold Schwarzenegger, local politicians, and celebrities; planned and organized national and international meetings for major corporations; and operated numerous tour and transportation programs for national and international corporations and associations. Cappa and Graham plans, provides, and coordinates all of the services that clients need for successful meetings and events. This is done either in house or through qualified vendors, including motor-coach companies, production companies, sound and light companies, printers, florists, caterers, entertainment companies, furniture rental, private yacht providers, and venues. Cappa and Graham also provides staff for all events and activities. Staff can include dispatchers to assist with directions and passenger transportation, tour guides, hostesses, registration staff, and on-site managers.

Business Advice and Plans

In the destination and event management industry, there are no opportunities for second chances, nor can a business offer a product that can be recalled or exchanged. Their staff members are young, enthusiastic, and eager to learn, ensuring that the work environment is always fun and exciting. Even so, through normal attrition (marriage, childbirth, and relocation), their most highly skilled team members had to be replaced on average every three years. Consequently, the management challenge was to ensure they constantly had a dedicated, skilled, and happy team in place capable of exceeding their clients' expectations with less involvement on the owners' part. Cappa and Graham has a very strong university internship program, which is a wonderful way to observe and train potential entry-level staff.

Photo courtesy of Linda and Gordon Thompson.

business. In most segments of the RET industry, there are fewer franchises than in other economic sectors, but recreation businesses for sale are easily found on the Internet or through industry associations, such as America Outdoors (www.americaoutdoors.org). Small Business Administration statistics (2005) show that more than half of small businesses fail within five years, while franchises have a much better success record. There are clear advantages to starting your own RET business, but there are also disadvantages compared with purchasing a franchise. Starting your own business provides maximum flexibility in what services you offer and how you create them, but it is also the greatest challenge and risk. Buying an existing business, especially a franchise, limits the services you offer and how you offer them, but you inherit a successful (hopefully), fully operating business, and this makes start-up much easier. But buying an existing business is often initially more expensive. Table 2.1 provides insights into the advantages and disadvantages of starting your own business versus buying a franchise.

Many good sources of information are available to help you learn more about the trade-offs between starting your own independent business and buying an existing one, as well as finding a business or franchise to purchase. Following are a few:

- U.S. Small Business Administration (www. sba.gov)
- Industry Canada Small Business (http://strategis. ic.gc.ca/epic/site/csbfp-pfpec.nsf/en/Home)
- International Franchise Association (www. franchise.org)

- Caffey, A. 2001. "Top Ten Signs of a Shady Franchise or Business Opportunity." *Entrepreneur.* March 12.
- BizBuySell (www.bizbuysell.com)

CONSIDERATIONS IN BUYING AN EXISTING RECREATION BUSINESS

A business for sale may present an outstanding profitable opportunity, or you may fall victim to a fraudulent scheme that makes a quick profit for the seller and leads you into failure. So it is very important to consider the basic factors shown in figure 2.1 and to take some time to conduct research.

- *Why is the owner selling?* A person sells their business for a reason; sometimes it is clearly stated, and other times it is hidden. A smart buyer will find out the real reason for the sale. Most owner motives are self-serving and not a golden opportunity for the buyer. However, perhaps the owner has undervalued his company. It could also be a **distressed business sale**, where they must sell to raise funds for personal reasons and are willing to take less than market value for an otherwise profitable company. Investigate by

Table 2.1 Advantages and Disadvantages of Starting a Company Versus Buying a Recreation, Event, or Tourism Business Franchise

Potential advantages of starting own business	• Maximum flexibility to create own concept • Opportunity to meet unique consumer needs • Flexibility to create and modify services, decor, equipment, or suppliers • Few initial fees or ongoing royalty payments to others
Potential disadvantages of starting own business	• Concept and operating systems are untested • Higher failure rate compared with franchises • Lack of brand awareness • Lack of support, training
Potential advantages of a franchise	• Much higher rate of success • Instant brand-name recognition, customer loyalty • Proven service system, reliable products • Support to help select site, train employees, and identify suppliers
Potential disadvantages of a franchise	• Cost of initial franchise fee and royalty fees • Saturation of market is possible (e.g., fast food) • Limited by contract on what you can do • Lack of flexibility in changing decor, products, or systems

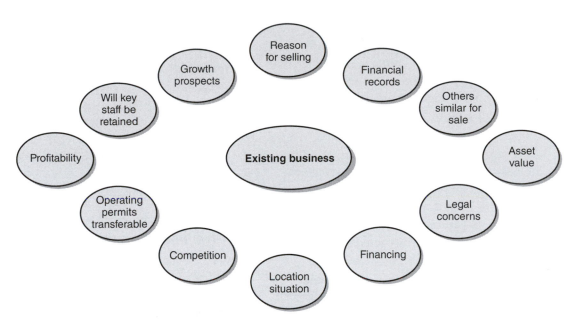

Figure 2.1 Factors to consider in buying a recreation business.

directly questioning the owner, and verify the sale motive yourself.

• *What are the future prospects for growth?* This is a fundamental and extremely important question. Is there a growing market for this service, or is it shrinking? Have sales been declining recently? If so, is it an aberration or a long-term trend? Determine where the best chances for growth exist.

• *Are there similar businesses for sale?* Are there other similar types of businesses for sale in and outside the area? Develop a comparison chart of strengths and weaknesses of each in comparison to asking price. You could use the items listed in this section as comparison factors or specific characteristics of the type of business. This may help you decide if this is the right company to buy and in negotiating the final price.

• *What is the company's financial strength?* The seller should be providing detailed financial statistics on sales history, expenses, and federal taxes paid to show financial strength. These should be documented with tax returns, bank statements, and other objective measures. If the company is weak financially, then there may be room for negotiating a lower price.

• *Is the business profitable?* The profitability of a small recreation company that is family owned is often masked by formal and informal payments and benefits to owners. Most of these are legitimate, but others may be of concern. A good basic measure of profitability is

income before taxes and depreciation, but add to this things such as auto and house payments and insurance coverage for the owners. Recreation businesses may show large sales, but profit margins can be too low to justify the purchase. Chapter 11 describes financial characteristics of recreation businesses in detail, but a general rule for profitability is a rate of 3 to 10 percent after taxes and depreciation.

• *Are the operating expenses reasonable?* Operating expenses for a business, such as wages, utilities, and rent, can be out of line with industry norms. If you purchase the company you may be locked into these arrangements. Do they pay excessive wages or supply amounts? Are there contracts that prohibit you from reducing expenses? For example, the direct unavoidable costs, excluding wages, to run an adventure tour should be 30 to 45 percent of revenue.

• *Are the fixed assets in good condition?* **Fixed assets**, such as company-owned buildings and major equipment, are critical to long-term profitability. Will you inherit old, worn-out gear and unmaintained buildings? Has the company been consistently replacing and maintaining equipment and other assets? This is determined through site visits and observing the operation in detail.

• *Is the owner assigning too much value to "goodwill"?* If a company has an excellent reputation and a solid customer base that returns frequently to make purchases, then this has value called **goodwill**. Check not only the number of clients in the company's database but also how current the contacts are and if they would follow the seller and not stay with you. You can determine this through discussions with the owners and key clients and by terms of the purchase contract.

• *Are government operating permits exclusive and transferable?* Operating permits, as will be discussed in more detail later in this chapter, give legal permission for companies to serve alcohol or operate certain types of activities, such as adventure outfitters and lodging operations in a public park or private reserve. Is this an exclusive permit to the company, or can other companies get these permits? Are they transferable to you? This can be determined by contacting the government agency responsible for the permit.

• *Are there pending legal actions and commitments?* If you buy the stock (see later section in this chapter "Legal Considerations and Forms of Doing Business") of a company, you need to be sure there are no pending legal actions. You would inherit these problems. Will you be bound by contracts or other legal commitments? If unsure, then consider buying just the assets instead of the stock. For example, you could purchase just the land, building, equipment, and vehicles of an ecolodge, but not the stock (and its bills, legal problems, and contracts) of the corporation that currently owns it.

• *Is the owner willing to sign a noncompete contract?* It is critical that you obtain a **noncompete agreement**, which is a signed legal agreement from the seller that they will not compete with you in the same type of business for at least three years. Otherwise, the seller may take the clients they promised to you with them to a new location and compete against you.

• *Are owners willing to finance part of the purchase?* If the owners are willing to finance a part of the purchase, even just 15 percent, then this could indicate that they are able to stand behind their promises and financial estimates. This will also help reduce the amount of money you'll need and associated interest costs to start the company.

• *Will key staff be retained?* A recreation business, even more than other types of businesses, depends on key staff members to know how to operate the firm and meet client needs. So it is critical to know whether two to five key staff will stay with the company after it is sold.

• *Is anything going to happen at the location in the near future?* Are there any proposed land use, competitor, or aesthetic changes anticipated in the next two years? Is that the real reason the owner is selling? Check with other businesses and local government officials in the area to determine future land use at the location.

Summarizing the concerns about owner motivation for selling, you should be aware of location, financial, and operational aspects of the company you might purchase. Otherwise you risk having some unpleasant surprises in the first year of ownership.

LEGAL CONSIDERATIONS AND FORMS OF DOING BUSINESS

Another critically important aspect for commercial recreation entrepreneurs is the legal form of business. As discussed in chapter 1, there are more client safety risks associated with commercial recreation than with many other types of businesses because of the participatory nature of RET. Therefore, it is critical that the personal assets of an owner or entrepreneur, such as her house and car, are shielded from lawsuits and other losses against the company. To do otherwise is to risk losing personal assets, despite having company liability insurance. The type of legal entity established also has direct effects on legal control of the business and owner taxes. The U.S. government has developed the following legal forms of business specifically with small businesses in mind to address the needs of legal control, double taxation, and shielding of personal assets. In Canada there are similar legal forms and names (see www.canadabusiness.ca/gol/cbec/site.nsf/en/bg00328.html). There is also a legal filing procedure for "**doing business as**," or DBA, that allows you to legally operate under a name other than the name of your legal form of business.

SOUND LEGAL ADVICE IS A MUST

Online legal resources and books are a good introduction to a subject but do not substitute for legal advice. Good legal counsel is essential, especially at start-up or purchase of a business.

Talk with other companies in your area about applicable laws. The following Web sites are excellent starting points for research:

- www.sba.gov (U.S. Small Business Administration)
- www.canadabusiness.ca/gol/cbec/site.nsf/en/index.html
- www.findlaw.com (a comprehensive source of federal, state, and local laws)
- www.canadainternational.gc.ca/dbc/how-to-establish-business-canada-en.aspx

SOLE PROPRIETORSHIP

A **sole proprietorship** is a business form that is not legally separate from its owner. It essentially means a person does business in their own name, and there is only one owner. Sole proprietorships are quick and easy to set up and do not require government approval. You do not have to share profits with anyone else. However, since there is no separation between the business and the owner, all debts or liabilities of the business are debts and liabilities of the owner. If a terrible accident were to occur to a client and they sued the company, the owner would be personally liable. Since accidents do happen, especially in more participation-oriented recreation, event, and tourism industries, a sole proprietorship legal form is not recommended.

GENERAL PARTNERSHIP

A **general partnership** is a legal business form in which all partners manage the business and are personally liable for its debts. Partners share with each other the profits or losses of the business undertaking in which all have invested. There should be a written partnership agreement, often registered with the state government, between the partners that identifies ownership and control of the company, contributions, who will operate it, and how to dissolve it. Partnerships can be preferred over corporations for taxation purposes, as a partnership structure eliminates the dividend tax levied on profits realized by the owners of a corporation. Drawbacks of a partnership are the unlimited liability of the partners for business losses, and it is not uncommon for disagreements to arise between partners that can cause serious disruption in operations.

LIMITED LIABILITY COMPANY

A **limited liability company (LLC)** is a legal form of business offering limited liability to its owners, and most states do not limit the number of investors. It is similar to a corporation but provides more tax and ownership flexibility than other ownership types. A limited liability company with multiple members may choose to be treated for U.S. federal taxation purposes as a partnership, as a C corporation, or as an S corporation. An operating agreement describes the company's membership and operational rules and how profits or losses are to be shared. The LLC form is very well suited for smaller RET companies with a limited number of owners primarily because of tax and limited liability benefits.

SUBCHAPTER S CORPORATION

Corporations are owned by **stockholders**, who purchase a stock certificate that allows them to receive dividends and have a voice in the operation of the firm. Legal control of the company rests with the majority stockholder. So, for example, an entity owning more than 50 percent of S corporation stock has legal control and can change the company direction by hiring or firing managers despite the wishes of other stockholders and staff. There are two primary types of corporations, C and S types. The C type is normally appropriate for very large entities and can result in double taxation of some company income. It is therefore not discussed here.

The **subchapter S corporation** has long been the most popular legal form of small RET businesses in the United States. It is a corporation that elects to be taxed under Subchapter S of Chapter 1 of the Internal Revenue Code. An S corporation is normally set up to not pay corporate income taxes on profits; rather, the shareholders pay income taxes on their proportionate shares of the S company's profits. The liability of the corporation is limited to corporate assets, and the personal assets of shareholders and employees are shielded from corporate losses. Another benefit of an S corporation is that during the early years when the company may accrue losses, these can be passed on to the owner as tax losses, offsetting personal income. The number of shareholders is limited to 35, so it may not be appropriate for very large companies. Articles of incorporation must be filed with state and federal agencies, and legal counsel is normally needed to properly set up this type of corporation.

It is possible to legally conduct business under a name other than your sole proprietor, partnership, or corporate name. This is referred to under the title of "doing business as," or DBA. When you register the DBA with the proper government agency (Secretary of State or county in the U.S.) it allows you to legally do business as a particular name at minimal cost, and without having to create an entirely new business entity. The regulations vary from state to state in the U.S. and province to province in Canada. With a DBA you can collect payments, promote, and represent your company under that name, as long as you are registered. Duplicate names in a state are not allowed and federal trademarks have precedence over a state DBA (discussed in next section).

PROTECTING YOUR IDEAS AND INVESTMENT

It is extremely competitive in the marketplace, and competitors are looking for almost any way to win business, so you must protect your property and ability to do business. Your product name, business name, logos, designs, concepts, and inventions are considered intellectual property. You must protect intellectual property from being stolen and ensure that you alone can continue to use it in the future. Intellectual property is protected in the U.S. through the following legal means (similar protections are available in Canada; see the Intellectual Property Office at www.strategis.gc.ca/sc_mrksv/cipo/welcome/welcom-e.html):

• *Trademark:* A **trademark** is a word, phrase, logo, or brand name for your product that is used to identify it and differentiate it from others. An example of a trademarked phrase is "Toyota: Moving Forward." A trade name is the name of your business. You should register these identifying items with the U.S. Patent and Trademark Office and use the federal registration symbol ® after a mark. For more U.S. information, see www.uspto.gov/main/trademarks.htm, or for Canadian information see www.bdc-canada.

com/BDC/services/Trademark_reg.htm, and consult a lawyer specializing in trademarks. Trademarks must also be registered in other countries to receive protection there.

An action of utmost importance for a new company is registering your business name as a federal trademark so that others cannot duplicate it and cause consumer confusion. If you do not do this in the beginning another company could register your name instead and potentially steal away many of your customer inquiries. Simply having a corporation name filed in a state is not adequate to guarantee no one will duplicate it outside that state. A federal trademark is required to ensure no one in any state or province can use your name. This is not related to, and is a separate process from, Internet domain name registration, which will be discussed later. Again, your trademarked business name must be registered in other countries if it is to have influence there.

• *Patent:* A **patent** is a right granted by the federal government to inventors for the making, selling, or use of an invention. An application must be filed with the U.S. Patent and Trademark Office, after which it conducts a search and issues a patent notice (for Canada information see www.ipic.ca/english/general/agents.cfm). This is a lengthy, complex process that normally requires a patent attorney. For example, if you design a new type of recreation gear, you should file an application with the U.S. Patent and Trademark Office, otherwise someone could copy it and claim exclusive rights to its design.

• *Copyright:* A **copyright** is an original expression of an idea affixed to paper or electronic media that controls the right to reproduce, sell, rent, and publicly display it. These include drawings, written text, computer programs, and advertisements. Copyrights cannot be obtained for factual information, short phrases, or words. It is suggested for significant or very important material that a copyright be registered with the Register of Copyrights, Library of Congress, www.loc.gov. For copyright information in Canada see the Intellectual Property Office at www.strategis.gc.ca/sc_mrksv/cipo/welcome/welcom-e.html). However, currently a copyright notice is not necessary to maintain copyrights. An example of a copyright is found at the beginning of this book.

• *Domain name:* A Web site on the Internet is essential for a company. When you establish a new Web site it is given a unique, lengthy numeric IP address so that Internet users can find or be transferred directly to your Web site. However, numeric IP addresses are difficult to remember and so domain names were created. **Domain names** are hostnames that are more memorable and stand in for numeric IP addresses. Your e-mail also comes to your domain name. The first part of the domain name is often related to or can be your actual company name. Every domain name ends in a top-level domain (TLD) code, which is always one of a small list of generic codes (e.g., com, biz, org, net, travel), or a two-character territory code (such as "ca" for Canada). For example, a Canadian company named "Yukon adventures" could have a domain name of "Yukonadventures.com.ca." It is critical for a new company to identify a memorable or easily associated domain name for their Web site and to register it with the international domain name registry. You should register domain names using all the related TLD codes, at a minimum com, net, biz, and travel. Licensed registration companies, like Network Solutions (www.networksolutions.com), act as agents and do the actual domain name registration for you. Many of the most simple and memorable domain names are already taken.

PERMITS, SERVICE CONTRACTS, AND LICENSES

If your company is offering services within a public park or natural area, such as a national forest or state or provincial park, you are required by law to obtain an operating permit from the appropriate land management agency, in addition to the normal local government business license. If the agency does not want to permit a certain type of activity you are proposing, such as guided backpacking trips, or does not want to allow any more companies to offer these services, you simply will not be able to provide them in that natural area. In most national parks, the U.S. National Park Service and Parks Canada have limited the number of permits to existing operators and in many cases have restricted use levels. As was discussed in chapter 1, these limits are in place to protect the environment and keep the quality of the user experience high. So to get started, entrepreneurs may need to seek permits from other agencies or buy a company with an existing permit.

Contracts must also be obtained from private land owners for desirable store locations and access to specific recreation areas, such as rock climbing or river rafting launch sites. Terms of the contract can make them exclusive to just one company or may be open to an unlimited number of providers. Frequently, federal and state agency contracts limit the amount of use allowed, when and where it can occur, and even the price that can be charged. Obviously, having a contract for exclusive or limited (one that limits the number of competitors) access is a desirable situation, but a contract may also place significant limitations on what you can do and how many guests you can take. As a prospective entrepreneur, you must check to see if permits are available, how many others are permitted, the permit requirements, and amount of use allowed. Other important concerns when buying an existing company are if the permit is transferable to the new entity, if it is automatic, and how complicated and lengthy the transfer process is.

STARTING YOUR DREAM BUSINESS IN AN EXOTIC COUNTRY

Many U.S. and Canadian residents have traveled in exotic developing countries and have dreams of starting a recreation business there. Some have succeeded, while other people have been frustrated and lost their money. One certainty expressed by all those who have tried to start a small recreation business in a foreign country is that it is not as easy as it appears at first. There are significant differences in the culture and economy where you'd be working, compared with your home country, which greatly influences the feasibility and profitability of a new company. In addition, there may be government regulations that directly or indirectly make it difficult to get started. Potential entrepreneurs cannot assume they can simply use their developed country money to buy their way to success. See Spotlight On Costa Rica Rios for a description of the start-up of an adventure travel business in Costa Rica by two U.S. residents and described in more detail in Case Study 2.3 in the online student resource.

Foreign countries can offer unique opportunities to start your own recreation company compared with your home turf. For example, government permits in the United States and Canada may be limited and already allocated, thus preventing your access. To buy an existing permitted company may be prohibitively

SPOTLIGHT ON

Costa Rica Rios

Location

The central office, warehouse, and bed and breakfast are located in the small city of Turrialba, Costa Rica, south of the country's capital, in Central America. They also have an adventure camp with tent cabins, a zipline course, and a kitchen in a remote location along the Pacuare River in the deep tropical forest.

Background

Costa Rica Rios began in 2001 after Bret Shelton, a young furloughed airplane pilot, Skip Harris, an expert kayaker, and Brian Cuttlers, a recent college graduate and Internet expert, met during trips to Costa Rica. They particularly enjoyed kayaking on the wild class IV (expert) internationally renowned rapids of the Rio Pacuare, hiking in the surrounding rain forest, and hanging out in the nearby historic city of Turrialba. There, Bret and Skip worked as river guides for an adventure company that offered

A guided rafting trip on the Pacuare River in Costa Rica.

Patrick T. Tierney

mostly one-day river trips and canyoneering down creek canyons using climbing equipment. When the owner became seriously ill, Bret offered to buy the company and went looking for partners to help him operate it. The resulting company incorporated in Costa Rica as Costa Rica Rios. Skip became the trip operations manager, Brian became the general and office manager, and Bret became the financial manager. After the sale, the management team made the strategic decision to consolidate the wide-ranging types of trips offered and to focus on the more profitable and longer trips. They concentrated on three- to seven-day kayaking trips and a program involving a week of adventures.

Products and Services

Costa Rica Rios now specializes in week-of-adventures programs. The week includes riding a zipline above a lush jungle-covered canyon, rafting through exciting rapids in a warmer-water river past waterfalls and colorful birds, plunging down a trail on the side of a smoking volcano atop a high-tech mountain bike, and learning to surf in the warm Caribbean Sea. They operate a shop and Spanish Colonial bed and breakfast for their guests in Turrialba, located close to the Pacuare River. They also contracted with a U.S.-based company to act as their booking agent and answer toll-free telephone lines, because it was extremely expensive to take or make calls from Costa Rica to the United States or Canada. (See case study 2.3 in the online student resource for more details.) Brian is now a full-time resident of Costa Rica.

Business Advice and Plans

Bret and Brian have plans to advance the company through fine-tuning and making their existing operations as profitable as possible. This could include purchasing real estate that supports these operations. They want to manage growth so they do not incur a large amount of debt that could put them in jeopardy during a down cycle in international travel. They hope to build a hotel on the Caribbean coast now that they have completed their Pacuare Adventure Camp.

expensive. The marketplace for your type of recreation service may already be saturated in your country compared with the growing demand for international travel experiences. For example, outbound travel spending by U.S. residents grew 21 percent between 2003 and 2005 (Research and Markets, 2006). The World Travel and Tourism Council research (2007) indicates that total international travel is projected to grow 4.3 percent per annum between 2007 and 2017. Overall tourism in some other countries, such as China, is projected to grow much more rapidly than in the United States and Canada (Varma, 2007), and this provides unique opportunities for persons who are willing to relocate. In addition, tourism and recreation resources, such as beachfront property, may be undervalued in developing countries compared with the United States. These areas may be the only places where you can afford to buy property with limited financial resources. Labor costs and some operating costs can be significantly less in many countries. Large corporations have recognized this and are outsourcing manufacturing and service jobs to places such as India and China, where labor costs a fraction of what it does in the United States or Canada. Finally, growing up in the United States or Canada allows you to better understand these source markets and the tourism system there, thus offering the opportunity for you to be much more effective in promoting and selling your services than is the isolated local resident.

But there are almost always significant unique challenges in starting and managing a recreation company in a developing country, especially a rural location. Language barriers may be significant if you are not fluent in the country's language. This can spell disaster in difficult business negotiations. Some other large challenges for U.S. and Canadian residents starting a company in places like Central and South America are to understand how to get things done in another culture. It often takes significantly more time to get through government red tape, local politicians, and a morbidly slow economy. They operate under a different system of laws and norms, with corruption sometimes a concern. The slow pace of a rural economy may be highly valued by visitors, but it can be very frustrating to a businessperson. The cultural meaning of time and work ethic can be very different in another country, and a businessperson cannot assume the local workforce has the same motivations and ideas they do. Another

challenge is meeting North American client expectations in a developing country, where service levels may be much lower.

The key to high service quality is your staff. You cannot import all key staff from North America without quickly alienating local residents and losing their support. Significant training of the local workforce may be needed, and this takes time and patience. Employees may be used to operating under a strict "top-down" management structure where they always wait for directions from supervisors. As one Costa Rica Rios manager reported that all the labor laws and government systems are designed to support a strong top-down labor structure, and this greatly slows down productivity. It may be difficult to attain the high service levels expected by sophisticated guests without staff taking more initiative in a flatter organizational structure. When a company finds well-qualified bilingual workers, it is often difficult to retain them because they are in very high demand by many types of businesses.

Learning how the local economy works is another challenge facing a North American start-up. Although labor costs can be a fraction of what they are in the United States, worker productivity can be significantly less. However, many goods such as computers and cars cost as much or more than in the United States. It may take a great deal of time getting needed equipment. Going out of the country and importing these back in makes them subject to import tax duties that can greatly increase their cost. If your equipment is expensive and poorly maintained and your service quality is low to the point where guests do not return and spread negative word of mouth, lower labor costs will not lead to profitability.

A tourism business located in a beautiful but remote third-world area at a great distance from major cities and their primary North American or European source markets is very vulnerable to drastic fluctuations in international travel. The events of September 11, 2001, and the subsequent drastic drop in international travel showed that many remote tourism destinations suffered worse than destinations within North America and Europe. Traveler safety, political turmoil, and terrorism are serious concerns affecting tourism in many parts of the world today. A small recreation business has little control over these factors, but they can greatly influence its viability.

The previous discussion was not meant to discourage you from considering starting an RET business in a foreign country but rather to offer considerations for you to think about when assessing feasibility and developing a business plan. U.S. and Canadian residents are successfully operating businesses internationally, such as Costa Rica Rios. But as Brian Cuttlers, general manager of Costa Rica Rios remarked, "Starting and running this company has been the hardest thing I've ever done, but also very rewarding."

INITIAL CONSIDERATIONS AT THE START OF THE PLANNING PROCESS

Starting a business takes passion, talent, motivation, research, and planning. As discussed in subsequent chapters, take time before you start your business so you can investigate your personal and business goals and write a comprehensive and thorough business plan. This will help you avoid potential start-up mistakes that, while not always fatal, make it much more difficult to succeed (see the earlier section on Fatal Start-Up Mistakes of RET Businesses on page 30). Here are some initial considerations at the start of the RET business planning process.

1. Identify the two primary reasons why you want to go into business: Is it creative freedom, to fully use your talents and skills, to be the best in a recreation activity related to your business, such as rock climbing; or is it to be your own boss? If your primary motive is to make a large amount of money right away, you are probably naive, as it usually takes years for a business to become successful, and recreation entrepreneurs often accept lifestyle benefits for lower incomes. Profits can be substantial once established.

2. Is this the correct business for you? What is your passion; how do you like to spend your time; do you have recreation skills that can generate income; do you have the time to put into a business; or what do others say you are good at doing?

3. What skills, experience, and resources do you bring to the business? If you are inexperienced, consider working for someone else and letting that person train you first as an employee. If you have few resources, you may need to wait to amass enough to see you through the start-up.

Once you have taken time to address these basic considerations and you are still enthusiastic about starting your RET business, then it is appropriate to think about the need for a **business plan** and its components.

NEED FOR A BUSINESS PLAN

Although planning cannot guarantee success, a thorough and well-thought-out business plan will significantly increase the chances of a thriving start-up or expansion. A business plan forces the entrepreneur to take more than a wishful casual look at the feasibility of the business. Love for a recreation, event, or tourism activity is not enough, and you can't eat beautiful scenery. So a plan must show how you will be able to support yourself through the first lean years and if the company will provide enough income once fully established. Although you may find owners who started without a plan, they are in the minority, and it is getting more competitive. Financial institutions and lenders invariably want to see a complete business plan before offering funding. Robert Krummer Jr., chairman of First Business Bank in Los Angeles, states it well: "The business plan is a necessity. If the person who wants to start a small business can't put a business plan together, he or she is in trouble"(Small Business Administration, 2005).

BUSINESS PLANNING PROCESS

A properly prepared business plan allows you to make a sound decision about the financial feasibility and profitability of your business concept. This section discusses the basic steps in the plan development process. Figure 2.2 illustrates how you'll need to get your ideas together, gather information from outside and inside sources, write up the plan, and eventually sign contracts and train new staff. This will take time, usually two to six months for a small business. The plan will probably end up being between 20 and 40 pages in length, including appendixes. But writing the plan should not be overly time consuming. Getting extensive data may not significantly add to the accuracy of the plan. You must move with calculated quickness or you miss the best opportunity.

So a balanced commercial recreation planning process is needed. It must result in enough depth of detail to answer critical questions (e.g., is there enough demand for your proposed service?) without

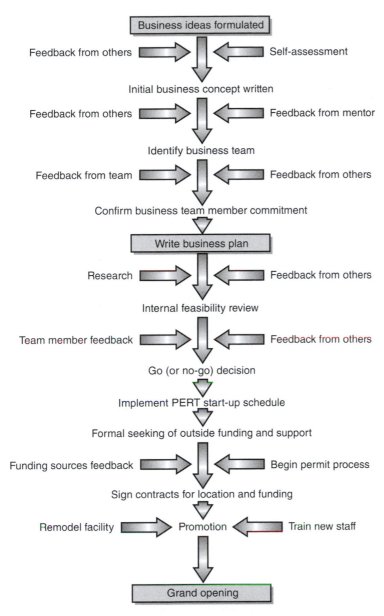

Figure 2.2 Steps in the business planning process.

overly holding back implementation. However, in the process of planning you may find that your business concept will not pan out because it will not provide you enough income or the consumer demand is lacking. This is commendable because you have learned during the process and saved yourself a great deal of money and effort.

Steps in the RET Business Planning Process

The RET planning process includes basic steps after which feedback and other actions are needed before proceeding to the next step. At first you take your

somewhat initial business ideas and get feedback from others and conduct the self-assessment described earlier in this chapter. Using this information you should develop a clear business concept. A business concept is a coordinated set of services and products built around one specific business theme. See chapter 3 for details on how to develop your concept. Feedback from a mentor and others is often very valuable before proceeding to the next stage. Seldom can a businessperson develop a company on her own. To develop this concept further, a strong start-up team of key professionals is needed before opening. You should contact these persons and get commitments and feedback from them. Together your team writes your business plan, conducting research and getting feedback from others along the way. Figure 2.3 describes the sections of an RET business plan. Chapter 5 of this book provides guidance for marketing analysis, identifying target markets, and competitor analysis. Chapter 6 describes marketing, promotions, and communications, while chapter 11 provides insights into financial planning and analysis.

Once the business plan is written, it should provide you and your start-up team with an initial financial feasibility of the proposal. Chapter 11 assists you in preparing financial statements and assessing financial feasibility of your RET business. Feedback from the start-up team, mentors, and others often requires you to make revisions to the initial financial section. After your best profitability estimates have been developed, it is time to make the go or no-go decision. If you decide to proceed, then develop a start-up schedule of key steps to opening. Here again chapter 11 will provide guidance and final actions needed for opening day. One critical step in the start-up schedule is seeking needed outside funding. This often involves a formal meeting with potential funding organizations and the presentation of your plan. Feedback from these financial representatives is frequently used to make revisions to your financial and funding proposal. Ideally this leads to a commitment of funds. There is no turning back now. All the pieces are in place to

Tech Application

Individual Technology Tool Kit for the Modern RET Entrepreneur

A recreation, event, and tourism entrepreneur or manager will face many challenges, not the least of which are multitasking and being ultraproductive with your work time. There will be a multitude of tasks to accomplish, but rarely will you have long periods of uninterrupted work time to complete them. You'll need to make the most of work opportunities when they arise, be it at the airport or waiting for a meeting to begin, or else you may find yourself working all the time just to keep up. A range of information technology (IT) tools for individual business professionals is essential for survival in the modern work environment. Listed below are some IT tool types, their uses, and specific software programs that an owner or manager can gain great benefit from by becoming proficient in their use.

Technology type	Uses	Specific tool or program
Contact management	Client and coworker contact info	Oncontact, ACT, Outlook
Calendar and scheduling	Scheduling, tickler system	Oncontact, ACT, Outlook
Word processing	Written communications	MS Word, Word Perfect
Budgeting and finance	Creating and analyzing financial data	MS Excel, QuickBooks
Web site editing and updating	Designing and updating your Web site	Dreamweaver, FrontPage
Digital photo editing	Manipulating digital photos	Photoshop, After Effects
Creating flyers, brochures, ads	Sale flyers, brochures	Publisher, Illustrator
E-mail management	Receiving and organizing messages	Eudora, Outlook
Presentations	Sales and info presentations	PowerPoint, Captivate
Making yourself mobile	Can be at work almost anywhere	PDA or laptop

This technology will require more than the average cell phone. A high-powered personal data assistant (PDA) with large internal memory and high-speed Internet connectivity is essential to glean critical information from e-mail and contact management programs. A laptop is even more powerful and needed to run all of these, but you may not want to carry a laptop everywhere you go on business. With wireless connectivity, you can choose to be "at the office" almost anywhere. But all this technology will do you more harm than good if you are not using the most up-to-date information or if you outright lose your valuable data. It is essential to synchronize (update) your PDA or laptop with the data in your office computer system on a daily work basis or a real-time basis. PDAs and laptops crash and are lost or stolen. So it is critical to synchronize your PDA daily, which acts like a backup, and then do a complete backup to a secure data storage device on a regular basis. If your PDA and laptop are lost or stolen, your data must be protected from exposure. Federal and state laws, as well as credit card companies, now require at least password protection of sensitive client data, not to mention your own private data. Finally, you may need to take a short course to optimize your effective use of the technology. So if you have the right technology equipment and software; are connected via wireless; and take serious precautions in case of equipment failure, loss, or theft, then technology can be a great tool to increase your level of service and productivity.

take the final steps, as described in chapter 12, before opening day. Final steps often include remodeling a facility, installing needed equipment, and instituting initial promotions as well as hiring and training new staff. Then it is the grand opening, and ready or not, the doors open to your first customers.

A review of this planning process for an RET business indicates that considerable lead time, feedback, and research is needed, as well as a concise, well-written plan. All this effort must be done expeditiously, usually in less than one year, often six months.

Components of a RET Business Plan

The following chapters in this book describe in detail the considerations, data sources, and techniques to research and write the business plan sections identified here. Your plan will consist of words (i.e., descriptions and justifications), numbers (i.e., trends and projections), and appendixes (for detailed data and supporting documents). You'll describe a business concept and the related set of services and products built around your business theme. Figure 2.3 shows the basic sections of a business plan.

The key sections of a comprehensive plan, discussed further in chapter 12, include a cover letter to proposed financial backers; a description of your RET business concept, services, and prices; a market, industry, and competitor analysis; a marketing and promotions plan; your management organizational team; environmental management standards; risk management; and the financial proposal, consisting of financial analysis and funding plan. Describing all the plan elements shown in figure 2.3 in sufficient detail is essential before a full commitment to a start of a new firm. Leaving out any one section or a lack of appropriate research could affect the success of your venture.

ASSISTANCE IN THE PLANNING PROCESS

You should be the primary author of the plan, but you will need help from information sources, other persons, and institutions, and you must employ appropriate software.

General Business Plan Resources

- U.S. Small Business Administration: www.sba.gov
- Canada Business Services for Entrepreneurs: www.canadabusiness.ca/gol/cbec/site.nsf
- U.S. Chamber of Commerce: www.uschamber.com/sb/business/sb/toolkits
- Money Hunter: www.moneyhunter.com
- Business Plans.Com: www.bplans.com

Organizations and Individuals

- Trusted colleagues: Colleagues can provide informal advice and unbiased observations.
- Banks and financial institutions: Banks may provide online business plan guides (e.g., Bank of America, www.bankofamerica.com/smallbusiness/resourcecenter). They also review nearly complete plans if the loan may be through them.
- Universities: Universities offer small business assistance programs, small business incubators, consultants, research, and student interns. For example, see the University of North Carolina, Small Business and Technology Development Center: www.sbtdc.org.
- Paid consultants: There are many companies offering these services. Depending on the complexity of your proposal, your experience, and their experience, they can provide very useful

---

1. Introduction
   A. Cover letter
   B. Executive summary
2. Business description
   A. Business concept, products, services, and experiences
   B. Market, industry, and competitor analysis
   C. Marketing and promotion
   D. Management practices, organizational team, service standards, environmental management, and risk management
3. Financial strategy
   A. Financial analysis
   B. Funding plan
   C. Key action steps

Figure 2.3 Sections of a business plan.

ideas and reviews. An example is Adventure Business Consultants, www.adventurebizsuccess.com. But remember, you must become a knowledgeable expert in your chosen business—no one can replace that.

- Industry associations: Recreation industry associations can provide statistics, consultants, and business planning assistance to members. Examples include the U.S. Bowling Association (www.bowl.com) and the Canadian Ski Council (www.canadianskicouncil.org).

BUSINESS PLAN SOFTWARE

Many software programs are available to assist in plan writing. But you must still do the research and compile the data that is asked for in planning software. So business plan software may be of limited value, especially if you follow the planning steps throughout this book and use the online commercial recreation business plan templates provided on the online student resource. Chapter 12 discusses finishing and funding your plan. The online student resource provides a business plan checklist and sample forms.

RELATIONSHIP TO OTHER TYPES OF PLANS

The most common goals of a business plan are to assess the feasibility of your business concept and how to fund it. But it often lacks detailed operating procedures and projections. Government permitting agencies, financial institutions, and partner organizations often require additional detailed operation planning documents before they will allow a business to start. For example, the National Park Service requires resource protection and risk management plans (see chapter 10) before approving a permit application. Financial institutions may want to see up-to-date financial performance statistics and an operations plan for the next one to five years when asked to provide funding for expansion. In addition, a company produces an operational budget providing very detailed projections of revenue and expenses for the upcoming year. All these operational documents must normally be consistent with the original business plans. Case studies in the online student resource and Spotlights On individual entrepreneurs and also specific RET companies in the following chapters provide examples of operational budgets.

SUMMARY

There are countless opportunities for entrepreneurs and intrepreneurs to start or expand a commercial recreation, event, or tourism business. Many sources point to growing global demand for these services. Consumer use and expenditure patterns in these fields are changing at a rapid pace. These changes provide openings for shrewd entrepreneurs to start their own business, buy an existing one, or grow a company in which they are employed. The benefits of each option are worth exploring. Do you have the characteristics of an entrepreneur? An entrepreneur must be concerned about the legal form of the business. Some forms are better suited for small RET businesses than others because they provide shielding of personal assets, clarify legal control of the company, and offer tax advantages. An important initial step in setting up your own recreation business is protecting your intellectual property. Another step is ensuring you can acquire the necessary permits and licenses that will allow you to operate when and where you want. Before committing, consider a number of factors about yourself and your proposed business in order to avoid making one of the common fatal mistakes of small businesses. Avoiding these fatal mistakes is often related to the preparation of a business plan. There are many good reasons to prepare a thorough plan, such as increased chances of a successful launch, profitability, and finding financing. This chapter discusses steps in the business plan development process and outlines the components of a typical commercial recreation business plan. The entrepreneur should be the primary author of the plan, but assistance in writing the plan is available from various sources. Finally, it is important to understand the relationships between a business plan and other planning documents, such as the annual budget.

 Check out the online student resource for additional material, including case studies, Web links, and more.

Part
II

Planning Basics

Chapter 3

Business Concept: Products and Services

Imagine this scenario: You have been recognized by your peers as an up-and-coming young entrepreneur at your school and invited to participate in a debate at the annual general meeting of the Association of Collegiate Entrepreneurs (ACE). It is quite an honor as you and three others will form teams to speak about the resolution adopted for this debate. You are assigned to be on the team that will present arguments in favor of the resolution. As a proponent speaking in favor of the statement, it will be your task to convince the audience your position is the correct point of view. The resolution reads as follows: "Resolved: Success for a start-up business begins with your business concept; a commitment to your vision; and a clear, easy to understand mission statement." Quickly you realize it will be important to define what each item is, how the business concept is strengthened by commitment to a vision, and whether or not evidence suggests a mission statement makes a difference in terms of measures of business success. There are two other points that need to be established—first, why is it important for a mission statement to appear at the beginning part of a business plan, and second, who passes judgment as to whether it is "clear and easy to understand"? You quickly realize you have some research to undertake in order to put together a convincing argument. The debate looks like a daunting but exciting opportunity to demonstrate the oratory skills you learned in your recent class on public speaking and debate.

In this chapter, we examine why you need to be able to describe your business concept, outline the mission statement, and identify how you intend to operate as a business. You probably will want to know why preparing a mission statement is considered a vital step to getting a start-up business heading down the road to success. To do this, we explore some examples of mission statements in the RET industry today and what research suggests is evidence of their importance. Given the range of stakeholders in any particular business, what do mission statements mean to customers, employees, investors, or the business owner? Most important, how is your statement tied to the vision of the business concept?

THE BUSINESS CONCEPT

One of the most exciting and creative stages of the business planning process is to clearly elaborate your unique and specific **business concept**. Your concept provides insights into identifying the key elements of your business plan: its purpose, products and services, name, and legal status. Under the heading **business description** (chapter 12), you are expected to outline important aspects of the overall concept and identify such things as name, legal status, and location, if appropriate. Essentially in this part of the business plan, it is important to clearly and precisely describe the purpose of the business because the goal is to sell the idea and to inspire the reader. At the core of explaining your concept is the **mission statement**.

A clear and easy-to-understand mission statement provides insight as to why the business exists and its purpose, the type of customers the business seeks to serve, and why the business does what it does. Altogether this chapter lays out the specific details, practices, and decisions you need to attend to in order to stake out your territory in the world of business. In terms of the business concept, it can be considered a two-step process.

BUSINESSES ARE CREATED TWICE

In business, a popular phrase coined to encourage business owners to plan ahead states that "those who fail to plan are planning to fail." Although there is no doubt you can learn a great deal from a business failure, it is not something you should plan to experience. Therefore, the careful description of the business concept is the first task. When it comes to planning for success, perhaps Dr. Stephen Covey (1992) stated it best when he said, "All things are created twice" (p. 99). His message is straightforward. First, you have to think, dream, or visualize what it is you aspire to do in life. Second, you implement that dream, aspiration, or goal. In other words, first comes the mental image, and second comes the reality. Stephen Covey's suggestion about first creating the mental image of the business can be applied to the step of thinking strategically about the business plan. In terms of a strategic planning process, people refer to the task of creating a vision as seeking to define a desired future state. "A vision is a marketing objective describing the organization's view of where they would like to be in the future" (Morrison, 2002, p. 601). As an analogy, you might consider building a home. First you have to create a vision of what kind of house you want, how you will live in it, and what kind of space is important for personal comfort. Next come the blueprints, followed by the actual construction of the home. A vision essentially means visualizing what the future of your start-up business will look like and explaining it in writing. Following are the initial two tasks involved:

1. Describe the purpose of the business and do so in a customer-oriented fashion. This means focusing on customer needs and the experiences or services that will be delivered. When you can state why the business exists, you give substance to the mission statement.

2. Create a concise, inspiring, and vivid image that best defines where this business is headed.

A **vision statement** is not about why you exist but rather an aspiration of where you are headed. It is often a creative, forward-thinking, value-laden, inspiring word picture that reveals an affirmation of an ideal the business seeks to achieve. The word image of a vision is most effective when it is valued and shared by everyone in the business because it creates unity and reinforces commitment to your mission statement. The vision statement provokes stakeholders to take ownership of the aspirations reflected within the statement.

The sequence in which these steps are undertaken is not important; however, the steps are linked and reinforce each other. Many times people with a recreation, events, tourism, and leisure studies education have an advantage when describing a leisure product because of the personal skills that initially drew them into the field as well as knowledge of what contributes to a satisfying customer experience. Often, you can draw on firsthand experiences, the knowledge of what you love to do in leisure, and the ability to match it to a consumer need.

FIRST ASK WHY

When you consider starting a recreation or tourism business, you have a rather unique opportunity to sketch a picture in words about *why* the business should exist in the first place. Basically the challenge is to answer the question "What is the reason for the business?" Consultants and business school gurus will consider it impressive and praiseworthy if you can write an answer to this question thoughtfully and in as few words as possible . . . provided you don't miss the point of answering the question. When you answer this question, you are taking the vital step necessary to prepare a mission statement. It's written for several purposes, but basically it serves to remind everyone involved what the purpose is when the time comes to enthusiastically implement the plan. It is entirely possible to believe the business will have more than one purpose, but it is necessary to focus on the core reason and then develop a set of principles to elaborate on important values. Other statements are drawn from the business examples introduced throughout this chapter because the case study often reveals important practices pertaining to the business concept, name, and legal status. Perhaps the best-known example of a concise and easily understood mission statement is the one attributed to Walt Disney, which will be revealed in more detail in the next several paragraphs.

MISSION STATEMENT: THE CORNERSTONE OF YOUR BUSINESS CONCEPT

Considerable literature suggests alternative ways of defining what a mission statement is or is not. Kotler (2005, p. 48) states, "A mission statement is a statement of organizational purpose—why do we exist and how do our core values fit into that purpose?" Thus, the basic question your mission statement should answer is "Why does this business exist?" and the purpose needs to be oriented to your customer. In other words, the mission should pay attention to satisfying the needs of customers because that is the foundation of the business. The purpose should not focus on the products because those things are a means to achieving your purpose, and it should reflect meeting a consumer need. The primary reason to focus on specific consumer wants and needs is they are long-lasting and more enduring over time. Products generally conform to a predictable life cycle and become outdated as times change.

NOW ASK FOR PROOF

If mission statements are such a good thing, where are they evident in RET businesses? Ask a previous visitor to Disney's Magic Kingdom to tell you what she remembers most about the experience, and you can expect to hear something about one or more of the product lines of the theme park, such as Adventureland, Frontierland, Fantasyland, Liberty Square, Main Street, Tomorrowland, and so forth. Each of the kingdoms in this popular destination can be described in terms of entertainment, what they contain, and how each area can capture customer attention with the diverse attractions and special features. Fjellman (1992, p. 16) provides a specific narrative on what Disney is able to do to attract large numbers of customers:

> *Disney is not just offering entertainment. The Company is also selling, to those of us that can afford it, an antidote to everyday life. Under the rule of the commodity, our lives have become fragmented and confusing. Our environments are dangerous and threatening. Our sense of powerlessness is fed by institutions of modern life and by the uncontrollable behavior of others. What we buy at Walt Disney World is not just fun and souvenirs but is also a welcome civility on a human scale.*

Stephen Fjellman's interpretation of Disney World is insightful and interesting. It captures some of the expectations visitors might have associated with Disney's Magic Kingdom, but does it actually represent the mission statement Walt Disney embraced? You will recall the question to be answered by a mission statement is *why* does this business exist? What is its purpose? If you know the answer as to why Disney World exists, write it down now. Walt Disney's mission statement as to why Disney World and Disneyland exist is simply "to make people happy." Now, it may appear to be too simple or too brief because it does not address *how* it

will be done or *what* exact services will be delivered to ensure visitors are happy. But it does tell us *why* the Disney Corporation exists, and it is a timeless statement that reminds customers and other stakeholders of the expected outcome of all organizational decisions. Of course, it is possible to identify other mission statements prepared for nonprofit organizations as well as businesses that produce specific products very different from Disney-type experiences. Several other such timeless statements of purpose address the question of why several other organizations exist, and they appear in table 3.1.

If you ask this question—what is the purpose of this business?—in the cases related to the mission statements in table 3.1, then you should be able to clearly understand *why* the businesses exist.

PR NEWSWIRE/Scott Brinegar

The mission statement for Disney World is simply "to make people happy."

Table 3.1 Sample of Mission Statements

Organization	Mission statement—*Our purpose is to*
United Way	*increase the capacity of people to care for one another*
Merck	*preserve and improve human life*
Celestial Seasons	*create a soothing, non-caffeinated after-dinner beverage*
Starbucks	*become the premier purveyor of the finest coffee in the world*
Sears Holdings	*be the preferred and most trusted resource for the products and services that enhance home and family life*
Harrah's Entertainment	*ensure each of our brands will be the overwhelming first choice for casino entertainment of its target customers*
Tesoro	*create opportunities that exceed yesterday's successes and maximize our potential*
Washington Mutual	*be the nation's leading retailer of financial services for consumers and small businesses*
Warm Rapids Inn	*help people experience the natural beauty of the Cowichan Valley*

PROFITABILITY AND LONGEVITY: MEASURES OF SUCCESS

In a recent study of major businesses, researchers wanted to find out whether or not the presence of a published mission statement had any correlation with the established success of a specific Fortune 500 company. The two measurements of success in terms of the company were longevity and profitability. In that study titled "Mission Statement Impact Assessment," (Mission Expert and Kinetic Wisdom, 2006), the researcher applied the two indicators to the top 50 companies selected from a sample of Fortune 500. The results reveal that when the two success indicators were examined for the businesses with published mission statements,

- 98 percent of the companies reported the highest five-year growth in revenues, and
- 90 percent of the companies had the highest one-year growth in revenues.

The researchers concluded that published mission statements apparently have a significant role to play in the profitability of major businesses. Apparently, being able to see the reason for a business to exist can make a difference in its bottom line. Or in the humorous and famous words of Yogi Berra, "You can observe a lot just by watching" (http://creatingminds.org/quotes/seeing).

On the other hand, the description of a vision for a business addresses the core values of the company. You might wonder at this point why you even need a vision if you have an effective mission statement. Is it really that important to bother writing one? The subject of vision statements is examined next.

WHY BOTHER WITH A VISION?

The creation of a vision has the capacity to generate excitement about the business concept. Ken Blanchard and Jesse Stoner (2004) believe a clearly stated vision is essential for success and greatness. Their reasoning is that when any member of a business team makes a decision with the end in mind (e.g., the vision of the business), then it will be a good decision because it is more likely to advance the long-term interests of the business. Making good choices based on a clear understanding of the core business values should be part of all decision making. That applies to small businesses as well as big corporations. Moreover, if a small business enterprise aspires to become a large business, the vision statement is a very critical component of the journey taken by the business. Table 3.2 presents a range of vision statements employing several of the tourism trade sector categories previously introduced in figure 1.4.

In a letter to General Electric shareholders, Jack Welch extolled the success of managers in terms of the new role the manager needs to perform:

Table 3.2 Sample of Vision or Value Statement for RET Enterprises

Accommodation	
Hilton Hotels http://hiltonworldwide1.hilton.com/en_US/ww/business/values.do	Hilton Hotel's vision is "To be the first choice of the world's travelers, building on the rich heritage and strength of our brand."
Food and beverage	
Starbucks www.starbucks.com/aboutus/environment.asp	Starbucks has six guiding principles to be employed in decision making. • Provide a great work environment and teach each other with respect and dignity. • Embrace diversity as an essential component in the way we do business. • Apply the highest standards of excellence to the purchasing, roasting, and fresh delivery of our coffee. • Develop enthusiastically satisfied customers all of the time. • Contribute positively to our communities and our environment. • Recognize that profitability is essential to our future success.
Celestial Seasonings	The vision of Celestial Seasonings is "to provide a high quality herb tea in beautiful packaging at a good price to the widest distribution as possible."
Transportation	
Norfolk Southern RR http://www.nscorp.com/nscportal/nscorp/	The vision of Norfolk Southern RR is "to be the safest, most customer-focused and successful transportation company in the world."
Virgin Group Company http://www.virgin.com/aboutvirgin/allaboutvirgin/whatwereabout/default.asp	Virgin's vision is "to create a brand that reflects value for money, quality, innovation, brilliant customer service, fun and a sense of competitive challenge. We deliver a quality service by empowering our employees and we facilitate and monitor customer feedback to continually improve the customer's experience through innovation."
Tourism services	
Time Warner www.timewarner.com/corp/aboutus/mission_values.html	The seven core values for success at Time Warner are creativity, customer focus, agility, teamwork, integrity, diversity, and responsibility. Each value has a statement elaborating on its meaning. For example: • *Customer focus*—We value our customers, putting their needs and interests at the center of everything we do. • *Integrity*—We rigorously uphold editorial independence and artistic expression, earning the trust of our readers, viewers, listeners, members, and subscribers.
Tourism Industry Association of Canada (TIAC) www.tiac-aitc.ca/english/welcome.asp	TIAC's vision is to ensure the following: • The government agenda is conducive to a growing and sustainable tourism industry. • An industry-led national tourism strategy exists that includes human resources, marketing, infrastructure, and the environment. • There is an effective advocate for tourism interests. • There is a national clearing house for information on tourism issues. • There is significant growth in the tourism industry in Canada. • Value is provided for membership investment.

Events and conferences	
Sutter Creek Theatre	Sutter Creek Theatre's vision is to be a vital, regionally recognized theatre of true artistic merit and a business that is acknowledged as being vital to the economic health of Sutter Creek.
Ramona Pageant Association www.ramonabowl.com/	Our Vision is two-fold: (1) to preserve, maintain and protect the Bowl—a 160 acre natural hillside amphitheatre and its supporting facilities; and (2) to insure the continued presentation of the historic outdoor play *Ramona*, community and educational programs and quality theatre entertainment.
Attractions	
Disney World	Walt Disney's vision is "to make people happy."
Polynesian Cultural Center	The cultural center's vision is to share with the world the cultures, diversity, and spirit of the nations of Polynesia.
Travel trade	
Canada West Ski Area Association	CWSAA's vision is to develop, coordinate, and vigorously promote superior programs that educate and enhance the well-being of the ski industry and its individual members.

In the old culture, managers got their power from secret knowledge: profit margins, market share, and all that. . . . In the new culture, the role of the leader is to express a vision, get buy-in, and implement it. That calls for open, caring relations with every employee, and face-to-face communication. People who can't convincingly articulate a vision won't be successful. (www.1000ventures. com/business_guide/crosscuttings/cs_leadership_ welch.html)

Advocacy for adoption of a vision by leaders within and outside of business can help focus on the value of the affirmation. Consider for a moment the circumstances facing Helen Keller (1880-1968), a world-famous author and American social activist who was both deaf and blind throughout most of her life. However, she was determined to learn about the world that she could neither see nor hear. She accomplished her aspiration by having words signed in the palm of her hand by her teacher. In her struggle to overcome adversity, Helen Keller became an inspiration to many observing her extraordinary achievements in life. When she was asked if "there was anything worse than being blind," she replied, "Yes, a person with sight but no vision" (www.quotationspage.com/ quote/25614.html).

GUIDELINES FOR A VISION

As priest, poet, and essayist Jonathan Swift wrote, "Vision is the art of seeing things invisible." Today in the business world, writing a vision is the art of making visible the important values chosen to guide business decisions and to clarify the contributions a business intends to make for an extended period of time in the industry of which it is a part. Such a statement is most likely to endure if it is carefully written to be understood by employees or shareholders. Questions to be posed when examining such a statement might include the following. The guides can serve as basic standards for judging whether you have prepared a good and effective vision.

- Is the statement of your vision concise and uncomplicated?
- Is it sufficiently inspiring to serve as an integral part of the business?
- Will it be appealing to your employees and those you contract for services?
- Does it make a commitment to quality and provide direction (e.g., a North Star in the sky)?
- Is it timeless, and does it possess the potential to endure for the lifespan of the business?

Chapter 7 gives attention to teamwork in business, so it is vital for employees to understand the core values of a business. In reference to the employees, Blanchard and Stoner (2004, p. 55) state a vision is important when it "provides a picture of the desired future, and offers valuable guidelines that help people make daily decisions." Another application of a vision statement is in the context of either strategic planning or a marketing strategy.

For example, take the case of a 21-year-old outdoor enthusiast and aspiring entrepreneur from Colorado who believed the trend in food products was toward healthy choices, and he truly liked the idea of natural food products. He visualized a need for the creation of a soothing, noncaffeinated, after-dinner beverage. He stated his vision for his marketing strategy would be *to provide a high quality herbal tea in beautiful packaging at a good price to the widest distribution as possible.* This entrepreneur, Mo Segal, founded a small business known today as Celestial Seasonings, and his vision guided the growth of his core concept for more than 30 years. He borrowed $500.00 to get started in business with a single tea, Red Zinger; however, he believed he would eventually distribute a variety of high-quality tea products. Accordingly, he set financial goals for the creation of more products. In spite of many obstacles, he never wavered in his aspiration to eventually reach $100 million in annual sales in his start-up business. When he sold his business in 1998 for $300 million, he exceeded his goal, and it was time for him to adopt another vision he entertained for quite some time . . . he envisioned himself reaching the summits of all mountain peaks over 14,000 feet (4,300 meters) in Colorado. He has successfully implemented that vision as well.

In terms of long-range planning, a vision can endure over time if it conveys three things: (1) a significant purpose, (2) a picture of the future, and (3) clear values. The Hilton hotel company probably accomplished (1) and (2) but not likely the third premise. Their vision is *to be the first choice of the world's travelers.*

BEYOND A MISSION AND VISION STATEMENT: A TIME-TESTED FORMULA

If a patented formula for success in business were to be revealed, its primary two elements would show some form of chemical bonding between (1) a well-defined consumer need and (2) something the business owner loves to do. As the saying goes, for lifelong growth and development, "Do what you love, love what you do." This also applies to business. Each of the following profiles provides an example where the owner gave attention to this motto to some degree. Three entrepreneurs from different countries and different circumstances capitalized on a love for out-of-doors experiences and opportunities. One was attracted to water sports (surfing), another was attracted to the mountains, and the third clearly loved high-risk adventure in the air and crossing the ocean (e.g., hot air balloons and seaworthy sailboats). In each case, the person found ways to build on his serious leisure pastimes and apply this to success in a business venture.

• Spotlight On Hobie Alter and the Hobie Cat Company: Building on the experience of being an accomplished California surfer, Hobart Alter started making surfboards in his garage, and he started to explore new avenues for building high-quality surfing products. His love of the surf and the creation of a team skilled with fiberglass products eventually led to the creation of several new lines of surfboards. He won surfing competitions, and his business took off. Later, he produced a racing catamaran that gained worldwide fame, and the product became a showpiece of the Hobie Cat company.

• Spotlight On John Gow and Silver Star Mountain Resort: John Gow, a Canadian mountaineer and certified ski instructor, established a small mountain guiding business focused on providing experiences in the mountains for youth groups. His small business venture required acquisition of many business skills over a decade. It eventually caught the attention of individuals in resort management, and he was invited to work his way up the ranks of a resort in the northern Rockies—Banff Hot Springs Hotel. Eventually he, and some partners, bought Silver Star ski resort with the idea of serving a wider range of customers and changing the area from a place for weekend ski outings into a full-service destination resort.

• Spotlight On Richard Branson and the Virgin Group: Across the Atlantic Ocean, a British adventurer loved the entertainment industry and thus established a mail-order record company. He signed up several upcoming but unknown musicians to cut some records in his new recording studio under his

SPOTLIGHT ON

Hobie Alter and the Hobie Cat Company

Location

In southern California, Hobart "Hobie" Alter founded his first business building 20 boards per year with very little advertising or promotion. After Hobie littered the family garage too many times with the material to build surfboards, his father moved him to a property on the highway in Dana Point, California. There he opened his Hobie Surfboards business in 1953. The original investment in the business was about $12,000.

Background

Hobie invested considerable effort over a five-year period in shaping, perfecting, and changing his surfboard line. By 1958, Hobie begin to manufacture the most successful foam surfboard line of the time, and the technique is still in use today. His personal interest was in surfboards that were lighter and more responsive than anything else at the time. It's said that he is one of the most successful entrepreneurs in surfing history because of the development of the foam-and-fiberglass surfboard.

In international surfing championships, Hobie placed in the top three in 1958, 1959, and 1962. He made the *Guinness Book of World Records* in 1964 by surfing for 26 miles (42 km) behind the wake of a motorboat from Long Beach to Catalina Island.

Product and Services

Today, the product line for the Hobie Cat Company extends into recreational and racing sailboats, paddle kayaks, fishing boats, and water-sport accessories. In the 1970s the Hobie 16 catamaran was one of the largest competitive sailboat classes ever created. It became the most popular catamaran ever. The company sponsored single-class regattas around the world and established regional, national, and international competitions. Demand for the product soared. Today a *Hobie University* booklet published by the North American Hobie Class Association assists all catamaran owners in acquiring the skills for competition and full enjoyment of the lifestyle associated with the product. The Hobie Web site is at www.hobiecat.com/sailing/index.html.

Besides successful promotional initiatives by the company, luck intervened as well. When the movie *Gidget* was released in 1959, actress Sandra Dee shed light on the beach culture of surfboarding as well as on finding love on Malibu Beach. One outcome was a rapid growth in demand for the product line of Hobie Surfboards and Flex-Fliers. The Beach Boys released their song *Surfin'* two years later, which represented another wave to ride in building the image of the surfboarding lifestyle. *The Endless Summer,* released in 1966, is considered the crown jewel to 10 years of Bruce Brown's surfing documentaries. Brown followed two young surfers around the world in search of the perfect wave and ended up finding quite a few waves in addition to some colorful local characters.

Business Advice and Plans

Hobie's love of surfing and using his new product to successfully compete in major national and international competitive events certainly advanced the visibility of his product line. When it came to seeking advice and getting a second opinion on some of his early business decisions, Hobie says, "Elwood Chapman, my business professor at Chaffey College, helped me a number of times when I was starting up my business and when I had to make some difficult management decisions."

Photo courtesy of Fly.

label, Virgin Records. The owner, Richard Branson, also decided to gain significant publicity for his new business by personally engaging in several adventuresome and exceptionally daring outdoor challenges that brought considerable fame to his company name and, of course, to him as well. Richard Branson was the first person to cross the Atlantic in a hot air balloon, made the fastest Atlantic sailboat crossing, and then participated with Richard Fossett to equip their unique aircraft that would circumnavigate the

SPOTLIGHT ON

John Gow and Silver Star Mountain Resort

Location

In Banff, Alberta, and the Canadian Rockies, John Gow was the third generation of his family to be a mountain or backcountry guide. Although his childhood was split between eastern Canada and a ranch west of Banff, the mountains were the great interest and passion in his youth. In 1964 John found employment in the ski business as a lift operator at Sunshine Village.

Background

John identified that success in the ski industry would require solid qualifications. At that time, there were no recreation management programs in Canada, so he pursued those available within skiing itself. He passed his first certification as a ski instructor in 1965, teaching skiing at Sunshine over the next four years. Summers were spent in mountain-related jobs. At the age of 22, John was a senior examiner in the Canadian Ski Instructors Alliance and a fully certified mountain guide through the Association of Canadian Mountain guides. He was one of only three people to hold those combined qualifications.

Product and Services

John and a partner launched their business, High Horizons, in 1967. The business offered mountaineering schools and camps for teenagers in the Rockies, and it grew into a successful mountain-guiding operation. In 1969 the owners of Sunshine Village offered him the position of assistant manager with the understanding that he would be trained to become president of the company upon retirement of the incumbent.

In the next several years he moved to general manager and then CEO of the expanding resort. During his entire period at Sunshine, John focused on skill development both through mentoring by his boss, the top Canadian ski resort operator of the day, and through courses and seminars run by Selkirk College, the Canada West Ski Areas Association, and the American National Ski Areas Association. There were a myriad of small-business skills to master, including marketing, finance, and human relations, in addition to the specifics of snow resort operations.

As John moved into the higher echelons of management, his grounding in the practical aspects of resort operations put him in good stead, providing the direct link between planning, supporting the aspirations of skiers, and dealing with the realities of operations. During his tenure as CEO of Sunshine Village, the resort grew with the addition of the world's largest gondola system as well as new ski lifts and terrain. The resort annually hosted the largest skier attendance in Canada.

In 1981 John, along with a small group of investors, purchased Silver Star ski area near Vernon, British Columbia. Once a prime British Columbia ski destination, Silver Star had been eclipsed by Whistler, Banff, and other regional destinations. A master plan was in place but it had serious deficiencies, failing to address shortcomings in terrain, vertical drop, and challenge. To John and his team, the proposed village was "cookie cutter" in style, and it isolated day visitors from resort facilities.

It was critical to develop a resort that would attract new, vacation-oriented skiers yet retain and strengthen the loyalty of the strong local customer base, the true backbone of the business. To achieve this, the village plan was revamped to bring day and resort guests together in the core and provide the necessary critical mass. New and exciting ski terrain was developed in the valley to the north, substantially increasing vertical drop and skiable acreage. The resort was rebranded as Silver Star Mountain Resort, nomenclature since copied by almost every ski area in western Canada.

Silver Star Mountain Resort's unique Victorian-style village and the terrain of Putnam Creek have been lauded by virtually every ski publication, and its clientele hail from around the world. Yet the locals are still fiercely proud of "their" resort. John credits his role in this success story to a solid grounding in the basics of the ski business, with a clear understanding of the needs and aspirations of a variety of client groups.

Business Advice and Plans

John's personal experiences in the mountains combined with various professional certifications as a guide and examiner led to his establishment of a small-business partnership. That led to his role as assistant manager, general manager, then CEO of a ski resort, and eventually a corporate owner and CEO of one of western Canada's premier mountain resorts.

Photo courtesy of John R. Gow.

Dr. Gerald Duggleby

Richard Branson and the Virgin Group

Location

Richard Branson's company, the Virgin Group, is based in London, England.

Background

As a young boy in London, Branson had an aunt who bet him that he could not learn to swim a set distance in the following five days. Since he did not know how to swim at the time, he knew it would not be easy. But he persevered, and on the fifth day he won the bet.

Richard Branson.

Richard Branson's first business venture while a teenager was a magazine titled *Student*, which he and a friend published for high school and college students from the basement of a London residence. This magazine business initiative was followed a year later by his mail-order record company called Virgin Records, which expanded into a recording studio in the following two years.

Daring adventures in highly visible settings became yet another risk-taking component that brought attention to his business name. In an interview, Branson admits he always liked challenges, and that fueled several attempts to break world records by crossing either the Atlantic or Pacific Ocean in a hot-air balloon. Successes occurred in 1986 and again in 1991. His attempts to circumnavigate the globe from 1995 to 1998 did not succeed.

When asked about the riskiest thing he has done, Branson says, "I couldn't tell you which was the riskiest because most of the decisions we have to make are risky. The very idea of entrepreneurship conjures up not only thoughts about starting up businesses and building them, but also the more frightening prospect of taking risks and failing. It's the last part that puts off so many people of taking a leap into the unknown and working for themselves. I'm having fun doing what I do, so the risk factor takes a second place."

Products and Services

Branson launched Virgin Atlantic Airlines, Virgin Holidays, Virgin Broadcasting, Virgin Hotels, Virgin America, and Virgin Airship and Balloon Company. During the last decade, many of these companies went international and he established the British Satellite Broadcasting Company. The list of companies operating under the Virgin banner totals over 60. One of the most recent tourism ventures in the United States was the announcement in September 2004 to form Virgin Galactic. Branson signed a deal worth up to $21 million with Mojave Aerospace Ventures to license the intellectual property behind the project, which will then establish the services necessary for space tourism.

The logical approach to understanding the structure of the Virgin Group is to consider Branson as a venture capitalist who unifies all of his ventures under a single brand name. The core of the Virgin Group is in travel, entertainment, and lifestyle. The product lines and services are too numerous to list. When asked what was next, Branson stated, "Starting businesses in new countries and markets rather than expanding the things we do. That gives us lots of opportunities to create a truly global presence and to do some good, too."

Business Advice and Plans

Branson believes in the importance of his highly visible media-catching adventures as a strategy in the branding of the name. He says, "If you get your face and your name out there enough, people will start to recognize you. Many people know the Virgin brand better than the names of the individual companies within the group." That is central to becoming a venture capitalist.

world—solo piloted, nonstop, without refueling. His company name was showcased in each of the adventures, and *Virgin* became a well-recognized brand name. Branson's latest well-publicized adventure is in the tourism field, Virgin Galactic, in which he will build five "spaceliners" to carry tourists into space within the next several years.

In each case, the entrepreneur found a creative way to incorporate his outdoor knowledge and experience into a business venture. The growth of the original business concept for these individuals is examined more closely in their respective profiles. Having a passion for something stimulates a creative, stimulating, and fulfilling force that gives purpose to what we do. Creativity can advance your business venture, and it can carry you a long way if you wish to grow from a small business to a bigger one. As Mihaly Csikszentmihalyi (1996, p. 2) wrote, when examining the psychology of optimal experiences, "creativity is so fascinating . . . [because] when we are involved in it, we feel we are living more fully than during the rest of life." A small business can provide such an opportunity.

VISUALIZE A DESTINATION

Experienced travelers recognize that a road map can be an asset when planning a trip, whether for business or for pleasure. The road map metaphor can be a useful asset in tackling the task of writing about your business description. Successful use of a road map requires you to have a clear *destination* in mind and to choose a time and place to *start the journey*. Your business plan will benefit from preparing a clear destination in terms of the vision you adopt to inspire others as well as highlighting the product and services that are likely to be part of the business concept. The range of choices in the RET industry today is as diverse as any of the choices you are likely to find in the business world.

PRODUCTS AND SERVICES

There is considerable latitude in the products and services an enterprise offers in order to become profitable. Just as recipes are important in preparing food, a mixture of goods and services can be specific to a business venture. Each of us can read a published recipe, but the final product from that recipe can vary greatly based on the time, talent, and "secret ingredients" that went into it. So it is with a product profile. You don't have to reveal your "trade secrets," but to complete other parts of the business plan, you will need to identify each of the products or services you feel will help the business achieve profitability. Your "secret ingredients" can give you a competitive advantage in the industry and may be related to programming skills or how you stage your experiences.

The philosopher Voltaire once said, "If you wish to speak with me, define your terms." This is good advice for effective communication with the diverse stakeholder in the commercial recreation and tourism field. Not everyone talks about products the same way. For example, a surfboard is a manufactured product to surfer Hobie Alter, whereas a *product club* is a relatively new term used to describe a small business marketing network that does not produce any tangible goods. It simply means "product development professionals," applying a label for network experience–based service providers as if they are involved with a manufactured item. It can be confusing when common terms are used in nonstandard ways. Therefore, this section will define basic terms related to the meaning associated with events, products, services, and experiences. These terms may have subtle differences in interpretation when considering factors such as production and consumption, quality control, duration of benefits, and so forth. It is also timely to clarify the circumstances where several components of services, attractions, and markets have been combined to create a label related to special-interest tourism. In chapter 8, considerable attention is given to this topic and particularly how value is added to intangible products by means of superior customer service.

Taken together, recreation, entertainment, leisure services, and travel are certainly at the top of the list of consumer industries. Clarke (1990) points out that (1) recreation, entertainment, and tourism enterprises are small and privately owned; (2) the businesses "produce" services rather than a trademarked or named product; (3) the public does not readily understand the structure and organization of the industry; and (4) the misconception persists that a variety of recreation services are tax-supported establishments. As will be seen later in the chapter, even the economic measures used by Statistics Canada and the U.S. Census Bureau divide the enterprise of the industry into unconventional categories. In terms of gaining recognition for the small and large business, it means that clear communication with stakeholders and interested parties is important to avoid confusion. In the next several paragraphs, standard meanings associated with several of the terms are described to address this problem.

A recreation, event, or tourism *product*, in traditional terms, means a tangible manufactured good, in contrast to the term *services*, which encompasses a wide range of intangible items that cannot be examined, touched, or tasted before being provided as part of the customer experience. Services come in many forms and are marketed in a manner to give them special characteristics. Products and services are essential ingredients in creating leisure experiences in recreation and tourism. *Programs* and *special events* come into existence as a result of a creative, and sometimes innovative, combination of products and services. Theater, surfing or sailing competitions, music festivals, craft fairs, cultural celebrations, and so forth are types of productions that bring together tangible and intangible elements to create focused, highly valued special experiences. Events have a long history in terms of leisure experiences, and the benefits were primarily focused on local residents—craft or agricultural fairs, holiday celebrations, school plays or sport competitions, harvest festivals, farmers markets, and so forth. A new phenomenon that appears to have burst on the scene is the mega-events that are viewed to benefit residents and tourists alike. This type of

event comes in all forms and generally requires the support of many community stakeholders and businesses. Roberts (2004) suggests there are a variety of ways to classify events, with the most common being to focus on the activity on which they are based.

Most are classified as based on either sport, the arts, other entertainment, heritage, or food and drink. Events can also be grouped according to their size, usually measured by the numbers of people who attend. In these terms the biggest events are the sport megas. The summer Olympics is the biggest of all the sport megas, and in recent decades each Olympics has been the biggest ever.

Music festivals and special events of all types are increasing in popularity and are programmed to attract target markets that follow the artists involved in the event. Perhaps the icon of pop music festivals was a three-day event outside Bethel, New York, in 1969 known as Woodstock. It attracted somewhere near 500,000 people and was covered extensively in the media for the great music, the environmental impact on the small area where it was staged, and the uninhibited behavior of the youth in attendance. Today considerable preparation and planning goes into organizing special events and festivals in order to be successful and to secure the permits necessary for them to be held. These events may cater to either pure leisure consumers or to business groups looking for commercial recreation activities to increase attendance at a meeting or conference or improve staff communications and teamwork. Providing recreation services to business clients, especially in urban settings, is an increasingly popular and lucrative part of the industry.

Event and meeting planners must combine the educational and pleasure-oriented goals of convention attendees. The convention sponsoring association has clear educational goals for attendees. Likewise the attendees, many of whom have the discretion to attend or not attend, also have at least some pleasure-oriented goals for the convention. Disneyland and Anaheim Convention Center managers know that often convention attendees want to bring their partners and even children, so they actively pursue this market and

Transporting travelers is the primary function of ferry systems; however, they may also advertise upcoming events such as the 2010 Winter Olympics.

J.S. Pfister

provide spouse and family alternatives before, during, and after the event. Finding the right balance between the educational and leisure goals—rather than a strictly "all business" approach—when creating a convention program is a key to attracting greater attendance and having satisfied attendees.

Several differences in the functions associated with the terms add clarity to the implicit meaning assigned to products, services, and experiences. In some cases, it helps to clarify the link between a manufacturer, a service provider, and the customer that seeks the experience.

Associated Press/Brent Hood

Events can range from the sport megas to the outdoor festival.

Experience-Oriented Services

Current marketing literature tends to focus on what is involved in creating and marketing the leisure experience (O'Sullivan and Spangler, 1998; O'Neal, 2001; McCarville, 2002). Today it is possible to describe key differences, as noted in table 3.3, in regard to the responsible stakeholder, the production process, ownership, quality control, and benefits derived (Janes, 2006).

A detailed description of the goods and services the business intends to offer to the consumer is important to the success of the business concept. For the owner, the range of goods and services to be offered means ensuring that frontline staff possess the passion and talent to produce and deliver the quality experience promised to the customer. For the profitability of the business concept, it is vital for the expected revenues to be greater than the cost of producing or acquiring the products and services incorporated into the experience expected by the customer. As you will learn in chapter 8, Pine and Gilmore (1999) have advocated that customers are seeking to purchase experiences and not simply products and services. When we reexamine the business principles that make up the vision statement for Starbucks (highlighted in table 3.2), it is evident that applying the highest standards of excellence in purchasing and processing a quality product is only one part of their operation. A separate Starbucks principle seeks to ensure they have a strategy to "develop enthusiastically satisfied customers all of the time."

Non-Experience-Based Services

A variety of recreation or tourism businesses are worthy of note because they provide specialized services that make it possible for the experience-based businesses to create and deliver their goods and services. For example, most recreation activities or travel need equipment manufacturers, information services, and places for the activities to be enjoyed. Motorized equipment needs to be serviced and repaired. The opportunities for small businesses in these areas are too numerous to mention. The Spotlight On John Avery and Roche Harbor Marine illustrates a vital business enterprise that is essential to all recreational and commercial boaters in the world. Roche Harbor Marine also reveals the elements of a lifestyle business as it provides the owner with opportunity to live, play, and work in a highly desirable location. It also reflects the conscious choice to provide services to a distinctive set of clients who are fun-loving and appreciative of the services provided for them. Further

Table 3.3   An Examination of Products, Services, and Experiences

Characteristic	Products	Services	Experiences
Focus	Manufacturer	Service provider	Consumer
Production and consumption	Products are manufactured in one place; products can be stored as well as shipped to another place for sale and consumption.	Service is realized at the time and place it is delivered by the service provider.	Experiences are created simultaneously by the interactions of the customer and service provider. An experience is consumed as it is being created but can endure partially as a special memory.
Ownership	Products are transferred to the purchaser along with all ownership rights.	Purchaser owns only a temporary right to have a benefit based on a promise of performance.	Rights to a leisure experience are jointly held and cannot be tied only to a promise of performance.
Quality control	Quality control permits mistakes to be discovered and corrected before the customer sees the product.	Mistakes are immediately evident in service delivery, so it is too late to implement quality control. Staff training can minimize mistakes in service delivery.	The quality of the experience is subjectively evaluated by the customer based on personal experience, expectations, and performance.
Benefits derived	Benefits accrue to the purchaser as long as the product is in use and tied to use of the product.	Benefits are based on the ability of the service provider to deliver on the promise made.	Benefits will be evaluated primarily by the customer based on the strength of the interaction of service provider and customer.

Adapted, by permission, from Janes 2006.

details on this business appears in Spotlight On in chapter 5 (see page 95).

Niche Tourism: A Mix of Services and Products

Tourism development and marketing professionals have been known to use the term *product* in unconventional ways. It is increasingly prevalent today to find types of special-interest tourism referenced as a consumer product. However, it is not a tangible manufactured product in the conventional sense. It is a label of convenience that permits a combination of attractions, services, and traveler motivations to be grouped together for strategic or marketing purposes. For example, one division in the Canadian Tourism Commission (CTC) financially supports businesses networking to encourage cooperative ventures by

helping them create a **product club**. The purpose of the CTC's product club initiative is

to help small and medium-sized businesses overcome impediments to tourism growth in a given geographic area or industry sector. Product-based "clubs" enable groups to present a united front in addressing issues of concern and to come together in partnering alliances to achieve common goals. If various sectors of our industry can create a critical mass through a Product Club, then they may be able to participate more effectively in CTC marketing programs (www.canadatourism. com/ctx/app/en/ca/marketing.do?cat=home.catalog. partnershipProgram.productDevelopment).

The goal of product clubs is to provide a practical method for improving the market competitiveness

J.S. Pfister

Heritage travelers are attracted to historic destinations such as Boston where the statue of George Washington stands in front of one entrance to the Boston Gardens.

of a sector or marketing area. A product club, for example, might form to promote winter tourism in the Northwest Territories. In reality, the term *product club* is a combination of business types and tourism services targeting a particular market segment. If a combination of services targeted a market desiring a visit to a unique natural setting that is protected for scientific reasons, and the tour operator provides the travelers with high-quality interpretative services that educate them about the setting, the package might fall under the label of *ecotourism*. If all the components essentially remain the same except the attraction is an operating farm, it might enjoy the label *agritourism*. When Hollywood films induce tourism to locations where the movie sets are built and segments of a motion picture production is filmed, the package may fit as part of *pop-culture tourism*. However, if the attraction is the site of a natural disaster, the package changes again and may best fit the marketing label of *disaster tourism*. In other words, the shift in one

of the ingredients, much like in food preparation, appears to result in a very distinct "product" in the tourism field.

New forms of special-interest tourism are gaining in popularity and recognition every year as new ingredients are combined to create a class of travelers that fit that "product" or marketing label. Another way to look at the special-interest phenomenon in tourism is as an initiative to create new niche markets for packaging a type of experience. In **niche tourism**, the enterprise has established a particular intangible specialty product that garners a reliable and substantial market share. However, the market is small enough that the business operating within the niche can be a viable enterprise but will not attract very much competition. The term was borrowed from the field of ecology in which a niche is the position that an organism can occupy within an ecological community and survive because of limited competition for scarce resources. Table 3.4 lists more than

Table 3.4 Niche or Special-Interest Tourism and Travel Products

Adventure tourism	Extreme tourism	Pop-culture tourism
Agritourism	Gambling tourism	Religious tourism
Backpacker tourism	Garden tourism	Sex tourism
Business travel	Gay tourism	Space tourism
Conference and incentive travel	Health and wellness tourism	Sports tourism
Cruises and voyages	Heritage tourism	Urban tourism
Cultural tourism	Inclusive tourism	Virtual tourism
Dark tourism	Mass tourism	Volunteer tourism
Disaster tourism	Medical tourism	Wildlife tourism
Ecotourism	Naturism	Wine tourism
Enclave/resort tourism	Pilgrimage tourism	Winter tourism

Source: www.intute.ac.uk/socialsciences/travel and http://en.wikipedia.org/wiki/Tourism

30 marketing labels to cover an ever-changing range of special interests found in the tourism literature today (www.intute.ac.uk/socialsciences/travel and http://en.wikipedia.org/wiki/Tourism).

The primary challenge in this area of tourism is to have solid information arising from market research to ensure your products and services can be matched to a viable and reliable market segment. The assessment of a target market is covered in chapter 5.

YOUR BUSINESS CONCEPT AND NAIC

As a final step in part two of the business plan (detailed in chapter 12), you should identify the business sector in which your type of service belongs using the **North American Industry Code (NAIC)** classification. The NAIC categories (displayed later in the chapter in table 3.6) are the same in the United States and Canada. The information adds considerable detail to where your business might fit within the general economy of the country, and it makes it possible to introduce the business to a potential investor or lender who knows very little about recreation and tourism businesses. In this part of the plan, you will want to write about the following:

- Your profile. This refers to giving your business name, its legal status, and a location where it will operate.
- The economic indicators for the industry sector. The plan should highlight several economic indica-

tors pertinent to the industrial classification systems applicable to your business. A business is not like an isolated island but rather is part of an ever-changing economic sector. This section of the business plan looks at the big picture of where your business fits within the larger part of the commercial recreation and tourism industry. Based on products and services it will offer, the business can be given a classification according to the North American Industry Classification System.

YOUR BUSINESS NAME

One of the most important and basic requirements of your business is to capture exclusive use of your name and concept and protect it from competitors. Unfortunately, you cannot proceed with complete freedom of choice because the choice of a business name will be linked to your legal status (see table 3.5). Chapter 2 identifies issues associated with acquiring a trademark for your company name and what you have to do when your favorite name is not your own name. Under such circumstances, you need to know about the process of **doing business as (DBA)**.

The situation may arise where you discover that you were not the first to reserve the name you will be using for your business. Duplication of business names may not be important if your market areas do not overlap or each business operates in a different state. Should you find a business in the vicinity that delivers the identical services you do, it probably represents a noteworthy concern. The solution will

Table 3.5 Legal Status and Naming Conventions

Legal status	Implications	Process
Sole proprietorship	There are generally no formalities if you are John Gow and want to be called John Gow Guide Service. Using your surname alone is possible too.	When a business name does not show the owner's surname or implies the existence of additional owners, then many states will require the owner to file a fictitious business name statement and publish notice. See DBA.
General partnership, joint venture, limited liability partnership	Generally, this option takes the path of having two names appear in the business name.	If you are not using your surnames in the partnership, you most likely will file for a fictitious business name. See DBA.
Corporation, limited liability company, S corporation	When you create a "recognized legal entity" the naming process is more involved. Laws and fees governing corporations vary from state to state. Most owners incorporate in the state in which they will conduct business. However, there are some other considerations. Nevada does not charge a state corporate income tax or personal income tax, and it allows for a higher level of privacy for a business. "Business-friendly" states do this to attract corporations to have offices in their jurisdiction.	Although you may have considerable choices for a name, there will be guidelines for **naming conventions** established by the laws of incorporation, which will vary by federal and state statute. There will be some words that will be restricted because they are reserved for nonprofit societies or associations. More important, you will have to research the availability of the name you have selected because it may not be available to be registered if an existing business has filed for it.
Doing business as, or DBA*	Of course, you may name a business something that simply sounds good such as Aardvark Adventures, Dianne's Dance Studio, Frank's Fly Fishing Shop, or Bertha's Restaurant. And your name does not have to be Aardvark, Dianne, Frank, or Bertha.	A business name that is not your own is known as an assumed or fictitious name. You will have to complete the DBA process, which varies from one jurisdiction to another. You can see DBA advertisements in the business section under DBA, which is the acronym for this process. Several states have online services that make the search process considerably easier.

* https://filedba.com/?r=overturead&OVRAW=Dba&OVKEY=dba&OVMTC=standard

depend largely on the ability of the owner to assess the consequences, adjust the business plan, and carefully select the best course of action. Michael Berry found another business several miles away that had an identical name to his business and decided it was time for a change after meeting the other owner. Cathy Fiddler discovered at a trade show that a well-established company with a different name but the same concept could move into her area and decided it was time to make a change. Diogenes was on the right track when he was quoted as saying, "There is nothing permanent except change." Each of the two businesses experienced a different outcome.

INDUSTRY PROFILE

It can be important to know where to find economic data about competitive businesses in your area. Just how you would tackle that problem depends on prior experience and familiarity with census information. As you will recall from chapter 1, the NAICS 71 category covers all establishments primarily engaged in operating facilities or providing services to meet the cultural, entertainment, and recreational interests of their customers whether or not they serve domestic or tourist markets. Once you identify the census district you intend to do business in, it is possible to identify the number of business establishments currently operating in that census district that represent the type of business you would like to create or purchase. Such data assist in describing the size of your sector to others and in considering competition. An exercise in the online student resource provides an opportunity to apply a particular North American Code to a district near you. The benefit of the NAICS data is that it can help you

- gauge the competition,
- calculate market share,
- assist in site location,
- design sales territories and set sale quotas,
- enhance presentation to bank and venture capitalists, and
- evaluate new business opportunities.

The good news is that several important changes in creating common economic indicators occurred because of the multinational signing of the North American Free Trade Agreement and the utility of the data will improve over time. There is now the prospect of two online options to help with information searches on business establishments, but only one of the two is operational as of 2008:

- *North American Industry Classification System* (NAICS) is a six-digit code in the United States, and it was approved just before the new millennium. The system is being jointly developed by the United States, Canada, and Mexico for the purpose of having a more uniform classification system than is available with SIC. An example of the three- to six-digit NAIC codes prepared for arts, entertainment, and recreation classification is presented in table 3.6.
- *North American Product Classification System* is described as a market-oriented hierarchical classifica-

Ski resorts appeal to a global market of dedicated skiers.

tion system for products (i.e., goods and services). The latter two systems will create consistency between the three countries in the classification of service products and notably strengthen economic measures needed for an overview of business sectors.

Trustworthy economic indicators in a business sector are desirable information for owners, money lenders, and financial professionals. When a specific business can be placed in a sector in which standardized economic account information exists, the business plan can be linked to the geographic data reported for the local, state, and national economy. The census Web site (www.census.gov/epcd/ec02/uses.htm) further describes how the economic data can be used.

The activities of recreation, entertainment, events, travel, and tourism are somewhat covered by national economic accounts designed to present industry statistics without regard to the purpose of the purchase of output. What it means is the economic indicators are values that do not distinguish between resident and visitor. So examination of the accommodation and transportation could not be attributed to tourism activity alone. It does however provide insights into the scope and magnitude of goods and services for resident and nonresident activity combined.

Table 3.6 North American Industry Code System and Schedule 71 Arts, Entertainment, and Recreation (U.S. Census, 2002)

NAIC code	Description
711	**Performing Arts, Spectator Sports, and Related Industries**
7111	Performing Arts Companies
71111	Theater Companies and Dinner Theaters
711110	Theater Companies and Dinner Theaters
71112	Dance Companies
711120	Dance Companies
71113	Musical Groups and Artists
711130	Musical Groups and Artists
71119	Other Performing Arts Companies
711190	Other Performing Arts Companies
7112	Spectator Sports
71121	Spectator Sports
711211	Sports Teams and Clubs
711212	Racetracks
711219	Other Spectator Sports
7113	Promoters of Performing Arts, Sports, and Similar Events
71131	Promoters of Performing Arts, Sports, and Similar Events with Facilities
711310	Promoters of Performing Arts, Sports, and Similar Events with Facilities
71132	Promoters of Performing Arts, Sports, and Similar Events without Facilities
711320	Promoters of Performing Arts, Sports, and Similar Events without Facilities
7114	Agents and Managers for Artists, Athletes, Entertainers, and Other Public Figures
71141	Agents and Managers for Artists, Athletes, Entertainers, and Other Public Figures
711410	Agents and Managers for Artists, Athletes, Entertainers, and Other Public Figures
7115	Independent Artists, Writers, and Performers
71151	Independent Artists, Writers, and Performers
711510	Independent Artists, Writers, and Performers
712	**Museums, Historical Sites, and Similar Institutions**
7121	Museums, Historical Sites, and Similar Institutions
71211	Museums
712110	Museums

NAIC code	Description
71212	Historical Sites
712120	Historical Sites
71213	Zoos and Botanical Gardens
712130	Zoos and Botanical Gardens
71219	Nature Parks and Other Similar Institutions
712190	Nature Parks and Other Similar Institutions
713	**Amusement, Gambling, and Recreation Industries**
7131	Amusement Parks and Arcades
71311	Amusement and Theme Parks
713110	Amusement and Theme Parks
71312	Amusement Arcades
713120	Amusement Arcades
7132	Gambling Industries
71321	Casinos (except Casino Hotels)
713210	Casinos (except Casino Hotels)
71329	Other Gambling Industries
713290	Other Gambling Industries
7139	**Other Amusement and Recreation Industries**
71391	Golf Courses and Country Clubs
713910	Golf Courses and Country Clubs
71392	Skiing Facilities
713920	Skiing Facilities
71393	Marinas
713930	Marinas
71394	Fitness and Recreational Sports Centers
713940	Fitness and Recreational Sports Centers
71395	Bowling Centers
713950	Bowling Centers
71399	All Other Amusement and Recreation Industries
713990	All Other Amusement and Recreation Industries

www.census.gov/epcd/www/naics.html

http://stds.statcan.ca/english/naics/1997/naics97-title-search.asp?criteria=71

SUMMARY

There is a Chinese proverb stating that a thousand-mile journey begins with but a single step. A well-planned thousand-mile journey can be a metaphor for starting up a new commercial recreation business venture in regard to planning ahead. Before you start packing for your journey, it is a good practice to consider all aspects of the trip. Part two of your business plan expects you to provide details of your destination and when you expect to begin. You should probably give a name to the trip as well. In this first part of the business plan, the author of the plan is expected to answer the following questions:

- Why should your business exist (i.e., your mission statement), and what are the basic details of the business concept? Can you describe it in 50 words or fewer?
- What products, goods, services, programs, and so forth are to be offered?
- What steps will it take to reserve your business name, and under what legal status do you intend to operate?
- Where does your business fit? Here is where an overview is provided of the industry trade sector in which the business will operate. No small business is an island unto itself but part of a business sector in the national economy.

 Check out the online student resource for additional material, including case studies, Web links, and more.

Chapter 4

Retail, Other Profit Centers, and Facilities

Learning Objectives

After reading this chapter you will be able to

- understand the importance of retail sales,
- explain why bricks and clicks (e-commerce) are important,
- describe how location and presentation affect retail success,
- identify six elements of successful retailing,
- discuss the importance of preventing theft,
- recognize income opportunities from rentals, and
- identify basic considerations for food and beverage service.

Key Terms

bricks and clicks

cost of goods sold

distributors

e-commerce

electronic merchandise
  surveillance systems

employee burnout

green cuisine

gross margin

inventory turnover (stock turn)

margin

payment dating

point of sale (POS) system

pro deals

trade shows

up-sell

Imagine this scenario:

You look at your financial statements again after one year in business, and a few surprises jump out. The largest shocker is the contribution your retail sales of clothing, equipment, and accessories make to the bottom-line profit. Having a retail sales component to your business was initially almost left out because the primary motive for starting your business was your love of the sport (e.g., snowboarding, rafting, or fishing) or activity (e.g., event planning or hosting people) and its provision and sales. But these did not have as high a profit margin as good old retail sales. Both your store and your online sales are stronger than you anticipated. At the last minute you decided to add equipment rentals for customers. Your equipment rental revenues grew fantastically over the year. Unfortunately, you had to overcome a few problems with retailing. The opening day of your store was delayed by local government development permits and regulations, and this cost you dearly because you had to get additional loans to carry you through until sales began. Later, food service became a frequent component of your events, and the city wanted you to get a food establishment permit. A second problem was that your wholesale purchases and merchandising were poorly planned at first. You found that the hot-selling items were frequently out of stock, while you had many other items you paid too much for, had a higher price compared to your competitors, and just did not sell. A compounding factor was that at first your sales staff was not able to turn lookers into buyers. Although it was personally painful and it took a while to catch on, you discovered that a few employees were stealing equipment from you and seriously eroding profits.

Although all the actions described in the opening scenario may not take place in such a short time frame, they do point out the importance of secondary profit centers (such as retail sales, rentals, and food sales) to the financial success of your recreation, event, and tourism company. Rentals and retail are the primary, not secondary, sources of profit for many RET businesses. In some cases the initial business concept later evolved into another different but related business. For example, adventure travel operators have transitioned into manufacturing their own outdoor retail equipment instead of buying it from others, and event planners have added a large equipment rental element to their business. So entrepreneurs should seriously consider the addition of retail and other profit centers into their business plan. In this chapter we explore key elements of the planning, development, and operation of retail and other secondary profit centers.

IMPORTANCE OF RETAIL SALES

Retail, rentals, and other secondary profit centers can add substantially to your bottom-line profits, even if your company is primarily a provider of activities and direct services. The revenue potential from retail is tremendous. For example, studies by the Outdoor Industry Association in the United States show sales of $33 billion at active outdoor recreation retailers in 2004, and this is growing at an annual rate about 1 percent greater than all retail sales (Outdoor Industry

Association, 2007b). Here are a few reasons to consider retail as a secondary profit center:

- Retail provides year-round and off-season revenue.
- Your activity customers now have other reasons to visit.
- Cross-sales are generated (one service needs related products for optimum benefits).
- Shopping is one of the most popular forms of recreation.

BRICKS AND CLICKS

When you think of retail, your favorite store in a nearby location might come to mind. But increasingly the emerging image is of your favorite retail Web site. So a retail strategy that includes both **bricks**, the physical store location, **and clicks**, the online sales Web site, is optimal. A good example is modern travel agents who counter large online ticketing Web sites by developing their own specialized e-commerce sites that enhance the options and services to the clients (see Corniche Travel, www.corniche.com). There are clear advantages to physical stores and online sales, but the synergy of both working in tandem is indisputable.

Stores allow buyers to see, touch, and try on or try out merchandise. Knowledgeable sales staff can help the clients choose what is best for them and provide

Internet marketing and online reservation capabilities are increasingly important for RET businesses.

low-cost but sophisticated e-commerce hosting company is Techwave, located at www.techwave.com. An online retailer can start out small, allowing only 5 to 10 items to be placed in the electronic shopping cart, or go with a full catalog using manufacturer pictures and product information along with personalized information from your staff. There are very few valid reasons why your company should not have an online retail sales component.

inducements for a sale. Clients can develop an emotional relationship with the staff and store. One recent study suggests cultivating an emotional relationship is more important than satisfaction with products in repeat retail purchase decisions (Outdoor Industry Association, 2007a). Once a decision is made, the buyer can immediately take away the item and start using it. Store location, displays, and activities encourage impulse buying. The traditional store is still perceived by the general public as a safe place to make a purchase; they and their credit card data are secure, and they can return merchandise with little cost. Sales staff can offer post-sale advice on how to best use the product.

E-commerce and online sales have revolutionized retail sales and now account for a significant portion of product sales. In some tourism sectors, such as domestic airline tickets, online sales will surpass offline bookings in 2007, according to research by PhoCusWright Research (Cannizzaro, 2007). Some advantages are 24-hour access, seven days a week; easy to navigate Web sites with knowledge databases; and no need to travel or find parking. Increased comfort with online security and next-day shipping have led to increasing online sales. The cost of developing and maintaining e-commerce sites has dropped substantially, and Web site design and hosting can now be contracted out at a reasonable cost. An example of a

COMMON ELEMENTS OF SUCCESSFUL RETAILING

Many experts agree there are six common elements of successful retailing (see figure 4.1), regardless of product type. To these you can add specialized elements for the unique nature of your business, such as outdoor equipment retailing. The six common elements are location, products, pricing of products, appearance, sales staff, and active management.

Successful retailing

Figure 4.1 Common elements of successful retailing.

LOCATION

Your retail store location is absolutely critical to its success. It is a place where you can maximize sales and exposure, customers can easily find you, there is adequate parking or public transit for clients and staff, you will be a welcome addition to the neighborhood, and you can get your business permits. What will be the distance between you and your best customers? Can you afford the lease? What are its terms? What is the reputation of the landlord? Where are your competitors? How important is foot traffic from a nearby central district or large employer? Is it necessary to be close to a trail or river for customers to try out items?

A key to any outstanding location is good visibility. Chapter 6 also discusses location issues and criteria.

PRODUCTS

The products and brands you carry are your central element. They must be closely aligned with your business concept, be complementary to your primary services, have strong positive brand recognition, be sought after by residents and tourists in the area, be within the price range of your customers, and be able to be purchased at a competitive price. Are they items you want to sell or products your customers want? Figure 4.2 shows 2006 sales by product category for

SPOTLIGHT ON

Scrapbook Your Story

Location

Scrapbook Your Story store and classrooms are located in Springfield, Illinois. Springfield boasts a population of 125,000; outlying communities raise the population to around 175,000.

Background

Jill Guinan previously worked as a medical practice administrator, which paid enough for her to eventually quit, follow her passion, buy a building, and open her own scrapbooking business. Jill was the youngest child in her family and said her mother made scrapbooks of her two siblings but never got around to making one for Jill. Jill made her own scrapbook years ago after finding photos in an old trunk. The term *scrapbooking* really started to take hold around 1998, and Jill started watching TV shows that spotlighted the hobby. She saw a need in her community for better access to supplies (she was starting to put books together for her two sons, now 11 and 13), and she felt passionate about helping families create better ways of documenting memories. Her bachelor's degree in business administration gave her the tools to do payroll, but she had no experience in retail or inventory.

With equity in their house, Jill and her husband, Kevin, bought a large building in 2003 on a main road at the edge of Springfield. About 40,000 cars pass by every day and a large billboard-like sign fronts the building. The location is only a 10-minute drive from the new Abraham Lincoln Museum and Presidential Library, which is a large tourist draw. Hotels are nearby as well. In additional to her regulars, Jill gets customers from the museum and from the Illinois State Fair. She has a tenant who owns a high-end cake business. The two businesses are a good fit and attract similar customers. In 2007 Jill and her husband opened a store in a mall but closed it several months later. Jill cited high rent and competition with Hallmark-type businesses as factors in closing.

Products and Services

Scrapbook Your Story offers a variety of classes and workshops. The two most popular are card making and anything related to pets. Several classes are also offered, which range from structured 60-minute programs to leisurely 3- to 4-hour open classrooms where participants work on projects. Six-hour classes are offered Friday nights, and it is a central socializing and gathering place. Jill likens it to quilting circles. The store offers an extensive inventory of supplies featuring the top names in paper, albums, rubber stamps, dies, and photo supplies. People of all skill levels in the craft can find what they need at Scrapbook Your Story. Jill has been very involved with customers from the start, finding out their needs in order to build her inventory. Other scrapbooking stores are organized by themes or brands, but Jill decided to go with themes only. She has sections devoted to Disney, graduation, pets, birthdays, and other themes. Customers find the story easy to navigate, and Jill is quick to point out that her strength is in customer service. Each customer will be helped with a scrapbook from start to finish, if needed. Jill's employees are creative and talented. A good location, radio and newspaper ads, and an informative Web site keep her connected to customers.

Business Advice and Plans

Running a scrapbooking business is more of a challenge than it looks. It involves good organizational skills and business timing. Jill has learned many things since opening her business in 2003; the two most important are to treat people with respect and base the business on customer service. Jill emphasizes that she does it for the love, not the money, and she won't retire rich. Her experience with the business has shown her children the importance of having a good work ethic. The business has a mascot dog named Mimi; she's pictured on their Web page. Customers stop in just to say hi to Mimi. Jill says that animals that are a part of a business tend to draw customers in. Having a business with her husband is both enjoyable and stressful at times, and it takes some time away from being with her sons. But having her own business and developing relationships with a variety of clients make it all worthwhile.

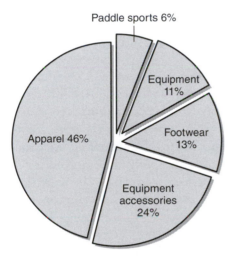

Figure 4.2 Distribution of sales across specialty retailer product categories.

Data from Outdoor Industry Association, 2006, *State of the industry report* (Boulder, CO: Author).

outdoor retailers. Can you get similar information for your type of business? Remember the 80-20 rule: 80 percent of your sales are from 20 percent of your shoppers. So you must do research to determine who your most frequent shoppers will be and what they are looking for. You must also see what other similar businesses are selling and what is being promoted nationally and locally.

A second critical element of retail products is where and how you buy them. You have a number of options, ranging from buying directly from the manufacturer, sales representatives, and distributors to making purchases at trade shows. You need to shop around to find the best combination of price, products needed,

shipping costs, and timing of delivery. Developing a good relationship and credit will improve your purchase terms and may help you get low-stock items. Before you make any major purchases, you should have a purchase plan, which identifies merchandise budgeted for purchase during a certain time period that has not yet been ordered (Waters, 2007). This plan is done in advance of your buying trip and outlines types, quantities, and your budget for each product category, thus allowing the buyer to just pick the best merchandise.

- *Manufacturers:* Advantages of buying from the manufacturer are knowledge of the product and customer service. The producer should have the best information about product features, testing, and composition. If something is damaged or not working as promised, it is often easier to deal directly with the manufacturer than an intermediary.

- *Manufacturer's representatives:* Many independent businesses represent or sell merchandise from a variety of producers. They may specialize in one type of product (e.g., outdoor footwear) or just one or two manufacturers. The advantages of using "reps" are that they have knowledge about which manufacturers' products seem to work better or are hot sellers; they will visit your shop and demonstrate products to your staff or clients; and they can sell you a number of types of merchandise at once, thus increasing your buying power (discount) and adding convenience.

- *Distributors:* **Distributors** buy products from many manufacturers, warehouse this inventory, and then resell it at wholesale prices. Examples of specialized distributors are Northwest River Supplies (www.nrsweb.com) for rafting outfitters and Party Pop (www.partypop.com) for event planners. You can buy many different product types from a variety of manufacturers and get immediate shipping. Distributors may also have stock when the manufacturer is out. Both reps and distributors charge something for their services above the price a manufacturer may give you. But many small retail businesses purchasing in lesser quantities, especially if retail is a secondary element, find the wholesale price difference can be very small or even nonexistent. But distributors may also be your retail competitor.

- *Trade shows:* **Trade shows** are large-scale, preseason, closed-to-the-public national or regional events where manufacturers and sales representatives show samples available for the upcoming season and take orders. Trade shows are very popular because of the huge selection of manufacturers, so a store buyer can make one trip and order almost all items for the next season at one time. Every industry has its primary trade show. Examples of popular trade shows are the national Outdoor Retailer Summer Market show in August and the Outdoor Retailer Winter Market show in January, both in Salt Lake City, Utah, and the EventWorld expo for special event planners held in August in the United States or Canada.

- *The Internet:* Specialized industry Web sites are becoming increasingly popular as a place to compare and shop for the best products and terms. Ordering is quick, and travel does not detract from your work time. However, you cannot have a demonstration or trial as you can at a trade show.

QUESTIONS TO ASK WHOLESALERS BEFORE YOU BUY

The purchasing terms and prices you receive can be the difference between profit and loss. When you are ready to buy, ask questions about the following issues:

- Minimum quantity required. Some companies will not take an order if below a stated amount.
- Quantity discounts. These are volume discounts.

- Payment terms. Net 30 means you must pay in full 30 days after receipt. Another common term is a discount for early payment. For example, 2-10 net 30 means a 2 percent discount if paid within 10 days or full amount is due in 30 days.
- Preseason discounts. If you order early at a trade show, you can qualify for a substantial discount and not have to pay until the merchandise is delivered.
- Closeout items. Products a manufacturer is marking down because they are being discontinued.
- Shipping date. You can state a specific delivery date, after which the order is canceled.
- Payment dating. Delaying your payment gives you extra time to sell the item.

PRICING OF PRODUCTS

Pricing is another key element of retail and is discussed in more detail in chapter 6. A key to success in the retailing area is maintaining a good **margin**, the percentage you earn above the price you pay. A long-standing rule involves doubling what you paid for an item, but this is not always realistic, especially with higher-priced equipment. When setting your selling price, you should consider consumer perception, the competition, turnover of the item, brand value (can you get a better price because it is a top brand?), and store atmosphere or setting. Be willing to reduce the price when sales are declining. Consider frequent buyer discounts and other pricing to build loyalty (see chapter 8). Maintain your highest price, and offer discounts only as a last resort. But always be able to quickly determine what you paid for an item, and use this to adjust any discounts.

A critically important retail concept is that people will pay more for items at the right time and in the right setting. When and where you present the items for sale are basic considerations. Highest prices tend to be paid in advance of the season when people are making plans. Many summer vacations that involve distant travel are planned four to six months in advance, so ads must be in place and products ready to sell well in advance of operating the services. For example, the months of March and April are big sale months for outfitters, resorts, and clothing retailers that provide or support summer programs. The appearance of the interior and exterior of the store (or Web site) is very important in creating an appealing setting.

APPEARANCE

The appearance of your store and the presentation of your product are critical for successful sales. Appearance must fit into the image you are trying to create through the store design. The look of your physical store or your e-commerce Web site should demonstrate the price level of your product lines, the level of service, the range of product offerings, and the specialized niche you are exploiting. How you display your products, the lighting, merchandise racks, color patterns, flooring, wall displays, and use of ceilings are all very important considerations. Research has shown that music strongly affects the atmosphere of your retail space. So music should be provided and perceived positively by your primary clients. Window displays can be a strong inducement to come inside

or a quick turnoff, so pay attention to them, just as the large retailers do. Consider hiring a professional window dresser to change your front window once a month to keep it fresh and appealing.

The internal layout of your store is obviously very important. Think about the entrance and how you can make it unique or enticing. Does it give the image of inexpensive products or of luxury products? Does it prominently convey your brand? Now think about how visitors will walk through your store. You should have a main path for them to follow, with a flooring color that is different from the rest of the store. This path should not be a straight line—research has shown that the straighter the path, the sooner the visitor will leave. So force visitors to navigate around racks and other displays with enticing side trails to themed merchandise sections. Face items so they can be seen from the main travel route. If you have exclusive signature items offered only by your company, they should be prominently displayed with better exposure than products of other suppliers. You might want to consider a discount rack or area for sale items. The size

A well-designed and stocked store can be personally and financially rewarding.

Robb Kendrick/Aurora Photos

and setup of your checkout area are also important. Locate displays of less-expensive impulse-purchase items near the register. Even after all your hard work to set up the appearance of the store, you'll need to change it on a regular basis, at least seasonally, to keep it from becoming boring to the client and to optimize seasonal sales.

It may be worth hiring a retail designer specializing in your niche to consult with in order to optimize sales potential. But your store should also reflect the unique "personality" of your business, not just what is done everywhere else. Designers may also provide tips on where to find needed merchandizing items and may be able to get competitive rates.

SALES STAFF

Not everyone is a great salesperson in a retail setting. Excellent salespersons have at least four characteristics: They are passionate about their products; they have a strong interest in serving customers; they put client needs first; and they are knowledgeable about the products and clients. Passion is an essential feature of a good salesperson because the fervor is contagious to the client and revs up sales opportunities. Passion and superior product knowledge are reasons why so many specialty retailers hire skilled mountain climbers, snowboarders, fishers, or activity experts to staff their stores. They must genuinely like people, greet them by name, be fun and upbeat, understand their products from the customer perspective, treat each guest as an appreciating asset, and be willing to listen to clients and address their individual needs. Although product price and quality are critical, your retail sales staff, like your activity staff, can make or break the experience, and clients judge your store through their interaction with staff.

Hiring the right person is the first step in gaining a strong sales staff. Conduct interviews with at least several staff persons the potential employee might be working with, and compare observations. Assess people and sales skills by asking candidates to do role-playing of common sales scenarios. See chapter 7 for additional interviewing procedures. The second part of getting a solid sales force is through training. New and experienced staff should learn the basics of soft selling: Offer a genuine greeting within 60 seconds of entry, engage in casual conversation about things of interest to the client, focus on customer wants, make it fun, don't try to "one-up" the guest (i.e., my story or experience is better than yours), and treat clients with respect. Knowledge of products is absolutely critical, so send sales staff to trade shows and organize seasonal product training updates. Help your staff know how to deal with difficult clients. There seems to be an increasing percentage of customers who "talk down" to staff, make outrageous demands, or are just plain unpleasant. It is becoming more difficult for staff to handle these challenges on a daily basis without lashing out at the customer or becoming demoralized, which often results in **employee burnout**.

To be able to serve customers well, your staff need to know what clients want and what they might be interested in purchasing. Employees should encourage the customer to do most of the talking by asking open-ended questions ("What can I help you find? Who are you getting it for? What's your price range? In what situations do you want to use it? What type do you prefer?"). Armed with this additional knowledge about the client, the staff member can offer suggestions that might satisfy his wants. Closing the sale is a necessary part of most sales situations. See the discussion of closing techniques in chapter 6 in the section on personal sales. Train staff to always **up-sell** by suggesting complementary items to the purchase, such as "Do you need a floating fishing line for your new reel?"

ACTIVE MANAGEMENT

The store manager must actively manage staff, monitor sales and inventory, and ensure that retail standards are upheld. Every store should have a procedures manual that outlines how the store will be operated. The manager must work with staff, equipment, and guests to ensure standards described in the manual are maintained. Management through example is a great way to convey the importance of standards.

In active management, the manager or owner must employ the very best technology to increase productivity and effectiveness. An example of critical technology is a computerized **point of sale (POS) system** to calculate and record client sales, as well as to measure and monitor sales, profitability, and inventory levels (see Tech Application). A Web-based POS system, such as MerchantOS (www.merchantos.com) goes well beyond an electronic cash register because it integrates customer checkout with inventory control and a client database. POS systems are often specialized for a specific type of retail product,

Tech Application

Advanced Point of Sale Systems

A point of sale (POS) system is the hardware (cash drawer, receipt printers, barcode scanners, label printers, computer, and so on) and software that is integrated to allow a retail business to record sales, keep track of inventory, record customer data, and track orders, thereby reducing lost sales and overstock. Some basic features of a modern POS system include the following:

- *Inventory control*—A database that tracks inventory levels, uses purchase orders for inventory replenishment, and produces sales and inventory reports that allow you to know when to order and how much to order.

- *Employee accountability*—Maintains records of who made the sales, what was sold, and where these transactions took place.

- *Payment facilitation*—Processes credit, debit, and gift cards.

- *Customer data*—Creates a database on each customer containing past purchases, preferences, and contact information.

- *Reports*—Should offer real-time inventory levels, what items are selling, and who the big spenders are, as well as data on profit, loss, and taxes due.

- *Tags, labels, and signs*—The system is capable of printing price tags, labels, and signs quickly, often using vendor-provided data.

- *Remote access*—Many programs allow access to your POS data via the Internet so you can access it from home or while traveling.

- *Service department work orders*—Places and tracks work orders for service to monitor completion progress and notify customers.

Some POS system software is housed in your own in-store computer; others are operated via the Internet, and the software and your data are on high-speed servers of a third-party contractor. Both types have advantages and disadvantages. If you have poor-quality Internet service and want to be independent of other providers, then in-store systems are best, while online systems allow you to operate on the latest software and high-speed servers with remote access. Some combine the two approaches and utilize your store-based software, such as QuickBooks Point of Sale (see www.quickbooks.intuit.com), to get your POS and inventory data from the third-party provider's computers. POS systems, such as MerchantOS (www.merchantos.com) and NitroSell (www.nitrosell.com), are popular Web-based providers. Gone are the days of a stand-alone cash register. To compete with big retailers and provide superior customer service, you need a sophisticated POS system.

or you can customize off-the-shelf systems to meet your needs. They can also be combined with small business accounting software, such as QuickBooks, to form a comprehensive package for monitoring all financial aspects of the business (see chapter 11 for more details on accounting software). Each item sold is deducted from inventory, thus providing real-time inventory management. Systems can be set up to notify management and even automate ordering once a minimal inventory level is reached. Discount sales can be programmed into the system to avoid confu-

sion and maintain pricing. Retailers can also capture customer e-mails and buyer behavior in the system for later promotional efforts. See chapter 6 for ideas on promoting your retail establishment.

RETAIL FINANCIAL RATIOS AND INDICATORS

An active retail manager must monitor the retail performance of the store and maintain control of inventory. A means of doing this is employing financial ratios and indicators. Following are some commonly employed ratios and financial indicators used to manage retail operations.

• Average ticket size (ATS): The average transaction size. This is determined by dividing total sales for the period by the total number of transactions. An increase in ATS can have a significant impact on profitability. There is no good or bad level for ATS; it varies with the types of products you sell. ATS levels from the previous years form a benchmark for comparison.

• Retail **gross margin**: A measure of profitability determined by subtracting total sales from **cost of goods sold**. Gross margin will vary with the types of products you sell and your volume. The margin is typically lower for more-expensive sporting equipment than for lower-cost impulse items. For example, margins on tents and packs range from 30 to 40 percent. The average margin of the sporting goods industry was 37 percent in 2006, according to the Retail Owners Institute (2007).

• Units per transaction (UPT): Average number of items per transaction. Again, there is no good or bad UPT level. It varies with the type of products you sell, with higher-priced items normally having a smaller UPT.

• **Inventory turnover (stock turn)**: How frequently inventory sells. Turnover is equal to net sales plus average retail stock. A high rate (more than five) may indicate low stock levels, while a low rate (less than two) suggests overstocking or sale problems. The sporting goods industry turnover rate in 2006 was 2.4, according to the Retail Owners Institute (2007).

Employ these statistics to monitor the retail performance of a store and assist with inventory control. For example, the Outdoor Industry Association gathered data from outdoor specialty retail shops in the United States and compiled performance statistics in 2006 (Townley, 2007). The findings indicate an average revenue growth of 8.5 percent over the year. Business expenses averaged 39 percent of revenue, gross operating margin was 44 percent, and there was a net operating profit of 5 percent. The importance of apparel sales was significant, accounting for 46 percent of revenue. Inventory turnover for accessories was 4.3, while it was 3.2 for apparel and lower for more-expensive equipment. An outdoor retail store owner can contrast her retail performance with these national benchmark studies to assess the performance of her store. Or a new start-up can use these statistics to help project sales, inventory, and profitability.

PREVENTING THEFT

An unpleasant but important part of retailing is preventing theft. Only a naive small recreation business owner assumes he will not be a target for theft. There are two types of theft: (1) theft by clients, such as shoplifting and burglary, and (2) theft by employees, such as stealing your client list, charging a customer one sum and ringing up a receipt for less, and shoplifting. According to a national survey (About.com, 2007), theft costs U.S. businesses more than $29 billion a year, the average dishonest employee steals $1,023 before being caught, and the average amount stolen by a shoplifter is $128. Theft can have a big impact on a small business. For example, if you have a 10 percent profit margin and someone steals a $128 item, you will have to sell $1,280 in merchandise to make up for that loss.

U.S. Small Business Administration provides some guidelines for helping small businesses minimize the potential for theft (Small Business Administration, 2007). To reduce client theft, greet customers within 60 seconds of entry; install security cameras, burglar alarms, and **electronic merchandise surveillance systems** (merchandise tags). The guidelines for preventing employee theft include watching for the telltale signs of internal theft; finding people you can trust (weed out dishonest people by performing thorough background checks on all new-hire prospects); having a management-level supervisor oversee inventory and bookkeeping; providing alternatives to stealing by offering generous employee discounts on all merchandise and **pro deals** from manufacturers; having clear policies on ethical behavior signed by each employee; and ensuring that management sets an example by not dipping into petty cash, fudging on expense accounts, or taking candy bars without paying.

OTHER COMMON SECONDARY PROFIT CENTERS

Three additional secondary profit centers commonly found as part of commercial recreation, event, and tourism companies are rentals, small scale

Alaska River Outfitters Recreation Equipment Rental and Shuttle Service

Location

The summer home of Alaska River Outfitters is in Haines, Alaska, the southeast part of the state near Glacier Bay National Park where the Alsek River empties into the Pacific Ocean. The only highway providing access to the Tatshenshini and Alsek rivers starts in Haines. There are regularly scheduled flights from Juneau and well-stocked grocery stores, so it is a convenient starting point for river trips in this remote part of Alaska.

Stan Boor, owner.

Patrick T. Tierney

Background

Stan Boor, owner of Alaska River Outfitters (ARO), was part of an elite crew of rafting guides who were exploring river trips worldwide for a pioneering company called Sobek Expeditions. He guided trips in South America, Africa, Asia, and Canada for many years. One of his most memorable expeditions was an exploratory first raft descent of the Tatshenshini River, which started in the Yukon Territory in Canada. On the 10th day the rafters continued on the Alsek River, and they floated into Glacier Bay National Park in Alaska. This trip was spectacular because the river cuts through four mountain ranges, has glaciers flowing into the river, features frequent viewings of grizzly bears, and traverses some of the wildest alpine areas left on the planet. After working for other rafting companies in the summer and ski patrolling at the ski areas outside of Salt Lake City, Utah, in the winter, he decided to start a company of his own. He thought back to the trip on Tatshenshini River and began a company to support groups who wanted to float the river, but he chose to guide only part time. He moved to the isolated coastal Alaskan town of Haines that had excellent road access to the start of the Tatshenshini trip, bought a dual-axle flatbed truck and van, and started offering an equipment and passenger shuttle service. This met with immediate success and the company has provided steady income. Haines has been a wonderful place to live since then. He and his wife, Kate, an expert climbing guide who takes groups on mountaineering trips throughout Alaska in the summer, have built a log home and small warehouse overlooking the Pacific and glacier-crowned peaks near Haines for their summer residence. They continue to spend winters at their home near Salt Lake City, where Kate is on ski patrol at Snowbird Resort and Stan manufactures small batches of custom equipment and takes reservations for the summer in Alaska.

Products and Services

Alaska River Outfitters supports 10- to 15-day Tatshenshini River trips by supplying rental rafts and gear, purchases and packs food for the trip, drives the group to the start of the expedition, and gives an orientation before he returns to Haines. These services make it extremely convenient for groups coming from the lower 48 states to organize a complex river trip. The time-tested gear and equipment systems are designed especially for the extreme environments found on a typical river trip in this region. Examples of the specialized equipment he rents are blowhorns and pepper spray to ward off bears.

Business Advice and Plans

Stan strongly feels that a small RET business owner must really care about the work and enjoy it. He likes meeting new people, being able to work outside in a fantastic natural environment, setting his own schedule with much of the year off, designing his own gear, and turning people on to the beauty of the Tatshenshini River.

manufacturing, and food service. The trends and basic components of each are presented in this section.

RENTALS

The rental of equipment can be a profit center alone, such as a company that rents party supplies and equipment. Rentals can also be an indirect revenue source by encouraging trial use and adoption, promoting retail sales, and increasing customer loyalty. There are good reasons why a customer wants rentals. For example, a beginner at a new recreation activity often does not want to make a substantial financial commitment in gear before they are sure of their level of interest. An expert may want to rent or demo a specialized equipment upgrade before they purchase. The client may need the equipment for only a very short period of time. If you do not provide rentals, your customers may go to a competitor who does. However, companies are reluctant to rent equipment because of the potential for damage to equipment, the concern that rentals may detract from sales, and the perceived liability they might assume. Special liability insurance policy riders, or additional coverage for equipment rentals, and valid liability waivers can minimize liability exposure (see chapter 10 on legal issues). Getting a customer to try a new activity through low-cost rentals often leads to adoption and new sales. So equipment rentals can be a lucrative element of some commercial recreation, event, and tourism businesses.

There are many commercial recreation businesses whose income relies heavily on equipment rentals, such as event equipment companies, winter sports shops, outdoors shops, and kayak or bicycle rental shops. A hot trend in equipment rentals is for companies to rent all the required gear and even buy and pack food for multiday recreation experiences, such as backpacking, bicycling, or river rafting, so that clients can get on a plane without lugging around gear. They can just show up at your shop, your company shuttles them to the start, and off they go on their excursion without delay. See Spotlight On Alaska River Outfitters for an example of a company that is successfully responding to this opportunity (see also Case Study 4.1 in the online student resource for a detailed dis-

Bridget Besaw/Aurora Photos

Equipment rentals can encourage trail use and adoption, promote retail sales, and increase customer loyalty.

cussion of the company). You will need to assess if rentals will add value for your retail customers and if there is sufficient demand for equipment rental as its own profit center. If you are situated in a desirable outdoor location along a trail, river, or popular area for events, rentals may be a viable option.

SMALL-SCALE MANUFACTURING

An increasingly common profit center opportunity is small-scale manufacturing of specialized recreation products. For more-experienced RET professionals, this is a very viable alternative because their years working in the industry have alerted them to the shortcomings of available equipment and the new types of products consumers want. An entrepreneur can make this a secondary component of his business or possibly one of the primary profit centers. There are many examples in the RET industry of persons starting out focusing their business on service provision in the outdoors only to later start a new company that manufactures specialized products sold by specialty retailers or used by outfitters and guides, with the bonus of allowing the owners to keep regular work hours and not be on the road or ocean for weeks at a time.

The options available in small, specialized RET equipment manufacturing are really quite varied. Examples include a company that designs and manufactures specialized mountain climbing equipment and clothing; a firm that designs padded mats used in gymnasiums and health clubs and imports them from China; an organization that makes high-end graphite fly fishing rods; a white-water photography business that takes, prints, and sells photos to rafting customers the day of their trip; and an enterprise that designs and helps manufacture waterproof tip-over indicators that send to the home base, via wireless connections, a signal when a rental kayak or canoe overturns so the rental shop employees can offer assistance. The Seattle area is a particularly good example of small outdoor recreation manufacturers who achieved more than $195 million in sales in 2001. Examples of these businesses follow:

- Camping gear, from mountain climbing equipment to sleeping bags. Washington's manufacturers supply an assortment of products designed for safe enjoyment of the outdoors.

- Mountain biking gear. Equipment for the increasingly popular sport includes bikes and the necessary accessories.

- Recreational boating. Options include pleasure craft and custom-designed boats for whitewater, freshwater, and saltwater recreation.

- Fishing equipment. Specialized rods, lures, tackle packs, and other fishing accessories are in demand.

- Recreational snow equipment, including innovative designs for skis, snowshoes, and snowboards. Large growth in the snowboarding industry complements an already strong Alpine skiing industry. Washington's manufacturers supply the gear to meet their demands.

- Outdoor apparel and sportswear. Attire specifically designed for extreme weather and other outdoor conditions is now available.

- Outdoor footwear. Products include state-of-the-art hiking and trail footwear.

An RET manufacturing company can engage in product design only, or on-site manufacturing, direct importation, contract manufacturing, and the formation of critical alliances to develop and distribute its products. A common business model is to design the product in Canada or the United States; arrange for contract manufacturing in China; and then distribute the products in North America, Europe, Asia, and around the world. An unwavering commitment to quality, a pool of talented engineers and product designers, and efficient mail-order distribution can all influence the strategic direction and profitability of the company.

FOOD AND BEVERAGE SERVICE

A common secondary element of a recreation, event, and tourism experience is food and beverage service. This could vary from all meals provided over a three-day guided wilderness fishing trip to a huge dinner and open bar at a corporate event. Catering events is big business in urban areas. But client expectations about the food quality have risen tremendously in recent years. Government agencies require permits or licenses when serving food and have stricter regulations and more frequent inspections. For example, the National Park Service now considers backcountry guides without electricity subject to many of the same food service requirements that traditional restaurants must follow. This is because there have been numerous instances, in settings ranging from cruise ships and corporate events to rafting trips, where poor food sanitation has led to sick clients, aborted trips or programs, and unhappy customers. In addition, guests more frequently have special dietary health restrictions that must be considered in menu planning. So companies need to acquire information about client dietary concerns before client arrival and provide alternative meals during the experience. Employees are often required to have "food handler sanitation" certification and follow food sanitation regulations. See Case Study 4.2 in the online student resource for more details on food sanitation and service.

The cost of buying raw food ingredients has been increasing rapidly and is expected to continue to do so in a high oil price and global warming world. Careful planning and purchasing of food is critically important in order to contain food costs. Buying food from wholesale distributors can save up to 50 percent in raw ingredients, and the savings can be passed to the bottom line (profit). It is also important to consider the types of raw food products you purchase for your operation, because how these are grown, harvested, processed, packaged, and sold affect not only your purchase cost but also the environment. See the green tip for information on **green cuisine** and how to support a healthy planet and client.

A license to make, serve, or sell food is normally required by the local city, county, or provincial government. Mobile food servers, such as catering companies and even rafting outfitters, must also have special permits. These licenses often require payment of application and inspection fees, a minimum level of insurance coverage, and adherence to strict sanitation and storage standards. Inspections are undertaken to ensure compliance. Obtaining a food facility license is normally not restricted in the number offered. This is quite different from the permit required to sell or serve alcoholic beverages. The number of alcoholic

beverage licenses issued is frequently limited, and once the permitting agency deems the area is adequately served, it will not issue new licenses. An alcoholic beverage license is also required for so-called off-premises sales or liquor service, such as serving beer or wine at events. In many U.S. cities, the maximum number of licenses has been reached, and to secure a license a new business may need to buy an existing business and transfer the license. This can be an expensive, frustrating, and time-consuming process; a transfer is not automatic, and the new business must still qualify. An entrepreneur would be wise to first check with the local Alcohol Beverage Control agency to learn about specific permit requirements and if permits are available in the area.

So it is imperative that commercial recreation, event, and tourism providers carefully plan the cost of quality food and beverage service into their programs; plan menus to serve a range of dietary needs; purchase sustainably produced ingredients at wholesale; abide by strict food sanitation guidelines; and get proper permits, staff training, and credentials.

Green Tip

Green Cuisine

What food supplies you purchase and how they are grown, harvested, processed, packaged, and sold affect the environment. Two common food items, seafood and coffee, illustrate this situation well. According to the Marine Stewardship Council (www.msc.org), our oceans are being seriously overfished, and some aquaculture seafood is laced with hormones and antibiotics. Fishing industries and marine environments around the world are being affected, and unless action is taken, some of our favorite fish may disappear from the seafood counter. To help care for the health of the oceans and your guests, you should consider following the recommendations of the Seafood Watch guide to sustainable ocean fare and purchase wisely for your next event or for your daily programs. Forget the Chilean sea bass and order the wild Pacific salmon.

Coffee is hugely popular, for most events and meals a necessity. But the global demand for coffee has resulted in production, harvesting, and sales techniques that unnecessarily hurt the environment and local communities in developing countries. Shade-grown coffee does not require clear-cutting tropical forests and heavy applications of fertilizers and pesticides (which can hurt wildlife), and it is cost competitive. Organic coffee is not produced or processed with harsh chemicals. Fair-trade coffee, which is purchased from cooperatives of small farmers to eliminate much of the middleman costs, provides the growers with a stable price that ensures a reasonable standard of living while adding only a very small additional cost for coffee buyers (see www.grinningplanet.com for more details). You can order shade-grown, organic, and fair-trade coffee online if your local supplier does not offer it.

SUMMARY

In this chapter we explore the importance of retail sales, rentals, small-scale RET product manufacturing, and food service as primary or secondary profit centers for commercial recreation, event, and tourism businesses. Retail sales of accessories, apparel, and equipment complement the provision of activities and events because they create more year-round and off-season business, support the primary service by providing needed equipment and gear, and bring in new customers. Both physical stores and e-commerce on the Internet are essential complementary locations for retail sales. Setting up an e-commerce shopping cart and inventory system is inexpensive and easy, even for small recreation businesses. The chapter describes six essential elements of successful retailing, including location and visibility, superior products and where and how to purchase them, pricing of merchandise, appearance and presentation of merchandise, sales staff, and active management. Retailers employ point of sale systems to measure and monitor sales, profitability, and inventory. You can use these POS systems to calculate basic financial ratios and statistics to manage store operations. The statistics can be compared with industry metrics to benchmark and identify your retail performance.

Theft in a retail setting is a common and potentially large problem for retailers. The chapter discusses guidelines for helping small businesses minimize theft by either clients or employees. Information about RET equipment rentals and how these can be a primary or secondary profit center is provided. In addition, the opportunities provided by small-scale RET equipment manufacturing are briefly discussed. The chapter concludes with a section on one of the most common secondary elements of many RET businesses, food and beverage provision. Although we do not address food service as a primary element, such as a restaurant, the chapter does discuss some basic regulatory, food purchasing, and catering considerations.

Check out the online student resource for additional material, including case studies, Web links, and more.

Chapter 5

Market Analysis, Target Markets, and Competitive Analysis

Learning Objectives

After reading this chapter you will be able to

- apply market segmentation techniques to two prospective business case studies,

- acquire market data for a commercial recreation business opportunity and use the data to make decisions about the target market for an RET enterprise,

- identify most common characteristics and factors for segmentation of the consumer population,

- describe application of market analysis techniques to business decisions, and

- explain how to acquire information for evaluating your competition and for identifying your competitive advantage.

Key Terms

behavioral variables	geographic variables	psychographic variables
benefits variables	market analysis	SWOT analysis
catchment area	market research	target market
competitor analysis	market segmentation	triangulation
customer profile	market share	
demographic variables		

Imagine this scenario:

You are an active road racing cyclist in your age class, and you have been contemplating opening a bike shop. You have good friends who are cyclists as well. However, they are a different breed of cyclists as they are dedicated BMX racers. They have ample opportunity for competition but have limited access locally to the clothing, gear, and bike equipment they need for BMX competition. The local bike shop is owned by an elderly person who enjoys the "fix-it type" bicycle service and is not particularly interested in the retail side or staying on top of the trends associated with the industry. Last week when you went into the local shop, the owner told you that he would like to sell the business and retire to the Sun Belt in the next several months. You're excited about the possibility of this store because he has an excellent location, and the owner is motivated to sell. This is truly an appealing opportunity because you are very familiar with bicycling. You also realize there are untapped retail markets, and the BMX trend is one of them. However, there are other considerations on the horizon that must be taken into account.

With the recent passing of your grandmother, you and your sister have inherited her large well-constructed heritage house. Although it certainly is very spacious, attractive, and filled with happy memories, it will be difficult for you and your sister to pay property taxes, maintain it, and live in it together given each of you has an independent lifestyle. Fortunately, your sister is interested in exploring whether or not it might present a business opportunity for her. The good news is the community you both live in has lots of travelers that come for summer and winter vacations to enjoy the year-round festival events. This is a large home with five good-size bedrooms, and with some remodeling, your sister could create a bed-and-breakfast (B&B) and rent the extra rooms to guests. As a cook at a specialty restaurant, your sister has always enjoyed being a host, and she previously worked at the visitor information center during her college days. The issue, however, is whether it is financially feasible to start up a B&B in view of the fact that so little is known about this customer market. What do travelers look for and expect from a B&B experience?

When thinking about the bicycle shop you would like to own, you realize that in terms of the retail component of the store, the same kind of questions exist about the nature and number of the potential market. You ask yourself just how similar or just how different the market analysis will be for each of these RET businesses.

Market analysis would be considerably easier if organizing data about your target market were as simple as being dealt the right cards to create the winning hand in a card game. In a game of cards, success is readily evident when you hold a winning hand. Selecting the "right cards" out of a very large deck (e.g., consumers of products and services) to create a winning hand in business is a suitable metaphor for your task of describing your preferred consumer market.

Several similarities are worthy of note. Just as a winning hand is not the identical combination of cards for every card game, the winning hand in business depends on the type of business (e.g., products and services) you are trying to succeed at. The cards you want to hold will vary from one type of business to another. Because the application of the principles of market analysis also vary from one business to another, two different types of businesses will be used to provide a context to the market analysis tasks. When you have a well-defined and viable target market in business, you do have a winning hand in terms of designing your marketing plan, adopting

your pricing strategy, and developing a loyal customer base. Another analogy is that the winning hand in a card game is not a certainty every time but is relative to the cards held by the other players in the game. In business, your preferred target market is relative to the target market that other businesses seek to capture and dominate as their share of the market. This analogy is important for understanding competitor analysis—another task described in this chapter—which occurs when you lay your cards on the table to see if "your winning hand" is actually better than the hand held by your competitors. This task will be discussed further at the end of this chapter.

ONE UNIVERSAL TRUTH OF BUSINESS

As a potential entrepreneur, you will share a common and very important task faced by all persons seeking to start up, or buy, an RET business. You, and your sister, as set out in the opening scenario, need to understand

Business assets are like the hand you hold in a card game. The strength of your hand (e.g., entrepreneurial assets) is relative to the cards held by others and this can influence the market share you need to secure to be profitable.

market research: the process of gathering customer data, organizing it by describing market segments, and then analyzing the data in regard to the size and location of the audience you will need to attract for the business to be profitable.

One universal truth for owners of a new RET venture is you have to know your customers if you intend to be successful! If you don't know what it takes to attract and keep your customers, your business will probably lose money. As you undertake the task of assessing market potential, you will discover that beyond the customers, you will also want to give attention to the competition out there in your area serving some segment of your target audience. Therefore, market research is essentially a double-edged sword that can be swung one way to assist with market analysis and swung another way for competitive analysis. The purpose of the opening scenario is to set the stage to examine the key concepts of market analysis, market segmentation, and competitor analysis in a meaningful way. As noted in the scenario, business opportunities may arise for

you in random and unexpected ways. This chapter focuses on the best practices for market analysis and competitor analysis in a general way as well as in a specific context. Your effort to describe preferred consumers, and to seek answers to the questions about them, will certainly influence the feasibility of the business opportunity.

UNDERSTANDING THE MARKET

Realistically, continuous up-to-date market information is valuable to every entrepreneur because primary customer markets change over time, as do the products they purchase. Therefore, you need to be mindful of the customer at each of the five stages of the recreation or tourism experience (figure 1.1, page 5). Once your business plan contains a statement of purpose along with a detailed description of the products and service you will provide (chapter 3), then examination of customer information is the next logical step in your business plan, and that step takes you down the path of market research.

WHAT IS MARKET RESEARCH?

Market research is an essential and deliberate process to acquire, examine, and document information about consumers that will be used to make marketing decisions. A wide range of decisions in business can benefit from market research. Carefully thought out and executed consumer studies are initiated for a variety of purposes, and each market study has the potential to provide an entrepreneur with valuable information for planning a business. There are at least a half-dozen important areas where market research is utilized in business planning.

Market research helps business owners identify and assess the following:

- Consumer needs, preferences, and behaviors
- The communication and media avenues best suited for marketing and promotion of products
- Client satisfaction with the products and services
- The factors influencing customer loyalty to a brand and likelihood of repurchasing a product
- The image the consumer holds concerning a business or destination that influences their decisions in regard to purchases or travel
- Market trends in the economy and shifts in consumer spending
- The competition and how to differentiate your own products and services

The task of describing consumer needs and preferences means putting into use some tools of **market analysis**. This technique refers to the collection, organization, and interpretation of consumer data that delineate the characteristics of the consumers making up the target market for your business. Thus, market analysis is a vital step in the preparation of a business plan. The results of analysis of market data can contribute to at least three fundamental business decisions that are elaborated on elsewhere in the text.

- How do you design an effective marketing strategy to reach the target market (chapter 6)?
- Can my business capture the necessary market share to achieve profitability (chapter 11)?

- Do I have a competitive advantage in the marketplace (later in this chapter)?

Market share is a measure of how dominant a business is within its service sector. Generally, a market share reflects a percentage of consumer spending for a product or service that a business captures, or intends to capture, in the course of serving its target market. Therefore, it is evident that market analysis is an essential task for planning a new business and also for evaluating the merits of acquiring an existing business. Moreover, it is linked to other parts of the business plan involving finance, marketing, and operations. As noted later, the underlying rationale for market analysis is the recognition that scarce resources can be stretched only so far.

PURPOSE OF MARKET ANALYSIS

The purpose of market analysis is to get to know the potential demand for your product and the ability of your preferred customer to pay for it. This task, carried out by you or a consultant, asks for an assessment of the proportion or percentage of the potential market you can rely on to build your business. You want answers to a common set of general questions pertaining to the characteristics of the market to be served. The basic questions, which would be modified for an existing business, include the following:

- Given the size of the market, how much of the market can I capture?
- Who are the customers to be served (or that are being served)?
- What are their needs in terms of travel services, leisure, or recreation?
- Given what I have to offer, how much are they likely to purchase?
- How often can I expect the market to purchase my service or product?
- What is the potential for building a repeat customer base?

By acquiring this type of information about the people to be served, you are in a better position to divide the potential consumers into segments and to identify one or more target markets. A **target market** refers to a particular market segment that your com-

Entrepreneurs that provide services needed by recreational boat owners will find a marina is a ready-made market for such businesses.

mercial leisure services business can aim its product at. The task of segmenting the market and creating a customer profile for the target market is described later in this chapter.

WHERE TO FIND MARKET INFORMATION

Market information can come from several sources. Depending on what business you are in, you can expect to find data from public, private, and nongovernmental sources such as

- the university, college, or public library;
- the business sections of bookstores;
- leisure market and tourism magazines and journals;
- Web sites (e.g., www.bicycleretailer.com);
- small business administration in the United States (e.g., www.sba.gov);
- small business administration in Canada (e.g., www.canadaone.com/index.html);

- associations of retired business executives (e.g., www.SCORE.org);
- business services for Canadian entrepreneurs (e.g., www.canadabusiness.ca/gol/cbec/site.nsf/en/index.html);
- census data (www.census.gov or www.statcan.ca/start.html);
- trade associations;
- convention and visitors bureaus;
- destination marketing organizations;
- consultants specializing in market research; and
- other businesses in the same service sector.

Look closely at other businesses and what they are offering; examine their marketing materials, and seek answers to the question of why customers go to them. The premise of looking systematically at other specific businesses as a source of information is referred to as **competitor analysis**, and it will be covered in more detail in another section.

THE SEARCH FOR TRUSTWORTHY DATA

The task of sorting out the reliable information from the less-reliable information (e.g., distinguishing fact from fiction) can be challenging at first because the quality of the data is not always the same. Therefore, you may need to examine and document multiple sources of market information to ensure it sheds light on the audience you intend to serve. **Triangulation** is a term that may help in several circumstances. When people want to get oriented in an unfamiliar environment, they will use several points of reference within the line of sight in the horizon. Using multiple references is a good navigational strategy to "get a fix" on one's exact location. It means taking a compass bearing on several fixed points to refine the information as to where you are located. A compass bearing allows you to draw a line connecting two points; where a combination of compass lines intersect with one another, you can reliably mark a specific point where you are located. Using multiple sources of consumer information can help you reliably identify some of the specific characteristics or attributes of the target audience that you are most interested in. John Naisbitt has written extensively on changes in the global economy and the nature of important changes in consumer patterns and trends that influ-

ence society. As a futurist, and author of *MegaTrends* and *MegaTrends 2000*, he points to the changes arising from the era of the Internet and the "information superhighway." Although access to information today provides many benefits, the trustworthiness of such information was questioned more than several decades ago by the author when he noted "we are drowning in a sea of information and yet starving for knowledge" (Naisbitt, 1982, p. 24). For a business owner, that statement is a cautionary warning about the possibility of being inundated with a sea of information about market characteristics but struggling to find trustworthy knowledge about a primary target market. It can be expected that detailed, reliable consumer data that a new entrepreneur is likely to depend upon will be harder to find and extract from the "sea of information." To a market researcher, quality data means empirically verifiable facts that originate from investigations carried out in a careful and systematic manner. As to be expected, quality has its own price tag; therefore, you can expect to pay for it in terms of market data.

WHO DOES MARKET ANALYSIS?

Every owner actively engaged in a commercial leisure services or tourism enterprise should be able to

Examination of market data by team members can assist in its interpretation and lead to thoughtful suggestions.

Reza Estakhrian

initially answer two questions: Who is buying, or going to buy, your product? What does the "typical" customer look like? If the answers to these questions are detailed, accurate, and reliable, then you can begin to tackle some of the decisions highlighted on the previous pages. The premise underlying market analysis involves segmenting your market, generating a customer profile for each segment you intend to serve, and setting some priorities for the target markets you would rate as the most important. Once completed, you will be able to design your marketing strategy for the year. This chapter helps you address the size, distribution, and characteristics of your preferred market. For example, it will soon be evident how you might attempt to answer these questions for both a bicycle shop and a small tourism enterprise (i.e., a bed-and-breakfast).

When you ask questions about the size and distribution of the preferred market in the case of the bike shop, you will look for information gaps pertaining to retail since the business does provide repair services but not retail sales. When potential markets have been ignored, it may be an excellent growth opportunity. Since the bike shop already exists, it may be possible to benchmark the bicycle business against equivalent businesses in other geographic locations. Benchmarking is a means of comparing one or more performance measures of your business against similar operations in the sector or assessing the measures against an

industry average. As a prospective owner of a business in the RET industry, you will have to collect some market research information if you are going to be successful. Of particular interest to the business plans will be obtaining as much data as possible about the characteristics of the primary and secondary target audience who will purchase what the business has to offer. A primary first-stage strategy in market segmentation is to organize the consumer market into groups with common attributes important to your product or service. Profiling the customer is a reality that the successful commercial enterprise needs to understand if it is to provide a value-added, personalized guest experience that cannot be readily purchased in the public sector.

Although your sister will be looking more at tourism and travel data for a B&B, you are more likely to focus on new consumer data that originate from a trade association such as the U.S. Bicycle Retailer and Industry News, National Bicycle Dealers Association, and perhaps the U.S. Cycling Federation. In conducting an Internet search, you will be able to find specific data on particular demographic age groups (e.g., Gen X or the Millennium Generation) and their level of participation in the cycling market. This will be examined more closely when discussing the segmentation of the market. With some market data on the BMX target audience combined with the purchasing patterns of the existing customer base,

Many travelers enjoy inns and B & Bs because they are perceived as intimate and safe, and they are hosted by individuals who know the area.

Associated Press/William Lauer

No matter the business, every business owner needs to conduct a market analysis by grouping people into several homogeneous groups with similar interests.

you will be able to assess the future profitability of the enterprise and then negotiate a purchase price if buying an existing business.

By contrast, your sister needs to consider a business that is at the initial start-up phase. There is no guest registry based on prior operations, so it is necessary to examine the customer database by employing a different approach to assess the feasibility of the B&B idea. Your effort in gathering information could involve new data that you might personally collect yourself (i.e., primary data) or it could be data that someone else has collected (i.e., secondary data). It is often expensive to carry out a research project to collect your own information, so initially a search for secondary sources of consumer data is a preferred way to proceed. In the case of your sister, one of the best practices in the accommodation trade is to search for a bed-and-breakfast guidebook (Stankus, 2004; Taylor and Taylor, 1999); examine suggestions from the industry associations; and track down a recent regional traveler and tourism survey that describes some, or all, of the following information:

- Total number of visitors to the area
- Preferred type of accommodation
- Length of stay
- Reason for travel
- Methods of booking
- Transport options

In many jurisdictions, local convention and visitors bureaus (CVBs) and tourism offices that market destinations (e.g., regional, state, provincial, and national) regularly conduct such surveys in order to describe modes of travel, preferred destinations, and spending patterns. Membership in B&B associations as well as CVBs can provide access to such information. What should be evident at this point is that secondary data on a particular market may be available from a variety of sources—an industry or trade association, a convention and visitors bureau, a marketing professional, a government agency, or a combination of stakeholders seeking to understand the consumers of RET products and services. You can gather the information in multiple ways, and tailoring your research to answer customer-oriented questions is vital for matching your product with its market. Once the information is collected, the next step is to organize it to create a picture of your preferred market (e.g., a customer profile), and that is what you should consider next.

SPOTLIGHT ON

John Avery and Roche Harbor Marine

Location

If you're cruising in the idyllic San Juan Islands and choose to dock at Roche Harbor Resort for equipment services, you'll find Roche Harbor Marine (RHM) ready to serve your needs. RHM was established as an S corporation in 1992 by John Avery. However, the origin of this business began 16 years earlier when John opened a business in Santa Cruz, California, in partnership with his brother. Their idea was to work on cars with the occasional repair of outboard motors. After a year or so, they serviced only boats. This shift of business purpose made sense. John notes, "I've always loved boats and always lived near the water. We found the marine work much cleaner and the people more appreciative, and most of all we enjoyed the whole boating atmosphere. We found not nearly as much competition, and it seems people enjoy spending money on their toys much more than on their necessities, and this makes bill payment for the services a lot easier."

John Avery.

Background

The Santa Cruz business was at the yacht harbor and their shop was one of only two providing marine engine services in town. "There wasn't much competition, so growing was easy as we started up," John recalls. "We could not believe our good fortune! We were each doing something we loved, working in a place we loved to be (on the water), and getting paid. I remember we always had the VHF radio on. When the salmon were biting, we would leave the secretary there to make excuses. Then we would jump in the boat and go fishing, usually back in a couple of hours with our limit. Also many of our customers became our good friends. I bring these things up only to highlight how much fun one can have while still making a decent living."

In 1988 John and his wife, Vicky, took a vacation to San Juan Islands, Washington, and both instantly fell in love with the place. They noticed there were boats galore with very few repair facilities on the island. In fact, the only boatyard on the island at the time was Jensen's Shipyard, and they really didn't do engine or drive repair. There were only a few people in the area who were doing that kind of work. Although Santa Cruz was where John and Vicky had lived most of their lives and they loved it there, they realized the San Juan Islands were a place they could live and have fun making a living. Within a couple of years, the Santa Cruz shop was sold and they moved to San Juan Island.

The first step for John was to be strictly mobile and work out of his truck all over the island as a sole proprietorship. The best opportunities were at Roche Harbor, so John tried to concentrate most of his efforts there, sort of becoming the resident marine mechanic. Fortunately in 1997, the owners of Roche Harbor built a new marina, and that changed everything. John opened a small shop on the premises and took on a partner. John specialized in stern drive and diesel, and his partner concentrated on outboards. A partner also allowed John to periodically take time off knowing full well the business was in good hands.

Products and Services

With the new marina came many new customers. The business moved into a larger building, and within a year John found it necessary to start hiring to keep up with the workload. In addition, the business picked up marine dealerships for Yamaha Outboards, Onan Generators, Yanmar Diesel, and Cummins Diesel. The next step was to add a retail component and open up a small chandlery and a well-stocked engine parts department. Today RHM employs eight people (six technicians, a parts and service manager, and a secretary) and is open year-round. Besides engine, stern drive, outboards, and generators, the added technicians have allowed RHM to expand into more specialized fields such as diesel heating systems, waste systems, and onboard electronics (navigation systems, autopilots, and radar). As a result, the business has become more of a full-service facility.

Business Advice and Plans

John says, "When I look back on the last 30 years, I realize how much I have enjoyed what I do. I realize how fortunate it is to make a living working on the water and around people who, for the most part, are fascinating and fun-loving. There is tremendous opportunity in the marine propulsion field, but it does seem that there are not a lot of young people getting into the field. I'm not sure why that is because the demand is certainly there. I do hope that changes in the future."

Photo courtesy of John Avery.

PROFILING A PREFERRED CUSTOMER

Over time it is evident that different leisure services are purchased, in large part, by a particular segment of the market. Based on a set of characteristics or attributes, a customer profile can be compiled. A **customer profile** is a detailed description of your typical customer. The 80-20 rule of business implies that 80 percent of your revenue will be generated by 20 percent of your customers. It falls to reason, therefore, that your ability to identify, describe, and understand that 20 percent of the market is central to the long-term success of the business. In the case of marine services in popular destinations, it is evident that Roche Harbor Marine decided to focus on a core set of customers, recreational boaters, and then located the prime market. Their success was to start small and then expand as major growth occurred with a resort complex (see Spotlight On Roche Harbor Marine). Essentially, a customer profile asks for you to identify the characteristics of the core customer who is most interested in buying the goods and services you offer. Chapter 6 explains how good marketing programs focus on the segments of the population that are most interested in your business. The identification of that segment of the population begins with segmentation and follows with building a customer profile.

SEGMENTATION OF THE MARKET

Market segmentation is a process that divides the entire market into groups that possess common or alike characteristics. It involves identifying a set of attributes or characteristics (i.e., age, product preferences, spending patterns, etc.) that allow you to divide customers into those you are likely to pursue and those you will not. The goal is to describe the core customer group of your business (i.e., the target market). It may be based on the segment you believe you can effectively serve together with knowledge that they are looking for the type of services you are able to offer. This information is the foundation of your marketing plan.

You might observe three broad categories, each containing a wide range of variables, when you consider the segmentation process. The headings of demographic, geographic, and benefit desired—including psychographic and behavioral factors—are displayed in figure 5.1. Each of these major headings can be seen as a component part of the pie that can be used

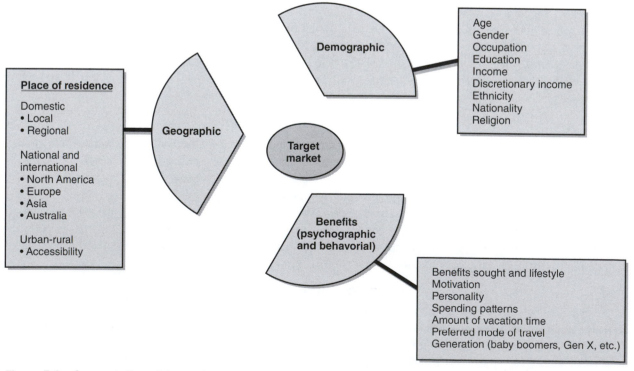

Figure 5.1 Segmentation of the market.

in building a profile. The relative size of "a piece of the pie," or the importance of any particular heading that covers a set of population characteristics, depends entirely on the nature of the products and services that a business offers or plans to offer. That is to say, the process of building a customer profile is carried out within the context of the type of business, its services, and its geographic location within the country. Figure 5.2 reflects the importance of particular segmentation headings when you apply the segmentation process to your bicycle shop or to the B&B. The presence, or absence, of a particular set of segmentation variables can be influenced by the nature of the existing market research. For example, prior studies initiated by the bicycle trade association suggest that benefits sought (love of the sport of bicycling, improved health, competition) and geographic factors (accessibility, location in the community), together with the anticipated growth of your youth or adult segments (age, gender, discretionary income, the boomer population), will be dominant factors in gaining an understanding of the core of your target audience. On the other hand, your sister will improve her chances for success if in building her customer profile she can acquire local data that describe benefits sought by those choosing B&B lodging over other choices (e.g., intimate, personal and safe, accommodation together with the opportunity to gain knowledge of area from the host), behavioral factors (lifestyle, discretionary travel time), and geographic factors (growth in the domestic and international travel industry, origin of the travelers).

As an illustration, we return again to the metaphor of holding a winning hand in cards. The segmentation categories are represented by one of the four suits in a card deck (i.e., hearts, diamonds, spades, and clubs), and the variables are represented by the value of each card within each suit, which ranges from deuce to ace. Holding a winning hand in a specific game is influenced both by the suit as well as the value of the cards you hold. As noted in figure 5.2, the different businesses rely on a different combination of cards.

Benefits Desired

The most attractive segmentation criteria relate to the benefits desired by customers, or **benefits variables**. The benefits approach groups customers according to an understanding of the benefits they seek in an event, product, activity, or experience. For example, as an outfitter on the Frazer River offering family-oriented trips, you would ideally identify persons who are looking for the benefits associated with the types of experiences you can provide—a one-day, interpretive river trip on a scenic, calm river, perfect for families. Alternatively you may also offer a high adventure, multiday trip with wild rapids on a swift moving river through wilderness areas with gourmet food served and having the unique itinerary of beginning in the Yukon Territory, flowing through northern British Columbia, and ending in Glacier Bay, Alaska. Researching only demographic information would not be an effective way to identify the right match

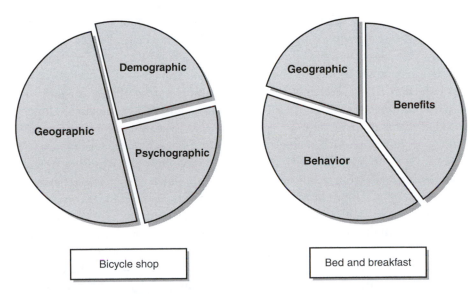

Figure 5.2 Relative importance of segmentation variables.

because your potential customers are likely to be not just young families; they may include grandparents taking their grandkids. The key information is the types of benefits sought (in this example, a scenic, short, mild family-oriented adventure). But a business manager must really dig deep to identify the real benefits sought, not just what appears on the surface. This is difficult information to obtain because market research in this area is not extensive. As pointed out by Morrison (2002), "The problem is that, although this type of information exists, few marketers have taken the next step of identifying and pursuing specific benefit segments. . . . As with psychographic, a major drawback in this type of segmentation is the lack of uniform definitions for . . . benefit segments" (p. 188).

What Morrison's comment highlights is an all too common lag between the time when benefits-based outcomes were first published in the literature and the time when market research was initiated to provide empirical evidence that reports on specific benefits identified by a type of consumer. It could be that the segment interested in BMX racing seeks the benefits of self-esteem, positive self-image, and the development of riding skills. However, those benefits are hypothetical until such time as market research confirms it. Although benefits segmentation makes considerable sense, it remains an elusive variable until there are data to support it.

Geographic Variables

A geographic market variable generally divides the customers according to where they originate or live. If the attractions in the vicinity of your business bring in visitors from Europe, Asia, Australia, and elsewhere in North America, then geographic segmentation may assist in segmenting the domestic customer from the international segment. Accessibility to your sister's B&B lodging could segment those arriving by personal transportation from those coming to the area via the local airport.

Geographic variables most commonly reflect customer origin. Depending on the product, it could be a local neighborhood or a particular region, state, province, or country. Without doubt, the attractions at a travel destination (e.g., cultural or natural assets, theme parks, heritage or historic features, special events, outdoor theaters) have "drawing power," and certain segments of the market will travel some dis-

tance to purchase the services or leisure experience. Obtaining information about where the customer originates creates an opportunity to assess growth in the geographic area. When a business collects ZIP or postal code information from its customers, a geographic software program can create a map of the consumer market, or catchment area, for the product or service. In this case, **catchment area** refers to the boundaries of a geographic area from which a business attracts its clients, visitors, or customers. For example, major tourist destinations will likely have many small leisure service businesses or perhaps a destination resort, each with its own distinct catchment area of variable geographic size. In a similar fashion, local government and community service organizations often define catchment areas, or service areas, for public safety (fire, police) and emergency medical services.

Demographic Variables

Researching **demographic variables** refers to profiling such details as age, gender, income, education, occupation, marital status, ethnicity, nationality, religion, and other attributes of the person. This information is helpful for describing the characteristics of the most common potential users found in a benefits segment. Demographics are generally not appropriate to use as the primary segmentation factor, as benefits desired are normally the key consideration in segmentation. For example, all ages of people take river trips, so you cannot say only the young or old go rafting. But the average age of participants in specific river trip segments could be quite different. Demographic variables are helpful segmentation factors because of the availability of such data from public records such as the U.S. census. The census has two important features worthy of note for some businesses. First, it is an enumeration and not a sample. An enumeration means the data cover everyone within the household; it is not a sample of select respondents. Second, the data collection procedure is geographic (e.g., by household), which means the demographic variables are place specific. For local commercial leisure services, the availability of census data at the neighborhood level means a business can accurately describe the size, distribution, and significance of the potential customer living within the census tract. The census information contains characteristics important to a consumer profile (e.g., family size, income, education, home ownership), and such data can be displayed for a potential catchment area as described previously. Another source of demographic information is EASI Demographics (www.easidemographics.com). Surprisingly, market share and expenditure data on tourists is available on the Internet by county for the state of Michigan thanks to the Tourism Resource Center at Michigan State University (www.tourism.msu.edu/t-aoe/html-aoe/members.htm). For a market profile, click on a particular county, and you can immediately examine data reflecting market share, trip volume, and expenditures of tourists within the county based on actual travel patterns (see www.msu.edu/course/prr/840/econimpact/michigan/countyprof98.htm).

Psychographic and Behavioral Variables

Psychographic variables are characteristics or attributes that relate to attitudes, opinions, lifestyles, personality, and interests. When a complete assessment is made of a person's psychographic makeup, it is referred to as a psychographic profile. One of the better known psychographic profiles is a typology by Stanley Plog of two consumer profiles describing their preferences and interests when selecting a travel destination. His profile describing an allocentric traveler

and psychocentric traveler consists of seven or more attributes based on lifestyle, interest, and personality variables. See figure 5.3 for a comparison of the psychographic type his research revealed about the typical visitor who chooses one type of destination versus another destination.

Behavioral variables refer to the recording and classification of consumer purchasing behavior. Behaviors are recorded in numerous ways, and each record-keeping strategy seeks to document customer actions related to online and offline purchases. The records may reflect supermarket cards that discount sale items, product surveys and warranty registration cards, contest entries, eBay purchasing records, property records, U.S. census records, motor vehicle data, automatic number information, credit card transactions, phone records, and so forth. The databases created from this information involve segmentation of the population based on one or more characteristics associated with buying habits and product preferences. Consumer purchasing habits and patterns represent extremely valuable information in business, and most of the research documents will be proprietary. Access to these data will come at a price, and the least expensive choice is likely joining a professional association that serves its members by conducting market surveys. This option is illustrated later in the text in the case of the bicycle business and the B&B opportunity.

Psychocentrics	Allocentrics
• Familiar travel destinations	• Nontourist destinations
• Common activities at destinations	• New experiences
• Sun and fun spots	• Sense of discovery (*visit before others*)
• Relaxation	• New and unusual destinations
• Prefers driving	• High activity level
• Heavy tourist accommodation, such as hotels, family-type restaurants, and tourist shops	• Prefers flying
• Family atmosphere/familiar entertainment	• Tour accommodations should be good and not necessarily modern/chain-type hotels
• Complete tour packaging with a lot of scheduled activities	• Enjoy meeting and dealing with people from another culture
	• Tour arrangements should include basics and allow considerable freedom and flexibility

Figure 5.3 Psychographic profiles reflecting choice of travel destinations.

Adapted from S. Plog, 2001, "Why destination areas rise and fall in popularity," *Cornell Hospitality Quarterly* 42(3): 17-18.

THE SEARCH FOR AND INTERPRETATION OF SEGMENTATION VARIABLES

Insight into what segmentation variables have been important in the past, and remain important today, can come from various sources. Unfortunately most textbooks are simply too general in their focus. Far more helpful in getting you started are trade associations and self-help books by experienced professionals. For example, Taylor and Taylor (2004) created profiles for B&B owners by describing several basic attributes of customers (e.g., gender, trip purpose, services preferred, family status). By examining the experiences of other operators, the authors document segmentation attributes that describe typical customers of bed-and-breakfast operations, such as the following:

- Adults who travel to enjoy the history and heritage of the area as well as observe and participate in special cultural events

- Retired couples with plenty of discretionary travel time who seek the personalized benefits of the relaxed atmosphere associated with a B&B

- Business and professional travelers looking for friendly hosts together with the comfortable homestyle setting similar to what they experience when they return from their trip

- Women travelers looking for safety and security, which is commonly part of the B&B environment

- Older adults (e.g., "empty nesters") seeking the B&B style of accommodation while visiting nearby friends and relatives

In terms of geographic factors, tourism researchers have documented that international travelers spend more and pay higher prices on vacations than do domestic travelers, and local residents spend by far the least. There are various reasons for this higher level of spending per capita among tourists, so if you will serve this market segment, it is important to consider not only their spending patterns but their preferences as well. The respondents in one market research study of ecotourism travelers visiting western Canada for nature-based travel reported spending on average $315 per day and enjoying trips of a week or longer. They listed their preferred type of accommodation as cabins, bed-and-breakfasts, and inn-type facilities;

at the bottom of their preference list was hotels. The sociodemographic data indicated these were professionals who enjoy taking such trips three or more times a year (B.C. Ministry of Tourism, 1995). Even when your core market may be local residents, there could very well be a proportion of your income from international travelers. Table 5.1 reveals the results of a community study in the state of Missouri that examined types of businesses in the commercial sector that derive a percentage of their income directly from tourist spending.

One lesson to be drawn for someone entering the bed-and-breakfast business is that a significant market segment and revenue stream will depend on the travel trade. Although figures on the number of visitors to the areas may be readily available, the important step is to estimate how many are potential B&B customers. Thus, it would be wise to draw on the resources of the trade associations created to support this sector of the trade. Your sister could join, and enjoy the benefits of, the National Bed-and-Breakfast Association, the American Bed and Breakfast Association, or the Professional Association of Innkeepers International. Professional associations can also be found in each Canadian province and each state in the United States. One association newsletter, titled *Yellow Brick Road*, offers vital data from a nationwide survey that

Table 5.1 Tourist Contributions to Community Businesses in Missouri

Business	% of income from tourism
Motel/Hotel/B&B	94.5
Restaurants	49.4
Taverns/Bars/Liquor Stores	34.8
Amusements	33.1
Gasoline Stations	31.5
General Merchandise	18.6
Auto Dealers and Garages	15.8
Food (retail)	13.8
Apparel and Accessories	13.6

Source: U.S. Dept of Commerce in *Community Tourism Assessment Handbook*, 1996.

assists new B&B owners with details about daily room rates, occupancy, purchase price, operating finances, return on investment, marketing budget, staffing, and amenities offered by respondents. In another example, Superior Small Lodging (www.superiorsmalllodging.com/about.html) will match travelers with B&B lodging at the destination.

Segmentation in the bicycle business needs to take into account the trends in the industry and possible new markets. If you purchase such a business, segmentation variables should include a mix of local residents and particular segments of the cycling market from out of town. Some of the local market would be known from the sales records of the current owner. In general, the goal is to understand the local and distant (tourist) markets and find answers to some key questions:

- Who is going to buy your product line?
- Will you market to BMX consumers, or is the market too small?

- What traits do you think your "typical" customer or client will have?
- Is there a common need for a particular service among your customers?

To obtain reliable and accurate data that reflect the national population in the cycling market, you may wish to purchase a market study prepared by the National Bicycle Dealers Association. This report illustrates the value of trade associations to market analysis, as they can tap a national audience. Of course, a full report with a complete database prepared for bicycle retailers may cost an individual retailer about $2,000. However, such a study can be invaluable if it assists in determining what product line is suitable for particular target markets as well as profit margins for products. It is generally possible to obtain highlight information from the executive summary of the study, such as presented in figure 5.4, but the more-relevant data will be in the content of the report.

The baby-boom generation dominates consumer spending on bicycles, as it has for 30 years. This domination will continue. Despite their advancing ages, most boomers who ride and buy high-tech cycling gear will continue to do so for at least another decade.

Older consumers are growing more educated, and one result is increased interest in promoting health in simple, low-impact ways. Cycling is already positioned to cash in on this trend.

About 24.6 million U.S. adults own a bicycle they bought new, a significant decrease from 1990.

The riders who dropped out during the 1990s appear to belong primarily to the "Infrequent" segment of bicyclists. Other segments of more-involved riders actually increased their participation in bicycling.

"Enthusiast" riders, who ride and spend more than other segments, tripled in number during the 1990s.

One-third of adult bicycle owners own more than one bicycle, but there are more than three million committed cyclists who own just one bike.

Bicycle owners spend more time in bicycle stores than they did in 1990. They spend less time thinking about making a purchase before they shop, and more time shopping, than they did in 1990.

Recommendations from salespeople or friends are by far the most important influences on a shopper's choice of bicycle brand.

Enthusiastic bicycle owners recommend a bike brand to 6 people in an average year. More than three people follow their advice, translating into sales of $2,100 a year.

The Executive Summary is based on a fall 2000 survey of 2,809 adults in the U.S. who bought their last bicycle new, with references to a similar survey taken in 1990. The authors analyze these results in the context of demographic and consumer information from the U.S. Bureau of the Census and other sources. The surveys do not include adults who bought their last bicycle used, who received it as a gift, or who bought or received a bicycle for a child.

Figure 5.4 Executive summary of a national bicycle trade association.
Reprinted, by permission, from National Bicycle Dealers Association, 2000, *The cycling consumer of the new millennium* (study highlights). [Online]. Available: http://nbda.com/page.cfm?pageID=41 [April 23, 2008].

COMPETITOR ANALYSIS

You have every reason to be excited about your business priorities and the steps you have undertaken to define a target market. However, your competitors probably feel excited too. It is important to accept the existence of competitors who feel the same enthusiasm for their enterprise as you express for yours. Acceptance of this premise means you must take a closer look at the competition. This step involves an analysis of your business's strengths and weaknesses against those of your competitors in the field. It would not be uncommon for a new business owner to believe his success is assured by comparing his strengths against his competitors' weaknesses. However, that strategy is flawed. The task is to match your strengths and their strengths and to examine your weaknesses against their weaknesses. An assessment of business strengths and weaknesses provides the opportunity to

carefully document whether or not you can conclude with confidence that you have a competitive advantage in business. Believing in yourself is important in business, but it is not a substitute for a careful examination and assessment of what advantage you may have over the competition. Figure 5.5 identifies 14 criteria suitable for competitor analysis of a variety of retail businesses as well as tourism service-oriented enterprises. When any or all of the criteria are selected for use in an analysis of competitors, it is necessary to define the criteria and address their relevance to the businesses under examination.

SWOT ANALYSIS

The process of determining if a discernible advantage exists over a competitor will require you to ask questions about your competitor and perform the first two parts of a **SWOT analysis**. SWOT analysis is

Competitive Analysis Worksheet

Factor	My business	Strength	Weakness	Competitor A	Competitor B	Competitor C	Importance to customer
Products							
Price							
Quality							
Selection							
Service							
Reliability							
Time in business							
Expertise							
Reputation							
Location							
Appearance							
Credit policies							
Advertising							
Image							

Figure 5.5 Use this worksheet to compare your business to other similar businesses.
Reprinted with permission of SCORE, "Counselors to America's Small Business."

an acronym that means examination of a business in terms of its **S**trengths, **W**eaknesses, **O**pportunities, and **T**hreats. The first two parts of this examination, strengths and weaknesses, are the external components that belong in a competitive analysis. *External* refers to looking outward for the purpose of scanning the external environment to assess the competition in the context of your own business. The latter two components, opportunities and threats, are initiated in business planning when you define the products and services (chapter 3), and the purpose is to ask questions about what opportunities are available for the business. The underlying rationale is determining what you can do successfully in either or both areas in a strategic context. In other words, opportunities and threats are the internal cornerstones to help a business develop a preferred future. You will recall that chapter 3 sets out the best practices to ensure that the opportunities component of SWOT analysis is carefully addressed. Threats require you to determine how you will respond to them, and these strategies are found in the chapter that addresses risk assessment and protecting your assets (chapter 10).

A competitive analysis is, therefore, a systematic gathering, organizing, and evaluating of the strengths and weaknesses of a specific business together with its competitors for the purpose of determining if a competitive advantage exists. The criteria employed to carry out the analysis will vary based on business type and the primary product or services it will offer.

GATHERING INFORMATION

Identifying the competitors is the first step. It may not be as simple as it might appear at first glance. If a detailed market analysis has been completed, it should be evident that the interests, preferences, and expectations of the customer will define what constitutes the competition. Thus, competition does not just arise from a list of identical "business types" in the vicinity. In the case of your sister, her focus should be on distinct benefits and amenities appealing to most B&B customers. An example might be a combination of personalized service and a memorable homestyle breakfast not present in other B&B operations. Assume that a cursory inventory of accommodations in the vicinity reveals a small rustic inn offering an individualized decor, a personalized service, and

a kitchen area where travelers can put together their own breakfast in the morning. Although this inn is not a B&B, it may very well be a competitor for the type of experience noted in the B&B customer profile. Therefore the inn would be included in the competitor analysis.

The first step in using the worksheet is the identification of competitor A, competitor B, and so forth as noted on the top line of the form (figure 5.5). The next step is to obtain information about each competitor for the appropriate evaluation criteria in view of your type of business. Essentially, the task is to know as much about their businesses as you do about your own. Printed material and the Internet will display what the target audience is able to examine when considering the purchase of a service or product. Other approaches involve familiarization with competitors at trade shows or putting on the "silent shopper" hat at a competitor's place of business. The objective is to see what is offered and the quality of the service. Some of the options for accomplishing this step are now briefly outlined.

Attend Trade Shows or Local Business Fairs

Competitors attend trade shows and local events to display their product offerings and to network with other businesses and suppliers. An observer at the trade show should focus on the message of the competitors and how they sell or market themselves. Trade show publications and materials often provide insights into pricing, length of time in business, advertising strategies, image, and their expertise in the trade.

Be a Customer

Every establishment listed in the AAA/CAA Tour-Book is evaluated by their inspectors. The inspectors arrive unannounced and silently evaluate the business on each of the criteria created for its one- to five-star rating system. In a similar manner, business owners can themselves hire a firm (e.g., www.mystery-shoppers.com) to evaluate various aspects of their business to improve customer service and to recommend strategies for staying ahead of the competition. If you are a new business owner, it is feasible to become a silent shopper and visit a competitor's place of business or conduct a "customer" inquiry over the phone. Draw your own conclusion about the benefits. Your sister may wish to stay at a local B&B in order to gain knowledge firsthand about business practices and level of service. To apply such criteria as quality, appearance, services, or expertise, it may very well require firsthand knowledge of a competitor's enterprise. As for your prospective business, you have the advantage of knowing segments of the cycling population (e.g., road racers and BMX riders). Although it may be helpful to "shop" at other bicycle stores, you have the opportunity to collect information based on that prior experience and active participation with elements of the target market.

Talk With a Competitor's Customers or Suppliers

As an alternative to a direct visit, information can be gathered based on conversations with the customers or suppliers. Discrete observations by the customers and the business network within the service sector can address questions about service quality, pricing, location, and so forth.

Go to a Franchise Show and Talk With Vendors

Most likely, you will not be specifically interested in the type of franchise a vendor has to sell, but vendors are very familiar with what is going on in the consumer market. They have to stay on top of trends, growth markets, and consumer behavior, so they carry out detailed assessments with certain local market areas or territories. Treat the vendors to coffee and chat about what they think about openings in the market of interest to you or needs your competitors don't fill. They are likely to provide suggestions that will assist in assessing competition since it is central to what they do for people purchasing a franchise from them.

In the course of gathering information, the goal is to have sufficient detailed information to answer most of the following questions:

- What is my competition doing right? Can I duplicate and improve on it?
- Do I have something to offer that my competitors cannot, or do not, offer?

- How can I differentiate myself from the competition?
- Does it appear that the target audience is growing and expanding?
- Is it evident that I have a competitive advantage in one area or another?

ORGANIZING INFORMATION

Organizing the information means placing it in your worksheet so that you can uncover a competitive advantage. A competitive advantage can mean drawing on the assets, special features, and resources of the business to put in place the operational practices and marketing strategies that distinguish you from your competitors. The process involves answering the previously noted questions as well as examining the criteria contained in the competitive analysis worksheet. The number of individual cells in figure 5.5 to be completed depends on how many competitors are evaluated and the number of criteria used in the analysis. The 14 items in the worksheet are examples only, and the left-hand column should reflect the most relevant criteria in light of the type of business being examined. When feasible, criteria should be based on benefits sought and amenities, not simply demographic or psychographic variables. Of course, it is the customer's preferences and values that are most relevant here. If you provide services rather than a product, then the criteria in the worksheet should focus on service-oriented criteria.

This exercise will help you discover just what you might focus on as a competitive advantage. The question you are trying to answer is if you and your competitors offer the same service for the same price, would it make any difference to the customer whom they bought from? If "individual and personalized service" is important, and it is not the same among the competitors, then perhaps a competitive advantage exists.

Evaluating the Data for Analyzing a Competitor

As an illustration, assume two B&B competitors should be included when filling in the competitive analysis worksheet for your sister's business venture. She chooses to simply use a plus (+), minus (–), and no difference (=) rating system for comparing the competition. After doing her preliminary worksheet, several of the criteria are dropped because there is no difference (=) between what she intends to do and the primary features of the competition.

The distinction she made in the case of one competitor relates to the B&B operator who lives in a separate home a block away from his B&B operation. He hires a housekeeper to come in and help with breakfast and daily maintenance. You could conclude that this is not customer friendly and enter a minus (–) in the service category because market analysis reveals that B&B customers value personalized service and direct contact with their resident host. Customers have indicated that getting to know their host, having access to information about the community, and being a guest in someone's home is an important part of the B&B experience. Your sister plans to live in her B&B and definitely provide individualized contact with her guests. In turn, she believes this will be a competitive advantage for her.

Eliminating a Competitive Advantage

When a competitive advantage is documented, the follow-up question to consider is whether you, or your competitor, can readily duplicate what created the advantage and thereby eliminate what was initially considered a competitive advantage. When the competition sees that you have something going for you that creates an advantage, it will not be long before she looks for a strategy to neutralize or eliminate the advantage you enjoy. But if the competitive advantage is location and exclusive product line (e.g., your bike shop), it will not be easy for your competitor to duplicate either of those factors. Your sister's competitor would have to sell his other home and move into the B&B in order to provide the on-site personalized service your sister has noted as an advantage she enjoys. That is not likely to occur, but it could and thereby change the rating to "no difference" across the board.

Identifying competitors and organizing information about them are critically important. A first step in a competitor analysis is identifying distinguishing benefits and amenities criteria that your target market is looking to receive. Gathering information on competitors can be achieved through attending trade shows, being a customer, doing Internet research, and talking with suppliers. Competitor data are organized into a worksheet or matrix. Your purpose is to identify a competitive advantage you might have among your top competitors.

SUMMARY

Business opportunities surround each of us every day. Our attraction to select one commercial recreation venture over the other can be influenced by our knowledge, skills, training, and personal preferences. Inevitably, however, there will be a need to focus on the patrons of the products or services who support the existence of the recreation or tourism business. Thus, the focus of this chapter does not ask why a particular leisure-oriented enterprise appeals to you, but instead asks why it appeals to the customer.

Market research can be initiated by anyone—an industry or trade association; an individual owner; a marketing professional; a government agency; or a combination of stakeholders seeking to understand the consumers of recreation, leisure, and tourism goods and services. The information can be gathered in multiple ways, and organizing it to answer customer-oriented questions is vital to matching your product with its market. The value of the information can be judged by the degree to which it assists in answering some of the following questions:

- Given the size and distribution of the market, how much of the market can I capture?
- Who are the customers to be served, or what do typical customers look like?
- What are their desired benefits, needs, and preferences in terms of travel services, leisure, or recreation experiences?
- Given my goods and services, how much are the customers likely to purchase?
- How often will they purchase my service or product?
- What is the potential for building a repeat customer base?

One certain way to fail is to try to please everyone. You must be able to identify good market descriptors so that a few specific markets can be actively cultivated. Good market analysis allows you to do the following:

- More effectively offer or create products, programs, and services with specific customers in mind.

- Adopt appropriate strategies for reaching these groups, and design marketing materials that appeal to what they value, prefer, and want to purchase.

- Direct scarce resources where they will produce the highest return.

- Monitor changes in the business environment that may affect existing customers or define a new target market.

- Focus attention on who is important, where they are located, and what it will take to satisfy their needs.

The purpose of market analysis is to thoroughly immerse yourself in the world of the customers and understand what is important to them. For a business owner, the market information is a way to adopt and strengthen operational and marketing practices that ensure the customers will select you over your competitors.

 Check out the online student resource for additional material, including case studies, Web links, and more.

Chapter 6

Marketing, Promotions, and Communications

Learning Objectives

After reading this chapter you will be able to

- understand the concept of marketing;
- explain the marketing mix of product, price, place, and promotion;
- summarize the promotional elements of advertising, personal sales, publicity, and sales promotion;
- identify basic and cost-effective promotional media for small recreation, event, and tourism businesses; and
- describe applications and tactics for marketing through the Internet.

Key Terms

advertising	marketing	qualifying customers
advitorial	marketing mix	return on investment
banner ads	media kit	RSS (Really Simple Syndication) feeds
blog	opt-in lists	
conversion studies	organic search engine placement	sales promotion
cost per impression		social media
familiarization (FAM) tours	press releases	travel trade
full cost price	price point	uniform resource locator (URL)
global travel distribution systems (GTDSs)	promotion mix	word of mouth (WOM)
	publicists	worldwide travel network (WTN)
intrinsic price theory	publicity	yield management systems

Imagine this scenario: The grand opening of your new recreation business was held yesterday. The company team worked overtime to try to make the event memorable and informative about your new services. The grand opening venue, food, and decor cost more than you originally thought it would, but you believed it would be worth the extra expense. Today you are reflecting on how it turned out. The venue was well decorated, the food was excellent, the staff were all in place and looked great, and even the March weather cooperated. The guests at the event were excited about your new services, and many made reservations or wanted to partner with you. There was only one problem: Not enough people attended. At times you could have shot cannons through the center of the room and not hit anyone. In your discouraging staff meeting this morning, everyone agreed the lack of attendance was due to poor promotion. It appears to be a combination of things: There was no organized plan for promoting the event; the timing of promotions was poor; the range of promotions was too narrow; the messages you tried to convey were not understood; the event promotions lacked a "call to action" or special offers to compel attendance; and you did not set up an evaluation system to track how your promotions performed. Now you have to rebuild your staff confidence and possibly revise your sales projections downward for next month. But on the positive side, you also learned the need for effective marketing and promotion planning.

This scenario illustrates that without effective marketing and a fully integrated promotions strategy, your company is invisible to most of your potential buyers, and sales lag as a result. Conversely, organizations that have effective marketing, evaluate the success of their promotional efforts, and make changes based on evaluations have seen amazing results, immediate spikes in reservations, and sales exceeding projections. For example, one small RET business sold out almost its entire summer season after the excitement and subsequent sales generated from a successful media publicity campaign that resulted in a four-page article about the company in a national travel magazine. In this chapter we discuss the marketing concept, the mix of marketing actions, the five Ps of marketing, background and examples of the different types of promotions, steps in creating an advertising campaign, Internet marketing basics, evaluation techniques, and developing the marketing component of a business plan.

Companies recognize the importance of marketing and promotion and spend a significant portion of their budget on it. For small organizations that market to consumers (versus business to business), the percentage of net sales spent on marketing ranges from 5 to 15 percent after a few years of operation and up to nearly 50 percent during the introductory period (Jacksack, 2006). These are general small business averages; a better source for small- to medium-size RET companies may be found in the Spotlight On businesses positioned throughout this book and in Case Studies located in the online student resource.

Experience has shown that not all marketing needs to be costly to be effective (Levinson, 2007). However, as a small business owner, you are always significantly outspent by the large corporations that dominate the media. So you must conduct research, know your customers well, plan your promotions, and evaluate the effectiveness of your marketing efforts.

At times promotional efforts do not generate the desired impact, and occasionally a promotion is a failure. Since some small organizations do not objectively evaluate their marketing efforts, they fail to recognize there is a problem or how to improve promotional effectiveness. Another factor contributing to the lack of successful promotions that was discussed in chapter 5 is a poor idea of who their most likely customers are and how to best communicate benefits to them.

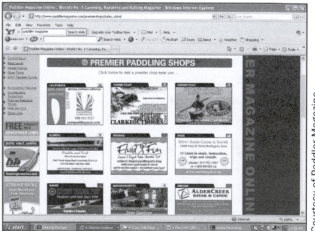

A sample classified ad in the back of a specialty magazine.

Courtesy of Paddler Magazine.

Leading organizations conduct **conversion studies** that quantify the percentage of inquiries generated from a promotion that eventually led to the purchase of a company service. By knowing how many people were converted by a promotional campaign and the average purchase made, you can calculate return on marketing investment. In this current Internet age, some company owners who sell to consumers have the mistaken idea that a company can rely exclusively on the Internet for all its promotional efforts. Studies show that many customers use the Internet for only certain activities and products, and companies must still employ traditional print or radio media, the travel product distribution system, and other channels to increase sales directly or drive traffic to their Web sites (PhoCusWright, 2007). This chapter discusses the needs and techniques for an integrated promotional media strategy of "bricks," "clicks," and good promotional tools to communicate effectively with your clients and stakeholders. This marketing mix then becomes an important part of the marketing element in your business plan.

MARKETING AND THE MARKETING MIX

Marketing means much more than just paid promotional advertisements. It is the process of identifying consumers' wants; developing products or services to satisfy those wants; promoting, selling, and distributing the product or service; and evaluating your efforts. Marketing begins with the products you offer but further includes how best to communicate or promote your services, their pricing, and the places you'll sell the products. The **marketing mix** consists of four components: product, price, place, and promotion (see figure 6.1).

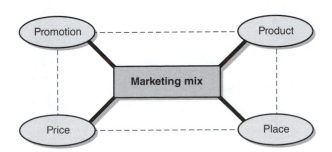

Figure 6.1 The marketing mix.

PRODUCT

Your product or service is a most basic, but critically important, part of the marketing mix. In chapters 2 and 3 we discussed the tangible and intangible elements of a good or service and how commercial recreation, event, and tourism services differ from other types of "products." Your service is a result of how you program, or combine and coordinate your company resources, into something the consumer is willing to pay for. The intangible elements are very important in the recreation, event planning, and tourism profession. In many instances we manage intangible elements in order to stage a positive emotionally charged experience for the guests.

It is not possible in this text to describe the myriad RET services and products. But it is safe to say that the company owners and key managers will all need to be technical and operational experts in the services they provide in order to offer quality products and services. Expertise is typically gained through work experience and training. But as you see in the profiles throughout this book, the providers of RET products and services must be open to modifying and creating new offerings in order to meet the changing wants and needs of consumers.

A company can change its product in many ways to appeal to new clients or retain existing customers. One strategy involves modifying tangible elements, such as buying a new fleet of tour vans. You can also train staff to be more friendly and receptive to guests, an intangible element. Following is a list of potential ways to change a product or service:

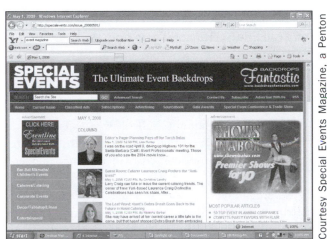

Courtesy Special Events Magazine, a Penton Media publication

An advertisement placed with an online magazine.

- Improve the facility
- Change instructors
- Provide new program content
- Modify the program duration
- Change the atmosphere through new decor
- Add new food dishes to the menu
- Conduct programs in a new location

It is critical that a company objectively evaluate its services in order to recognize if change is needed and what elements to modify.

PRICE

Price has many different connotations for consumers: direct and indirect, implicit and explicit. All these elements can greatly influence buying propensity, as the continual price-reduction sales at retailers illustrate. Only the admission fee or the most basic costs of participation are shown in promotions. But other indirect costs can greatly increase the total price paid by consumers, such as transportation to the program site, equipment needed, taxes, and surcharges. These are generally not mentioned in promotions because they can discourage consideration of your service by indicating to potential buyers that your service is above the **price point**, the price at which consumers are familiar with such products and at which your competitors price similar services. Some advertised cruise prices are good examples of a common strategy to keep competitive at the price point because the ads show the cabin price in large bold font but place port charges, which can significantly increase the ultimate price a consumer pays, in small font in a less-visible place. Ethical and legal considerations can enter into pricing, ranging from the questionable ethics of suggesting (but not actually stating) in an ad that the resort price is per room rather than per person, to the illegal activities of false advertising or the infamous "bait and switch," where a lower-priced trip is advertised but not available when a buyer goes to make a reservation, and the only alternatives are paying additional hidden costs or buying a higher-priced service.

There should be a clear rationale or strategy behind setting a price. Is it an "introductory" price strategy that is meant to drive sales, with the trade-off of breaking even or possibly incurring a small loss? The strategy is to appeal to consumer price sensitivity and steal customers away from other businesses for a short period of time. Such a strategy may be appropriate at the start-up of a company. Another alternative is a "profit maximization" pricing strategy used during the high-demand season. This is used when there is more demand than supply, and you need to price to generate the most profits you can earn without losing past clients. Many resorts and lodges now have tools to help them with the implementation of a profit maximization strategy. They employ **yield management systems** that identify and automatically set the highest price that can be charged for a particular room or program on a specific night with a high probability that it will be sold. These pricing systems rely on databases with 3 to 5 years of sales history to identify the best price (see tech application for details).

But even if you cannot afford a yield management system, or there is no software for your type of business, you should seriously consider using the yield management concept in setting your prices. Instead of having the same price year-round, set prices higher in the prime season, especially if you sell out often, and reduce the price asked during the lower-demand period. Ideally, you should sell the last place on your trip (or room in your resort) at the highest possible price, based on past experience. A potential disadvantage of such a pricing system is it can confuse repeat consumers who paid another price at a different time during the same year. A yield management price strategy also requires an interface between your office computers and your Web site's host server and additional training for reservations staff.

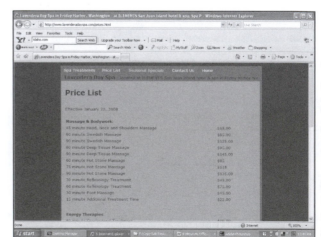

Price list for spa treatments.

Courtesy of Lavendera Day Spa, San Juan Island, Wahington

Tech Application

Setting Price Through Yield Management Systems

If you operate an RET business that is capacity constrained (i.e., with a limited inventory of service opportunities, tour seats, rooms, seats on an airplane, or rental items), then yield management has the potential of greatly assisting you in setting the highest price you can charge for a specific date and time. Tour operators, for example, often find that some dates (weekends) and times (9:00 a.m. to 2:00 p.m.) sell out more quickly than other times. Computerized yield management programs, also known as revenue management systems, are a tool for better understanding, anticipating, and responding to consumer demand in order to maximize sales and profit. These systems basically review demand and sales history from the past two to five years for each day, trip, or room type; identify the types of customers who buy; and suggest the highest price that can be charged to fill the tour, room, or seat. A historic user of yield management systems is the airlines. They set prices based on past sales history, then monitor how seats are being reserved and take appropriate action, such as offering discount pricing, if it appears that seats will not fill otherwise. Resorts use yield management systems to calculate the rates for specific room types and restrictions, such as a minimum night stay, to maximize their return and profit.

There are a number of important considerations in a yield management system. Yield management results can be influenced by several factors, such as number of inventory classes (first, second, and so on), whether the inventory is fixed at a location, whether more capacity can be developed rather quickly, and the number of potential prices that can be charged. The following table provides a comparison of yield management factors that would influence optimal pricing for a resort and a tour operator.

Factor	Resort	Tour operator
Unit of inventory	Room	Tour
Number of inventory classes	2-8	2-10
Fixed or adjustable capacity at location	Fixed	Somewhat adjustable
Mobility of capacity	Small	Large
Number of potential prices	2-3	2-5
Duration of use	Changeable	Changeable
Group discounts	Yes	Yes

Yield management systems can be stand-alone tools or a component of a larger business or property management system. One of the most popular yield and property management systems for resorts and lodging properties is OPERA (see www.micros.com). Advantages of this system are that it's both modular and scalable. Smaller independent RET businesses can choose a scaled-down, pay-as-you-go version at a lower price that requires less information technology expertise on-site. This version is hosted remotely and is accessed using the Internet, thus enabling import and export of the required data from the on-site property management system to a central server operated by MICROS. After the initial installation, a small business would pay for just the server time used, making it more affordable. A company can also select just the modules or components that are best suited for the business. Modules include yield or revenue management, property management, sales and catering, quality management, gaming accounting, and mixed-use vacation ownership and transient room management. The OPERA reservation module also sells and reserves space for group functions. An activity scheduler can be used to list and reserve activities, such as spa treatments or rounds of golf.

(continued)

Tech Application (continued)

Modules in the OPERA Business Management System

- Reservation system
- Yield/Revenue management
- Customer information system
- Sales force automation
- Sales and catering
- Vacation ownership system
- Activity scheduler
- Financials

The basic component of any yield management system is the reservation database, which holds the inventory and pricing information. The yield management element then saves and analyzes demand and reservation data taken from the reservation module.

There are also extrinsic (overt, listed) and intrinsic (implied) elements of price. For many people, a high advertised price implies high quality, whereas a lower price means inferior quality. The **intrinsic price theory** states that if your price is too much below the competition, then the price alone conveys a message that there must be something wrong with the service. This is an especially serious concern for small local businesses, with little name recognition but lower overhead and pricing, that are trying to compete in a national market with many larger firms with higher prices bolstered by strong brand image and awareness. One RET business owner was surprised when during a call the consumer said she liked the small company's product better than one from a national company but was concerned about booking because the price was lower. High prices can also convey status. Signature label clothes, which are priced at a premium because they are supported by a national image campaign, are good examples of this principle. So owners must also consider the intrinsic component of pricing.

Pricing your services and taking into account all these considerations is a more complex process than outward appearances would lead you to believe. A company manager must know the **full cost price** (lowest price that can be charged to cover production costs); understand what people in the target market want, their ability to pay, and their price point; identify a clear pricing strategy; and have a keen sense of competitor pricing.

PLACE AND DISTRIBUTION

The place concept in marketing refers to where, when, and how you sell your services and products. Your office is no longer the only place where sales are made. There are three parts to the place theory:

1. Physical locations where your company sells its services

2. Partner organizations that sell your services through the travel distribution system and at nontraditional places

3. Cyberspace, or the Internet, which is becoming an increasingly common means or channel of distribution

Distribution refers to the use of a distributor, or middleperson, between the supplier and retailer, who sells and then delivers proof of service purchase to the ultimate consumer. An example of distribution is a travel counselor (agent) who makes reservations at transportation, lodging, and attraction companies and then provides an itinerary and confirmation numbers to the client. Travelers today are multifaceted as to what part of the travel distribution system they use to buy travel services, selecting certain channels (online or offline, direct or intermediaries) and types of sites based on their destination, whom they are traveling with, and trip type (PhoCusWright, 2007).

Physical Locations

The physical locations where sales can take place are retail locations with high consumer traffic levels or a company's headquarters. We explore location considerations in more detail later in this chapter. The traditional and still very important means of selling the services of many recreation, event, and tourism (RET) businesses are walk-in and telephone sales. Some types of small recreation businesses that appeal to impulse purchasing behavior and have remote participation sites, such as white-water rafting or climbing guides, continue to rely heavily on special sales offices, or kiosks, in the tourist districts of vacation destinations (see figure 6.2). But downtown city sales offices of a growing number of national and international tourism businesses, such as Club Med and American Airlines, are closing because of increased use of the Internet and the ability of their high brand visibility to drive inquiries to their Web sites.

Place also includes locations away from company-owned property. Catalog shopping is now a billion-dollar business that extends your sales reach.

Toll-free phone numbers also extend the reach of your sales office and are inexpensive to set up. But the toll charges from customer calls can be very high for the service provider, sometimes exceeding $1,000 per month for some small recreation businesses that sell to a national market. However, if the type of information provided on toll-free calls is closely monitored, unnecessary chatter reduced to a minimum and sales result, then almost any RET business can afford a toll-free phone line.

Internet

Cyberspace, commonly known as the Internet or World Wide Web, is an increasingly common "place" for sales to be made. Almost every recreation, event planning, and tourism business in the United States and Canada has its own Web site, although content, presence, and sophistication of direct online sales, or e-commerce, varies greatly. PhoCusWright (2007) conducted an annual survey of travel consumers in 2006 and found that more than half of all travel to consumers in the United States will be purchased

Figure 6.2 A tourist kiosk in Aspen, Colorado.

Patrick T. Tierney

online. Online travel sales are expected to top US$136 billion in 2007. These statistics clearly show that it is absolutely essential for almost every commercial recreation, event planning, and tourism business to have a presence on the Internet, including direct sales e-commerce capabilities. Marketing through the Internet is so important that there is an entire section later in this chapter devoted to that topic.

Partner Organizations That Sell Your Services

Sales of your services by others often makes a significant contribution to the bottom line. Whether your company sells primarily to travelers or local residents, sales partnerships are important. Here are just a few examples of how important distributors, or partner organizations, can be to a recreation, event, and tourism business. Theme parks are increasingly working with large local employers to have them sell park tickets to their employees. In 2004, more than 75 percent of international airline tickets were sold by travel agents and only about 24 percent by the airline companies. The cruise industry relies heavily on travel agents, who accounted for nearly 95 percent of their total sales (Morrison, 2002). Events and meetings generated more than US$136 billion in revenue in 2006, the majority of which are planned and facili-

tated by independent professionals (Meeting Planners International, 2007). In each of these situations, travel distributors sold more volume for the industry than was done through the Internet, and in the case of cruises, much more than the service provider itself. These cases suggest that a recreation, event, and tourism business cannot afford to ignore the sales opportunities offered by partnering organizations. The key point is that both the Internet and partner organizations are important to RET companies.

The central idea behind using partner organizations is that your business cannot effectively promote and sell in all locations (even with the Internet) or to all large local groups. For example, travel management companies (agencies) are located in every major city worldwide; they have a loyal customer base and cover the initial cost of promoting and selling your services to their clients. Travel counselors are one of several key components of the **worldwide travel network (WTN).** This network consists of buyers, both individual consumers or businesses; intermediaries (distributors), such as travel counselors and visitors bureaus; and suppliers, such as airlines, local resorts, and recreation and entertainment companies (see figure 6.3). Intermediaries in the WTN, such as event planners, sales representatives, destination management companies, and visitors bureaus, do not own the means of production; they act only as agents

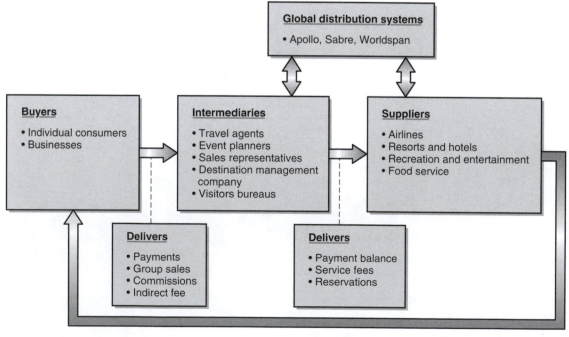

Figure 6.3 Worldwide travel network.

for the suppliers and buyers. Suppliers at a destination, such as a local commercial recreation company, could develop an informal relationship or possibly even a formal partnership through a signed contract, where they agree to allow the intermediary to sell their services. Direct sales to travel management companies and other nonelectronic partner organizations are still effective for small business.

One important part of this travel system is **global travel distribution systems (GTDSs)** consisting of interlinked, highly sophisticated computer systems containing the inventory and pricing of suppliers (primarily airlines, large hotels, and rental car companies at this time). The GTDSs also facilitate the purchase of travel services, ticketing, and transfer payments between buyers and suppliers. Some examples of a GTDS are Apollo, Sabre, and Worldspan. GTDSs were at one time available only to travel agents, but now anyone can get limited access to these databases through the Internet and electronic travel sites, such as Travelocity.com and Expedia.com. The GTDS companies require direct electronic communication of your inventory and pricing between your computer system and theirs. This takes more-expensive, sophisticated computer software systems beyond what many small companies can use and afford. The GTDSs also want a larger year-round inventory than most small companies have to offer. So until recently it was extremely difficult for small RET businesses to be listed in a GTDS. An exception to this now is Travelocity.com, which will include your traveler services in their database for free, but you are required to sign a contract and pay a 25 percent commission on any sales.

Whether the partner organization you are working with has access to travelers or locals, it requires some type of benefit (usually a payment) for its efforts on your behalf. In exchange for staff time, effort, and expense (e.g., promotions, ticketing costs), the intermediary requires the suppliers to pay a commission or a booking fee. Travel counselors (agents) normally require a standard commission of 10 percent of the total cost (except for electronic travel agencies), which the consumer pays. But since airlines have discontinued paying travel agent commissions, many agents now require a $30 to $60 airline booking fee to help cover their ticketing costs.

Event planning companies usually bid on the planning and operation of an event in a different way from travel counselors. Their bid usually includes the hourly wages for staff time, as well as other direct operating costs (e.g., food, lodging, shuttles). Then a percentage is applied to these direct costs (total staff time and operating expenses) to cover overhead costs and provide a profit.

There are clear advantages to using partners in the travel distribution system, especially for small local recreation businesses. There are often no up-front costs for their services, they require payment only when a sale is actually made, and they can promote your services to a much wider audience. The challenge for relatively unknown local suppliers is to get the attention of and develop a strong relationship with intermediaries so they will sell your services rather than those of your competition. You can develop these relationships by making direct sales calls to local travel counselors, event planners, visitors bureaus, and destination management companies that are bringing buyers into nearby destinations, as well as by attending national **travel trade** shows where you can meet with representatives from larger travel agencies and tour operators who have offices and clients in distant source markets.

A small commercial RET company can also develop formal and informal partnerships with organizations outside the electronic distributor to help sell their services. Some examples of nonelectronic organizations that are selling recreation provider services are grocery stores and large employers. It has become common practice in the Rocky Mountain states of the United States for winter sports resorts to have nearby grocery stores sell their lift tickets. Local theme parks, such as Great America in Santa Clara, California, work through the human resource departments of large technology companies in California's Silicon Valley to sell tickets to their employees. In these two cases, the human resource departments require discounted rates as a benefit to their employees, such as admission discounts and special employee events. The grocery stores also earn a small commission and offer something unique to their shoppers, thus giving them another reason to shop and distinguishing the store from its competition. Providing sales aids, such as point-of-purchase displays at partner locations, can be effective. Coming up with creative offerings that have value for a potential partner organization is critical to developing a successful sales relationship with nontraditional sellers.

PROMOTION

An average citizen of Australia, Europe, Japan, or the United States is bombarded by hundreds of promotional messages every day. They come through billboards, banner ads, Web sites, newspapers, telephone solicitors calling at dinner hour, e-mail, magazine **advitorials**, and sponsored listings on your favorite Internet search engine. We all would go crazy if we tried to fully process each promotional message. Most messages are ignored, and only a very few are processed and lead the person to take action, other than switching off radio stations or hanging up the phone. So each of these promotions competes for your attention, hoping to spur you to take action, but ultimately most don't succeed. So this implies that a business, especially a small recreation business with very limited funds, must carefully determine and accurately use the best promotional technique for a given market segment to relay a message that is deemed relevant and results in the desired action.

Promotion is the art and science of communications. Goals of promotion are to inform, persuade, and remind. You want to communicate a favorable image of your company to your previously identified target market through a mixture of media and activities.

PROMOTIONAL ELEMENTS

How you mix or balance different types of promotion can greatly affect your marketing effectiveness. The **promotion mix**, according to Semenik (2002), is a combination of techniques or tools selected to communicate with a target market (see figure 6.4). Your promotion mix is the combination of four elements:

1. Advertising
2. Personal sales
3. Publicity
4. Sales promotion

ADVERTISING

Advertising is widely used and consists of any form of paid nonpersonal communications placed in the media. Usually ads are placed in the mass media, such as radio, TV, the Internet, newspapers, or magazines. But there are many other alternative locations for ads besides traditional media, such as on taxicabs, on billboards, on signs towed behind airplanes, or almost anywhere consumers might be able to see your message. They are paid, either in currency or in barter, so you can say almost anything you want, within truth-in-advertising law limits; and you decide where and when an ad will be placed. Advertising is nonpersonal because neither the sponsors nor their representatives are present, and communication is strictly one way. A coordinated ad campaign can be much more effective than several individual ads.

Steps in Creating an Advertising Campaign

An advertising campaign is a basic element of promotion that integrates several types of media ads around a common goal and theme to synergistically create a coordinated and more-effective promotion than can be done with individual ads. Advertisements can also be combined with other forms of promotion, such as personal sales and sales promotion, to further enhance effectiveness. Often there is a common campaign tagline, or message, prominently shown in all the ads. The seven basic components of an ad campaign follow.

1. *Set campaign objectives.* What are you trying to accomplish with the campaign (e.g., increase awareness of a certain service, change the image of your company, or inform past visitors about new attractions)? Objectives should be as specific as possible, be measurable, and have a definitive completion date.

2. *Establish a budget.* The limiting factor in any campaign is the budget. At the very least, you should estimate the amount of funds you have available at the beginning.

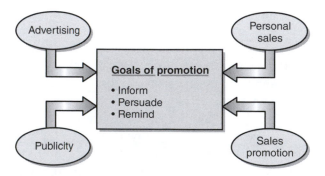

Figure 6.4 Goals of promotion and the promotion mix.

3. *Develop a theme.* To be most effective, a campaign should have a consistently presented theme or message that runs through all the promotions. Themes must be related to the campaign objectives. Examples include "priced right," "located closer," "more exciting tours," or "offer more."

4. *Select media.* The media you use to display your ad can range from the traditional forms of radio, TV, Yellow Pages, newspapers, and magazines to the Internet (see following section on Internet marketing), travel guides, transit buses, and movie theater screens. Each medium has its own advertising requirements and costs; a specific reach, or number of persons who see or hear it; and a unique viewer or listener profile of interests, area of residence, and household income levels. Reach and viewer or listener profile are important considerations to see if there is a large enough number of potential buyers and to determine if your target market matches closely to the medium's user characteristics.

5. *Create advertisements.* This is the fun, creative, and technically difficult part of a campaign. The ad message, tagline, look, and call to action should all be pretested to ensure their effectiveness. An ad agency or graphic artist is often employed to create the final advertisement, which is sent to a newspaper or Internet Web site.

6. *Decide on number and timing of placements.* The number of ads you pay for are referred to as *placements.* The timing of your ad placement is critical to its success because you want it seen or heard when your target audience is most receptive to your ad message. For example, if your business is operating three-day snowboarding packages in Wisconsin, your ad should be in front of viewers during the August to October period because that is when many winter sports enthusiasts are thinking about and planning their winter vacations. For other short-duration recreation programs sold to resort visitors, guests may not be receptive to your ad message until the day they arrive in a resort area.

The second part of timing is knowing how far in advance you need to place ads to meet media requirements to get them seen or heard at the correct time. National magazines, for example, normally require your print-ready ad and payment as much as six months in advance of the issue delivery.

7. *Evaluate the response.* It is extremely difficult to objectively judge the effectiveness of an ad campaign without a preplanned method of evaluation. Evaluation is critical because an ad sponsor could be wasting money on a poorly designed ad without realizing it. It can be difficult to distinguish how callers or Internet searchers got your information and whether it was from a specific ad, so you must build the evaluation method into your initial promotion plan.

Some Advantages of Advertising

- *Potential low cost per impression.* Although the total cost of an advertisement may run into the millions of dollars, such as during the Super Bowl football game or international soccer matches, the total cost per contact can be small. For example, a full-page color print ad in *Outside* magazine may cost $50,000, but it is seen by as many as 500,000 readers, resulting in a **cost per impression** of about 10 cents.

- *Ability to present images and reach locations a salesperson cannot.* Video and color images can be very effective in conveying a message about your company, compared with just voice communications. These can be beamed into homes or workplaces at all hours, where salespersons may have no access.

Potential Disadvantages of Advertising

- *Total expense of an ad.* The media have frequently priced advertising so high that only the largest companies can afford the prime placement locations, such as the first pages of a magazine or commute time for radio. Most new businesspersons do not realize how expensive it can be to create an ad—you might need an artist or ad agency—and to pay for enough exposures for it to be effective. Fortunately, stock photos (see www.corbis.com) and even stock radio or TV ads are available and can be altered to fit your specific needs.

- *A great deal of waste.* The media charge for all potential viewers or listeners of an ad even if a significant portion of them are not at all interested in what you are promoting. So in essence a good deal of the ad cost is wasted because it is seen or heard by persons with no interest in your service. It is critical that you choose a medium that reaches your target market with a minimum of waste.

- *Inability to close the sale.* Although an ad can be effective in creating awareness and increasing intentions to purchase, ads often cannot close a sale. The viewer or listener must call a salesperson or go to a Web site to complete the transaction. Personal salespersons are much more effective in closing sales than is advertising.

• *Repeat exposures needed.* Since many ads are seen or heard during times of distraction, such as driving to work or while talking to friends, multiple exposures are needed for the message to be comprehended and remembered. Radio in particular requires repeat exposure, from 5 to 20 ad placements, before it becomes effective.

Basic, Cost-Effective Ads for Small RET Businesses

The following advertising media have proven, in a variety of settings and over a period of years, to potentially be very cost effective for small RET businesses. Consider the characteristics of your marketplaces and product, and then create a well-researched ad for each of these media.

• Yellow Pages: The Yellow Pages list local telephone numbers and are frequently used for purchase decisions. Monthly payments help reduce initial outlay. You can have images and logos in the ads, and many reservations are made over the phone.

• Internet advertising: An informative and easily navigated company Web site that has high placement on Internet search engines is how many new clients find a business. See the discussion later in this chapter on Internet marketing.

• Industry co-op advertising: Cooperate to compete against larger destinations or corporations. Many small businesses from one type of business can get together on a co-op brochure and ad campaign. By combining ad dollars, the businesses can purchase bigger and better-placed ads, thus leveraging their contributions with those of other partners. An example of this is the Colorado River Outfitters Association, where members pay a relatively small amount to have a listing in a statewide rafting brochure and Web site, and the association places full-page ads in promotions for the state of Colorado and in other media directing consumers to the brochure or association Web site with company listings.

• Convention and visitors bureaus: The mission of convention and visitors bureaus (CVBs) is to increase visitor spending by bringing tourists to their destina-

tion, and by highlighting the recreation and tourism services in their area, they enhance destination attractiveness. So CVBs provide many options for members to be included in co-op marketing advertisements. Since most persons responding to ads are interested in visiting the destination, ad waste and costs can be reduced for a business. For an example of co-op advertising opportunities with a convention and visitors bureau, see figure 6.5, which features member options with the Seattle Convention and Visitors Bureau.

• Billboards: If your business has a great deal of walk-in business, then a strategically placed billboard could be very cost effective. Monthly payment plans can reduce up-front costs. This alternative is most affordable in rural locations near your store.

• Brochure distribution: Research continues to show that low-tech distribution of brochures in commercially served racks can be more effective for tourist-serving businesses than most other kinds of media (Tierney, 2003). Visitors readily pick up brochures (because they have place-relevant information and coupons), and you pay only for distribution in the areas from which you draw your clients.

Evaluation of Advertising

It is important to evaluate the effectiveness of all your advertisements and other promotions, whether they involve telemarketing to local employers or are targeted to visitors in other states. Cash registers should be programmed to accept promotional codes, and company reservationists and online reservation forms should always ask how an inquirer first heard or learned about the company. But these are frequently not enough to attribute the inquiry or sale to a particular ad. You also need to know if an inquiry was "converted," or resulted in a sale. Other more diagnostic methods for evaluating an ad include the following:

• Campaign-exclusive coupon or offer. Counting the number of redeemed coupons provides an estimate of the dollar sales volume associated with a promotion.

• Campaign-specific toll-free telephone number in the ad. Using a toll-free number unique to a particular campaign is gaining popularity because of its low cost and precise assignment of a booking or sale. The evaluation of promotions can be challenging and

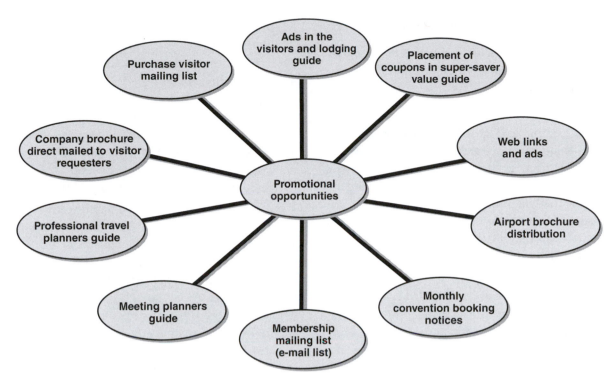

Figure 6.5 Advertising and promotion opportunities with the Seattle Convention and Visitors Bureau.

must be planned along with the initial marketing efforts. As you will see, the evaluation of Internet ads can be much easier.

Effectiveness is most often shown in financial terms. A frequently used metric of ad effectiveness is **return on investment**, or ROI:

$$ROI = \frac{\text{ad-generated sales}}{\text{total ad media and creation costs}}$$

Media costs include not only the ad placement fees but also the cost of producing the promotion. Any ad with an ROI of less than 2.0 should be discontinued or significantly modified.

Evaluation has demonstrated that, in many cases, advertising may not be the most effective form of promotion. The initial high cost and nonpersonalized nature are weaknesses of advertisements compared with other forms of promotion, such as personal sales.

PERSONAL SALES

Personal sales are oral presentations with one or more buyers. This includes the classic sales call, where a company salesperson travels by plane and rental car to the office of a potential buyer, and makes sales calls at buyer offices. A newer high-tech method is teleconferencing via the Internet. Telephone sales can be highly effective for prospecting (identifying prospective customers) and qualifying (determining the value and ranking of prospective customers). Once leads have been qualified, then in-person sales can be used to successfully learn about customer needs and wants in detail and hopefully close a sale. Teleconferencing allows two or more persons in different locations to synchronously converse and see each other, without the need for travel. If real-time video and voice features with electronic signatures are used, it can be effective for maintaining an existing client relationship, as well as closing a sale. See www.acttel.com for an example of the options available in video conferencing.

Some types of recreation, event, and tourism businesses by far prefer personal selling to other forms of promotion. In general, personal sales are most effective and are associated with high-priced purchases and businesses that sell to groups, while advertising is often used to contact the mass market or travelers making moderate- to low-cost purchases. The high degree of personalization with personal sales is both a strength and a limitation. Field sales are the most expensive part of promotion and are limited to situations where the presentation is made to persons representing group sales potential, such as travel counselors, travel program directors, and corporate representatives.

The Personal Sales Process

The personal sales process is not as simple or easy to master as a first glance might suggest. Following are the most commonly identified steps in the sales process:

1. Prospecting and **qualifying customers**: This involves exploration and research to find likely customers. Prospecting through telephone directories or other publicly available lists and cold calling are frequently used methods. Once sales leads are identified, qualify them to see if they are past customers, if they have needs the company can satisfy, the potential volume of business they could bring, and if they have the funds and authority to make the purchase.

2. Preplanning the sales call: Gather enough information to become familiar with the prospect's situation to generate interest in the company services. Have a specific purpose for every sales call. However, many sales representatives, such as your office or store staff, do not have the opportunity to preplan every sales situation, as unknown clients walk in the door.

3. Making an approach: This involves arranging the appointment, greeting the potential customer, making introductions, briefly describing your services that can meet the prospect's needs, and listening carefully to what the potential customer is saying. Establishing rapport and trust in the early stages of the conversation is critical. For sales representatives serving walk-in clients, a quick friendly greeting and eye contact are followed by a rapid assessment to learn about client needs and if assistance can be offered. Sales staff are usually trained to ask two or three key questions to quickly identify qualified prospects. Many callers or walk-in visitors are not truly interested in buying anything or are looking for free advice or directions. The monthly charges for a toll-free phone line can quickly amount to thousands of dollars. So if you are busy or the prospect is calling on your expensive toll-free telephone line, then you must politely refer an underqualified prospect elsewhere, get her e-mail or mailing address to send her additional information, or end the conversation once you have established they are not worth continued contact at this time.

4. Making the presentation: A sales presentation can be a "canned" or memorized presentation; a programmed presentation, such as using a flip chart or outline; or an audiovisual employing PowerPoint or multimedia.

5. Handling objections and questions: When the presentation is completed, the prospect usually asks questions and raises objections. There are two common ways of handling objections: (1) discreetly demonstrating the concern is not important and (2) using the "yes but" approach, where you initially agree then show the objection is not relevant.

6. Closing the sale: The all-important moment has arrived when your prospect seems ready to make the purchase or reservation. You must overcome fear of rejection and always ask for a commitment. Clues on when to ask for a commitment include questions from the prospect ("When is the deposit due?"), active processing ("This really sounds great"), requirements ("The departure will have to fit our available dates"), and nonverbal clues (posture changes). The salesperson can directly ask for the sale or attempt a trial close by asking, "Shall I see if space is available for the tour on that date?" or a special concession close by saying, "I can offer you a 10 percent discount if you reserve at least six spaces."

7. Following up after the sale: The final personal sales step is following up with the client to deliver required documentation, reassure him about the wisdom of his purchase, see if he actually used the reservation, or determine his evaluation of the service. The follow-up also includes the input of appropriate client data into the company database.

Some Advantages of Personal Sales

Personal sales are best suited to certain situations and environments. The following describes some of the strengths or advantages of personal sales:

• Highly persuasive. A personal sale involves two-way communication where buyer needs can be identified and quickly addressed by the sales representative.

• Great way to start a relationship. It can be an effective way of developing a personal relationship with a new buyer or identifying decision makers and qualifying buyers, in contrast to e-mail solicitations, which are often unwanted, impersonal, and limited in the types of information that can be gathered from a new contact. Your sales staff is a human reflection of

Frank Herholdt/Stone/Getty Images

Personal sales can be very effective to prospects representing group business.

your organization, and this can convey quality and assurance that other types of mass media promotion cannot.

- One of the most powerful means of closing a sale. Since there is two-way communication, if questions or objections arise during the presentation, they can be responded to immediately and a contract signed before leaving. Careful attention to individual needs and requirements by a sales representative is certainly one of the most potent forms of promotion. It is also used to follow up after a sale. Just one visit by a salesperson may end in a sale, whereas advertising may need to be seen several times before the message is understood and translates into a sale by the consumer.

- Provide up-to-date information. Personal sales allow a company representative to pass on detailed information about its products to other businesses, such as the travel trade, which can then more effectively sell the company's services. This is in contrast to ads, newsletters, and e-mail, where content is often limited. Salespersons can also make suggestions about selling techniques and present sales materials

and point-of-purchase materials to the travel trade during a visit.

Potential Disadvantages of Personal Sales

Just as there are situations where personal sales are particularly effective, there are other environments for which they are not well suited. Following is a list of disadvantages of personal sales:

- Expense. An oral presentation to one or two individual buyers is often not cost or time effective because of the inherent cost of personal sales. However, if the buyers represent group business or large expenditures, then it can be very cost effective. Expenses include staff wages, transportation, lodging, and food costs, as well as demo and support expenses.

- Limited reach. Through the mass media your company message can reach hundreds or thousands of clients in the time it takes to make one sales call. Balancing this disadvantage is the highly persuasive nature of good personal sales. The best personal sales prospects should represent significant group business.

PUBLICITY

Publicity is nonpaid, nonpersonal stimulation of demand by obtaining favorable coverage in the media. An example of publicity is when your company is featured in a newspaper or magazine article. The media are always looking for news and human interest stories, and they can be a ready promotional partner if you have truly newsworthy information about new and appealing services or activities. But the media are also very wary of ads couched as news and will quickly refer you to their advertising department if the item is not news. Publicity can be extremely important to small RET businesses because of its low cost and high potential returns.

Many small recreation, event, and tourism businesses, such as Adrift Adventures and Sea Trek, have recently decreased their reliance on advertising and now depend more on publicity to foster interest and sales. This trend is driven by their success in facilitating publicity, the strong interest media have shown in many of their adventure activities and special events, and the large response generated from it. Even if your RET services are not inherently very exciting, you can still stimulate publicity (e.g., through events and new product offerings). Potential benefits of publicity are enormous. For example, one small private golf club sponsored an event that received a great deal of press coverage, and this resulted in large sales increases for several years.

The challenges of publicity include getting the media's attention and interest, since many other companies are also contacting them. Getting positive coverage is also critical; unlike advertising, where you tell the media what to state, in publicity your company has no control over what messages the media convey.

Favorable publicity usually doesn't just happen on its own; it is often fostered and cultivated by an organization. A company must seek out and respond to opportunities for publicity. The basic needs for generating publicity include the following:

• *Issue press releases.* Professionally formatted **press releases** are essential to get the media's attention and interest and to provide them with the first level of information they may need. Figure 6.6 gives a sample press release showing the standard formatting, with a release date, contact information, a catchy and informative title, and simply stated but appealing information in the release body. The keys to gaining the media's attention are the title and the first two sentences of the release.

• *Develop a media kit.* A **media kit** is a packet that includes relevant and timely press releases, background about the company and its owners, unique features, testimonials, sample articles, a contact person, and photos. The kit must have a polished and professional appearance but not contain too much information. However, your media kit can also be on your Web site (as discussed later under Internet marketing).

• *Create a FAM tour.* **Familiarization (FAM) tours** are specially created low- or no-cost tours of your facilities or your programs for the travel press, travel consultants, and other partnering business representatives only. The theory is that the best way for the press or partner organizations to learn about the uniqueness and quality of your programs is to participate in one. The low-cost feature also provides an incentive for the writers to give you a little more positive coverage. Travel writers are another target for attention, as they are contracted to write stories on travel for newspapers and magazines. A word of caution: There are people who pose as travel writers and travel agents to take advantage of low-cost travel, but they never will be able to provide your company with favorable coverage. To protect yourself from these scam artists, always ask for a writer's credentials, samples of published stories, and if possible a letter from the media editor contracting the person to write a specific story.

• *Distribute press releases and media kits.* The press release can be mailed or e-mailed or accessed through a "pressroom" on your Web site (see the Internet marketing section later in this chapter). The challenge is to identify what media, who within the media would be most interested and authorized, and how to best contact them. For those who want to do a little independent research, *Gale's Guide to the Media*, a directory found in larger public libraries, lists the contact information of most newspapers and magazines in the United States, including the editor of the travel or related sections. The Web site www.travelwriters.com is a source for lists of active travel writers, stories in progress, and methods to distribute press releases. It costs money to subscribe and for individual services. One service distributes information about your press trips to the travel press and writers and allows you to select whom you would

Fishworks Fly Fishing Store
P.O. Box 182
Ferretville, UT 84070

CONTACT: Mary Jones
Phone: (800) 000-0140
E-mail: mjj@fishing.com

FOR IMMEDIATE RELEASE
March 17, 2009

Fly Fishing for Women Only

Exhilarating, Empowering Adventure for Mothers, Daughters, Friends

Ferretville, UT, March 15, 2009—Fishworks Fly Fishing Store is now taking reservations for a new four-day, women-only fly fishing trip launching June 24, 2009, on the spectacular Green River in Colorado and Utah.

Guests and an all-women guide staff will float fish in quiet sections and a few class III rapids through 2,000-feet-deep canyons in Dinosaur National Monument; learn the basics of fly fishing equipment, technique, and tactics; take side canyon hikes; see wildlife; discover petroglyphs; share experiences.

Fishworks co-owner Mary Jones was among the first female fly fishing guides in a predominantly male-oriented profession. Women's trips are a success today largely because of comfortable, state-of-the-art fishing equipment and insights into women's experiences with fly fishing. "The Green River is one of my personal favorites, a perfect setting for great brown trout fishing, awesome scenery, and quiet stretches made for conversation and contemplation," says Ms. Jones. "Grandmothers, mothers, daughters, and friends will connect with one another in a very special way on and off the water. The strong, hard-working young women on our guide staff are great role models, and at the end of the day we'll celebrate the grace, intelligence, and compassion within us all," she adds. Fishworks' all-women fly fishing trip is an active fishing adventure in oar-powered rafts and dories. No previous fly fishing experience is needed; women and girls 12 and older are welcome. The trip launches June 24 and ends June 27, 2009. It is a complete package that includes guides, fishing gear, shuttles from Fishworks's headquarters in Ferretville, Utah, and great meals from first day to last.

To encourage multigenerational participation, the package is priced at $699 for adults and $549 for girls 12 to 18 ($50 off Fishworks's already discounted kids' rate). For more information on this and other unique Fishworks programs, visit www.fishing.com or call toll-free (800) 000-0140.

Figure 6.6 Sample press release.

like to invite by reviewing each individual writer's resume and publishing history. Another is a type of press release distribution service that e-mails your press release to thousands of travel writers who have opted-in to receive information.

• *Get to know your local media editors.* Generate positive press about you or your company by developing a relationship with your local media editors. This may lead to you being called for an expert opinion on a news story related to your specialization and the featuring of your business in a story.

• *Hire a professional publicist.* **Publicists** specialize in knowing the media and what they are looking for to meet their editorial calendars and writing needs. Publicists can be a "one stop" business by helping your organization identify media interested in your company products, create appealing press releases and effective media kits, and distribute them to the media. The cost of their services is often affordable for small recreation businesses and can be very effective. Your best prospects are the in-person companies that specialize in the recreation and travel industries, such as the Fontayne Group (www.fontayne.com), or Internet-based firms, such as www.travelwriters.com.

In some instances the media are not interested in your services, but you still need to stimulate strong demand. Sales promotion provides another alternative to advertising and publicity, or it can be used in conjunction with them.

SALES PROMOTION

Sales promotion includes promotional activities that do not fall into previous promotional categories where the consumer is given short-term incentives to make an immediate purchase. Examples of sales promotion used by small recreation, tourism, and event businesses include trade and consumer shows, demos, coupons, contests, frequent buyer or flyer programs, travel clubs, direct mail, money-back guarantees, partnerships, networking, magnets and other giveaways, and trial offers. Merchandizing and point-of-purchase exhibits in a store, such as posters, menus, and merchandise displays, are also considered part of sales promotion. Creativity is critical in developing a sales promotion. It must catch and hold the attention of consumers and stimulate an impulsive purchase response or generate favorable recognition of your company.

Some time-tested and effective sales promotion techniques affordable to small recreation, event planning, and tourism businesses include the following:

- *Coupons:* Discounts and special offers on printed coupons, for example, have long been used to stimulate demand and call the consumer to action.

- *Direct mail:* Mailing promotional materials the old-fashioned way, by the postal service, can still be very cost effective, especially to past customers. Have realistic expectations, as a positive response rate of 2 to 5 percent is considered good. Your company should try to capture the contact information from whoever contacts you. Asking if they want to opt-in and receive future mailings is the best way to get a clean, effective mailing list. You can also buy focused mailing lists, for specific areas or activity preferences, from direct mail services. More companies are now mailing CDs or DVDs with a small printed insert because video is much more stimulating, and the price for large DVD production runs is low per item.

- *Contests:* An example of a contest is a radio station giving away a travel service you provide as a prize. The station trades air time for the value of your service. This is often an excellent way to increase awareness of your company at little cost to you.

- *Trade shows:* Trade shows can be a very cost-effective technique when the show attracts buyers interested in your product. You can also demonstrate the product and give away a small reminder of it (e.g., a poster or taste treat). Fishing services and adventure travel companies have gained significant business from consumer shows, such as the International Sportsmen's Exposition (www.sportsexpos.com) or the Adventures in Travel Expo (www.

adventureexpo.com). A well-known, highly effective business-to-business trade show to find companies bringing international vacationers into the United States is the International Pow Wow (see www.tia.org/powwow/Index.html).

- *Brochures:* One of the least costly means of getting tourist information to visitors is through brochures distributed in professionally managed brochure racks (Tierney, 2003). Coupons and other calls to action can be designed into a brochure to increase distribution and assist in tracking cost effectiveness. Brochure distribution companies, such as Certified Folder Display Service (www.certifiedfolder.com), have exclusive contracts to place brochure racks in hotels, restaurants, and visitor centers along major travel routes and at tourist destinations, and they keep a slot filled with your brochures for a reasonable cost. For a worldwide listing of distribution companies, visit the Association of Professional Brochure Distributors (www.iapbd.org).

- *Networking:* Networking provides a wide variety of opportunities to meet and talk with a broad range of persons who might be interested in your business. An example is going to a local chamber of commerce "mixer" where members meet each other and exchange information. A shrewd business owner makes a concerted effort to introduce the company services in many different environments and settings, from professional organization parties to trade shows. Develop the art of "working a room" to contact and get business cards from as many persons as possible.

ENHANCING WORD-OF-MOUTH PROMOTION

Most small recreation, event, and tourism business owners will confide that the two biggest sources of their sales are returning customers and persons referred by them. So providing incentives for past customers to tell others, referred to as **word of mouth (WOM),** can be the most effective form of promotion. The source (your past client) is trusted by their friends and family, and they can spread the word about your business rapidly and to a large number of people. Godin and Kawasaki (2006) have shown that the WOM marketing actions you take to get your customers talking to others about the benefits of your services can be very cost effective. Some managers think there is not much that can be done to encourage word-of-mouth business, but experience shows otherwise. The following are examples of techniques small RET businesses have used to generate WOM:

- Offer referral incentives to past clients, such as discounted future trips, invitations to a presale, or free T-shirts.
- Give group discounts, with the amount increasing with group size.
- E-mail a set of digital photos or a video of a participant taken during the activity, or create a Web page with images from the trip. Some companies encourage independent professional photographers to sell photos of visitors on a ski slope or in rapids.
- Give out free postcards with stamps after a trip. A related technique is allowing clients who reserve a trip to forward an electronic postcard to a friend via the company Web site.
- Offer frequent buyer benefits, including discounts and special offers.
- Provide parties or movie showings for past clients, with invitations to bring guests.

MARKETING VIA THE INTERNET

A strong, effective presence on the Internet is absolutely critical to a successful business in today's marketplace. Most small recreation, event, and tourism business owners will tell you that the majority of new inquiries and sales now come via the Internet. This factor, combined with the *relatively* low cost of Internet promotions relative to other media, means a business must be well placed on the Internet. Research shows (Tierney, 1997; Tierney, 2000; Forester Research, 2006) that search engines are by far the most frequently used means for consumers to find new Web sites and information on the Internet. But the competition to be placed highly on the most frequently used Internet search engines (e.g., Google, MSN, and Yahoo!) is fierce and becoming more costly.

It is easy to create a plain Web site, but the technical programming now required to make a Web site easy to find on search engines, to have a modern look that

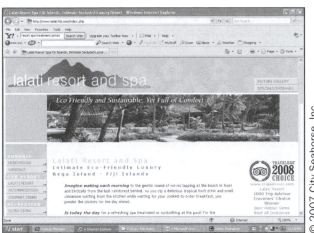

A well-designed Web site is critical to effective marketing.

impresses viewers, to permit the site to be effortlessly navigated, and to allow foolproof online bookings is growing increasingly complex and requires real technology experts. An advantage of Internet advertising is that evaluation is easier and more direct because you often pay only when a visitor clicks on your ad. After a Web site is created, its content must be frequently updated by in-house staff who are experienced with HTML editing software, such as FrontPage or Dreamweaver. You must be knowledgeable about the basics of Internet marketing, develop a sophisticated Internet marketing strategy, and have staff expertise in this area. Some aspects to consider with Internet marketing follow.

THE INTERNET ALONE IS NOT ENOUGH

The importance of the Internet to generate new sales is undeniable, but some recreation managers think they can rely completely on the World Wide Web for all their promotional needs. This is a big mistake for two reasons. You need to use other media and types of promotion to drive visitors to your Web site, since first-page search engine placement may not always be possible or affordable. Second, other forms of promotion, especially publicity, targeted personal sales, and a prime office location for walk-in business, can generate substantial sales that would not come through the Internet. Therefore, the Internet does not totally replace other forms of promotion; it is one of many media, albeit a very important one.

MORE THAN A MEDIUM FOR ADVERTISING

Another common mistake is to view the Internet as just an electronic brochure or a media for advertising. As figure 6.7 illustrates, the Internet offers far more opportunities than just advertising and online sales. Direct e-mail promotion, sales promotions, publicity, and low-cost research are other advantages of the Internet.

Figure 6.7 The Internet can influence many parts of marketing.

DIRECT MAIL

Direct Internet response refers to sending messages and offers via e-mail. E-mail is an incredibly important means of communication and in 2005 was second only to telemarketing in media revenue, low cost, and response rate. More than 2.6 trillion e-mails were expected to be sent in the United States in 2007; on average, an Internet-connected person receives 35 messages a day, opens two or three messages from **opt-in lists** (consumer selects the option to have a provider send more information in the future via e-mail), and clicks on one per day (Silverpop, 2006). However, promotion through e-mail has some challenges: It is easily ignored and often unwanted (known as "spam"); not all persons have an e-mail address; spam-filtering programs can block messages; and the government is now starting to regulate e-mail. E-mail marketing wizard Brian Baker (2006) offers the following tips for successful e-mail promotion:

- Always ask first: The consumer chooses to "opt-in" on your Web site or via other means to be sent future e-mail.

- Personalize the e-mail: Use personal names or products of interest to consumers in the message.

- Identify yourself: Use the subject line to identify yourself, not your offer. For example, a fly fishing shop might write in the subject line "Your Fishworks Fly Fishing Shop Insider Rate" rather than the offer "Special Spring Fly Rod Savings."

- Remind consumers that you know them: Early in the message tell the recipients, "You're receiving this e-mail because . . ."

- Get to know them better: Ask for their preferences. Almost two-thirds of opt-in respondents were willing to answer a few questions to get personalized responses or information.

- Help them tell their friends: Encourage word of mouth, also known as viral promotion, by providing the option to "forward this information to a friend."

- Don't send too often: Monthly or even quarterly e-mails are more likely to be opened than are ones sent weekly.

- Remember what they said: Store preferences and other consumer information in a database linked to your e-mail program.

PUBLICITY THROUGH THE INTERNET

A company Web site and actions via the Web should develop and promote getting free positive publicity to the extent possible. The following are some methods to do so:

- Create a robust Web site pressroom: At a minimum there should be a pressroom or media link on your home page linking to a page with press releases, photos, and company background information.

- Don't forget e-zines: The Web is full of Internet-based magazines that need stories and news, so e-mail press release announcements to them as well as to traditional media.

Green Tip

Reduce Direct-Mail Waste

Directly mailing printed information about your services to potential customers can generate new sales, but it can also be very wasteful and in total can have a large adverse impact on the environment. Mail that is unwanted and not opened is referred to as "junk mail." The amount of paper junk mail sent each year in the United States is staggering—some four million tons, nearly half of which is never opened. Even if a consumer recycles sent items, there are still enormous environmental costs in terms of ink; energy to produce, deliver, and recycle the paper; recycling inefficiencies; and loss of virgin forest to create the high-quality glossy paper much junk mail uses. There is a lot you can do to reduce waste, save your company's money, and reduce the environmental cost but still generate new sales. In addition, there is a growing movement and a set of federal regulations requiring that complaining consumers be removed from mailing lists. So reducing direct-mail waste can save a business money (lower printing and postage costs), help the environment, and be respectful of consumers but still enhance sales.

There are some specific things businesses can do regarding direct-mail items. First and foremost is to clean up your list or buy clean mailing lists, removing addresses that will be undeliverable. There are companies that specialize in list cleaning at a reasonable price. This saves you money right away, with no decrease in sales. You can also ask your clients if they want to receive information and thus create an opt-in list. Consider switching from mailing printed items to sending equivalent materials electronically. Finally, reduce the environmental cost of printed materials by using paper with high postconsumer content, nonpetroleum-based soy ink, and paper produced by chlorine-free processes. See the Code of Conduct for Scott Walking Adventures in the online student resource for chapter 9. Many printers have these products and competitive rates, or you can view the Web site of Oregon-based Environmental Paper & Print (see www.environmentalprint.com/index.php).

• Try an Internet publicist: Several Web sites specialize in announcing your information or new content to Internet-based editors, writers, and bloggers (a **blog** is a Web site where entries are made in journal style and displayed in a reverse chronological order). An example of an Internet publicist is URLwire (www.urlwire.com).

• Use the right format, with no attachments: Use the e-mail programs properly, create e-mail messages that are professional in appearance when seen by the receiver, keep content simply stated, and do not send attachments (because of virus concerns). Instead of attachments, refer consumers to your Web site or provide a link for additional details.

• Monitor groups: If you join, monitor, and become involved with select online affinity groups, such as newsgroups, Yahoo! groups, and discussion lists, you can generate positive impressions for your company.

BANNER ADS

At the top or sides of many popular commercial Web sites and search engine results are **banner ads** that can be purchased (see figure 6.8). A banner ad has very limited space for text and a small image (often with animation) that is linked to a Web page with more content, often the advertiser's home page. Advertisers usually pay for a banner ad by the number of times it is seen (views) or more commonly by the number of times a Web site visitor actually clicks on (links to) the ad. The Web site sponsor provides the advertiser with many metrics, such as the number of ad clicks and the characteristics of the viewers' Internet connection or **URL (uniform resource locator)**.

Figure 6.8 Banner ads appear on the right side of this Web page.

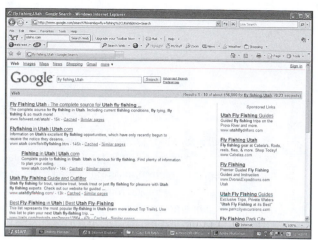

Figure 6.9 Search engine results show organic results on the left and sponsored ads on the right.

PURCHASING KEYWORDS

The primary search engines, such as Google and Yahoo! allow advertisers to bid on "keywords" that they believe potential clients would type into the search bar when they are looking for their type of product or service. For example, if an advertiser sells hot air ballooning trips, they would bid on the keywords "hot air ballooning," hoping a user would type those words in the search bar, see their ad, click on it, be directed to the company Web site, and buy the service. On some search engines these ads are called "sponsored links" or "sponsored ads" and appear next to and sometimes above the natural or organic results on the search engine page (see figure 6.9). Google AdWords (www.adwords. google.com) and Yahoo! Search Marketing (www. searchmarketing.yahoo.com) are the largest network operators and prime locations for keyword purchases. A great feature of purchasing keywords is that if you cannot get good **organic search engine placement** through programming of your own Web site, then this may be the only other alternative to getting listed on the first page of searches for your type of product at your location. Another benefit is that you pay only when the user clicks on the ad. The challenge these days for small businesses is that the purchase of keywords is through a continuous online auction where the price paid per click is often reaching high prices. For example, on Google AdWords, the price for first listing on the phrase "Utah rafting" exceeds $5.00 per click. This initially sounds low, but if you get 100 clicks in a week (maybe with a low percentage actually resulting in a purchase), the total cost is

about $500. If you bought five sets of keywords that perform similarly, then the total cost of all ads for only one month might be $10,000. So you must be very judicious in keywords you buy and careful with words placed on your sponsored ad. Frequently monitor the ad performance metrics (provided for free by the search engine or advertising company) and resultant purchases to ensure it is cost effective and affordable and to fine-tune your ads.

SOCIAL MEDIA

The World Wide Web has a number of very popular **social media** Web sites that are designed to facilitate social interaction between friends and build online communities of persons with similar interests where opinions and photos are easily exchanged. Examples of immensely popular general social media sites are MySpace.com, friendster.com, and facebook.com. Other sites specialize in building online communities and referrals based around an interest in travel. The most popular social media travel site is tripadvisor. com. A challenge with social media, like other forms of publicity, is that companies cannot directly "control" what is said about them on the social media, but they can enhance the likelihood of positive responses, and they can appropriately reply (without raising more negative comments) to negative statements to minimize damage. Some refer to this as managing your online reputation.

A promotional tactic used by a growing number of companies is to optimize the use of social media, online communities, and social travel Web sites in order to generate the greatest amount of positive publicity about the company. This is frequently done by providing **RSS (Really Simple Syndication) feeds**, offering a place on the company Web site for clients to comment about their experiences (without editing by company), encouraging a blog about the organization, and incorporating third-party communities to exchange information about the company. Frequently used exchange Web sites are Flickr.com for photos and slides and YouTube.com for videos. The results of successful social media optimization can be dramatic and achieved at relatively low cost. Many companies now have videos on YouTube and

---

SPOTLIGHT ON

Adrift Adventures, Inc.

Location

Adrift Adventures provides whitewater rafting, kayaking, and environmental learning programs in Utah, Colorado, and Alaska. Their headquarters, store, and warehouse are in Jensen, Utah, a very small town at the main highway entrance to Dinosaur National Monument. This location provides easy access to their three most popular rafting and kayaking trips.

Courtesy of Michael Powers

Rafting the Green River on an Adrift Adventures trip.

Patrick T. Tierney

The Yampa River Canyon in Dinosaur National Monument is famous for its rafting.

Background

Adrift Adventures started out as a very small whitewater rafting company called Colorado Canyons Whitewater. The business acquired another company, expanded to two offices in two states, and offered rafting and learning adventures on nine rivers in Colorado and Utah. At one time Adrift partnered with other companies to offer winter sailing and hiking trips in Hawaii, sea kayaking in Belize, and hot-air balloon rides around Fort Collins, Colorado. A key to their success was acquiring limited-operator permits from the National Park Service and other federal and state agencies to run interpretive whitewater river trips on nationally known rivers and parks.

Products and Services

Adrift provided their clients all boating equipment and related gear, licensed professional guides, meals, and shuttles. An important component of their trips was the opportunity to learn about the 2,000-foot-deep (610 m) canyons and its wildlife, 800-year-old Indian rock art, and colorful cowboy history. They had permits to operate in Dinosaur National Monument on the Green and Yampa rivers, in the Gunnison River Gorge National Conservation Area, on the Cache la Poudre National Wild and Scenic River, in the Arkansas River State Recreation Area, and on the North Platte River in the Routt National Forest and the Talkeetna River in Alaska.

The keys to client safety and enjoyment and company success were the spectacular natural settings, their outstanding guides, and training and management. It is a labor-intensive, high-risk recreation business that demands continuous hands-on management and protection of the fragile park resources. The owners were actively involved in the designation of the Cache la Poudre River as Colorado's first national wild and scenic river. Their efforts were recognized through a nomination for the *Condé Nast Traveler* magazine International Ecotourism Award (see Case Study 9.1 in the online student resource for a discussion of Adrift's sustainability report).

Marketing and promotion were done mostly through viral marketing (encouraging word-of-mouth promotion) from past clients, a strong Internet presence, group sales, and securing publicity. They used many strategies to encourage

(continued)

Spotlight On . . . (continued)

word of mouth, including photos of guests' own rafting experiences, referral rewards, and group discounts. By 2000 the Internet was the greatest source of new clients. High placement on search engines was a key Internet strategy. The company paid technical consultants who knew the latest search engine requirements and opportunities to maintain high placement on Google, Yahoo, and other portal sites. Where high organic placement was not possible, they purchased keywords on search engines. Personal sales to group representatives were another promotional activity. A few ads were placed in national travel magazines. The company evaluated return on investment for all major promotional expenses and made adjustments because of a limited marketing budget.

Business Advice and Plans

After 25 years of operation, the owners of Adrift Adventures sold the company in 2006. The business was a small family-owned and -operated entity; therefore all family members had to be happy with the needs, challenges, and rewards of the company. The family agreed it was time to change directions and sell. It was a very difficult decision for some of the family members because, besides being an important source of income, the company had become like a member of the family and it was a part of their lives that they enjoyed very much. Another consideration was that, in order to receive the best price, company profits should be peaking and the operation should be running well. Finally, it was realized that sale of the company was just another, albeit the last, stage in the entrepreneurial cycle.

photos on Flickr and encourage their guests to place their own materials on these sites.

SALES PROMOTION THROUGH THE INTERNET

The Internet can be a fertile ground for promoting your business through sales promotion tactics, such as online coupons, contests, virtual tours, sponsorships, trial offers, and other giveaways. The opportunities to increase traffic to your Web site or generate direct sales are varied, from contest Web sites to offers placed in newsgroups. An example of how small RET businesses use the Internet for promotion is illustrated in Spotlight On Adrift Adventures and described in more detail in Case Study 6.1 in the online student resource.

SALES AND WORKPLACE OFFICE LOCATIONS

The location of your business office is very important to RET businesses that want clients to visit them to make purchases. Your office location also can have significant affects on your employees and, if you want a home office, your family. The following section describes office location considerations and home offices.

OFFICE LOCATION CONSIDERATIONS

Location of the recreation, event, and tourism office is an extremely important consideration for the marketing and financial elements of a business. Visibility, access to clients, safe neighborhood, proximity to trails or rivers, adequate parking, and public transportation nearby are all vital to the successful promotion of your services. But the perfect location is different for every business. The ideal location for some tourism firms is in the heart of a tourism district at a resort area where there is tremendous walk-in business potential. In contrast, an urban event planning company might best be located in the downtown business district close to the headquarters of major employers and the convention center. A suburban snowboard shop might best be located next to a freeway or busy street with great visibility and quick road access. This compares with a rural fly fishing guide service, whose perfect location is along the access road to a gold-medal trout stream. A start-up walking touring company might be headquartered out of the owner's home because she meets clients at tour locations. Each type of business has unique considerations as well as requirements common to all businesses. Here are some items to consider when determining where to locate your business.

• Access to clients: How close are your potential patrons, and how far are they willing to travel to get to your business?

• Competitors: Often you do not want a competitor next door, but sometimes being located in a district with many similar businesses can actually draw clients your way.

• Transportation: What is the ease of access by road and public transportation? How is the road to drive in the winter when conditions are icy? Is the site accessible by freight company trucks? Is there adequate parking nearby for clients and staff?

• Neighborhood: What is the composition of the neighborhood? Is it up and coming with an upscale demographic, or is it a downtrodden older business district with narrow streets? Will nearby businesses draw in customers or repel them? Who is the anchor tenant or key attraction in the neighborhood? What are crime levels in the area, and do visitors perceive it as a safe neighborhood to visit?

• Access to educated workforce: Are there many potential well-educated workers nearby, such as near a university campus, or is the site in a remote area with a very small labor pool where you will need to import workers?

• Regulatory restrictions: What are the zoning and related restrictions on business activities? Restrictions might affect type of uses permitted, signs, parking, and changes to building exterior.

• Space: An obvious concern is adequate space in the short term as well as for future expansion.

• Costs: The most fundamental consideration is cost related to the location. This might include monthly rental or purchase price, lease terms, and needed building improvements as well as who pays for utilities, insurance, and taxes.

You will need to enlist the help of an experienced commercial real estate agent for the search and an attorney to review the lease or purchase contract. Normally, a new business does not buy property until it has a proven record.

HOME OFFICES

Many a small business has begun in the owner's home because of the low costs, an extremely short commuting distance, and the advantages of writing off a portion of your house payments on your tax return. However, operating a business out of your home does require careful planning and a healthy dose of ethical behavior. It is simply illegal to operate a business that draws clients in many residential neighborhoods, or the business size and type may be restricted. Operating without a business permit is illegal and unethical and can cause you legal and neighbor troubles. Residential neighborhoods often have poor visibility and limited parking. Do you have enough separate office space and appropriate telephone lines and Internet access? How will your family accept strangers constantly coming into their home? Then there is the consideration of how you will be able to separate your personal life from your work life. An entrepreneur with a home office will need to learn how to "close" the office, or all their family and personal time could become work time.

DEVELOPING A MARKETING ELEMENT FOR THE BUSINESS PLAN

A very important component of a business plan is the marketing element. Chapter 12 provides a discussion of the overall business plan and where the marketing element is integrated. Following are the components of an RET-focused marketing plan.

• Industry overview: Describe the nature, characteristics, and trends of the industry in which you intend to be involved. Is the industry growing or declining, what are key growth factors, what is the size of the industry, what about seasonality? How does your business fit within the big picture?

• Products, services and your market analysis: What is your business concept, and what general types of products, services, or experiences will you offer? Identify the size of the market, and describe market segments within a geographic region you intend to serve. Describe the unique benefits sought by each market segment. Which segments will you target for your business? Why? Profile your primary customers in each segment.

• Location and competition: Where do you plan to locate your new RET business? Why there? What is your primary competition for the selected services and target segments? Develop a competitors matrix, and identify any gaps or opportunities. Describe how your business will compare with competitors. How will you position your company in the marketplace? What entrance strategies might you employ?

• Marketing mix and promotions: Describe the key elements of your marketing mix, consisting of pricing, place or distribution, and promotion for each of your targeted market segments. What do you propose for the specific promotional elements of advertising, publicity, personal sales, and sales promotion? How will you evaluate the effectiveness of your promotional efforts?

• Budget: Provide an itemized promotional budget for the year with a monthly schedule of promotional activities and ad placements, and their individual costs and expected ROI.

• Evaluations: Describe how you will evaluate your promotional effort, and what specific methods will be employed.

SUMMARY

A recreation, event, and tourism business needs to communicate with a larger audience than your existing customers and their friends, and this is done through marketing. Marketing includes more than promotion via advertising alone. A well-designed and well-researched marketing mix of innovative product, price, place, and effective promotions is much more successful. Technology is becoming increasingly important in marketing, such as yield management systems for determining price to charge. Promotional elements vary from advertising, publicity, and personal sales to sales promotion. The Internet has become a much more important component of the marketing mix. An example of Internet promotion is online auctions that buy keywords on Internet search engines. Yet some traditional nontechnical forms of promotion, such as brochure distribution and personal sales, continue to rank very highly as sources of new sales. This suggests that you must research what your clients want, identify messages that best facilitate the sale, develop effective forms of promotion, and conduct evaluations of promotion effectiveness. Therefore, it is critical to develop a comprehensive marketing plan in which you identify the mix of strategies and techniques for best communicating and promoting your services. This chapter describes the components of a marketing plan and guides you through important components of marketing plan development.

 Check out the online student resource for additional material, including case studies, Web links, and more.

Part

III

Management Principles and Practices

Chapter 7

Management, Leadership, and Team Building

Learning Objectives

After reading this chapter you will be able to

- define the terms *management, leadership, managerial duties, organizational chart, team building, job analysis, position description, recruitment,* and *mentoring;*
- identify the significance of management and leadership in a business setting;
- describe managerial duties and the lessons learned from businesses that did not succeed;
- describe steps in the process of building a team, such as the best practices for recruitment, the role of training, the merit for hiring versus contracting, and compensation strategies; and
- identify managerial self-assessment tools and choices one has for strengthening management leadership capability.

Key Terms

Blake Mouton Managerial Grid

business team

independent contractor

leadership

management

managerial duties

Myers-Briggs Type Indicator (MBTI)

organizational chart

position description

profit sharing

recruitment

team building

Imagine this scenario:

As the owner of an event management company, you just delivered all the contracted logistics and support services for a major nonprofit fund-raising festival. Your client approaches you after the event and says, "I am so pleased with the services you provided, the capability of your staff, and how effectively every member of your team worked with my contact persons. I heard many times how thoughtful your staff were as they kept us well informed throughout and responded positively to our last-minute requests for adjustments because of unforeseen circumstances. We would like your company to continue as our supplier for this annual event, and we have a much larger event that we would like to talk with you about as well."

As you head back to your office, elated by the satisfaction expressed by your client, you reflect on the key steps you initiated in the previous month to provide effective leadership, hire the right people, compensate your staff properly, provide the appropriate training, dedicate time to several team-building activities, and put in place a solid contract with the necessary independent contractors. Your attention to details ensured a seamless delivery of critical services by staff and others. Now is the time to communicate the successful comments and outcomes to your staff. It is also an ideal time to ask them to brainstorm what improvements we can make in serving this highly satisfied client with the even larger event she has in mind.

The opening scenario illustrates some of the positive outcomes related to a well-managed company with solid human resources, expertise, and leadership. However, it is not unheard of for the exact opposite to happen where an organization has weak leadership and ineffective management, resulting in employees delivering poor service and leading to unhappy customers, even lawsuits from both clients and employees. In fact, lawsuits brought by employees against their employers are one of the fastest-growing forms of litigation. Successful management starts with a clear understanding of management and leadership principles, resulting in the building of an effective management team, and culminates with well-supervised employees delivering exceptional service. This chapter outlines successful practices covering primarily the following questions:

- First, what do you know about the art of management and leadership?

- How can you proceed to build an effective business team?

- What are the management pitfalls or "lessons learned" by other small businesses that deserve your attention?

- How can other "lessons learned" be applied to the task of building, training, and rewarding your business team?

- Finally, if you want to enhance your management and leadership knowledge, skills, and abilities, what are the choices?

WHAT IS MANAGEMENT?

Management is probably the most important single word for an entrepreneur to embrace and understand. The word today appears regularly in both the print and electronic media of a business because effective management, or the lack of it, influences so many business functions. A brief and simple approach to defining the term would say that management is simply the art of getting things done through people. However, over time the definition has been refined both in scope and significance by pointing out there is a lot more to it than just getting things done. Managers are clearly responsible for looking outward at the external working environment of the business, setting priorities, and then making sure the most important things get the attention they deserve. In the following pages it will become evident that management is central to the success of a recreation, event, and tourism business.

LEADERSHIP IN BUSINESS

Leadership is the second most significant word in today's competitive business environment because it directs the manager of a business to focus inward on their personal capabilities and style. Experts on leadership will quickly point out that "how things get done" influences the success of the outcomes and indicates a right way and a wrong way to do things. When a noted leader on the art of management, Peter Drucker, coined the phrase "Management is doing things right; leadership is doing the right things," he was seeking to clarify the distinctions he associates with the terms.

When Stephen Covey, founder and director of the Leadership Institute, explored leadership styles in the past decade, he focused on the habits of a great number of highly effective individuals. His *Seven Habits of Highly Effective People* became a popular best-seller very quickly. His ideas forced a reexamination of the early leadership paradigm, which he observed centered on traits found in the character ethic and the personality ethic. The former ethic suggested success was founded on integrity, humility, fidelity, courage, patience, and so forth. The personality ethic suggested it was one's attitude, not behavior, that inspired success, and this ethic was founded on a belief of positive mental attitude. In contrast to each of these ideas, Covey advocates that leaders need to understand universal principles of effectiveness, and he highlights how vital it is for leaders to first personally manage themselves if they are to enjoy any hope of outstanding success in their work environments. To achieve a desired vision for your business, it is vital that you have a personal vision of where you are headed and what you value. Business leadership means that managers need to "put first things first," which implies that before leading others, you need to be clear on your own values, abilities, and strengths and be seen as trustworthy.

STRIKING A BALANCE

Management decisions are about doing the right things and doing those things the right way. Stephen Covey's leadership paradigm for personal effectiveness is about gaining the confidence of others to get things done. Put into perspective, leadership skills should be viewed as a necessary but not sufficient condition for the success of a business. The point of view recently put forward by Mintzberg (2004) is that management and leadership are complementary attributes needed to succeed. "I use the words management and leadership interchangeably. It has become fashionable to distinguish them. Leadership is supposed to be something bigger, more important. I reject this distinction, simply because managers have to lead and leaders have to manage. Management without leadership is sterile; leadership without management is disconnected and encourages hubris. We should not be ceding management to leadership . . . ."(p. 6). The literature in both

areas is worthy of critical examination, and mastery in one area does not diminish the relevance of the other area. Articles that bring the qualities of a leader and manager together in the context of entrepreneurship can be found in several places on the Internet, and one such source is available at www.aykya.com/leadership/managers_leaders.asp.

It would be difficult to combine all the current advice on management into this chapter, but it would be fair to say that management decisions are about doing the important things the right way, with a substantial amount of personal attention to self-discipline and self-knowledge. Self-knowledge implies being fully aware of your strengths and weaknesses, your skills and abilities, and your managerial style.

How an entrepreneur can gain self-knowledge and why it is important to being personally successful is at the heart of building a business team. When the management overview component of your feasibility study is prepared, you reveal how work will get done through people; what positions will exist; and how decisions about personnel, marketing, finance, risk management, delivery of goods and services, and daily operational matters will receive the attention that each function deserves. The management component of the feasibility study addresses the planning and the decisions you need to undertake for the business to prosper and succeed.

MANAGERIAL DUTIES

Numerous decisions will be made every day in business, with important tasks initiated based on those decisions. Anticipating what has to be done, and how it will get done, is fundamental to ensure your vision for success in a small business is achieved. People seeking to own and manage a commercial recreation, event, and tourism business must acquire knowledge of the industry along with certain skills and abilities to manage it effectively. Figure 7.1 identifies eight **managerial duties** that are part of the management and leadership experiences you will face as a business owner.

Examination of the following managerial duties illustrates the interrelationship of the concepts of management and leadership. Each of the concepts can be transformed into an area of managerial responsibility. Taken together, the eight areas of responsibility offer an overview of the opportunities and the challenges that rest on the shoulders of the manager.

Figure 7.1 Managerial duties and responsibilities.

Neglecting one or more of the responsibilities has consequences that deserve equal attention.

PLAN AND ORGANIZE

The ability to plan and organize gives structure to the business, creates an important and clear image of certainty, and keeps the business in working order. In defining roles, working relationships, and the implementation of the team-building process, organizational skills will play a major role in ensuring a functional and integrated operation. Every component of marketing, finance, training, risk assessment, and so on must be planned for and organized. It is a managerial duty to ensure this occurs either by delegation or by performing the task.

INNOVATE AND EVALUATE

Being innovative is part of being entrepreneurial, as it permits corrections and adjustments in business activities when they are needed. Evaluation is a means of discovering improved ways to stimulate growth, to assess customer satisfaction, and to support new product development.

MAKE DECISIONS

Reflective thinking is very important, but managers must analyze information and make careful timely decisions. Decisions are part of a manager's everyday activities, such as work scheduling, allocation of resources, or adopting strategies to achieve financial objectives. Clear and decisive actions are vital elements to keeping things moving forward and in creating a proactive work environment.

COMMUNICATE

An absolutely essential skill is the capacity to effectively communicate organization decisions, plans, and actions to team members. It is of vital importance to possess the interpersonal communication that builds trust, harmony, and rapport among team members. Praise and acknowledgment of the contribution of each and every team member are the keys to successful program, product, or project delivery and are vital to retention of staff.

RECRUIT, TRAIN, AND RETAIN

The ability to recruit, train, retain, and motivate the members of the team is fundamental to getting work accomplished. The potential to expand the capacity of a small business is fully dependent on skills related to personnel management. This pertains to recruiting, training, and even replacing individuals as the circumstances require. One example of team training is making sure your business "goes green," and this is illustrated in the green tip on the following page.

Green Tip

Building Environmental Management Into Employee Training

Minimizing a company's impacts on the environment can be thought of as the "job" of the operations and maintenance departments of an RET company. Establishing clear policies and practices for environmental protection and recycling is fundamental in the operations division. But the leaders of top RET companies are now making environmental management a job requirement of all staff and are building it into their employee manuals and training. This way everyone knows the importance the company places on environmental management and ways they can contribute to reducing adverse effects. A good example of this is Alpine Meadows ski area (www.skialpine.com), awarded top listing in the 2007 California Ski Area Environmental Scorecard. On page five of their employee handbook, listed ahead of topics such as attendance and scheduling, is an extensive discussion of the company's environmental philosophy and values, and their "Environmental Code of the Slopes." The code covers topics such as

- respecting wildlife,
- properly disposing of waste,
- encouraging employee and guest carpooling,
- using washable utensils in cafeterias,
- supporting cleanup days,
- turning off lights and machines when leaving rooms for long periods,
- establishing an extensive education and recycling program,
- encouraging guests to help protect the environment, and
- providing feedback on how to improve the company's environmental performance.

These same principles are a significant component of preseason orientation and training for new and returning employees. These actions clearly demonstrate to all employees the company's commitment to protecting the environment.

Alpine Meadows can be a model for other RET businesses. Their actions point out how important it is for company owners, the board of directors, and executive managers to understand and commit to environmental management as well as strong fiscal management.

RESOLVE CONFLICT

One of the more demanding and important talents of a manager is conflict resolution and the capacity to create win–win scenarios when conflicts arise. People management problems can occur in many forms in the workplace, as disputes may arise between you and a supplier, your employee and a customer, or between overly competitive employees. In the workplace, conflict is more likely to be evident when highly motivated team members are new or have not worked together long enough to value the differences among each other.

BE PROACTIVE

Taking action can be considered either reactive or proactive. Leadership in business today rewards the proactive person who anticipates issues looming on the horizon, prepares for them, and does not wait until there is an immediate crisis. Strengthening your managerial skills to be prepared for contingencies, setting the direction, and putting the business plan into practice are important. Networking skills are critical components to being a proactive leader because you can learn from others about what they see on the horizon or what they think may affect the business climate in the short term.

BE A CHANGE-MAKER

Trends, fads, and changes in commerce are happening continuously. You must not only observe indicators of change or listen to messages indicating potential changes in the business climate but also tap into your intuitive capacity. The synergy of drawing upon many sources of information can expand your awareness of potential changes and enhance your creativity when formulating a response to anticipated change. Later in the chapter, the Myers-Briggs Type Indicator (MBTI) is discussed. The MBTI identifies the degree to which you prefer to first employ your intuition or one of your other senses when faced with interpreting new information and assessing a major change. Identifying, anticipating, and assessing the consequences of the changes occurring in the economy or with consumer preferences can influence the products, services, or mission of the business.

PUTTING FIRST THINGS FIRST

As Stephen Covey advocated, it's a matter of "putting first things first." If you are not clear about your decision-making ability, interpersonal skills, or ability to plan and organize provisions of the business plan, then the first priority should be an assessment of your overall managerial capability. There will undoubtedly be the fundamental desire to acquire critical thinking and interpersonal skills that allow you to successfully implement your ideas and goals. Along with this desire will be the opportunity to become involved with your professional associations which in turn develops a network of professional peers that can exchange information and share in your professional goals.

Leaders seeking to acquire portable skills and managerial experience will find it occurs at various stages of their career path. Chapter 13 examines several paths for acquiring relevant work-related experiences as part of a postsecondary education. Nonetheless, the initial ingredient to begin with is a passion for the business concept and an ability to listen to trusted advisers. Chapter 3 suggests that if you are passionate about your vision for the future, then you are more likely to make wise choices in your decision-making activities. Such enthusiasm is also associated with being creative in the actions you take every day. Creativity "provides one with one of the most exciting models for living," according to Csikszentmihalyi (1996, p. 11). He further suggests: "Each of us is born with two contradictory sets of instructions: a conservative tendency, made up of instincts for self-preservation, self-aggrandizement, and saving energy, and an expansive tendency made up of instincts for exploring, for enjoying novelty and risk—the curiosity that leads to creativity belongs to this set. We need both of these programs. But whereas the first tendency requires little encouragement or support from outside to motivate behavior, the second can wilt if it is not cultivated. If too few opportunities for curiosity are available, if too many obstacles are placed in the way of risk and

Professional networks will be important for a new business and a sensible management decision would be to join a local DMO and advertise through your tourism visitor center.

J.S. Pfister

exploration, the motivation to engage in creative behavior is easily extinguished" (p. 11).

The path explored and taken by Mary Mahon Jones helps to reveal the unlikely choices one might follow in terms of discovering opportunities to build upon the creative skill and knowledge associated with art appreciation and cultural tourism. After working in art galleries and performing leadership functions in professional associations, Mary was presented with the opportunity to become CEO for the Council of Tourism Associations, an organization representing and lobbying on behalf of tourism associations in British Columbia. This management experience was

then followed by a decision to build upon that experience by focusing consulting expertise on cultural tourism and the arts as an important and growing industry sector. See Spotlight On Mahon Jones and Associates.

As noted in chapter 1 (figure 1.7), the best scenario for living life more fully is when you are able to match your love of a business purpose (i.e., commitment) with your personal talent to do it well (i.e., capability). The reality is the most basic of managerial duties and practices of a business do not come instantly, and if one tries to move too quickly down the path, some of the failures illustrated in table 7.1 could occur. It

Table 7.1 Nineteen Management-Related Reasons for Business Failure in Rank Order

Management reasons attributed to the failure of small business	Frequency
1. Poor cash flow management skills or poor understanding of cash flow	82%
2. Starting out with too little money	79%
3. Lack of a well-developed business plan, including insufficient research on the business before starting it	78%
4. Not pricing properly; failure to include all necessary items when setting prices	77%
5. Being overly optimistic about achievable sales	73%
6. Not recognizing, or ignoring, what they don't do well and not seeking help from those who do	70%
7. Denying problems in the business until it's too late	66%
8. Minimizing the importance of promoting the business properly (marketing)	65%
9. Ineffective prioritization for the use of both time and money	64%
10. Insufficient relevant and applicable business experience	63%
11. Insufficient entrepreneurial instinct about how to run a business	63%
12. Not paying attention to the plan after it's developed	60%
13. Inability to delegate properly—micromanaging work given to others or overdelegating and abdicating important management responsibilities	58%
14. Hiring the wrong people—clones of themselves and not people with complementary skills—or hiring friends and relatives	56%
15. Falling in love with their idea and losing objectivity and customer focus	55%
16. Poor people-management skills	54%
17. Not understanding or recognizing, or ignoring, competition	53%
18. Not knowing when to hire or fire employees	48%
19. Too much focus and reliance on one customer or client	47%

Adapted, by permission, from John Murphy, Murphy Associates, Your Marketing Department, "19 Habits of Not Terribly Successful Entrepreneurs" (Brookfield, WI: Author).

Mahon Jones and Associates

Location

Located in North Vancouver, British Columbia, Mahon Jones and Associates (MJA) is a new face to the consulting world but not new to tourism or the arts. The firm is centered on Mary Mahon Jones' experience of more than 16 years as a chief executive officer in tourism and the arts as well as 10 years as an arts educator.

Mary Mahon Jones.

Background

When Mary Mahon enrolled in university, she lacked a clear direction of her future other than the fact that she loved to draw. What followed was the first of many periods in her life of intense personal growth. While at the university, she learned that her real talent lay in learning theory, strategic thinking, and communications. When she obtained her degree from Queens University, her academic path should have led to a career in teaching. However, fate intervened as it did many times when, after motherhood and a change of address, she enlisted as a volunteer animator at the MacKenzie Art Gallery in Regina, Saskatchewan. In less than five years, she headed up the gallery's education department, overseeing a small army of paid and volunteer gallery educators. Inspired by the work of Edmund Burke Feldman, she created a methodology called the MacKenzie Method, which inspired appreciation of art works.

While at the art gallery, Mary became involved in several profession-related associations, including the Museums Association of Saskatchewan and the Canadian Association of Gallery Educators. As board chair of both associations, Mary entered into a new world of experience in government relations and advocacy. It was because of her work in both that she was offered the position of general manager of the Saskatchewan Council of Cultural Organizations (SCCO) in 1991. The job was to manage the allocation of about 40 percent of the net proceeds of Saskatchewan Lotteries to nonprofit organizations working in the arts, heritage, and multiculturalism. Over five years, SCCO and Saskatchewan's cultural community were restructured to become SaskCulture, a new organization with improved relationships to other cultural stakeholder groups in the province as well as the lottery-funded sport and recreation community.

In 1997, Mary looked westward to British Columbia for new challenges and applied for the position of CEO of the Council of Tourism Associations (COTA). In 1998, she arrived in British Columbia as COTA's first full-time employee, ready to build a new organization that would provide unity and advocacy for the province's growing tourism industry. For a decade, Mary led and helped build a strong organization with a record of success in creating land-use agreements with other resource-based industries, a vibrant annual tourism conference, several programs to assist industry development, and a sustainability-based plan for the future of British Columbia's tourism industry. After a decade with the tourism association, Mary reassessed her skills and assets to discover a wealth of knowledge and experience gained over the course of her career, which could be the foundation of a solid consulting business.

Services

MJA provides consulting services to business, nonprofit groups, and government agencies. The services include conducting focus groups or workshops, research on issues affecting a client, advice on government relations, and assistance on issues and events affecting tourism or arts organizations. Combining her cultural and tourism backgrounds led naturally to a special expertise in cultural tourism. The greatest asset is her extensive network of contacts in the British Columbian and Canadian tourism industry. Her project management training and her experience as a teacher and leader permit her to assemble and manage project-specific teams of experts simply by tapping into this network when responding to requests for proposals. As with every aspect of her life, this has opened up new opportunities for personal development as she manages these teams through a myriad of topic areas, addressing a range of issues important to the development of tourism and the arts. As the saying goes, "It just keeps getting better."

is often said that many new entrepreneurs start out without sufficiently investing in real-life experiences to make good business decisions. Making good business decision needs to be explored next.

FATAL MISTAKES AND MISADVENTURES IN BUSINESS

Every year, some businesses succeed while others do not. The important question is what can be learned from those that fail. As briefly highlighted in chapter 2, one of the fatal mistakes for a small business pertains to the failure to plan and organize the business. This section addresses what we can learn from other businesses that did not succeed. Once you open your doors to customers and get started down the path to success, the question shifts to what activities you need to monitor and pay attention to if you are to avoid the fatal pitfalls common to businesses. If, for example, you take one of the managerial duties too casually (e.g., neglect to recruit a solid team), then you may want to know just how frequently that pitfall tends to contribute to business failure (see table 7.1). So it will be helpful at this point to review what causes businesses to fail.

WHY NEW BUSINESSES FAIL

Every business manager needs to know why businesses fail. To be sure, businesses fail for a variety of reasons, and it is probable there will be more than one. What is not in dispute is that the majority of the reasons can be traced back to action or inaction on the part of the individual responsible for managing the start-up business. For example, table 7.1 sheds light on 19 managerial duties, many of which have been previously noted in figure 7.1. In this table, the percentages are listed for a wide range of specific factors that contribute to the failure of a small business.

Close examination of these 19 specific management factors helps you see the role of managerial duties as you get started in business. What is the likelihood that you will make any one of the mistakes on the list? What does each fatal mistake most closely represent, given the eight managerial skills? Does the item symbolize a failure to execute a decision, a failure to communicate effectively, or inattention to the documented financial practices contained in the business plan? Once you are able to associate the failure with one of the managerial duties, then you can contemplate the actions necessary to avoid these mistakes.

DANGERS AND RISKS OF A FRANCHISE

One of the appeals of buying a franchise is that you are not beginning from scratch. In terms of the managerial duties, a buyer of a franchise believes what is being purchased is a proven business strategy that has been shown profitable time and time again. In most cases, a franchise represents a reliable investment but it is definitely not risk free. While several management issues can be mitigated by the suggested strategies provided in a franchise opportunity, there remains pitfalls that can lead to failure. Gaebler Ventures offers assistance to entrepreneurs, and they have identified several reasons why franchises can fail (www.gaebler.com/Gaebler_Entrepreneurs.htm):

- *Proven versus unproven franchisors:* While there are proven franchisors selling time-tested strategies for operating a business, there are also the unscrupulous types trying to make a quick buck and they will not provide what is promised. As noted on one Internet blog (www.franchisepick.com), the Internet has changed the game for individuals choosing to operate in an unethical manner. Controversial franchises are now exposed for what they have done, and the Web site blog annually identifies the best and the worse examples engaged in selling a franchise.

- *Market saturation:* While an exclusive territory is offered as part of the deal, you will need to possess the same knowledge of a start-up operation. If the market area is saturated with the businesses in your industry sector, then you need to consider an alternate location. Location is a critical aspect of a small business, so enter into the idea of a territory with open eyes (item 17 in table 7.1).

- *Inadequate marketing:* While a franchisor might have name recognition and offer you the opportunity to buy into a market campaign, neither is sufficient for success. When a franchisee fails to get the word out locally the profitability is undermined. Owners cannot forego the cost of an effective and efficient marketing plan (item 8 in table 7.1).

- *False expectations:* When a franchisor creates the image of certain success, it leads to unrealistic aspirations for the new owner. A franchise will demand the same dedication, hard work, and focus that is required of a start-up business.

BUILDING YOUR TEAM

Although it might be ideal to do everything you can yourself, there will come a time in the life span of a business to build a rock-solid management team because that represents an opportunity to have other people buy into your business concept and help it succeed. Planning to have the right people involved in your business is one of the most valuable components of your business plan and vital to building your team. Readers of a business plan, such as a venture capital company, will not want a listing of all employees; their concern is the level of knowledge, skills, experiences, and responsibilities of your business team. Consider your **business team** to be a small number of people, with complementary customer knowledge and technical skills specific to your type of business, who are committed to your business concept, hold themselves mutually accountable to their defined responsibilities, and adhere to your standards of operation. Your success depends on energetic people who can work together well and produce exceptional results in terms of your products and services. For this to occur, every independent small business owner needs to recognize that **team building** is a planned, continuous, and deliberate process that progresses through several stages of development and takes time

to do well. A common mistake is to hire your personal friends without looking at what knowledge, technical skills, and experiences they will be able to contribute to the business. Whether or not the members of your team are part-time employees, full-time employees, or contracted, each person will need to be clear as to his or her responsibilities or assigned tasks.

Building a complementary team means knowing the abilities of everyone involved—including yourself. With that information, you can then identify how to address all the business functions that will contribute to overall success and how to build the team needed in the short term and long term. Of course, identifying your team is carried out concurrently with writing the other sections of your business plan. The goal in plan preparation is to have the preliminary results of your team-building strategy carefully described in the management section. The management section is where you identify the key functions, outline the position descriptions, and highlight the credentials of your team members. To write the management section of a business plan, you need to see the "big picture" of what has to be done in the business, assess the talent that will be needed, describe the positions to be filled, and lay out the strategy to get them filled.

The process of building your team often involves three steps:

1. Preparing an organizational chart together with position descriptions for key functions

2. Carrying out a recruitment plan to bring on board talented people for each position

3. Outlining a training plan to reinforce team building, validate or certify the talents of the team members, and retain key individuals

ORGANIZATIONAL CHART

The preparation of the **organizational chart** requires you to describe how the key functions identified will be assigned to a specific position. Following are some of the most common functions:

- *Operations:* creating and delivering exceptional goods and services

- *Finance:* preparing the financial records and monitoring profitability

- *Marketing and sales:* designing and implementing a marketing and promotion plan

- *Legal and risk management:* providing myriad legal advice, assessing risk and liability factors, and overseeing risk-reduction strategies

- *Administration:* networking with the suppliers that provide the business with the materials or knowledge needed to operate

- *Human resources:* overseeing and assisting with hiring, supporting, disciplining, and terminating employees

Responsibility for each of these functional areas will need to be assigned in this organizational chart. An organizational chart also shows responsibility areas and formal lines of communication. Just how simple or complex the organizational chart is depends on the legal form of the business, the size of the organization, the number of staff, and the specialty of the firm. This chapter focuses primarily on small to medium limited liability and S corporations because they are the recommended form for most small RET businesses (see chapter 2).

For the small S corporation, the organizational chart can vary greatly depending on the size, specialty, and seasonality of the business and the range of skills possessed by the business owner. As an illustration, the pool management company described in this chapter (see Spotlight On on page 147) is a microsized company of 140 seasonal employees and 20 year-round staff members. The most critical aspect in the organization is having the right ratio between the number of staff in a team and the number of facilities each group will be responsible for in delivering the contracted services. Of course, the reliance on seasonal help would be quite different for the bicycle store or the bed-and-breakfast introduced in chapter 5. If a business owner has little inclination for the bookkeeping tasks, then that function would be incorporated into financial staff positions or outsourced to a professional accountant. The organizational chart simply shows the key supervisory and technical staff positions within the structure and the responsibilities they have. Figures 7.2 through 7.4 display the possible structure

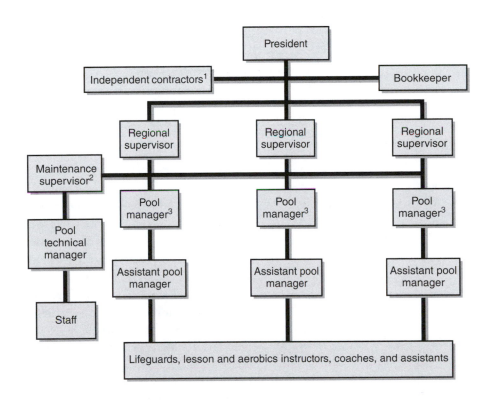

1. Some involvement of electricians and plumbers as independent contractors.
2. Maintenance supervisor and staff are responsible for repairs throughout all three regions.
3. Each pool manager has an assistant manager and lifeguards as well as some or all of the following—swim or water aerobics instructors, team coaches, and coach assistants.

Figure 7.2 Example of an organizational chart for a pool management company.

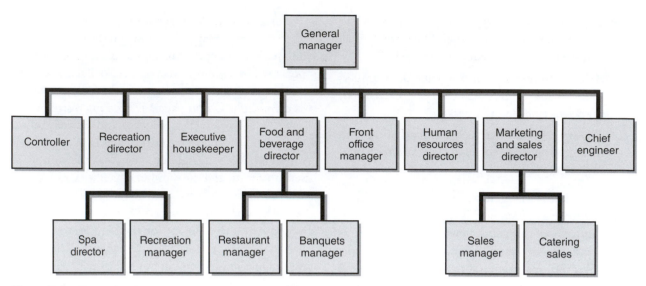

Figure 7.3 Example of an organizational chart for a resort.

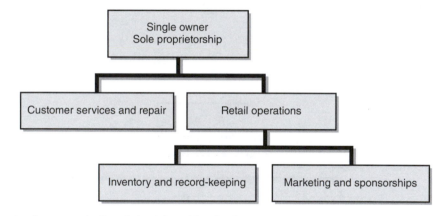

Figure 7.4 Example of an organizational chart for a bicycle shop.

for three different businesses: a pool management company, a medium-size resort, and a bicycle shop. The resort chart is much more specialized because of the business size and the complexity of different operations.

Use these sample charts to develop your own organizational chart. Once the overall organization is identified, then the most crucial jobs should be analyzed in more detail.

Prepare a Description for Each Position

Naturally, the basic concern for any small business is how it can afford the help it needs to succeed. This chapter is designed to answer that question and show you how to make the well-informed decisions necessary to build a management team. Whether or not you have the benefit of a professional for a very

specific task or enjoy the benefit of an employee for the long run, it is important to remember that when you pay people for their time, you should treat them as an investment as well as an expense. It is similar to allocating your money in marketing in the context that you are essentially making an investment in developing a loyal and satisfied customer.

Each **position description** in the organizational chart will identify assigned duties and responsibilities and outline the reporting and working relationships between the individual and other team members. Once this is completed, the next step is an analysis of the job to be performed.

Perform a Job Analysis

Job analysis takes the duties and responsibilities that need to be performed and carefully examines the knowledge, skills, and abilities required to successfully

Blue Water Pool Management, Sales, and Service, Inc.

Location

For Blue Water Pool Management (BWPMSS), it all began in a single county of east-central North Carolina in the summer of 1982. Bob Wendling started the business working as a seasonal operator of country club swimming pools. The business provided spring cleaning and opening of the pool, lifeguard services, daily maintenance, and end-of-season winterizing.

Background

After four years as a sole proprietorship, the company became an S corporation in 1986, which provides tax advantages and limited liability. By then it had expanded its clientele to include homeowner association swimming pools (both guarded and unguarded), hotels, and residential pools. In 1989, the company expanded its operation to include a retail pool store and pool construction company.

Bob Wendling.

In 1994, because of rapid growth and overextension of its resources, the company refocused its energies solely on pool management and operation. Its clientele were identified as country clubs, homeowner association pools, wellness center pools, hospital therapy pools, and public pools. It began operating several pools on a year-round basis.

Products and Services

BWPMSS' services include standard facility management duties and staffing and training. Facility services involves draining and cleaning of pools, repairs and painting, daily pool maintenance, meeting and maintaining pool health code requirements, closing, and winterizing. Personnel services include staff training; training and management of lifeguards, swim instructors, water aerobics instructors, and swim team coaches; and providing classes for certified pool operators, CPR, first aid, and lifeguarding. By 1996, BWPMSS managed swimming pools in 10 counties from eastern to central North Carolina and employed over 140 seasonal workers and 20 year-round workers. (See figure 7.2 for the organization chart.)

Business Advice and Plan

When reflecting on the growth and success of his business, Bob lists the following as among the most important considerations:

1. Customer service has to be your main goal. There will be very little, or no, profit without satisfied customers.
2. Screen and hire great pool managers and then train them to hire their staff.
3. Spend time training and making sure managers and staff know how to do things right. Set standards and make sure they know what those standards are.
4. Document, document, document everything you and your employees do.
5. Write an employee manual and go over it with your staff. It must clearly identify policies as well as many, many other things.
6. Hold managers and staff accountable for their responsibilities.
7. Hold periodic staff meetings with your managers and require that they do the same with their staff. Establish agendas and take minutes.
8. Reward staff for going the extra step, not for just showing up on time. (Being there on time is expected.) Make a concerted effort to retain your outstanding staff through promotions, pay increases, and other rewards. (I had many seasonal employees—that is, high school and college students—return for three, four, and five years.)

Photo courtesy of Robert C. Wendling.

fill the position. There are several basic factors to consider, such as the amount of work to be performed, working conditions, the strategy you will follow to advertise effectively, and the date you would like this position to be filled. Table 7.2 describes key questions to consider, based on the job analysis. Essentially this step will help identify performance-based criteria you will be able to use when the time comes to fill the position. Review the identified job requirements to clarify whether or not these criteria can be fulfilled by an independent contractor (e.g., bookkeeping or marketing) or whether it will be necessary to directly employ someone.

When a position in the organizational chart has been described and analyzed, then you are ready to implement the recruitment process.

RECRUITMENT PROCESS

For a commercial recreation, event, and tourism business, it is not likely that you can post a "help wanted" advertisement and expect the right person to show up. As the owner, you need to know what is involved in **recruitment** and give this activity your careful attention. Blue Water Pool Management Inc. places recruitment at the top of the list in regards to challenges faced by a business owner. In fact, the recruitment and management of staff is a business commitment that ranks ahead of the customers for a number of reasons everyone should think carefully about. It will also be important to confirm there are good reasons to employ someone versus having an independent contractor. When the recruitment process begins, you will also need to be well informed about the laws governing hiring practices.

The recruitment process is highlighted in figure 7.5, and it starts with the results of the job analysis. As you prepare a position announcement, you will extract from the job analysis some of the knowledge, skills, and abilities you expect applicants to possess in order to be eligible for an interview. At the same time, you will need to have an application form, if you so desire, and it is wise to organize an information kit that you can place on a Web site so that applicants understand the purpose, structure, and goal of the business. Once the announcement and information kit are completed, you proceed to advertise the position. Managing the applications will be influenced mostly by the number you receive and whether you have decided to acknowledge receipt of each application. With the effectiveness of the Internet, more people are likely to submit resumes or e-portfolios

Table 7.2 Key Questions to Consider Based on Initial Job Analysis

Factor	Questions
Amount of work	Do you require the position to be full time, part time, temporary, or contract? What are the needs of the business? If part time or temporary, is there merit in looking at cooperative education programs through universities and colleges?
Working conditions	What are the expectations in terms of the combination of skills, abilities, and knowledge? Will they be entry level or have supervisory duties in the absence of the owner? Will the incumbent be required to work a split shift or expected to be readily available for overtime? If so, how frequently?
Search strategy	In light of the skill level, should the recruitment effort be targeting the newsletters of professional organizations, online employment listings, university placement offices, newspapers, Internet list servers, job fairs, the referrals of business contacts or employees, and other sources? Consider this question: How would suitable candidates generally get job information? What would be the primary source of information for suitable candidates in regard to the employment opportunity you have available?
Start date	What will be the start date? How much time do you have to complete a search and to fill the position? Is there a significant cost in not filling the job by the target dates? Perhaps the person you want is not readily available. Are there others who can help in the search process? Who is best suited to serve on the selection team or to be on the interview panel?

Adapted from M. Beauregard and M. Fitzgerald, 2000, *Hiring, managing and keeping the best: The complete Canadian guide for employers* (Toronto: McGraw-Hill).

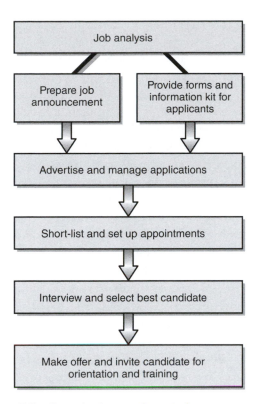

Figure 7.5 Steps in the recruitment plan.

electronically, and this can greatly assist in the communication process.

Once the application process is closed, you need to shortlist and set up job interviews. The interview with each candidate should be carefully prepared so you have sufficient information to select the best person for the job. The final step is to make an offer to the successful applicant. It may be important to make a *superior* offer to a specific person much in the same fashion you make a *superior* offer to your target markets. This is especially critical for stealing away talented persons from other firms who will form key members of your business team during the start-up phase of a company. A company can offer profit sharing as one alternative to a very high initial salary. **Profit sharing** is the potential for a key staff person to earn much more than the base salary by working very hard and making the company successful. Examples of profit sharing range from year-end bonuses based on performance, to stock options, to actual employee-owned companies. Stock options are the option to buy stock at a fixed lower price in the future. These profit-sharing options provide an extra incentive to work because if the company wins, the employee wins.

Once your offer has been accepted, you will probably want to identify what orientation or training activities are scheduled to welcome your new employee to your team. When Bob Wendling of Blue Water Pool Management Inc. reflected on 25 years of managing seasonal staff, he offered specific advice on the importance of establishing management practices that will reinforce reliable communication among staff. (See Spotlight On Blue Water Pool Management, Inc.)

Building your team and staff require that you follow a legal recruitment process. Your goal in the hiring process is to hire people who will be with you for some time. For this to occur, there needs to be a match of their characteristics with those of the position description and appropriate compensation. A most important step in the interviewing of applicants is recognizing there is a legal way to get information about their reasons for applying, their problem-solving skills, their personality, and how well they might work with your team. See the following list for hiring cautions and other sensitive issues.

- Protect privacy of employee information.
- You cannot gather information about or discriminate based on
  - nationality,
  - race,
  - age,
  - gender,
  - religion,
  - ethnicity or skin color,
  - disability, or
  - pregnancy.
- Provide equal-opportunity employment.
- Check for citizenship and work visa.
- Conduct background checks for sensitive positions (for employee screening services, see www.avert.com or www.order.choicepointinc.com).
- Hire as "employment at will."
- Ensure a drug-free workplace.

Today, the United States is the only major industrial power that maintains a general employment-at-will rule. Canada, France, Germany, Great Britain, Italy, Japan, and Sweden all have statutory provisions that require employers to show good cause before discharging employees.

CONTRACTING FOR PROFESSIONAL SERVICES

When seeking additional help, you can choose to have the required skills provided under contract or by an employee. The most common functions to be contracted out involve specialized services or projects that are task specific such as filing of annual taxes, some bookkeeping, journal ledgers, and legal matters. The most common reason for hiring employees is to have them available on an hourly basis (e.g., sales) so they can be continually involved with the delivery of either the goods or services that are the core of your business. Selecting an independent contractor or employee is not a process to be rushed because it could be very costly if not carried out in a systematic and careful manner.

There are both advantages and disadvantages to utilizing independent contractors versus employees in your business. But first it is important to know the legal differences between the two, otherwise you may be subject to large fines by state or provincial employment agencies and the U.S. Internal Revenue Service or Revenue Canada. Figure 7.6 provides guidelines for determining if a person is an employee or an independent contractor. A true **independent contractor** provides his own tools (e.g., computers, rafts, climbing gear), sets his own hours, has specific work tasks, and provides his own workers' compensation insurance and federal tax identification number. Check with the IRS and state or provincial employment agencies for specific rules. There should always be a written contract for every independent contractor. Figure 7.7 provides examples of the components of a contract with an independent contractor.

Using independent contractors offers many advantages: You save money by not having to pay employment taxes and workers' compensation insurance; you can shop around for the services that best match your existing short-term needs; you can negotiate for payments for those services in a manner that best suits your cash flow; and you can secure the expertise you need in a timely manner. Independent professionals

Many facilities often hire personal trainers or activity coordinators as independent contractors to provide services directly on behalf of the wellness center or resort.

Bill Crump/Brand X Pictures

- Work is task or project driven.
- Worker sets own hours.
- Pay is by the job, not by the hour.
- Worker provides own equipment, tools.
- Contractors must normally have their own workers' compensation insurance and file their own taxes.
- There is a written contract.

Figure 7.6 Criteria for determining if a person is an independent contractor.

- Employee compensation
- Method of payment
- Ownership: trade secrets and client lists
- Holds employer harmless
- Termination at will of either party
- Arbitration, attorney's fees, and settlement costs
- Role of employee
- Best effort required
- Noncompete clause
- When they must report
- Must adhere to employee policy manual
- Satisfactory performance or termination by company

Figure 7.7 Contract components for an independent contractor.

can provide you with the precise skills you need at the time you need them, with no promise of long-term employment. If you have learned of an opportunity to enjoy free publicity but need a marketing professional to help you frame a story that will showcase your business in the best light, you can purchase that help quickly. It is not at all uncommon for new businesses to make mistakes in marketing in general and particularly in choosing the best advertising of their services.

Some new RET owners might be tempted to make almost all their workers be independent contractors, the so-called virtual organization. But there are also some clear limitations and disadvantages of independent contractors: lack of worker control by employer;

a contractor does not have to work more than stated in a contract; lack of flexibility (for employer) in job tasks that can be done by contractor; lack of loyalty to company; lack of continuity and history of service; and they are more likely to steal your clients. The bottom line is your company will still need frontline staff to be there *all* the time, who have the flexibility and training to do whatever needs to be done to serve the client. And in many cases those workers are employees, not subcontractors. However, European-based companies and international cruise ships frequently use contracted frontline staff.

THE CULTURE OF THE WORKPLACE

Whether big or small, a business exists for a reason, and that reason is most evident in the mission statement (chapter 3). The mission statement helps to create a business culture. The culture of a business provides a basis for attracting, recruiting, and hiring the people that will help advance the vision and be the most successful in your work environment. The leadership ability of the manager sets the tone for the work environment and the actions of all involved to help maintain it. Finklestein (2005) has examined qualities he believes successful managers tend to have in common. The qualities he notes are balance in work and life, a team of advisers, and attitude.

- *Balance in work and life.* It's said time is money, and every person has 1,440 minutes in any given day. Leaders in business know that how employees spend their time directly affects how successful the business can become. It is common for business owners to integrate their social lives into their business lives. Thus a client who purchases a product today is later invited to the waterfront cabin the following weekend. In this scenario, clients become close acquaintances, and coworkers become like family. Over time, business managers build their lives around their businesses, and it's very difficult to distinguish between their social lives and their business lives. But to remain healthy and have successful personal relationships, there must be balance between work and leisure time.

- *Team of advisers.* Business owners know they cannot do it all. Therefore they seek to create a team of trusted advisers within the company which represents the executive committee consisting of top managers who will challenge them, ask critical questions, and hold them accountable for actions taken in the course of managing the business.

- *Attitude toward team members.* The owner of the company must have a positive can-do attitude and accept 100 percent of the responsibility for the results of his business decisions. However, when success is achieved, it is appropriate to give credit to others within the organization. Without exception, the most successful business owners understand that it's all about people: hiring and retaining the right people, replacing ineffective people, and providing the necessary resources for employees to master their tasks. The managerial duty is to get the best people to work and collaborate with you and to put in place management strategies that ensure your cast of capable individuals work together and contribute to the success of the business.

DEVELOPING A MANAGERIAL STYLE

With the search engines available today for published material of all kinds in libraries and bookstores, Web sites, blogs, and other electronic media, anyone searching words such as *management* or *managerial style* will find volumes of information. For most people, it will be difficult to know where to begin with the range of material. There are as many ideas as to the best theory, or practices, as there are authors writing about them. When it comes to reducing the risk of making a fatal management mistake, there is no substitute for some form of progressive practical experience.

There may be, however, a combination of sensible ways to approach the personal task of strengthening managerial capability. These approaches would include the following strategies:

- Find yourself a mentor willing to work with you for a specific period of time as you implement the business plan you authored.
- Complete online self-assessment tests to examine your strengths and weaknesses in specific areas of management and team building.
- Participate in formal management workshops or courses offered by "business incubator" centers or at a nearby college or university.
- Identify an experienced business manager, discuss your aspirations for experience, and then

work for this person to gain firsthand practical work experience.

Each of these options could be combined or effectively integrated to some degree. The exception perhaps is the last one, since you would be working with a second party's business plan and under the conditions that were agreed on. Additional details to be considered in the case of the first three options are now described.

MENTORING

Mentoring is an option for a less-experienced person. Ten useful steps are identified at the following Web site: www.secretsofsuccess.com/article/rdmentor.html. You can either select someone you know or someone you have never met. Next you would approach the person with a letter stating your achievements and your aspiration to establish a mentoring relationship, and ask for 30 minutes to meet with her to discuss the mentoring opportunities. It might be wise to indicate why you are asking her to be a mentor. Perhaps she is considered a good role model or a good listener, or she would be candid with you in terms of putting managerial skills into practice. Selecting someone you have a lot in common with is not the best strategy because your goal is to address weaknesses or unknown areas. Instead, seek out someone who possesses strengths you lack. This means you would find someone likely to challenge you to acquire new strengths instead of reinforcing existing ones.

EXPLORING YOUR CAPABILITY WITH SELF-ASSESSMENT TOOLS

Many brief online assessment instruments or tools can be found on the Internet, but the relative quality and measurement behind the assessments will be unknown. Two assessment instruments that are identified here have a substantial body of literature about them and address two different aspects of leadership and management. Generally these assessment tools are readily available to you from various sources, including online.

Blake Mouton Managerial Grid

Drs. Robert Blake and Jane Mouton are two accomplished pioneers well known for examining the role

There are a variety of management and leadership self-assessment programs which can be completed online by each team member.

that personal values play in a manager's preferred style of leadership. The methodology of the **Blake Mouton Managerial Grid** (www.gridinternational. com/values2.html) is founded on proven theory of human behavior, and the online self-assessment tool evaluates the leadership style most valued by people completing the test. When presented with specific management scenarios, you will be asked to select one and rate it, with the end result revealing your preferred course of action in the case of 60 or more practical managerial situations. The results of the combined choices then place you in one of seven positions on the "management grid." Your dominant classification on the management grid can then be examined and interpreted more in depth by consulting their book *The Power to Change*. The self-assessment information permits a prospective or current manager to anticipate how others may respond to his management style together with the strengths and weaknesses of the approach in team situations.

Myers-Briggs Type Indicator

The **Myers-Briggs Type Indicator (MBTI)** has many individual and team-building applications. It is often administered to university students to assist them in career counseling at the campus career center. The most important application in terms of managerial duties involves proactive leadership and the team-building process. The team-building aspects and team-development application of using MBTI relates to distinct benefits of improving communication, enhancing team problem-solving skills, valuing diversity in team decision making, and resolving conflict. These benefits are realized when each team member understands their own type and the consequences of their preferred style on the tasks assigned to and shared by the team. A half-day or full-day workshop can make a notable difference in team performance and the leadership capability of the manager to delegate tasks. Another assessment tool of a similar nature called True Colors is administered in a similar way. It focuses on building communication skills, valuing differences, strengthening teams, and creating a productive work environment.

SUMMARY

This chapter examines the terminology, duties, and common pitfalls that are prevalent in business management and managerial leadership. The overriding personnel question in regard to building a business team is what is the plan for securing the most capable talent needed in every key function or area of responsibility? The effort devoted to addressing that question will be time well spent. The initial examination of the personnel strategy might include the following questions:

- How will the business be organized, and what positions will be established?

- What are the skills needed in each of the positions?

- When should steps be taken to fill the positions needed for the business team?

- What leadership strategies and practices will be put in place to strengthen and build the business team?

The one asset your business has, that your competitors do not have, is you. Management of a small business is very dependent on the talent of the manager and presumably the authors of the business plan. The hats you may wear in management will cross the spectrum at one point or another. Of course when you start up a business, it is important to have financing in place, reliable details on existing and potential customers, a plan to get the messages in the hands of the target market, and suppliers that will help you with what you need. Although all these tasks are important, the most important is how well you have prepared the management section of your business plan because it influences all other business functions. An examination of figure 7.1 reveals the spectrum of managerial duties that will arise as a business plan is implemented. Preparation for these duties is important, and it is worthwhile to consider the advice that "the skills to be a good employee are not the same skills required to be a good entrepreneur" (Kiyosaki, 2005, p. 4).

For team-building experience, MBTI or True Colors can be an effective strategy to build rapport, camaraderie, and effective communication among members. For knowledge about managerial style, the Blake Mouton Managerial Grid can offer valuable information for understanding the values underlying a preferred style.

 Check out the online student resource for additional material, including case studies, Web links, and more.

Chapter 8

Service Quality Management and Customer Loyalty

Learning Objectives

After reading this chapter you will be able to

- describe the importance of customer service in commercial recreation, events, and tourism;
- discuss today's service imperative;
- explain the cost of delivering poor service;
- evaluate service principles;
- describe the process of winning back clients through service recovery;
- understand the importance of developing and maintaining relationships and loyalty; and
- evaluate RET service, why it is needed, and how to do it.

Key Terms

added value

client safety orientation

customer loyalty

empowerment

experience

experiential dimension

mass customization

moment of truth

relationship

service

total quality management

Imagine this scenario:

Your spa is celebrating its third year, and business is brisk. You have just left your office after being engrossed in paperwork and company financial data and are walking past the reservations area, when a customer you have never seen before asks if you are the manager. You are tempted to keep going, but she seems concerned about something, so you ask how you can be of help. She apologizes and tells you that she just wanted you to know how great an experience she had with your company today, and she has been a client with you for several years. This time the guest brought along four friends who were so impressed with their treatment that they want to book an even bigger "girls week at the spa" with you next fall. They all gushed with praise for an employee you hardly knew. Interestingly, they did not even mention the brand new spa equipment you had proudly installed last month. Pleasantly surprised, you ask the guest again for the name of the employee whose service was so outstanding, and then you thank them.

When you get back to the office, your assistant asks you to take a minute to look at something. He gives you two piles of letters received from past clients. The first pile contains letters with positive comments: My therapist was spontaneous, very informative, on top of things, and she and I became good friends; the staff were so friendly and everyone helped me relax; the masseur I always request has gotten to know me so well that she is always able to understand my needs and goes out of her way to make me feel good; the spa treatments I had today were one of the most relaxing times in my life; the facilities and equipment were incredibly clean and just as spectacular as promised, but what really made it special was the terrific staff, so you can be sure we will be back; and we had a fantastic time with you last year and wanted to bring our friends with us this year. The second, smaller pile has letters with comments that are almost painful to read: I demand my money back because I never got what your reservationist promised; when I complained, the staff person gave me a curt response and then ignored me, so I am going to bad-mouth your so-called spa to everyone I know; I expected personalized service, but all I got was a masseur who cared more about going home than about listening to my health needs; the hot tub area was so dirty and gross, I am never coming back here again; and I was really upset that you were not able to keep my reservation at the scheduled time, but then the front desk attendant apologized, explained the problem, and offered me an upgrade and the next available time slot. After you finish reading, you think to yourself, *What is really making the spa successful?* Based on comments from guests, it is the quality of service delivered by your staff, the way your staff handle client complaints, and a team effort at service recovery that has led to loyalty and return business. Repeat visitation appears to be more related to the value added by your staff and, although still very important, less related to the flashy new facility you built.

The opening scenario is common in the RET industry, and it demonstrates the importance of staff and customer-friendly systems in the provision of quality service. In this chapter we explore what is considered superior service, the importance of service, costs of poor service, different levels and types of service, the underlying concept of staging experiences, features of outstanding service, service principles, managing emotionally charged client situations, recovering from service mistakes, and ways of developing client relationships and building loyalty. We offer examples from segments of the RET industry.

Superior service does not just happen on its own: The principles for superior service must be followed, customer-friendly systems must be established, and staff must be trained. Recreation, event, and tourism companies, more than almost any type of business, must provide positive and memorable experiences, not just a generic product. Another critical element of service is evaluation and dedication by management to change based on consumer feedback. If these things are done consistently well, then it breeds **customer loyalty**. Many of the customers quoted in the opening scenario indicate they have developed and want to maintain a relationship with the company, which will lead to positive word-of-mouth promotion and future purchases. These are good examples of what service means in this industry and how it affects customer loyalty. Small RET businesses live and die by outstanding customer service and loyalty. It is typical for more than 70 percent of RET sales to be what are called "returns and referrals," clients who are satisfied and returning again to purchase or are suggesting that their friends try your company. The chapter ends with a discussion of how to integrate quality service, developing relationships, and increasing customer loyalty into your business planning.

WHAT IS SERVICE IN COMMERCIAL RECREATION, EVENTS, AND TOURISM?

Entrepreneurial recreation, event, and tourism businesses are considered part of the service industry, according to chapter 1. But people working in the industry often have only a vague notion of what constitutes superior customer service. Yet a company's beginning, profitability, and continued existence depend on a deep understanding of not only what service means but also how to provide it, how to recover when there is poor service, and how to objectively evaluate the organization's level of service. As you will see later in this chapter, superior guest service can position your company in the minds of the consumers in a positive light and greatly influence their relationship and loyalty with your company.

SERVICE IMPERATIVE

Consumers are no longer satisfied with just the purchase of, for example, a new fishing rod from a fly fishing shop or a plan for a two-day festival from an event planner; they demand services that provide more than these purchases. There is a clear link between the physical product (the fishing rod) and the intangible personal service that goes along with and adds value to the product. Before your guests arrive, and certainly once they are at your recreation business, they expect you to know in advance what they will likely need and want. Moreover, they will expect your staff to be ready to provide it. If customers believe there is a large gap between what was expected and the benefits they enjoyed, then most customers will not complain to you or your staff—but they will never come back and will give negative feedback about your business to their friends.

COSTS OF POOR SERVICE

Service today is commonly so inadequate that you might think consumers have come to accept it. But poor service really can hurt a business, and surprisingly, much of the damage is not readily visible to the owners. Research cited by Bly (2002) found that:

- 26 out of 27 unhappy customers fail to report it to the business;
- 67 percent of those will not come back;
- each one tells an average of 9 persons, who then tell others (20 total); and
- in comparison, a satisfied customer tells an average of only 2 persons.

What are the implications of these statistics? If a business that consistently provides poor service does not have any idea it is considered below par, it will never again see the majority of dissatisfied customers, and those unhappy ex-clients will spread negative word of mouth. This level of negative word of mouth could potentially overwhelm increases from promotions, leading to a slow and agonizing company death.

A massage therapist giving treatment is an example of personalized service.

PhotoDisc

BENEFITS OF SUPERIOR SERVICE

What are the benefits of superior service? The opening scenario provides some immediate insights, but considerable research has been done on this topic. Research has found new customer acquisition, usage, and retention were greatly influenced by the customer service level, and companies rated high on service have the following characteristics (Bell and Zemke, 2007; Nam, Manchanda, and Chintagunta, 2007):

- Kept customers longer (50 percent longer or more)
- Have lower sales and marketing costs (20-40 percent lower)
- Experience higher return on sales (7-12 percent higher)
- Have better net profits (7-17 percent better)

Superior service is of utmost importance, especially to the small business.

These studies also indicate that businesses with superior levels of service could more easily differentiate their business from the competition, charged more, had high profit margins, and enjoyed stronger customer loyalty compared with businesses with lower levels of service. You cannot compete with the big box retailers on price, but you can compete with them on service.

In summary, superior service is of utmost importance, especially to a small business. It differentiates the company from its competition and generates positive word-of-mouth promotion. This free promotion leads to more loyal customers and lowers marketing costs, which result in higher profits.

BASIC SERVICE TYPES

As an RET service provider, you need to understand the different types of service and the fundamentals of service so you can manage your operations more successfully. When you provide a **service**, you per-

form work for another through helpful or professional activity. Service in RET often refers to anticipating the customers' wants and delivering desired actions in a manner that exceeds their expectations. In the manufacturing economic sector, a tangible good is the *product*. But in the service sector, the "product" always includes an intangible service. There are three main types of service, often with both tangible and intangible elements:

- Fix things
- Provide assistance
- Add value

The *fix things* type of service in the commercial recreation, event, and tourism industry includes businesses that repair customer products, such as ski repair shops or recreational vehicle mechanics. These are essential services, although not what the consumer expects to need or is building a dream vacation around, but when something breaks they are indispensable. See the green tip for a discussion on how to maintain or improve service and at the same time reduce toxins.

Barry Gnyp/Upper Cut/Getty Images

Green Tip

Maintain or Improve Service Levels While Removing Toxic Substances

Most RET businesses use some type of toxic substance in their workplace. These can range from toilet bowl cleaners to pesticides on a golf course. They can be used in operations, but frequently they are involved in maintenance activities. Often you do not realize their dangers. Drain cleaners are caustic, and they can damage the kidneys, liver, digestive system, skin, and central nervous system. Pesticides can be extremely toxic to humans and wild animals, impairing the central nervous system and causing cancer. Even with proper operator safety equipment, they are still released into the environment and can affect unintended life forms. Only the most toxic substances are regulated by federal and state laws, but the majority of other chemicals have never been thoroughly tested for toxicity. According to the U.S. Environmental Protection Agency, toxic substances pose a huge but largely unverified threat to the environment. The keys to reducing the critical problem of toxic materials are to substitute less-harmful alternatives, and where no reasonable alternative exists, to use the least dangerous application methods and amounts. A good example of what can be accomplished is the organic golf course maintenance movement. Many of the top golf courses are certified green courses. The renowned Vineyard Golf Course in Martha's Vineyard, Massachusetts, for example, won the 2008 President's Award for Environmental Stewardship from the Golf Course Superintendents Association of America (see www.vineyardgolf.com). The course has eliminated the use of the most toxic types of pesticides and treats turf with natural fertilizers, eliminating use of chemical fertilizers. This shows that you can maintain high service levels and a strong reputation while significantly reducing the application of toxic substances.

There are a number of things a small RET business can do to work toward a goal of reducing toxic materials. Listed here are just a few examples.

- Wash with washing soda (sodium carbonate) instead of toxic cleansers.
- Use pressed-wood products with low or no formaldehyde.
- Remove items that attract pests to reduce the need for chemicals.
- Take hazardous wastes to designated local collection sites.
- Choose pump-spray containers instead of aerosols.
- Ask for unbleached paper products.
- Purchase mercury-free thermometers.
- Pull weeds to reduce the need for herbicides.

In addition to these noncommercial alternatives, several companies, such as Ecolab (www.ecolab.com) and Sun & Earth (www.sunandearth.com), specialize in nontoxic maintenance products and systems.

The *provide assistance* type of service often involves professionals who can plan, prepare, or direct a person in his leisure pursuits. Examples of these services in the tourism field include event planners, travel agents, concierges, and information center staff. These professionals are frequently used and essential in many recreation settings. But almost any staff person who is visible to the public may be asked to play this service role. This suggests that customer service knowledge and training are essential for all employees of a service business, including maintenance staff.

Added value service providers give additional benefits to someone who has purchased a tangible good or, in other cases, enhance the visitor experience. In today's world of big-box discount retailers such as Wal-Mart and huge international chains such as Hilton resorts, adding value through customer service is critical for small businesses. Value can be added to a tangible product or service through many means. Here is just one value-added scenario, using a fly fishing specialty shop, looking at various stages in the purchase and activity process: Having a friendly staff person available to make a client feel appreciated when she arrives (at the fly fishing shop), helping her find the right product (e.g., fishing rod and reel), getting the correct fit (fishing rod flexibility and action), setting it up (winding fly line on the reel), offering (fly fishing) lessons on how to use it, providing guided (fly fishing) trips in the local area where she can use her purchase, having expedited repair service when there is a problem (rod cracks), providing exclusive offers for past clients (first chance to get new gear on sale before store opens to public), and offering opportunities to socialize with fellow clients and staff with similar interests (an event with other women fly fishers). An example in the event profession is where a company assigns an event planner experienced in a proposed event type to a client. This person antici-

pates accurately the size and type of venue that would be best for the event sponsor, knows the alternative locations in the region very well, and suggests the best venue for a specialized event. He might also design the decor that accentuates the venue features. Finally, the planner identifies vendors (electricians, florists, and so on) who are skilled at crafting the venue into a memorable event location. The end results are greatly impressed event guests and added value for the event sponsor, compared with using a rather bland hotel meeting room.

As you can see, all of these additional actions by the small recreation or event planning business add considerable client value. It is a matter of total value received, not just initial cost, that a consumer takes into account. It is less likely that a person could get the same total value at a big discount store, even though the initial price is lower. She could pick the wrong product on her own versus the perfect item at a small local specialty shop. The consumer is also

Joel Sheagren/Aurora/Getty Images

Offering guided fly fishing trips and lessons adds value to the basic fly rod product.

likely to get more-personalized local knowledge and prompt service at that small specialty shop than at a franchise of a multinational company located in the community.

Another perspective on different types of service is described by Peters (1987) and Kandampully, Mok, and Sparks (2001). They found that tourist services can be viewed at several levels. Figure 8.1 illustrates the concept of service levels and how they affect the prices that can be charged, which impacts profitability.

1. The *basic* service level has minimal facilities and outdated processes (e.g., winter sports area with a few slow short lifts, minimal skiing and snowboarding trails, minimal lessons, and a small lodge). Facilities and services are below average. Guests would be willing to visit only because it was nearby or the price (lift ticket) was very inexpensive. These types of service providers are disappearing because they are uncompetitive and unprofitable.

2. The *anticipated* service level is what might be found at the typical service provider. A person (snowboarder) would not dream about visiting this business, but he may patronize it because it offers some value (reasonable lift ticket prices, some close-by challenging runs, a good school for lessons at all levels of skill). This level of business can be quite profitable if competition is not too great.

3. The *augmented* service has added value over the expected level because it has superior facilities (high-speed four-person detachable chairlifts) and many amenities (complete ski school, modern spacious lodge with excellent meals and entertainment). Visitors are willing to pay a higher price for the augmented level. This business type often has the highest market share and profitability.

4. The *possible* product is the augmented service with leading-edge innovations that customers have not yet foreseen and no other competitors have developed. The RET business does everything professionally possible to exceed customer wants (e.g., heated chairlift seats, pay-per-run ticket pricing). These are the providers that potential users dream about visiting and that receive a tremendous amount of free media publicity. As such they can charge the very highest rates and have the highest profitability.

The demand for *basic service* comes when the consumer has no other choice and little free time. There is greater demand for *anticipated service* providers because they offer value and better equipment, amenities, and service. Demand for *augmented service* providers is always high because they have superior service and many amenities. Demand for *possible products* can grow rapidly once they exceed customer expectations by offering a "dream" destination or service, with the most advanced equipment and facilities and the most personalized service.

In summary, there are different types and levels of service in the commercial recreation, event, and tourism industry. The basic type and level has a large influence on the nature of the service, its importance in the industry, demand for the service, and profitability for the service provider.

STAGING EXPERIENCES

Tourism, event planning, and recreation services are primarily intangible and perishable. They may have few physical features and cannot be touched, stored, heard, or felt in the same manner as a manufactured product. They are perishable in the sense that they cannot be produced and stored for later sale. They tend to be delivered on demand. Seldom, however, are all recreation services purely intangible. Most likely it is a combination of tangible opportunity (e.g., ecolodge room and meals) and intangible elements (e.g., friendliness of staff, making your stay easy, or learning about wildlife in the area). This mix of tangible products and intangible service features, generated by service provider staff for an individual person, is the cornerstone of the recreation, event, and tourism service industry.

Experiences are intangible products created simultaneously by both the provider and the guest. This refers to the feelings, or the **experiential dimension**, generated in the consumer's mind because of the leisure service. An **experience** is defined as the

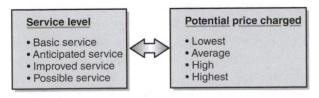

Figure 8.1 Service levels and potential price charged.
Adapted from T. Peters, 1987, *Thriving on chaos: Handbook for a management revolution* (New York: Knopf), 114.

process of personally observing, encountering, or undergoing something. Each leisure encounter has affective dimensions. Was the vacation exciting or boring? Did it build family bonding? Was it restful? The higher the positive emotional response generated the better. A comparison between offering a service and creating an experience can also be seen when we focus on the role of the seller and the buyer, attributes we associate with each, and the nature of the outcomes from the perspective of the customer.

The key element in differentiating between a service and the experience is the need for the active involvement of the guest in the latter. A service tends to provide an expected benefit for a target market, whereas an experience is created by the active participation of the guest in response to the staging of the engagement by the commercial operator. The operator functions as the stager of the engagement, and when the guest responds as an active participant, then the experiential dimension has the ability to transform the person's emotional, physical, and spiritual state. The collective sensations create a memorable experience that fulfills the psychic need of the guest that participated in its creation. Quality takes on an intrinsic and individual level of satisfaction, which a guest is willing to repurchase and share with others.

An important concept in service quality is the "experience ladder" because it conceptualizes the effects of service level, product differentiation, and price charged (Pine and Gilmore, 1999) (see figure 8.2). At the bottom level is a "commodity" that has very low product differentiation and price. The consumer can find little difference between the services of various companies, and their product is considered generic. At the next level upward, a "good" provides more distinction between companies, and the average price received is greater than at the commodity level. At the "goods and service" rung on the service ladder, company products are truly distinct in the minds of the consumers, and they are more willing to pay and can more easily find what they want. The top level is an "experience" that creates a very positive, hoped-for emotional state in the guest. The goal of a recreation business is to move its service up the experience ladder, from commodity to experience, so as to differentiate its service from competitors and be

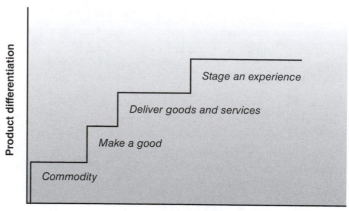

Figure 8.2 The service ladder and effects on product differentiation and price that can be charged.

Adapted, by permission, from B.J. Pine and J.H. Gilmore, 1999, *The experience economy: Work is theatre & every business a stage* (Boston: Harvard Business Publishing), 166.

able to profit more.

A key aspect of the service ladder concept is customization to meet individual desires. Consumers increasingly want it *their way*, not necessarily the way your company likes to do it. They are not willing to settle for one product applied to the mass market; rather, they want your service individualized to the extent possible for their unique wants. The more you customize, the more desirable it is to the client. However, the other side of customization is that it can make services very expensive and thereby price many potential buyers out of the market. So Pine and Gilmore present the idea of **mass customization** to represent the concept that service providers offer a range of service alternatives that allows consumers to mix, match, and individualize their experience to their desires, while keeping the price reasonable. Coffee is a frequently used example. A cup of plain coffee is a commodity, fetches a low price, and can be found at many locations. It is hard to make any money selling a plain cup of coffee. An average (better quality) cup of coffee is expected and costs a slight amount more. But if, like Starbucks and local specialty coffee shops, you can provide an array of high-quality coffee beans and many flavorings, the business can customize that cup of coffee to the unique preferences of each coffee drinker, offering as many as 300 variations. At the experience stage you are not just selling a custom cup of coffee, you are also setting the stage for a relaxed atmosphere to meet friends; complete a work task on your laptop via wireless access; and interact with the staff, who become almost like friends. This range of engagement creates an experience that is beyond just providing a cup of coffee, and people are willing to pay much more for it and return again.

COMMON FEATURES OF OUTSTANDING SERVICE PROVIDERS

A question that is commonly asked by entrepreneurs and owners wishing to grow their companies is whether there are service provision attributes that are universal to outstanding service companies. A number of researchers (Kandampully, Mok, and Sparks, 2001; Janes, 2006) have discovered three underlying factors of exceptional service organizations. A fourth service factor, also described in this section, is particularly germane to the RET industry.

1. A service-oriented company philosophy: a unifying recognition from top to bottom that service is important, valued, and rewarded. It is management's responsibility to instill this philosophy in all staff and operationalize it in planning and everyday guest interactions. The Ritz-Carlton resort company is well known for its fastidious adherence to the motto of "ladies and gentlemen serving ladies and gentlemen."

2. Customer-friendly systems: systems developed from a thorough investigation into how to make the entire customer service cycle as easy and convenient for the customer as possible and the implementation of these plans. Examples of company systems include the ease of accessing and reliability of the company Web site, record-keeping accuracy, refund policies, timely delivery, and adequate parking or shuttles.

3. Customer-oriented frontline staff. Almost every study of service quality points to the critical importance of frontline staff, such as reservationists, ride operators, servers, and guides, in making or breaking a quality customer experience. It may be better to have no one available than to have a substandard staff person. Examples of frequently cited poor frontline service include failing to greet the customer, giving inaccurate information, talking to another employee while the customer is waiting, displaying rude behavior, having an uncaring attitude or a sloppy appearance, and using high-pressure sales tactics.

Inherent in many challenging recreation activities, such as rafting, mountain biking, and snowboarding, are risks that cannot be removed without destroying the motivation for engaging in the activity. So a fourth and uniquely important characteristic of outstanding adventure recreation and tourism businesses is **client safety orientation**. This orientation means the company puts guest safety as the number one priority. If it is apparent to guests that your organization has done everything it can reasonably do to prevent injuries and maintain the fun and challenge, then an injured guest is not only much less likely to start a lawsuit but also much more likely to come back again and tell his friends about his excitement and your outstanding response.

Customer- and safety-oriented frontline staff are particularly critical to the successful RET organization. The inappropriate action of just one employee can overcome the benefits of expensive computer systems, million-dollar facilities, and dozens of staff. Bell and Zemke (2007) found that, as a service provider, you must do the following:

- Find and keep high-quality staff. Exceptional service starts with exceptional frontline staff.
- Hire frontline staff with great care (no panic hiring).
- Provide extensive training.
- Offer strong management support, as frontline jobs can be very challenging.
- Involve staff in decisions that affect their jobs, and empower them to make decisions and take responsibility for their actions.
- Do everything you can to retain your best staff.
- Provide opportunities for advancement of your best staff.
- Recognize and reward frontline staff contributions, and celebrate your successes.
- Be a visionary, a strong role model, and a leader that promotes your team's cause. Be energizing and inspirational.

These service principles are exemplified by many successful RET businesses. Spotlight On describes the Yangshuo Mountain Retreat, located near Guilin, China, and the unique services they provide.

Yangshuo Mountain Retreat

Location

The Yangshuo Mountain Retreat (YMR) is a small ecocultural resort located outside the small tourist city of Yangshuo in Guangxi Province of southwestern China. This area has a dramatic landscape of weathered limestone pinnacles and verdant forests through which the Li River traverses. It has a very rich cultural heritage dating back over 1,000 years and vibrant modern cities, such as Guilin.

Background

Owner Chris Barclay acquired the land rights for 30 years from the government and in 2000 built the 22-room resort. The YMR was conceptualized as a simple ecolodge where American and British expatriates in China could escape from the crowded, polluted megacities. At startup there was no air conditioning, or a Western-style kitchen, or even a computer. But when the retreat grew in popularity, they found it necessary to upgrade facilities. So they added air conditioning, computers and wireless broadband, and a kitchen for cooking local

Ms. Chun (Angel) Li, the front-desk supervisor and clerk, works five or six days a week.

Patrick T. Tierney

as well as healthful Western foods. Today the rooms remain simple in layout with limited amenities (there is no TV), but they are very comfortable and decorated with local artwork. Plenty of cultural authenticity, spectacular scenery, and friendly service have drawn people from all over the world. The resort has a wide international underground reputation and has consistently been rated the best accommodation in this region of China by tripadvisor.com.

Products and Services

The Yangshuo Mountain Retreat features 22 traditionally furnished rooms, a restaurant serving both local and Western foods, a comfortable dining room, a small bar, mountain bike rentals, guided hikes and tours, tai chi lessons, massage, and access to swimming and boating on the Yulong River. It employs a friendly staff of residents from the area. In some cases these families have lived in the region for over 500 years. A good example of the outstanding service is Ms. Chun (Angel) Li, the front-desk supervisor and clerk. She often is the first person a new arrival hears or sees at the resort. Very fluent in both Chinese and English, Angel answers the phone, makes room arrangements, and advises guests on things to do and places to visit in the area. Her warm personality, outstanding adherence to guest service, and keen knowledge of the area all contribute to making an outstanding guest experience. Her intimate knowledge of the area comes from the fact that she is of the 25th generation of the Zhao clan and was born in a nearby Ming Dynasty fishing village. This might be enough, but Angel does all these things while living with osteogenesis imperfecta (OI), a disease that causes dwarfism and bones that break very easily. She was the first hired staff member at YMR and is provided with an assistant, room and board, and a salary at the resort. Angel's guest service seems to be an important element of guests' experience at YMR and the main reason they return.

Business Advice and Plans

The resort's top rating on social media sites is a reflection of the high level of personal service that is provided to guests at the resort. There are many comments in their guest book and on their blog about how guests were impressed with the friendliness, helpfulness, and quality of service by the bilingual staff. The importance of service is higher in this remote, culturally distinct location where the native language is not spoken by the majority of international guests.

Another key point illustrated by YMR is the ethical and financial commitment to helping overcome the serious disease of OI. YMR owner Chris Barclay founded the Chinese-U.S. Medical Foundation (CUMF) to conduct research and help children with brittle bone disease across China. They donate 5 percent of their profits to CUMF each year. Through these efforts Barclay and YMR have sought to inform others of the disease and provide accommodations so that staff members with the disease can work there. Although his initial motivations for hiring were altruistic, the high level of service provided by Ms. Li has paid off financially for the resort.

SERVICE PRINCIPLES

Although services vary with the nature of the client desire, the service type, and the level of service, a number of critical customer service principles apply to any service industry. These are presented here and are followed by a recreation, event, and tourism business profile.

1. View your service quality through the customer's eyes. Left untrained, company employees will often "filter" how they evaluate their service based on their own needs (e.g., they are not feeling well) and the workplace environment (e.g., how their supervisor treats them) rather than what the client thinks. They may rationalize poor service by saying, "We are doing the best job we can." But clients don't care if you are having a "bad day"; they just want what was promised and superior service. So business employees must view every element of their operation through the customer's eyes.

2. There is a cycle of service. An RET firm must be effective at every stage in the cycle to provide an outstanding experience. The service cycle begins when a customer first tries to find out about your business. A critical element is the actual provision of service. It ends temporarily when service is complete and the guest leaves the property. But clients often desire continued contact with your organization—a *relationship* that continues into the future. The cycle ends only when the client decides to end the relationship.

3. Little things mean a great deal. Much of service is not "rocket science"; rather, it consists of many seemingly small things that add up to be very important to the guest.

4. Underpromise and overimplement. Consumers are used to organizations making promises but failing to deliver. So when a recreation business provides not only what was pledged but even more than promised, this engenders a very positive consumer response.

5. Human touch is powerful. According to Allen Tofler (1984), "The more high technology oriented we become the more we crave human touch." By human touch he means not just physical touch (e.g., that of a spa masseur) but also one-on-one, personalized interaction with a service provider. But in the drive to hold down prices through automation, many businesses have taken out much of the human interaction during a service encounter. A lack of staff opportunity to customize the service and respond to individual needs may actually backfire on an organization.

6. Treat customers as an appreciating asset. Studies in restaurants have shown that a regular guest who spends an average of $25 on a meal and often brings friends and acquaintances will directly spend and influence almost $500,000 over a 10-year period. Similar situations can be expected in commercial recreation settings. What would happen if your frontline staff viewed a guest who visits frequently, spends an average amount, and brings friends to your business not as a standard purchase but rather as a valuable appreciating asset? Would the staff act differently toward the customer?

7. Buyers' expectations are progressive. What works today to exceed guest expectations will be overlooked tomorrow because guests expect increasing levels of service.

8. Show enthusiasm toward the customer. Frontline staff must consistently convey to clients that they are very willing to assist them.

9. Keep the establishment clean and employees within company dress and grooming codes.

10. Be flexible to meet individual customer needs. Staff must indicate to guests they are willing and able to change to meet individual desires wherever possible.

11. Make guests feel welcome and appreciated. Many small actions, such as using the guest's name, smiling warmly, and offering a friendly greeting, add up to an initial strong positive feeling about the company.

12. Service should be convenient for the customer. Making service prompt and easy for guests is extremely important.

These 12 customer service principles are very important to RET business success. An excellent example of applying these service principles and forming them into a cohesive service model is Joie de Vivre Hospitality, as described in Spotlight On.

Most of these service principles involve small changes, but sometimes organizations must make dramatic and large-scale changes to increase service quality. A commonly mentioned model that has guided service industry change is the **total quality management** (TQM) approach described by Besterfield (2002). TQM is characterized by a complete

Joie de Vivre Hospitality Service

Location

The Joie de Vivre Hospitality headquarters are located in San Francisco, California. They have hotels, resorts, and campgrounds throughout northern and southern California. Their Web site is www.jdvhotels.com.

Background

Chip Conley, founder of Joie de Vivre (French for "joy of life") Hospitality, started his company at age 26, two years after his university graduation. Starting with the Phoenix, a rock 'n' roll–themed boutique hotel in downtown San Francisco, his company has expanded to 30 properties. They have built a unique collection of lodging establishments in California, each with its own personality, ranging from a luxury campground to the Hotel Kabuki, with a Japanese communal bath theme.

Products and Services

The company has expanded to 35 boutique hotels and one luxury campground. Joie de Vivre has this set of core values:

Create landmark destinations full of soul and personality.

We're in the business of creating dreams.

Every staff member can be the critical starting point for successful business.

Happy, enthusiastic employees translate to strong customer loyalty, which maintains a profitable and sustainable business.

These values are translated into the daily operations of the company and guide its managers led by JDV owner Chip Conley. These are expressed in their Heart of Joie de Vivre service model (see figure).

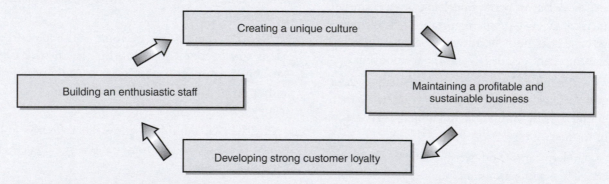

Joie de Vivre Hospitality service model.
Adapted with permission of John Wiley & Sons, Inc.

This model suggests that a profitable and sustainable business must first create a unique corporate culture. Profit will follow once employees are engaged and loyal to the company. A key element in creating engaged and loyal employees is the corporate culture, or the way staff feel about their work climate and the way they are expected to behave toward other workers and clients. This philosophy and culture can translate into enthusiastic employees through training and fair financial incentive and rewards. But the managers found that employees need more than just money; they desire recognition for the contributions to the guests and the company if they are to be responsive to customers and loyal to the organization. Their strong belief is that money alone does not motivate to provide superior service. Building an enthusiastic workforce comes from other staff and especially a supervisor who shows respect, fairness, pride, and camaraderie at work. Making it a fun place to work has been shown to affect staff enthusiasm. Working for a socially and environmentally responsible company also can create a sense of pride in an organization.

If employees are enthusiastic, have pride, and are engaged with co-workers and guests, then they develop a passion to exceed the customer desires. When staff are inspired by the workplace and their jobs, they find important meaning in their work. In his book *Peak: How Companies Get Their Mojo From Maslow,* Conley (2007) argues that finding inspiration and meaning in work is the highest level of self-actualization and key to successful service. With inspired employees striving to fulfill and exceed customer desires, they create customer loyalty toward the organization. Strong guest loyalty ultimately results in a profitable and sustainable business. This service approach seems to be very effective: Joie De Vivre Hospitality has grown to be the largest boutique hotel company in California with annual revenues of over $200 million.

Business Advice and Plans

Mr. Conley is the first to admit that the success of the business has been due to the dedicated staff who provide outstanding service. But underpinning and guiding the staff have been a clear company service philosophy and a unique service model. They believe that management's job is to take care of employees, who in turn provide superior service to clients, which results in happy, positive customer experiences, which leads to solid owner financial returns and company growth.

shift in company focus to maximizing customer satisfaction. This restructuring involves reversing traditional top-down management to more client-centered management. Managers become leaders who work continuously on improving the system and listen more to frontline staff about how they can better do their work.

MANAGING MOMENTS OF TRUTH

A regular leisure client is very upset over a problem with the service received, and she is demanding a full refund and apology. What should the company do? This is a **moment of truth** for the company according to Zemke and Albrecht (1990). A moment of truth is a personal, emotionally charged contact with a client where a timely and appropriate response can make a big difference in customer satisfaction. A high-quality service organization needs to identify in advance where these will occur and develop policies and plans to deal with them when they arise. A key element in managing moments of truth is empowering frontline staff to handle situations in an appropriate manner without having to automatically call a manager.

SERVICE RECOVERY

People make mistakes, and machines stop working. Even the best service providers have customer service breakdowns. So a critical component of customer service is a prompt, appropriate recovery from these

situations. If done correctly, a recovery can actually increase customer loyalty to the organization. An important first step in recovery is training the staff that a client complaint, in most cases, is really a "gift" from the guest, who is going out of his way to identify a problem with the organization's service and a potential solution. This contrasts with the common but wrong response of a staff person's becoming upset with the client and blaming the guest for the company-generated problem. Some companies have a "no questions asked" refund policy. But these types of policies may not always be appropriate for small event, recreation, and tourism businesses that offer expensive programs. Wal-Mart refunding a $15 retail item is a very different situation from a small seasonal guiding business giving a full $2,200 refund on a week-long program where the company provided what was promised. It may require active listening and negotiations by the supplier to make the client happy.

One common aspect of a successful service recovery is having well-trained, responsive staff readily available to assist. Colenutt (2000) found that technological distractions, such as TV shows on monitors in unexpected queues at attractions, did not influence guest satisfaction, but responsive staff positively influenced satisfaction, and guests were less likely to blame the company for the delay.

EMPOWERING STAFF

If a company is to be responsive to client needs, it must empower staff to act in service recovery and to improve systems and services. **Empowerment** is based on the beliefs that well-trained frontline staff are in the best position to understand client needs and know how to satisfy them quickly; that employees' abilities are frequently underused; and that given the chance, a responsible worker will take steps that benefit both the client and the company. This contrasts with an organization that fails to consult frontline staff on how to improve service, imposes overly burdensome bureaucratic policies, or always forces employees to seek out supervisor approval before they are allowed to take any action.

Empowering staff can be a way to resolve customer complaints effectively, but if not done properly it can lead to greater problems, such as offering things the company cannot provide, significant financial losses, and a lack of consistent and fair treatment of all guests. So a company needs to take specific steps not only to empower but also to manage the service recovery process so that it follows company policies. Following are the principles of empowering employees:

- Clearly convey to staff their responsibilities.
- Give them authority equal to their responsibilities.
- Set standards of excellence in service recovery.
- Provide staff with training and mentoring that will enable them to meet the standards.
- Set service recovery boundaries (e.g., one night free or 10 percent off next service).
- Role-play the most common service recovery situations and responses.
- Give employees feedback on their performance.
- Support staff on their recovery decision, if within designated boundaries.

Each of these principles can assist staff in their service recovery efforts and lead to improvements in the systems and services the company offers. But even with employee empowerment, establishing and training in service recovery procedures is needed.

SERVICE RECOVERY PROCEDURES

All service providers need to respond promptly to guest concerns in a service recovery situation. It is important for an RET company to establish a service recovery procedure that outlines the basic steps toward solving guest concerns. A frequently recommended course of action is to apply HEAT:

- **H**ear the person out.
- **E**mpathize with the person.
- **A**cknowledge the problem.
- **T**ake immediate action.

When you *hear the person out*, the client will often be very upset, vocal, and even rude to the service provider. Your frontline staff cannot take these attacks personally and become emotional themselves. Letting the client vent his frustrations and concerns and not trying to interrupt him is key at this stage.

To *empathize with the person*, staff must show that they understand why the client is concerned and the problems he must be facing. The service provider tries to see the situation through the client's eyes. Often a sincere statement such as "I can see how you would be upset" will convey empathy to the guest and help defuse the situation further.

When someone *acknowledges the problem*, the client recognizes that the staff person understands the situation. Succinctly repeating back to the guest the nature of the problem confirms that you understand what he is saying. This is different from admitting something was the company's "fault," which may have unwanted legal liability implications. Again, it is easy for a grocery store clerk to admit it was her error in overcharging $2 on an item shown on a receipt, versus a situation where a staff person admits that a client's injury during a guided tour at an ecolodge was the lodge's fault.

If the company doesn't *take immediate action*, the client will not be satisfied. Empowering the frontline staff in advance to make decisions on their own up to a certain monetary or replacement level is a critical part of this step. Beyond a specified level or in certain defined situations, a staff person may need to call a manager. But staff should not unduly delay a response, give the impression they are "putting off" the client, imply it is not their problem, or indicate they do not consider the situation a big concern.

Another commonly used service recovery system is the SMILE process. This system is used by a number of winter sports resorts to address guest concerns quickly. The SMILE system emphasizes small but important personal steps at the start, including smiling and positive eye contact with the guest.

- **S**mile.
- **M**ake positive eye contact.
- **I**nitiate conversation and solutions.
- **L**isten for guest responses.
- **E**nsure implementation of solutions.

Whatever recovery system you employ, it is important that after the initial recovery response has been completed that a tracking system and follow-up with an unhappy guest be undertaken to ensure they were satisfied with the recovery actions. Follow-up response, without a sales pitch, is a sure sign of an excellent service provider, and it generates customer loyalty. If all these actions are taken, the formerly upset client is actually more likely to come back and buy from the company than before her purchase. Why? Because the company showed it is concerned and willing to take action, and this is indeed rare in today's service environment.

CREATING POSITIVE MOMENTS

Emotionally charged incidents with clients need not just be negative in nature. Gross (2004) argues that a smart organization will strive to create positive moments, where you foster a positive emotional response from clients. This can be done through surprise (an unexpected offering), contests, and giveaway items (e.g., cookies or supplier demos). Contests have long been used to generate excitement about a company and increase interest in booking. Gross suggests that to be most effective, giveaway items should be offered at random times so clients do not come to expect them and they retain their surprise element.

DEVELOPING CLIENT RELATIONSHIPS AND LOYALTY

In past years some tourism organizations have placed more of an emphasis on attracting new customers than retaining existing clients. However, it can cost six times less to retain a current customer than to get a new one (Sawyer and Smith, 1999). How can a recreation business effectively retain customers? An increasingly recognized approach is to develop a **relationship** with the client. Developing a relationship can benefit the organization for years in the future.

A principal goal of a good customer relationship is to increase loyalty to the organization. Levitt (1991)

believes service is an ongoing relationship between buyer and seller that centers on keeping the customer happy with the seller after the sale. This is particularly important for many recreation and tourism businesses because they cannot appeal to the mass market, there is a limited potential client base, and client repeat purchases and referrals make up the majority of their sales. Tourism businesses large and small have tried to position their brands with a strong service element. The Ritz-Carlton brand, for example, has been created around superior service, and this is a key to the company's solid customer loyalty.

Besides providing consistently great service, a company needs to make past clients feel special and valued in order to foster a positive relationship. Morrison (2002) and others have suggested the following methods to build strong customer relationships:

- Make use of databases: Identify repeat visitors; track their preferences and interests in advance of arrival.
- Personalize: Have frontline staff know and use client names at arrival.
- Offer incentives: Provide incentives for continuing repeat purchases (e.g., frequent buyer programs, preferred supplier arrangements).
- Offer exclusive service alternatives: Offer extras to repeat visitors, including upgrades, free T-shirts, and preferred placements.
- Adopt repeat pricing: Develop special pricing, such as repeat buyer discounts.
- Communicate frequently: Send newsletters, opt-in e-mail updates, and birthday cards.
- Develop a buyer club: Consider starting a club of past clients who receive special offers, newsletters, and invitations to local social events (e.g., Halloween party for member kids or St. Patrick's Day party, prerelease movie).
- Develop companywide client retention strategies: Establish retention goals, and develop ways to help each department achieve them.

A growing trend in recreation, event, and tourism businesses is the use of guest relationship software. Most companies today have computerized database programs, such as guest or property management systems, that allow a company to quickly capture customer data, show marketing info, track inventory, and send reservation confirmations. But Gale (2005)

Tech Application

Customer Relationship Systems

A customer relationship system (CRS) is focused on sharing information between the employees of your company, from the frontline staff and sales staff to the marketing manager and owner. A CRS is designed to help an organization manage its relationships with customers and prospects. The basic components are hardware and software systems that provide the functions of collecting, storing, analyzing, and disseminating pertinent, detailed information. A common problem today is that basic information isn't always shared between employees, and this can lead to poor service or lost sales opportunities. If staff who deal directly with customers lack information about past customer preferences or special requests, the result is a downgraded service encounter, and the clients may go elsewhere next time. An organization can "lose" a potential client in the system, thereby not following up or not providing needed information or service in a timely manner. On the other hand, when needed information is quickly accessed in any location (office or outside), it can expand customer service capabilities, enhance the customer experience, and lead to greater customer retention and loyalty. For example, can staff see all instances where a customer or a prospect has interacted with the company, regardless of the employee or department it happened in? If you do have a service lapse but handle a complaint effectively and monitor implementation of the complaint resolution actions, it will improve the chances of retaining the client. CRS systems offer solutions to these business challenges and are now available at a reasonable price and with important features so they can be utilized by small- and medium-size RET companies.

An example of a CRS that is tailored to SMEs is Oncontact (see www.oncontact.com). Oncontact is powerful, flexible software that can run on stand-alone or networked computers. There are no required third-party or monthly service fees, an important cost factor for small companies. The software allows you to do the following:

- View a complete history of each contact.
- Manage contacts, e-mail, and calendars.
- Manage schedules and create recurring activities for multiple users.
- Automate scheduling of follow-up activities.
- Send, store, and retrieve e-mails, letters, and faxes.
- Record incidents, and create a complete service history.
- Schedule phone calls, meetings, or to-do lists.
- Assign tasks to team members.
- Prioritize support incidents, and establish a work queue.
- Record service problems and resolutions.
- Escalate urgent cases for immediate response.
- Search the knowledge base to locate similar cases and problems.
- Empower customers to solve their own issues via the Web.
- Designate contacts to an unlimited number of campaigns, and track results.
- Deliver targeted marketing campaigns to select customers or prospects.
- Create HTML e-mail campaigns.
- Track campaign budgets and cost per lead.
- Create marketing reports to examine a campaign's effectiveness.

The company offers online or in-person training. It can provide consulting to facilitate customization and implementation of the system, although this is not always needed.

This is an example of one CRS system. There are many others that may be designed specifically for certain types of business, such as country clubs. Some software systems provide CRS features and point of sale features. Investigate the range of alternatives and speak to others who are using that specific CRS system before you purchase.

found that companies in the forefront have advanced the basic database system into customer relationship systems (CRSs). When you purchase a CRS you get powerful database management software, specialized for a segment of the recreation, event, and tourism industry. It offers all the standard database actions but also provides more depth in the amount and type of guest information that can be stored, combines all client data from different databases, coordinates client and staff communications, provides easy data retrieval in all departments, sends post-stay thank-you notes and service evaluations via e-mail, and helps a company identify its best customers through the "lifetime value of a guest" metric. Lifetime value is determined by adding up all purchases made by the client, or by the group, room, or event. Since CRSs involve advanced technology, some small tourism providers have outsourced database and CRS tasks to independent providers, such as Digital Alchemy (www.data2gold.com), who then provide Web-based and wireless access for company staff. Personal digital assistants (small handheld computers) and wireless access extend the reach of these CRS systems to anywhere on the property, such as the golf course, spa, or highway.

A critical period for retaining new clients and developing a relationship, especially for certain types of recreation organizations such as health clubs, is during the initial membership or purchase period. Businesses need to have new clients bond with staff and assimilate into the organization right away. Guests may need to receive extra attention in the initial purchase stage, while longtime clients need to be made to feel they are important and not forgotten after a period of time. To do these actions well and provide consumer-responsive service, the company needs to know a great deal about what the guests desire and what they think about current company service quality. This means you must evaluate the quality of your service.

WHAT IS QUALITY SERVICE?

How does a company know if it provides high-quality service? Quality management grew out of the need in the manufacturing industry to ensure product standardization and zero defects. This model can be characterized as a production process, with quality assurances and the training of operational staff

to ensure every item is identical with no faults. It should be noted, however, that this manufacturing model is probably not suitable for the many aspects of the service industry, and in particular leisure and recreation experiences, for two reasons. Standardization is not what most clients are seeking, and "producing" an experience is a multiparty collaborative process. Because of participant involvement, specific standardization is probably not as attainable. Instead, the service industry tends to address quality as the task of reducing or minimizing the gaps between the perceptions of quality service held by the provider and by the customers.

In proposing a model for service quality, several studies (Parasuraman, Berry, and Zeithaml, 1991; Morais, Zillifro, and Nyaupane, 2004) suggest that gaps can be considered between perhaps three variables: customer expectations, provider perception of the expectations, and any service quality conditions or specifications that exist (timeliness, cleanliness, safety, and so on). In this context, two important gaps might arise: (1) between the expectations of the participant and the staff (e.g., employee understanding of customer expectations) and (2) between the expectations of the participant and service quality specifications (e.g., safety label). In addition, gaps may arise in service delivery because of perceptions communicated to the customer during marketing of the services, as well as how the services were rendered (e.g., staff were impersonal or rude).

These studies point out the importance of using a client-centered approach to identify service gaps when determining if an organization offers quality customer service.

EVALUATING RECREATION, EVENT, AND TOURISM SERVICES

It is extremely difficult for staff to objectively evaluate their service quality because they unknowingly filter their assessment through internal lenses, such as budget limitations, staffing problems, or manager–employee relationships. Company staff tend to believe they provide outstanding quality service, but significantly fewer of their clients believe they received outstanding service. In addition, companies do not often have much in-depth information about their guests or desired guest changes. So the consumers are in the best position to determine if their unique needs and wants have been met or exceeded. Therefore, the most accurate way to evaluate service is through the eyes of the consumers.

But many elements of RET services are intangible, so does that mean it is impossible to measure and evaluate all of them? Effective evaluation of all elements of service is not only possible but also must be done. An ideal service evaluation should

- be representative of all clients, not just those who complain;
- evaluate the full cycle of service;
- be unbiased and not likely to be falsified by staff; and
- provide specific enough client feedback to help improve service.

Evaluation should consist of important criteria rated by the guests on the amount these factors have been met or exceeded and by how important each criterion is to them. Without an importance measure, a company will not know if the criteria are relevant to the customers or not and which of all criteria are considered most critical. The results can be presented graphically, as in figure 8.3, to help in understanding the implications.

Figure 8.4 describes service evaluation methods that have been employed. Comment cards are the most frequently used method because they are inexpensive and can capture many of the most flagrant problems that guests are willing to discuss. But remember that only a small percentage of unhappy guests report their feelings, so comment cards miss feedback from most of the unsatisfied customers. They can also easily be altered, removed, or "stuffed" by employees whose job may be affected. Methods that provide data from a representative sample of guests, such as valid e-mail or telephone surveys that are collected by a contractor, are accurate in tracking service quality but more expensive. It is easy to get

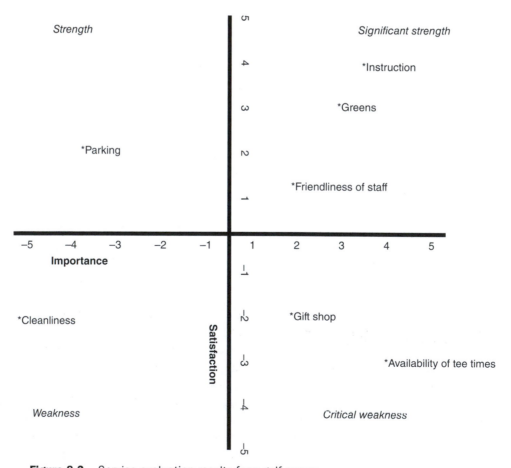

Figure 8.3 Service evaluation results for a golf course.

Service Evaluation Methods

- **Comment cards**—Posted in conspicuous location on property; voluntary compliance. Many potential problems, but inexpensive.
- **Secret shopper**—Trained person experiences service and secretly evaluates it.
- **Exploration group**—Small group of employees sent to evaluate leading competitor.
- **Mail or e-mail survey**—E-mail survey sent. Can be confused as spam.
- **Phone survey**—Contractor surveys sample of past guests by telephone.
- **Online survey**—E-mail with survey link sent to a sample of or all past clients.
- **Focus group**—An in-depth qualitative group interview of (paid) past clients.
- **Consumer panel**—A group of customers is paid to visit and periodically evaluate.
- **Compile verbal complaints**—Frontline staff report consumer complaints.
- **Observation**—By management or outside party.
- **Intercept on site**—Ask guests when on site.
- **Ask staff**—Formally or informally survey frontline staff.
- **Toll-free hotlines**—For consumers to management.
- **Employee teams**—Staff from other company location visit and evaluate.

Figure 8.4 You can employ a wide variety of service evaluation methods.

a representative sample with an exit survey given as guests checkout or just before they leave, but it can slow down or interrupt your guest if completed on-site before they go.

Surveys on the company Web site are problematic because those who respond are often not representative of all guests, despite acquiring a large number of respondents (Tierney, 2000). Another approach is to use on-property methods, such as the secret shopper technique, because actual staff interaction and equipment operation can be readily and comprehensively evaluated. Price, Arnold, and Tierney (1995) found that using multiple methods of tracking customer service levels and taking surveys at different stages in the client experience (including focus groups; pre-service surveys; observation at sample times during the experience; and follow-up telephone, e-mail, and mail surveys) provide a much more complete picture and can be done with minimum interruption of the guest experience.

Following are some suggestions to consider when setting up a service evaluation program:

- Include *quantitative questions* to calculate averages and numerically track change over time.
- Include *qualitative open-ended questions* to get in-depth detail to help explain observations.

- Evaluate the full cycle of service—from information seeking through to follow-up after the sale.
- Consistently gather data to allow for comparisons over time.
- Evaluate monthly to see changes.
- Use results to motivate staff and make changes in the organization. For example, you could base management bonuses on achieving a certain level of guest satisfaction.

HOW TO INTEGRATE CUSTOMER SERVICE EXCELLENCE INTO A BUSINESS PLAN

Most actions related to developing excellent customer service and strong client loyalty fall under the heading of company operations. This is appropriate, but because of the absolutely critical importance of outstanding service provision, it should also be part of your business plan. Although there is generally no heading or section in a business plan titled "customer service," key factors that will help bring about superior guest service are found in various sections of the business plan. First, in the description of your business and the services you provide, show that you are aware of the importance of service, the critical role it will play in your success, and how you will evaluate service on a regular basis. You might include key service standards. When you discuss competition, you will certainly be identifying and comparing the service features and quality of competitors. In the management and personnel section, you may identify a customer service manager in your proposed organizational chart or at a minimum show the customer service experience of your proposed key managers. Finally, the appendixes to the plan may contain letters of reference elaborating on the excellence of manager knowledge of customer service or the high quality of customer service while working for previous employers.

SUMMARY

Recreation, event, and tourism businesses cannot develop, grow, or maintain profitability without excellent customer service. Outstanding service does not happen on its own; it is a managed endeavor. Service providers can add value by giving additional benefits to someone who has purchased a tangible good or, in other cases, enhance the visitor experience. Consumers are more willing to pay top prices for augmented and leading-edge services because they exceed their expectations by offering the most advanced facilities and services. Outstanding service can lead to the client having an exceptional experience with a company. Experiences are positive, emotional, intangible "products" created in the mind of the consumer simultaneously by both the provider and the guest. To achieve outstanding customer encounters, a company must move their services up the service ladder from commodity to experience. A key aspect of moving up the service ladder is customization to meet individual desires. Consumers increasingly want it *their unique way*. Outstanding service builds an ongoing relationship between buyer and seller that focuses on keeping the customer happy with the seller after the sale. All levels of an organization must have a thorough understanding of the importance of superior service, how to provide it, how to recover when there is poor service, and how to accurately evaluate your organization's level of service and make changes based on service evaluations. If these are done consistently well, then it fosters customer loyalty. Key features of outstanding service providers have been identified, and examples of their application are provided. A number of service evaluation methods are described, along with the advantages and disadvantages of each.

 Check out the online student resource for additional material, including case studies, Web links, and more.

Chapter 9

Ethics, Environmental Management, and Sustainability

Learning Objectives

After reading this chapter you will be able to

- describe the importance of having a code of ethics and providing ethics training;
- critique an ethical and regulatory basis for environmental management;
- explain how organizations are defining and measuring environmental and social sustainability;
- describe how triple bottom line accounting expands the ways an organization measures its success;
- identify green business practices and how RET businesses can reduce their environmental impact;
- apply carbon offset principles to help make a business travel carbon neutral; and
- describe the key components of a sustainability report and the use of environmental and social performance measures.

Key Terms

carbon neutral

carbon offsets

code of ethics

ecotourism

environmental management

ethics

International Organization for Standardization (ISO)

Leave No Trace

neutral third party verification

sustainability

sustainability report

triple bottom line accounting

Imagine this scenario:

As a small manufacturer of sports clothing and recreation products, you have just been named in a lawsuit for human rights abuses by your own shareholders. The pending court action seems unbelievable given the fact your business has a published code of vendor conduct prohibiting child labor, forced labor, and discrimination, and it's been one of your corporate goals for five years. However, you are to learn that it is not just about good intentions; it requires complete and accurate knowledge of compliance with the business principles set out in regard to being a responsible corporate citizen. Social responsibility as a statement of intent is one thing, and compliance with it is another. You discover this as you review a sustainability report prepared by an external compliance team that documents noncompliance with the adopted standards. It is very evident from the lawsuit that the premise of commitment to a "triple bottom line" can be not just a public relations effort but also a serious element of business success, and transparency in reporting on operational practices is important along with profitability.

Henry David Thoreau once commented: "What is the good of having a nice house without a decent planet to put it on." Today, growing concerns about unethical behaviors by business managers has led to a severe decline in public trust in business leaders, their motivations, and the accuracy of information they provide. At the same time the dire environmental impacts of human activities, such as global warming, have caused many citizens to call for significant changes in businesses' operations so they are more environmentally and socially sustainable. Federal, state or provincial, and local government agencies now require RET companies operating in public facilities and on public lands to have a comprehensive environmental management system and report their performance on moving toward sustainable operations. In this modern time, more than ever, the consumer is well educated and will select a provider based not just on price, value, and quality of the services but also on the company's record of ethical behavior as well as its efforts at reducing environmental impacts and helping the local community. Companies with a strong record in these areas have competitive advantages, stronger growth, and higher profitability than those firms that do not. Therefore, ethics, environmental management, and sustainability are bottom-line considerations for how a business plans and operates.

In this chapter we cover the topics of ethics and ethical business behavior, provide examples of the business code of ethics, and show how ethics training can help an RET business prosper. This discussion transitions into the related topics of environmental management systems. Examples of government environmental management systems requirements and RET business responses are included. The chapter also provides details and examples about how innovative, profitable RET businesses are measuring their environmental and social performance, setting goals, and taking actions to improve their output. We discuss how a triple bottom line approach is more commonly being used to identify the true success of a company and convey that to the public. Businesses are reporting their efforts toward sustainability in order to be ethical and advance the organization.

ETHICS ARE IMPORTANT

From predatory lending practices in the 2008 subprime mortgage foreclosure crisis, to home-decorating guru Martha Stewart's insider trading, to the Enron accounting fraud, to Watergate spying, a continuing barrage of corporate and government scandals has led to an erosion of trust by North American residents in leaders of their private and public organizations. The need to restore trust by the public, employees, and other stakeholders is considered one of the great challenges faced today by national and multinational corporations (Murphy, 2003). A lack of trust is not just a concern for big businesses; it certainly affects small RET companies as well. No business can operate unethically and expect to continue to keep its consumer and business customers. People do business only with organizations they trust. The public looks for adherence to high ethical principles by businesses, along with value and quality in the services they purchase. Therefore, ethical behavior is a bottom-line consideration for a business.

WHAT ARE ETHICS?

A lack of trust in an organization results from its leaders or employees taking unethical actions. But just what are **ethics**? A common definition sees ethics as a set of principles of "right conduct." Added to this is the idea that an ethical act causes the greatest good for the greatest number of people. Ethics fall outside of strict, narrow legal and policy definitions. What is considered "right conduct" that causes the greatest good is identified by society, and in the case of a private company, the organization also implicitly or explicitly defines it. Identifying and conveying its ethical principles is a way for every business to guide stakeholders into deciding what it considers ethical behavior. Companies have found that ethical standards can and must be adopted, communicated, and constantly reinforced in a business setting.

CODE OF ETHICS

A national report on how to rebuild trust in business has strongly recommended that companies develop and adopt a set of ethical principles and train all their employees in its application (Lorsch, Berlowitz, and Zelleke, 2005). A **code of ethics** is a written document that provides guidelines to encourage ethical behavior by company stakeholders. Examples of topics in a code of ethics are shown in figure 9.1. Fruitful areas of discussion include conflicts of interest and how to avoid them, gifts, entertainment of business associates, and the privacy of organization records. A small RET business can use these topics to help develop its own specific code of ethics. Another helpful source of information on developing a business code of ethics and its contents can be found at www.managementhelp.org/ethics/ethxgde.htm.

ETHICS TRAINING

Companies recognized for their commitment to ethical practices have made a solid effort in ethics training. Training must start with a strong commitment of support from the owner or CEO followed by the development of a set of programs for all employees. Examples of where and how ethics training can be offered include the following:

- Hold an orientation to ethics program during new employee orientation.

Topics for a Code of Ethics

- General employee conduct
- Conflicts of interest
- Outside activities, employment, and directorships
- Relationships with clients and suppliers
- Gifts, entertainment, and favors
- Kickbacks and secret commissions
- Organization funds and other assets
- Organization records and communications
- Dealing with outside people and organizations
- Prompt communications
- Privacy and confidentiality
- Service to community
- Protection and conservation of natural resources

Figure 9.1 When developing a code of ethics for your company consider these topics.

- Review ethics guidelines in management training retreats.
- Involve employees in reviewing the codes and the training.
- Role-play potential ethical dilemmas during ethics training.
- Incorporate ethical performance in performance appraisals.
- Owners and managers demonstrate ethical behavior through their actions.

These examples deal primarily with ethical issues related to business administration practices. However, the concept of ethics as actions that cause the greatest good should also extend to protecting public resources, such as the natural environment, vulnerable clients, and the community a company operates within. Ethical principles imply its operations must not diminish public resources, and should even try to improve them, thus allowing the business to operate for a long period of time. A good illustration of how an RET company integrates ethics into its services is provided in Spotlight On Geriatric Healthcare Consultants and Scott Walking Adventures.

Geriatric Healthcare Consultants, LLC.

Location

The office headquarters are in Oakland, California. Geriatric Healthcare Consults also has 500 active contracts in 27 states.

Background

There is an increasing trend for commercial recreation companies to conduct services that formerly were provided by public agencies. Some of these operators are offering services to the growing number of aging baby boomers in North America who desire and need health and therapeutic recreation services. Two critical concerns when working with the elderly are enhancing their quality of life and the ethical care and treatment of these vulnerable clients. Geriatric Healthcare Consultants is a good example of how a privately owned, commercial therapeutic recreation company has recognized the growing demand for these services and at the same time has made a strong commitment to ensure the ethical and caring treatment of clients while expanding rapidly and realizing a reasonable profit.

Products and Services

Geriatric Healthcare Consultants (GHC) provides comprehensive therapeutic recreation, leisure and activities, social services, and dementia care consultation and training to improve the quality of life for residents in skilled nursing and assisted-living facilities throughout the continental United States and the Hawaiian islands. Their mission is accomplished through best-practice consulting support, which provides training, education, and oversight of those responsible for the delivery of psychosocial services within these settings. GHC does not operate a facility; rather, the company provides specialized training and support for the staff who are managed by other organizations.

GHC has experienced steady growth since it began operation in 1990. It is now the largest consulting group of its kind in the United States: It has more than 500 active contracts in 27 states, including the Hawaiian islands. Their team of 20 full- and part-time consultants is composed of therapeutic recreation specialists, social workers, and dementia care specialists. They have had to do very little marketing of their services because in this growing part of the industry, the agencies desiring their services often approach them first and request that the company respond to a request for a proposal. GHC then submits a proposal outlining services and their budget in a competitive selection process.

Business Advice and Plans

GHC serves staff who are responsible for the care of elderly residents in assisted-living and skilled-nursing facilities. The frail elderly are a very vulnerable segment of the population whose psychosocial and quality-of-life needs have traditionally received very little attention. Regulatory agencies are increasingly aware of the need to support quality of life (as well as quality of care) within the nursing home industry and are paying close attention to the delivery of services within this industry. But even without the regulatory oversight, GHC provides consulting and training on policies, procedures, and programs that ensure the ethical and appropriate care of the residents their clients are responsible for. As the owner and chief executive officer, Keith Savell states, "Our success lies in our ability to develop trusting relationships with those we serve and to offer best-practice training and resources in support of the center's efforts to facilitate optimal quality of resident life." Quality of life is now much more than a catchphrase. It is widely accepted as a core value in the delivery of care for frail and dependent elderly.

ENVIRONMENTAL AND SOCIAL SUSTAINABILITY: NEW ADDITIONS TO THE BOTTOM LINE

There is mounting evidence that human and business activities are having profound effects on our global environment. It is now recognized that the tourism industry is not as clean as it was once profiled, and in fact, it is contributing to environmental concerns, ranging from global warming to adverse impacts of tourism on host cultures. This growing recognition by the public and government has fostered a significant movement toward more-sustainable and earth-friendly travel, recreation, events, and tourism that also respect and reward the host community. Such efforts are attempting to make the RET industry more sustainable. Although there is frequent disagreement about what constitutes sustainability and how it can be accomplished, many businesses are working toward more-sustainable operations.

A process or state that is sustainable can be maintained at a certain level indefinitely. The Canadian Institute for Research and Innovation in Sustainability (2008) defines **sustainability** as "Living and working in ways that meet and integrate existing environmental, economic and social needs without compromising the well-being of future generations." Author Andres Edwards (2005, p. 11) says our society is undergoing a "sustainability revolution." More people, businesses, and government leaders now recognize the dire situation we will leave the next generation in if we do not make changes. A growing segment of the public is demanding sustainable RET opportunities, regulators are requiring stricter environmental protection practices, and communities are rejecting development that does not benefit them.

MOTIVATIONS FOR GOING GREEN

Many businesses are "going green," or adopting sustainability, because it can save them money in the short and long run (see chapter 11), improve their competitiveness, and increase sales, but it is also a moral imperative and the ethical thing to do (Barnett, 2007). RET businesses are finding that many of their best employees and customers keep asking what the company is doing to help the environment, if it is selling products with high postconsumer content, if the firm is green certified, and how it contributes to the local community. If you are able to answer positively to a range of eco-friendly questions, your employees may become more enthusiastic and loyal, the number of your clients then increases, and you often get a positive article in the local newspaper about your efforts. All of these outcomes can substantially boost your competitiveness, sales, and profitability. So environmental and social sustainability is very much a bottom-line part of a business today and, therefore, should be an important part of an RET company's business plan and management practices.

ENVIRONMENTAL MANAGEMENT

One important aspect of moving toward a more-sustainable company is environmental management (Higgins and Duane, 2007). A definition of **environmental management** is the identification and management of the impacts of a company's operations on the environment, with the goal of reducing any adverse effects. This is both a voluntary ethical choice and a strict regulatory requirement of contemporary businesses. There are a myriad of federal, state, and provincial laws, ranging from the clean air act and hazardous waste regulations to the clean water act, that require any business to measure its impacts on the environment and to minimize adverse effects. Once thought to be limited to smokestack industries, environmental management is now also a significant concern and requirement for all RET businesses, especially those that operate in public facilities (e.g., event centers) and protected areas, such as national and state or provincial parks, forests, wildlife refuges, and recreation areas. Protected areas are key attractions and settings for many RET businesses, and government management agencies have clear legislative mandates to protect these natural and cultural resources for future generations. There are also additional laws that influence how businesses operate in protected areas, such as the Wilderness Act, Endangered Species Act, Wild and Scenic Rivers Act, Antiquities Act, and Marine Mammal Protection Act, just to name a few. To put it bluntly, if you wish to operate an RET business in a protected area, you must have a very strong understanding of environmental management and clearly describe and practice minimizing potential impacts to the protected area. Otherwise

To operate a business in a protected area you must understand and practice environmental management and be aware of additional laws governing the protected area.

you will never be awarded a permit to operate; if you do manage to secure a permit, then the government agency has the legal authority to force your business to change or your operational permit will be revoked.

COMPONENTS OF ENVIRONMENTAL MANAGEMENT

Environmental management is the result of a comprehensive planning process incorporating standards or protocols and then implementing an operating system and auditing results, with feedback on the effectiveness of minimizing impacts. The **International Organization for Standardization (ISO) 14000** guidelines are the most widely used standard for environmental management systems in North America, and they are compatible with the European Eco-Management and Audit Scheme (EMAS). The ISO 14001:2004 consists of a *framework for a holistic, strategic approach* to an organization's environmental policy, plans, and actions. The ISO information provides a guideline from which each business must develop a plan based on its unique environment and potential impacts. The level of effort and sophistication of the environmental management system varies with the size and potential impact of the business operation. Because of the diverse settings and level of

detail required, it is beyond the scope of this section to delve more deeply into this topic. For guidelines, interested readers should visit www.iso.org and contact the U.S. National Park Service or Parks Canada for more details. For another example, Scott Walking Adventures developed an environmental, social, and business code of ethics to guide planning and operations ensuring they act in an environmentally and socially responsible manner (see figure 9.2). Case Study 9.1 in the online student resource describes environmental management, sustainability efforts, and the sustainability report of a rafting company.

TRIPLE BOTTOM LINE

The goal or ultimate output of any business is still financial profitability, as discussed in chapter 11. But a growing chorus of voices (Henderson, 1991; Hawken, 1993; Dean, 2006) are saying that in our contemporary world, stockholders and society must demand more than just profitability as the sole measure of business success. Author Ralph Buckley (2003) refers to the growing trend of adding a business's contributions to environmental conservation and community or society to the standard financial profitability measures, thus creating a **triple bottom line accounting** system. Figure 9.3 describes how the success of using resource inputs should result in a triple bottom line output for businesses in the tourism industry. For example, a tourist attraction located in a city uses its own facilities, equipment, and financial and human resources along with energy and environmental resources (publicly held clean air, wildlife) and community resources (airport, friendliness toward visitors, water treatment plant) to produce profits that are shared by owners and employees. The venture would not be sustainable, however, if it did not also conserve resources—even attempt to renew the surrounding environment—and if it did not respect and benefit the local community (more than just by providing jobs for a few employees and paying their taxes). The output is a triple bottom line for the attraction.

Triple bottom line accounting has its roots in the parks and ecotourism movements. The International Ecotourism Society (2006) defines **ecotourism** as "Responsible travel to natural areas that conserves the environment and sustains the well being of local people." The demand for ecotourism experiences continues to grow. In 2006 the *New York Times* declared ecotourism the "buzzword of the year" (Higgins, 2006). Ecotourism is among the fastest-growing travel trends and is estimated to be a US$77 billion market (International Ecotourism Society, 2007). There are plenty of business opportunities for ecotourism guides and outfitters, as well as in retailing and ecoresorts. An outstanding ecotourism experience is a fundamental component of conserving resources. Research has also shown that participation in ecotourism is significantly related to the willingness of the public to protect natural areas in the future (Tierney, Price, and Arnold, 1994). Although not all RET activity providers visit natural areas, the principles of ecotourism are transferable to other situations and have been used to develop the modern triple bottom line accounting approach.

Environmental, Social, and Business Code of Ethics for Scott Walking Adventures

- To ensure that the environmental, social, cultural, economic, and aesthetic needs and expectations of the community and our customers are included in our policies, plans, and decisions and result in the provision of quality goods and services.
- To ensure operations are designed and conducted in a manner that will conserve resources, minimize or eliminate environmental damage, and, where possible, enhance environmental situations.
- To continually evaluate new information, technologies, and services, thus providing our employees and ourselves with opportunities for development, environmental education and protection, and improved customer service.
- To act with a spirit of cooperation within the industry and related sectors to foster greater public awareness of the economic, social, cultural, and environmental significance of tourism.
- To enhance our natural, historic, cultural, and aesthetic resources as a legacy for present and future generations, through encouraging establishment of parks, wilderness reserves, and protected areas.
- To ensure that the privacy of our guests, potential guests, and guides is maintained and follows the directives of the Privacy Act of Canada.

Figure 9.2 An ethics code can guide planning and operations in an environmentally and socially responsible manner.
Adapted, by permission, from Scott Walking Adventures, 2006, *Responsible travel policy.* [Online]. Available: http://www.scottwalking.com/travelpolicy.cfm.

Figure 9.3 Triple bottom line input–output model for sustainable tourism businesses.

Ralph Lee Hopkins/National Geographic/Getty Images

The principles of ecotourism are transferable to other situations and have been used to develop the modern triple bottom line accounting approach.

FOUR GREEN BUSINESS PRACTICES FOR RET PROVIDERS

Four increasingly common "go green" business practices are described here, including resources for obtaining additional information. The section that follows this discussion provides material on how to develop a sustainability plan and report. These can all be elements of an RET company's efforts toward triple bottom line accounting and sustainability.

• *Green your building.* The design and operation of a building can have a large impact on the health of the occupants inside and the outside environment, as well as on operational costs. So there is a strong push toward making buildings greener. The best-known green building certification system is the Leadership in Energy and Environmental Design (LEED) Green Building Certification and Rating System, which encourages and accelerates global adoption of sustainable green building and development practices. The LEED certification is designed to guide and distinguish high-performance commercial and

institutional projects, including office buildings and recreation facilities. It measures and encourages use of sustainable sites and transportation, promotes water efficiency, optimizes energy performance, encourages renewable energy, protects natural resources, reduces construction waste and encourages reuse, minimizes resource consumption, discourages reliance on toxics, and improves indoor air quality. The process can be used by even small RET businesses. See the LEED Web site (www.usgbc.org/DisplayPage. aspx?CategoryID=19) for more details.

• *Leave no trace.* For many years, ecotourism tour outfitters have tried to minimize their impacts on the natural environment and other users. Now there is a comprehensive system designed to inform both professional guides and individual wild land users on ways to plan ahead and prepare; travel and camp on durable surfaces; dispose of waste properly; leave what you find; minimize campfire impacts; respect wildlife; and be considerate of other visitors. The **Leave No Trace** Center for Outdoor Ethics has training available for company employees at reasonable rates. See www.LNT.org for more details.

• *Operate carbon neutral.* There has been a strong new trend toward assessing environmental impacts before implementation and then determining ways to reduce nonrenewable energy use, carbon dioxide emissions, and unsustainable resource use. Companies are designing green buildings, airlines are reducing carbon output from jets, and small companies are switching to biodiesel fuel and hybrid cars. Alpine Meadows resort (www.skialpine.com/winter/mountain/oneplanet), awarded top listing in the California Ski Area Environmental Scorecard, is 100 percent wind powered. More companies are attempting to be **carbon neutral** (not contributing a net gain in carbon dioxide to the atmosphere through their travel or events) by reducing carbon dioxide emissions to the extent possible and then including the expense of carbon offsets in their cost of doing business. **Carbon**

offsets are payments made to finance new renewable energy sources and planting of carbon-absorbing trees that counterbalance carbon emissions from travel. For ways to make your travel more sustainable, see www.sustainabletravelinternational.org and figure 9.4. Another similar alternative that can be used to offset carbon dioxide production from operations is to purchase renewable energy credits (RECs) that allow you to buy renewable wind power–generated electricity. Using this method, the Stratton, Vermont, and Alpine Meadows ski resorts are 100 percent wind powered. If your company is not adopting these technologies and practices, then you may be losing employees and customers who expect you to be a leader—and a loss of customers translates to a loss of profits. These actions may still be the right thing to do, even if there are no direct immediate financial rewards.

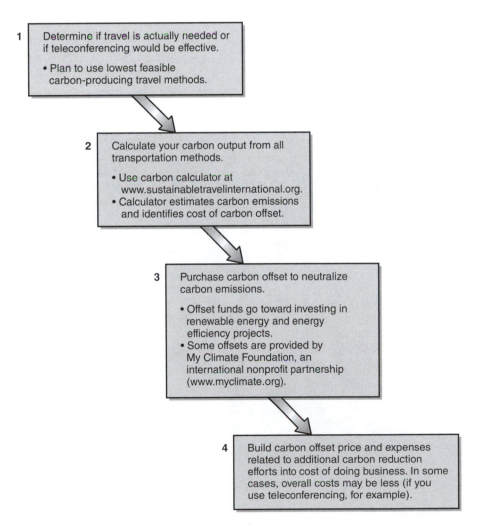

Figure 9.4 How to make your business travel carbon neutral.

• *Green your event.* The trend is clear: Demand for greener events is growing. The examples are numerous, from mega-events such as the 2006 Olympics in Turin, Italy, 2010 Winter Olumpics in Whistler, British Columbia, and a "carbon neutral" Rolling Stones concert to smaller local events, such as environmentally friendly meetings and weddings (Davidson, 2007). Your company can plan the program or hire a growing number of event planners who specialize in green events. Some basic considerations for greening your event include sending electronic invitations rather than paper, using biodegradable plastic tableware, featuring live plants as part of the decor, serving condiments in bulk containers instead of individual packets, booking your event at an eco-certified hotel, using green power, and featuring sustainable seafood in meals. For additional details on making your event greener, see www.itsyournature.org/files/NRDC-GREENGUIDE-FINAL_0.pdf.

Located throughout this book are more green tips that offer specific examples of how RET businesses can incorporate environmental conservation and community benefits into their planning and operations. But one of the basic needs for going green is to compile a comprehensive sustainability report and integrate resultant information into their planning.

SUSTAINABILITY REPORT AND PLAN COMPONENT

A growing number of successful RET companies, such as Xanterra, are already producing special sustainability reports documenting their triple bottom line approach to measuring organization success and outputs (see www.xanterra.com/Environmental-Action-364.html). A **sustainability report** clearly presents the company's environmental and social sustainability vision, goals, policies, and performance over a period of years in one comprehensive document. The extent and depth of the report will vary with the size and complexity of the company operations. Here again, small- and medium-size RET businesses can engage in this effort, as it is not just for large corporations. For example, the sustainability report summary for a small seasonal rafting outfitter is shown in Case Study 9.1 in the online student resource.

A sustainability report starts with a long-term commitment from the owner and top management and an

Managers of many golf courses have become concerned about their impacts on the environment and have sought green golf course certification.

Photodisc/Getty Images

allocation of funds. These are needed to complete this substantial effort and to get all parts of the organization involved. Another basic need is a commitment to have sustainability data and results verified by an independent auditor. **Neutral third party verification** is an essential component of the process to ensure accuracy and accountability and to make sure the report is not really just a public relations action. However, the cost of a formal independent audit by one of the national accounting firms, such as KPMG Performance Registrars (see www.kpmg.com), may be too great for a small RET business. But the use of nonprofit organizations, land management agency representatives, or industry associations for auditing can help keep the cost affordable. But even with independent auditing, some authors have questioned the accuracy of company-provided data (Sullivan and Gouldson, 2007). Finally, get your staff involved in finding creative and cost-effective ways to achieve company goals. Most companies have found current employees very enthusiastic, and sustainability efforts have even resulted in the organization's attracting top job candidates.

CONTENTS OF A SUSTAINABILITY REPORT

There is no one generally accepted table of contents or format for a sustainability report; rather, different businesses have developed their own reports. Some organizations rely on the International Organization for Standardization (ISO) 14000 guidelines for environmental management systems (see www.iso.org for more details). The ISO 14001:2004 provides an outline for an organization's environmental policy, plans, and actions. Following is the outline for a sustainability report for an RET business:

1. Company profile
2. Reporting methods
3. Verification
4. Company's long-term environmental and social (E&S) goals
5. Summary of progress toward meeting E&S goals
6. Key company E&S policies and management actions
7. Environmental and social performance
8. Regulatory compliance

Your company's environmental and social (E&S) goals should focus on key concerns related to the type of business and its location. There are two elements to each goal: a nonquantitative goal and a quantitative measureable objective. The following two examples show an E&S goal and its related measurable objective.

- Slow global warming—Reduce the company's total gasoline consumption by 15 percent by the year 2010.
- Enhance education in the local community— Increase the number of student internships or cooperative education placements by 50 percent by the year 2010.

PERFORMANCE MEASURES

A very important and challenging component of a sustainability report is the measurement of environmental and social performance. Choose performance measures that address E&S goals with reasonable accuracy and cost. Based on a review of sustainability reports and ISO recommendations, some typical E&S performance measures were identified and are presented in table 9.1. Measures can range from kilowatt hours of renewable energy generated on company lands and gallons of water consumed to cash contributions to community organizations. This is not considered a complete set, and other measures can be developed.

Once you have quantified your performance measures, then you should adjust (normalize) them to account for annual changes in the size or overall output of your company. This allows a consistent basis for comparing the current year's performance level with the initial performance level. Measures can also be adjusted to show the data on a per unit output basis, by taking the total amount of the measure and dividing it by the total number of units of production, such as tons of CO_2 produced per room night, per dollar total revenue, or per client user day. Otherwise actual achievements could be overstated when your company grows significantly. The end result is a benchmark that provides a more accurate picture of change in a specific performance measure over a multiyear period in order to show progress or backtracking in regard to the related company E&S goal.

Table 9.1   Environmental and Social Performance Topic Areas and Measures for RET Companies

Topic area	Performance measures
Company profile	• Total revenue ($) • Net profit ($) • Number of employees • Total user days, room nights, or event attendance
Environmental measures	
Greenhouse gas emissions	• CO_2 produced by corporate air travel (tons) • Use of fossil fuels (gallons of gasoline) • Electricity used (kWh) • Carbon offsets purchased ($, CO_2 tons)
Renewable energy	• Solar, wind, other generation (kWh)
Transportation	• Average company vehicle fuel efficiency (mpg) • Bio/alternative fuels used (gal) • Employee subsidy using public transit ($)
Solid waste	• Solid waste to landfill (lb) • Solid waste recycled (lb)
Hazardous waste	• Electronics recycled (lb) • Solvents used (gal) • Pesticides used (gal)
Water	• Water use (gal)
Green procurement	• Organic, fair-trade coffee (lb) • Certified sustainable seafood (lb) • Green cleaning products used (lb)
Volunteerism	• Volunteering by company staff (hours)
Contributions to projects	• Cash contributions to environmental organizations ($)
Social measures	
Workplace conditions	• Workforce retention rate (%) • Workforce safety (# accident lost days) • Staff/client serious injuries (#)
Support for community organizations	• Cash contributions to community organizations ($) • Product contributions to community organizations ($)
Support for education	• Student interns hosted (# interns) • Field trips to company facilities (# students) • University research grants ($)
Volunteer leadership	• Managers who volunteer in leadership positions with professional or community organizations (#, % of total)
Support for at-risk youth	• Complimentary/discounted programs ($) • Summer employment (# youth)
Support or access for low-income families	• Complimentary/discounted programs (in-kind $)
Support for disabled	• Employment (#) • Complimentary/discounted programs ($)
Volunteerism	• Volunteering by company staff (hours)

SUMMARY

Ethics and ethical business practices influence the success of a business. You must identify your company's core values and what you consider "right conduct" that causes the greatest good through a code of ethics reinforced by a strong training program. A company, small, medium, or large, must work hard to promote ethical behavior among its staff or else risk short-term gains for long-term pain that could threaten the organization's existence. A logical extension of ethical business behavior is promoting environmental and social sustainability. Government agencies now require comprehensive environmental management by permit holders to minimize impacts on public resources.

Financial performance is still a very important measure of private company success. But this chapter also discusses how innovative RET businesses are measuring their performance in a triple bottom line approach. The chapter provides background and examples of how an organization can set environmental and social goals, measure performance, and take actions to improve its output. A very valuable activity for moving toward sustainability is to compile a sustainability report. A sustainability report clearly describes your company's environmental and social sustainability vision, goals, policies, and performance over a period of years in one comprehensive document. Despite the limitations of today's methods, the attempts at measuring environmental and social performance, as well as sustainability and timely actions by your business, will ultimately lead to better management, and what is reported will be better understood.

 Check out the online student resource for additional material, including case studies, Web links, and more.

Chapter 10

Protecting Your Assets: Liability and Risk Management

Learning Objectives

After reading this chapter you will be able to

- identify types of liability that affect RET businesses;
- explain key elements of contract and tort law applicable to commercial recreation, event, and tourism businesses;
- discuss the methods for protecting your company assets, guests, employees, facilities, and funds; and
- describe principles of risk management and their application in preparation of a risk management plan.

Key Terms

accident report form

acknowledgment of risk

business interruption insurance

commercial general liability
  insurance

contract liability

errors and omissions insurance

guest medical insurance

insurance

liability

liability waiver

negligence

product liability insurance

risk management

standard of care

tort liability

workers' compensation insurance

Imagine this scenario: It has been a really bad week at your recreation, event, or tourism business. A guest was injured during one of your programs, and you have just received notice of a lawsuit; a hailstorm broke windows and made large dents in all your company vehicles; an experienced employee suffered a knee injury that requires a $30,000 surgery, and she will not be able to work at full capacity for five months; your most lucrative client announced that he wants out of his contract with you; and you caught one of your employees stealing money from the cash register, but you do not know how much has been taken. How will you fight the unjustified lawsuit, find the money to fix your vehicles, pay for the health care and lost wages of your injured employee, negotiate a new contract with your big client, and figure out how much money was stolen? To financially and emotionally survive this awful week, you need to already have a solid risk management plan in place.

All too often an owner or manager does not fully appreciate how important risk management is until a catastrophe, such as any one mentioned in the opening scenario, strikes a small business and puts it into a financial nosedive. Chapter 2 discusses appropriate ways to set up your new business to minimize potential liability of company owners, while this chapter discusses protecting your assets and risk management during operations of a commercial recreation, event, and tourism business.

OPERATIONS RISK MANAGEMENT

Risk management is the process of doing everything you can to protect your guests, employees, client property, company assets, and equipment from losses. It involves much more than just responding to guest injuries. In this chapter we investigate four specific areas of concern:

1. Relevant laws, legal concepts, and contracts
2. Losses and injuries to clients
3. Injuries to employees
4. Financial and asset losses

RELEVANT LAWS, LEGAL CONCEPTS, AND CONTRACTS

Recreation, event, and tourism (RET) providers operate within a legal system and must be familiar with laws, court decisions, and regulatory agency policies. Ignorance of the law is no excuse for not following the law, and this could result in contract violations, lawsuits, loss of operating licenses, and bankruptcy. You must be well versed in the most applicable laws

and regulations for your particular type of business, as well as retain qualified legal counsel. In this chapter, our goal is to help you understand some fundamental legal terms and concepts.

The **standard of care** required to prevent and respond to accidents is determined by operating requirements set forth in laws and regulations, or if these are not available, by identifying the common practices or standard operating procedures of companies that provide similar services in comparable environments. These industry standards of care are determined by documenting the safety policies, staff qualifications and training levels, facility requirements, and types of equipment normally used by providers of this type of service.

Liability is a critically important concept affecting RET owners. It refers to a situation in which a company is subject to a lawsuit because of a failure to carry out certain responsibilities as defined by law, standards of practice, or contractual agreement. A *contract* is a written agreement between two or more parties enforceable by law. A person who does not live up to her responsibilities, through negligence or intent, must compensate the other parties. There are two general types of liability: contract liability and tort liability.

Contract liability refers to lawsuits based on charges of failure to perform as directed by a contract (e.g., between concessionaires and land management agencies or with partner organizations, suppliers, or transportation carriers). When an RET company desires to start providing services for an organization, a new contract is usually negotiated and signed with the venue, funder, owner, or land management agency. Contract law is highly technical, so you should always consult an attorney to develop and execute a new contract and for issues related to contract performance.

Tort liability is a lawsuit based on a wrong committed by an employee or company outside of a contractual agreement. A tort may include a violation of a person's legal rights or a breach of some public duty or responsibility that results in injury or loss. Intentional torts, such as assaults or slander, are treated as criminal and require proof of an intent to harm. Unintentional torts are related to negligence and typically result in the payment of damages to the injured party (Kraus and Curtis, 2000). The latter are more common in RET settings where a guest is unintentionally injured during a recreation activity.

Negligence is a key legal principle in tort liability, and it must be proven before a company or person can be held legally responsible. It is often defined as an unintentional act of omission or commission in which a person fails to do something that a "reasonable" person would do under similar circumstances or does something a "reasonable person" would not do (Kraus and Curtis, 2000). Very often a lawyer trying to prove negligence will determine the common practices or standard operating procedures of companies that provide similar services in comparable environments, then compare the defendant's policies, staff training, employee actions, and equipment to these industry standards of care.

LOSSES AND INJURIES TO CLIENTS

Owners and managers in the commercial recreation, event, and tourism industry must pay focused attention to risk management for many reasons common to all businesses, but in particular because guests are often active participants, there is a greater risk of injury, and worksites may be in remote nonoffice locations. Guest and employee safety must be of paramount importance in the decisions managers make. Frontline staff must be thoroughly trained, and in many cases certified, in leading higher-risk activities—so as to reduce the likelihood of injury—and in proper emergency response if an accident should occur. You must balance the actual risk present in the program or activity with the competency of the program's leaders (Nicolazzo, 2007). If staff persons are not well trained, their training is not documented, guests are not warned of hazards, participants use improper or poorly maintained equipment, and a client suffers additional injuries during the emergency

response, then the company is open to a lawsuit and subsequent financial loss.

A component of risk management for clients that has taken on new importance is protection of guests against terrorism and criminal acts. Today a company operating global programs needs to consider prevention and liability for theft, terrorist acts, and guests contracting diseases, such as severe acute respiratory syndrome (SARS), during a program. Most commercial insurance policies exclude terrorism from coverage, leaving companies vulnerable to severe losses (Mansfield and Pizam, 2005). This is also a potential argument by an RET company against a lawsuit under these circumstances.

INJURIES TO EMPLOYEES

Harm to guests during a recreation activity is not the only legal risk to be concerned about. Chapter 7 discusses concerns related to employment laws in which an employee can bring a lawsuit against his employer. More and more employees are being injured in the workplace, whether an office, a spa, an event, or a wilderness area. These can result in time lost on the job, higher insurance rates, lower guest service, and lawsuits. In fact, employee injuries are one of the fastest-growing types of lawsuits and now make up an increasingly significant cost for employers. Injuries to recreation providers can be more serious and expensive, such as broken legs or even death, than the sore wrists associated with carpal tunnel syndrome in office workers. Employees can be injured during a recreation program, sustain a gradual loss over time from stress or repetitive motions, or believe they have been wronged by company policies or actions, such as wrongful termination or discrimination. Most states and provinces have passed laws that require organizations to create a safety committee, made up of frontline and management staff, that meets regularly to discuss employees' workplace safety concerns.

FINANCIAL AND ASSET LOSSES

A final area of concern for risk management is losses of buildings, equipment, and other assets from a variety of causes, such as theft, fire, the actions of others, loss of a key employee, or severe weather. The immediate loss of a major asset could not only cripple a company financially but may also adversely interrupt longer-term operations and lead to bankruptcy. Policies to minimize losses, training, and supervision of staff, and adequate insurance coverage are all important means of preventing financial and asset losses. For example, employee theft is very common, and systems must be in place to minimize actual losses. Strategies for dealing with all these concerns are addressed in subsequent parts of this chapter.

MANAGING RISK

A company cannot eliminate all risks without destroying the inherent nature of recreation activities. No recreation activity is 100 percent safe. So a company must manage risks through transferring some risk to insurance firms and by conducting basic risk management operational procedures (see forthcoming sections of this chapter). Programs and procedures to prevent losses, supervision of staff and guests, and adequate insurance coverage are all important elements of risk management (Leemon and Schimelpfenig, 2006). Bringing together all these elements in a comprehensive risk management plan is imperative and will be described near the end of this chapter.

SUPERVISING GUEST AND EMPLOYEE BEHAVIOR

People, be they guests on your property or your staff, sometimes do foolish or prohibited things that result in their own injury. Some examples of this kind of behavior include a snowboarder who goes past a closed area sign and gets caught in an avalanche, or an employee who fell while having fun chasing his girlfriend during work hours, and his injuries required knee surgery. In these two situations, as in many others, the company and employer are expected to supervise guest and employee behavior to prevent or minimize the chances of injuries. The company is set up for serious injuries to guests and staff and the resulting bad publicity, emotional distress, and financial losses if it cannot be shown that the organization made consis-

tent reasonable efforts to manage behavior, especially in high-risk situations.

INSURANCE COVERAGE

A legitimate company owner in the United States and Canada would be foolish to operate without any insurance coverage, and in fact it is illegal to do so in many instances. There are stark examples of fires destroying company buildings and their contents; or errors in planning a corporate event that resulted in demand for a large financial reimbursement, where no or too little insurance coverage was in place. These can result in severe financial losses. Most regulatory and

Supervising guest behavior, especially in high-risk situations, is important for their safety and for risk management.

Jose Azel/Aurora Photos

permitting agencies also require minimum insurance coverage to protect public health and safety. For example, the National Park Service requires a minimum of $1,000,000 of liability insurance coverage to operate many concessions in a park. Workers' compensation insurance is required by law in every U.S. state and Canadian province. However, lack of available liability and workers' compensation insurance at an affordable price has been a significant concern in the past for almost all RET companies.

Insurance companies transfer or share a portion of the risk of loss with a recreation provider for a fee that is usually based on loss history for that type of service and for the specific business and its business practices. A business can normally absorb smaller regularly occurring losses, such as from shoplifting or bad debts, in the cost of doing business. But where unpredictable or very high losses may occur, then purchasing more than adequate insurance to cover potential losses is prudent. There are many types of insurance, and limitations on coverage can vary widely, so you must purchase the correct type and often customize coverage to your particular situation through insurance riders, or coverage extensions (see figure 10.1). It is important to develop a good relationship with an insurance agency that specializes in policies for your kind of RET business.

TYPES OF INSURANCE

You can purchase insurance for almost any type of risk. RET business owners typically protect themselves with the following coverage.

Commercial General Liability Insurance

Commercial general liability insurance covers injury or loss to the public when they are participating in your recreation programs or events with your equipment and staff or on your property. This is a basic but very important coverage for any company to have, but especially those offering recreation activities and adventure programs. Regulatory and permitting agencies often require this coverage as a condition of providing a permit to operate. In case of a serious accident, the insurance company will investigate the incident, make recommendations on how to work with the injured party, defend your company in a lawsuit if it should be necessary, and pay any awards or expenses from the lawsuit up to the policy limit. Protection limits are stated per occurrence (for one incident) and aggregate (total coverage limit). In most cases to acquire coverage, the insurance carrier will place limitations and operator requirements. For

Understanding Insurance Terms

- Aggregate limit—The maximum total amount of dollar coverage provided by a policy in the policy period.
- Per occurrence limit—Maximum dollar coverage for any one claim.
- Insurer—The company that sells the insurance.
- Premium—The amount charged for a certain amount of insurance coverage.
- Endorsement—A written or printed form attached to the policy that alters provisions of the contract.
- Exclusions—Events and activities not covered by the policy, stated in writing.
- Insurance company rating—A measure of the insurance company's financial strength, which measures its ability to pay claims.
- Umbrella liability coverage—Provides excess liability protection to provide excess coverage over the "underlying" liability insurance you carry; provides automatic replacement coverage for underlying policies that have been reduced or exhausted by loss.
- Collision coverage—Provides coverage for an insured's vehicle that is involved in an accident, subject to a deductible.
- Comprehensive coverage—An auto policy that covers the insured's vehicle that is damaged by incidents that are not considered collisions, such as fire or theft.

Figure 10.1 Familiarity with the terms that appear in your insurance policy can assist in asking the right questions about the coverage.

example, a horseback riding outfitter may be required by the insurance company to have all children under 16 years wear a helmet and every group be led by a guide. Excluded from commercial general liability coverage are serving alcohol, automobile use, and worker injury.

Guest Medical Insurance

Guest medical insurance is a no-fault policy that covers the costs of any initial medical treatment and emergency transportation related to a guest injury. It is designed to ensure that treatment is secured immediately without consideration for who was at fault. Typically, the policy covers only the deductible and any additional costs not covered by the injured person's medical insurance provider (primary policy). This is a particularly important type of policy for recreation providers because it often limits injury by getting the best medical treatment as quickly as possible, which reduces the chances of further injury and a subsequent lawsuit.

Errors and Omissions Insurance

Errors and omissions insurance covers against claims from customers who suffered losses because of errors you made or things you failed to do but should have done. This coverage is very important for event planning companies, travel agencies, and other intermediaries who do not directly operate programs but plan, give advice, make educated recommendations, design solutions, represent the needs of others, or prepare for services done by others. Errors and omissions policies are designed to cover legal defense costs and ultimately the final judgment if the business owner does not win a lawsuit.

Product Liability Insurance

When you purchase **product liability insurance**, the policy covers injury to customers from their use or misuse of products you made or sold. This type of policy is especially important for small or large manufacturers and for retail operations.

Commercial Automobile Insurance

If you are transporting paying customers or require that staff travel in company vehicles during a program, the company must have a commercial automobile insurance policy, as private insurance is voided in commercial settings. Commercial automobile policy providers may restrict who can drive company vehicles based on driver age, driving record, or the need for a commercial license.

Fire and General Property Insurance

Fire and general property insurance protects against loss from fire; vandalism; and wind, hail, and storm damage (but not from flooding). It covers replacement or repairs for physical damage to your assets. Company assets must be listed on the policy if they are to be covered by it.

Business Interruption Insurance

A policy for **business interruption insurance** covers financial losses, up to a stated limit, in case the business cannot continue as before during emergency repairs and recovery. The interruption could be caused by a natural or man-made disaster (e.g., fire).

Crime Insurance

Crime insurance protects against losses resulting from burglary and theft. Documentation of losses and a police investigation are required for payment. Fidelity bonds can be purchased to cover employee theft. They protect an employer against employee theft, larceny, or embezzlement committed by a covered employee. Bond cost is based on the value of the property at risk.

Workers' Compensation Insurance

Workers' compensation insurance provides no-fault coverage for employees injured on the job, including paying for medical expenses and reimbursement for wages lost because of the accident. This mandatory type of insurance is the primary policy for covering employee injuries and is administered and often provided by a state or provincial agency. Worker injuries can create huge expenses, such as with a lifelong disability, that are well beyond the means of small businesses to cover. So workers' compensation policies spread this risk among the pool of all employers, making it more affordable. A business pays different rates for employees in distinct job categories, with coverage for some job categories being much more expensive (e.g., ski patrols that use explosives to control avalanches at winter resorts) than other types, where accident rates and payouts are much less (e.g., clerical office workers). Workers' compensation insurance is a particularly significant cost to recreation service providers and leaders because there is a greater chance of serious injury, as compared with other types of business. The cost of covering adventure guides in rafting and climbing, for example, ranges from $0.15 to $0.40 per dollar of payroll. So your "payroll" expenses for riskier jobs may increase by a third because of workers' compensation. Rates paid are also dependent on the dollar amount of claims made in the past by a particular company. This experience adjustment could result in one company without any claims in the last five years paying a third less for coverage compared with a company with numerous losses in similar job categories.

In summary, insurance coverage is necessary but also very detail oriented. So it is very important that you work with a qualified insurance agent who specializes in your type of RET business to identify risks and provide adequate insurance coverage.

RISK MANAGEMENT IN GUEST RECREATION SERVICES

A good place to start understanding risk management related to operations of an RET activity, event, or adventure program is by looking at the seven most common allegations of a lawsuit against a service provider (see Spengler, Connaughton, and Pittman, 2006).

1. The injured person was not adequately *warned and informed* of the inherent dangers.

2. The injured person did not receive *proper instruction* on skills and use of equipment.

3. The program or trip was in the *wrong place at the wrong time* (cold air and water temperature, wrong size building, and so on).

Ron Koeberer/Aurora Photos

Crime and natural disasters can seriously interrupt business unless crime and business interruption insurance has been secured.

4. The leader, guide, or planner *used bad judgment or was inexperienced.*

5. The *rescue was overly lengthy and complicated*, subjecting the injured person to undue pain or suffering.

6. The equipment or product was *defective or not maintained properly* and caused injury.

7. The service was *not what was contracted*, and this caused pain, suffering, or financial loss.

Some of the previously presented allegations might arise in every type of RET business (employees used bad judgment; not what was advertised; not what was contracted), while others are more applicable to recreation and adventure settings (wrong place and time; improper instruction; rescue complications). However, let's use an example to illustrate how most of these allegations could be present in a nonadventure setting. Let's say you are planning a wedding in an outdoor setting, a park with a lake. There is a small stage for the ceremony and a dance floor setup. In the ultimate awful wedding, what could go wrong and result in a loss? Well, the bride fell off the stage during the dance (not warned; no safety railing) and was injured, the golf cart used to carry the groom to the stage tipped over on a steep hill because of low tires and a broken spring (no instruction or no warning about driving fast down a hill; poorly maintained equipment); it rained and everyone got soaked because no shelter was set up (planner used poor judgment on her first outdoor wedding; it was the rainy season, should have scheduled event for another time or had it in a large tent); there were no company employees trained in even basic first aid at the scene, and it took 20 minutes for an ambulance to arrive to attend to the bride (rescue was overly lengthy); and the alcohol and food was considered by the bride's father to be lower quality than what he had specified, and considering everything that went wrong, he refused to pay. As you can see from this nonadventure event scenario, every type of RET business needs to be concerned about risk management, and there is a lot more to risk management than just buying insurance. The first step involves prevention of accidents.

GUIDELINES FOR PREVENTING ACCIDENTS

The following are the most commonly employed methods or guidelines for preventing accidents. Specific methods vary with the type of service.

Provide Proper Staff Training and Foster a Cooperative Team Spirit Among Employees

Adequate staff training is the most basic requirement of a service provider. If inexperienced staff are used, they must have a very experienced leader. Developing a cooperative, versus a competitive, attitude among coworkers is very important in recreation settings so that staff have others to back them up in case of questions or emergencies. Regular staff training and adequate supervision are expected. Competency-based hiring and promotional standards together with an effective staff development system help ensure consistent program quality and safety (Nicolazzo, 2005). To avoid serious errors or omissions by an event planner or travel agent, for example, have policies that require a quick review by a senior staff member before the contract or plan is sent to the client.

Document Staff Training and Experience

Companies must set up a system for documenting staff training, especially for program leaders, equipment use, and maintenance. A written record of train-ing received, the instructors, topics covered in basic training, and total hours of work experience in similar situations will be demanded for involved employees after a serious injury by law enforcement, regulatory agencies, and attorneys in a lawsuit. Therefore, it is best for you to require written documentation of all previous training and experience and then place descriptions of any company-provided training in each employee's file. Course syllabuses and rosters, copies of certifications and experience logs, and payroll records are commonly used to document training and experience. For example, if your business is a go-kart track, documenting the amount and type of training given to the staff who are loading and orienting guests into the go-karts is important and would be relevant if an accident should occur. In adventure settings, both program leaders and the company should keep a training and experience log. River rafting companies in Colorado, for example, must provide specific types and hours of training and guiding information in order to adhere to state outfitter licensing laws. These logs are inspected and used to document guide training and experience in case an injury should occur during a rafting trip.

Frequently Inspect and Maintain Equipment, With Documentation

All equipment must be checked frequently and maintained on a regular basis if it is to remain safe to use. If staff do not know equipment is broken, they may inadvertently use it, which can contribute to employee and client accidents. You must establish a regular schedule for checking important equipment and identifying the hazard level of problem vehicles and gear. Pull very hazardous equipment from active inventory, and document maintenance or repair that has been completed. You cannot wait until something breaks; the expectation is for the company to discover problems before they present a serious hazard.

Federal and state laws now require commercial vehicle drivers to conduct pre-trip inspections and report vehicle maintenance needs to the manager supervising that part of the business. Vehicles with hazardous conditions must not be used for trips until repairs are made. A log of major recreation equipment used and its condition is also essential. A commonly used approach is to conduct a pre-trip inspection, and then at the end of each program, the leader notes any

Theo Helmann AFP/Getty Images

Truthful advertising, guest orientation, regular and documented maintenance, and accident responsiveness are required to minimize liability in mountain bike rentals.

equipment maintenance needs and forwards these to management.

Warn Guests About the Hazards and Have Them Assume These Risks

RET providers should never state in writing or say verbally that an activity is "safe." A brief listing of potential risks should be included in promotional materials for all adventure activities. When clients are involved in active programs, certainly adventure programs, they should be required to read and sign a legal document before they start that, at a minimum, describes the risks associated with the activity they willingly are about to undertake. There are two general types of notification forms: an **acknowledgment of risk** (AOR) and a **liability waiver**. The AOR identifies the risks associated with the activity, then states that the guest is aware of these risks and chooses to participate despite the risks. A sample AOR for a rafting operation used for trips through national parks in the western United States is shown in figure 10.2. A waiver includes the AOR components and goes further to describe how the client waives, or relinquishes, her legal rights to bring a lawsuit against the service provider.

The wording of AORs and waivers is very important, and their use effectiveness varies by situation, state, and country. Although some attorneys suggest AORs and waivers are of no use, the general practice of the recreation industry in the United States and Canada, backed by numerous court cases, suggests they have value in either reducing damages or even getting lawsuits thrown out of court. But the AOR or waiver must be a legal document (consult a lawyer to ensure this), and clients must not be coerced into signing them. Youth under 18 years present unique, heightened liability concerns, and parents or legal guardians must sign for children under 18 years (Van Gorder, 2007). However, having the client sign an AOR or waiver is not always convenient; you may not want to scare away potential business, or the activity is considered to be of low risk (e.g., a retail setting). Consult your attorney to see if the problems that arise from having your guests sign one of these forms are worth the protection it could provide.

Finally, a guest must be verbally warned of potential hazards and how to avoid them before the start of a recreation activity.

Provide a Complete Preprogram Safety Talk for Guests

Adequate instruction provided before any guest participation in a recreation program is an essential element of risk management. This talk should

In consideration of the services of _____ , Inc., their officers, agents and employees, and stockholders, and all other persons or entities associated with those businesses (hereinafter collectively referred to as " _____ "), I agree as follows:

Although_____ has taken reasonable steps to provide me with appropriate equipment and skilled guides so I can enjoy a rafting activity for which I may not be skilled,_____has informed me this activity is not without risk. Certain risks are inherent in each activity and cannot be eliminated without destroying the unique character of the activity. These inherent risks are some of the same elements that contribute to the unique character of this activity and can be the cause of loss or damage to my equipment, or accidental injury, or in extreme cases, permanent trauma or death._____ does not want to frighten me or reduce my enthusiasm for this activity but believes it is important for me to know in advance what to expect and to be informed of the inherent risks. The following describes some, but not all, of those risks.

1. White-water rapids will be encountered. You can be jolted, jarred, bounced, thrown to and fro, and otherwise shaken during rides through some of these rapids. It is possible that you could be injured if you come in contact with other passengers, paddles held by a passenger, food boxes, frames, or other fixed equipment necessary for the operation of the expedition and the outfitting of the raft.

2. Boats could turn over or you could be "thrown" overboard as a result of unexpected wave action or your guide's misjudgment of the rapid or the terrain. This could result in "mental anguish" or trauma; injuries sustained from collision with the raft and its supplies or equipment, or from items in the river bed; and prolonged exposure to cold water (hypothermia) leading to impaired health or, in extreme cases, death. Accidental drowning is also a possibility.

3. Accidents can occur during off-river hiking excursions. Trails are not maintained, and you can slip or fall during a hike, resulting in damage to equipment or personal injury.

4. Accidents can occur at camp and when getting on and off the raft. Rafts are slippery when wet and can drift a distance when you try to climb on. You might slip and fall, in which case you might damage or lose equipment you are carrying (such as a camera or day pack), you might injure yourself by falling against some object, or fall into the river. River currents are swift, so all persons, especially children, must wear a life jacket when on or near the river.

5. Exposure to the natural elements can be uncomfortable or harmful. You should be aware that this exposure could cause sunburn, dehydration, or heat exhaustion and heat cramps.

6. Rafting trips often occur in wilderness settings a long distance from roads and medical services. Evacuation and medical treatment may be delayed, causing additional trauma.

7. Some rafting trips use one- and two-person inflatable kayaks. Operation of these boats requires quick and vigorous paddling. There is no guide in these boats, and participants are on their own when maneuvering. Therefore, riding in kayaks has a greater risk of injury than in guided rafts.

I am aware that white-water rafting entails risks of injury or death to any participant. I understand the description of these inherent risks is not complete and that other unknown or unanticipated inherent risks may result in injury or death. I agree to assume and accept full responsibility for the inherent risks identified herein and those inherent risks not specifically identified. My participation in this activity is purely voluntary, no one is forcing me to participate, and I elect to participate in spite of and with full knowledge of the inherent risks.

I acknowledge that engaging in this activity may require a degree of skill and knowledge different from other activities and that I have responsibilities as a participant. I acknowledge that the staff of _____ has been available to more fully explain to me the nature and physical demands of this activity and the inherent risks, hazards, and dangers associated with this activity.

I certify that I am fully capable of participating in this activity. Therefore, I assume and accept full responsibility for myself, including all minor children in my care, custody, and control, for bodily injury, death, or loss of personal property and expenses as a result of those inherent risks and dangers identified herein and those inherent risks and dangers not specifically identified, and as a result of my negligence, in participating in this activity.

I have carefully read, clearly understood, and accepted the terms and conditions stated herein and acknowledge that this agreement shall be effective and binding upon myself, my heirs, assigns personal representative and estate, and for all members of my family, including minor children.

PRINT PARTICIPANT NAME: _____

PARTICIPANT SIGNATURE: _____ DATE: _____

(If under 18, guardian signature required.)

PRINT ADDRESS: _____

CITY: _____ STATE: _____ ZIP: _____

CONTACT NAME/PHONE IN CASE OF EMERGENCY: _____

Figure 10.2 A sample visitor's acknowledgment of risk for a rafting company.

involve identifying hazards and how to avoid them, demonstrating proper techniques, and showing what to do in an emergency. To ensure that frontline staff cover all critical topics, companies are now requiring leaders to rely on printed safety talk cards, with little improvisation allowed.

Learn About the Special Medical Considerations of Guests

Before the start of the activity, you must learn about any medical or physical conditions that may affect the ability of a client to safely participate in the program. These conditions could include medications, allergies, dietary concerns, and prior experience in similar activities. Company staff members are expected to make accommodations for these conditions, such as plan contingencies in case of an accident or change menus, or not accept the client's registration. Organizations acquire this information at registration and during the preactivity safety talk.

Set Special Policies for Riskier Program Elements

You are expected to anticipate hazardous situations that may arise during a recreation program and create specific staff and client policies designed to reduce the risk of injury. What is low risk for one type of person or in one setting may be much higher risk for other persons or in different situations. Two examples of this need are the increased risk (and excitement) of rafting during peak spring runoff or allowing young children to participate in an activity that may be appropriate for adults only.

Alcohol consumption during a program is another important risk consideration. Your guests are often on vacation, and many desire to relax with a favorite alcoholic beverage. Alcohol consumption by clients on trips can be a safety problem and can increase company risk and liability, even if you do not serve them. Drinking during activities may be unacceptable, while at camp or lodging it may be more reasonable. Therefore, companies must have clear alcohol consumption rules, especially during activities. An example of where this can be an issue is wine tasting during a bike tour in the Napa Valley, California, wine-producing region. Special alcohol insurance riders or provisions must be included in your policy.

You must also establish policies for staff alcohol consumption on multiday programs where they are with clients 24 hours per day.

EMERGENCY RESPONSE

Although very infrequent, accidents can occur even with the best-trained staff and most modern equipment. So another element of risk management is emergency response. How your organization responds, provides first aid, seeks medical help, assists in any evacuations (in remote areas), and communicates with the patient and media have a huge impact on guest health and safety but also in the likelihood of a subsequent lawsuit.

The three basic elements of effective emergency response are (1) providing proper medical treatment; (2) documenting accident details; and (3) properly handling and communicating with victims, relatives, agencies, and the press. Each is described here in more detail.

Provide Medical Treatment

Providing prompt, proper emergency first aid, contacting the emergency medical system (EMS), and if in a remote setting, taking evacuation actions is the first element of an effective emergency response. If your service is adventure oriented or in a location 30 minutes or more from medical assistance, you must have staff trained and certified in first aid onsite and generally cannot rely totally on local EMS providers.

Get Proper Medical Treatment Regardless of Fault

Get the best possible emergency medical treatment as quickly as possible and worry about who pays later. Determining subsequent medical care after initial medical treatment has been given is a doctor's decision. If the accident is serious, then you must immediately contact your insurance company, which should provide guidance about who will pay for the follow-up care. In many instances the guest's own insurance should cover these expenses.

Provide a High Level of Care and Show Concern

Lawsuits are entered by injured parties when they believe the service provider has not demonstrated the highest level of care and concern for their well-being and personal safety. This care and concern starts before the accident and should be an ongoing element of the entire program. Prompt, correct first aid by trained and certified medical first responders is a requirement. Injured persons respond better and develop lesser degrees of shock if one individual is assigned to that person, stays with him in the ambulance or vehicle to the hospital, checks him into the hospital, remains in the waiting room, and gives him the same kind of care and attention that a parent would give her child. This is often the most important factor in discouraging accident victims from going into litigation (Hronek and Spengler, 2002).

Document Accident Details

Documenting accident details on an **accident report form** and obtaining witness statements is the second element of an effective emergency response. You must have established procedures and forms for recording what happened; when, where, and how it happened; who was involved; first aid given; and follow-up actions taken by the company. Getting several signed witness statements is highly recommended in any serious accident situation.

Complete an Accident Report Form

The program leader who was overseeing the injured person should begin to make field notes about the accident as soon as possible. Of particular concern is answering the basic questions of what, where, when, how, and who was involved in the accident. The program leader should note the time of the injury and the time of any evacuation, as well as make notes about the details of what happened and possibly things that were said. An example of an accident report form is shown in figure 10.3.

Gather Statements and Photographs

It is extremely important to acquire witness statements, and if helpful, statements from the injured party and family members, about how and why the accident occurred. These documents should be signed by both the witness and the company representative. Take pictures of the accident site. However, the company should recognize that whatever statements are gathered will be subpoenaed in a court action.

Prepare a Full Written Accident Report

An assigned company official should undertake a thorough investigation of any serious accident. Utilize the initial accident report, the witness statements, and the written accounts of the service provider or leader to develop a complete written report of the accident and follow-up care. Develop a file of the accident that includes the full report, the signed waiver form or acknowledgment of risk, witness statements, insurance agent instructions, the doctor's reports, and any other pertinent information. Make a backup copy, and store each file in a different location in case of future legal action.

Communication

Properly handling and communicating with victims, relatives, agencies, and the press is the third element of an effective emergency response. It is critically important to be respectful of victims and their relatives and to not cause undue suffering by the inappropriate release of accident information. Yet you must fully cooperate with law enforcement and regulatory agency personnel.

The opportunity to defend an RET service provider against frivolous litigation often slips away in the few days after an accident occurs. As time goes by, memories fade, details are forgotten, and the opportunity to put a professional face on the entire incident is lost. Litigation attorneys often wait until the statute of limitations (time after which a lawsuit cannot be filed) almost expires before they file the lawsuit. Their hope and the reality, unfortunately too often, is that by the time the lawsuit is filed, so much has been lost and forgotten that it becomes impossible and impractical to defend the provider against the lawsuit. The sooner information is gathered and obtained about the accident, the better your chances are of effecting a positive outcome if faced with potentially damaging litigation. The following guidelines will help you handle accident situations properly and avoid litigation.

Communications With Injured Person After an Accident Occurs

Training should be provided so that staff communications with an injured person are carefully considered and guided. Staff should never make guarantees of a speedy evacuation. You can say that you are doing the best you can and that you have sent for help. Do

River: _____ Weather: _____

Location: _____ Date: _____

Type of vehicle/boat: _____

Injured Person

Name: _____

Address: _____

City: _____ State: _____ Zip Code: _____

Phone: _____ Age: _____ Sex: Male Female

Parents (if under 18): _____

Patient's description of accident:

How patient could have prevented the accident:

Witness to Accident

Name: _____

Address: _____

Phone: _____

Name: _____

Address: _____

Phone: _____

Describe possible injury:

Similar injury occurred to person prior?

First aid given at river: _____ By whom: _____

Transportation to medical facility: (how, time, who, and so on)

Doctor's diagnosis:

Name of doctor who attended patient: _____

Name of guides involved and the trip leader: _____

Description of accident:

Photos of site taken?

Signed witness statements attached.

The above information is correct.

_____   _____
Signature of trip leader   Date

Figure 10.3   Sample accident report form.

not make any admission of guilt or wrongdoing, such as "We've had problems here before" or "This horse has been a problem for us in the past." Comments of this nature will be very damaging in litigation. Do not make statements about what happened. It is okay to say you're sorry the person is hurt, to say you are doing everything you can to get help as fast as you can, and to show empathy and sympathy.

Communications With the News Media

If there has been a serious injury, the wise service provider can almost count on some contact with the news media. Often this contact leads to poorly documented facts of the accident and results in bad publicity and potential litigation problems. You should have a clear policy that designates only one person as the spokesperson with news media. The spokesperson should do the following:

- Prepare a factual statement to be reviewed by legal counsel, if necessary.
- Communicate the statement to media services, such as Associated Press.
- Set up a system for handling telephone inquiries.

A general policy is that no one, including the spokesperson, can release any information that identifies the responsibility for the accident without first consulting legal counsel.

Follow-Up

It is essential that a representative of the service provider make visits or phone calls to a seriously injured client concerning their welfare and well-being for a period of time after the initial medical treatment. Show personal attention, care, and concern, and they will be less likely to sue you. Remember, everything you say or do before, during, and after the accident could be scrutinized in detail, either by litigating attorneys or a court of law. Think about what you are doing and saying. All these risk management components should be brought together into a comprehensive risk management plan. An example of a risk management plan and program for an adventure ropes course is described in Spotlight On.

SPOTLIGHT ON

Fort Miley Adventure Challenge Course Risk Management

Location

The Fort Miley Adventure Challenge Course (FMACC) is located in Golden Gate National Recreation Area in San Francisco, California.

Background

The FMACC is part of the Pacific Leadership Institute (PLI) at San Francisco State University. PLI's mission is to provide leadership development, outdoor recreation, and experiential education programs to public, nonprofit, and private agencies meeting youth, recreation, and human service needs. The FMACC supports this mission by operating a challenge course (also known as a ropes course) that offers half-day, full-day, play-day, and multiday programs tailored to various types of groups (such as youth, corporate, and leisure) and their goals. *Challenge courses* are a team-based progression of low-elevation and higher-elevation elements built in the trees; they involve the use of cables, ladders, and ropes. These elements employ physical, emotional, and mental challenges to encourage team development, support, trust, leadership, self-esteem, and personal goal setting.

Photo courtesy of Drew McAdams

Products and Services

The PLI through FMACC provides the challenge course elements and a variety of programs that are operated by paid and volunteer staff. The ropes course challenges and motivates participants to achieve more and work together in new and creative ways.

The FMACC has a risk management program to minimize the risk of accidents and injuries while maintaining a reasonable level of challenge. Their risk management program consists of seven components:

1. *Management oversight and duties.* This includes statements by the director about the importance of safety and risk management. It assigns the responsibility for safety oversight to the FMACC director and outlines that person's responsibilities and those of other organization staff regarding safety and risk management.

2. *Hazards and risks.* Unique risks and hazards to both guests and staff associated with the FMACC are outlined. The plan describes specific policies and practices for reducing risks from these hazards. An example of a hazard is a participant falling off an element. One related safety policy is belaying participants with special climbing rope and gear and the commands used to start or stop participants from climbing. This ensures that if a user falls, he or she is held off the ground by the rope and safety system.

3. *Risk transfer.* PLI is covered by a $15 million insurance policy, which provides coverage not just for FMACC but for other activities at San Francisco State University. With ongoing clients, PLI often requires additional insured clauses in the contracts, which lists FMACC on their client policy. Another risk transfer mechanism is that all participants are required to sign a liability release before arriving at the course.

4. *Inspection and certification.* Many of the challenge course elements are anchored in living trees and use cables, bolts, ropes, wood bridges, and specialized hardware. To ensure the course is safe for use, the organization takes two primary actions: Staff inspection at the beginning of the day before clients arrive and a detailed inspection by an independent third party. This inspection is done at least twice a year and more frequently if needed.

5. *Accident reporting.* This organization, like other adventure operators, has reporting procedures and forms in case of an accident. An incident report must be completed for each accident that results in injury and for a near-miss (incident where safety was compromised but did not result in injury). If a serious injury occurs, the staff must obtain written statements from at least two witnesses.

6. *Training.* Adequate staff training is considered the main priority for the FMACC. The organization has developed a 50-page training manual and requires all staff to attend multiday training sessions, be tested on basic skills and knowledge, and go through an apprentice program before they can lead a group.

7. *Emergency procedures.* The organization has a set of clear policies, procedures, and written checklists in case of an emergency. Staff must have a certificate in standard first aid. They have a "cause no further harm" set of first-response procedures because there is a city fire station with advanced medical response just two blocks from the course.

Business Advice and Plans

A serious concern about safety in any RET business is the tendency to become complacent and let safety standards slip if a serious accident has not occurred in some time. It is management's duty to constantly maintain high safety levels for both clients and staff. Death and serious injuries to staff and clients have occurred at other adventure outfitters because of horseplay and disregard for safety guidelines. Industry statistics show that most accidents on challenge courses happen to the staff, so management must not let staff become complacent about safety standards.

PREPARING A RISK MANAGEMENT PLAN

Before you start your RET business, you should develop a thorough risk management plan (also known as a Loss Control Plan) and then update it annually. Property owners or land management agencies will always require a thorough risk management plan to be submitted and approved well in advance of a program or event. It is much more effective for a company to take a comprehensive look at risk management in the organization than to deal with issues as they arise (Spengler, Connaughton, and Pittman, 2006). The eight major components of this plan are described here.

1. *Purpose, management policy statements, and duties.* The first element of the risk management plan outlines the purpose of the plan and gives statements by executives about the importance of risk management. It also outlines responsible company positions and the responsibilities and duties in risk management. This component describes how your risk management program will be administered.

2. *Hazards and risk factors.* Each RET business has unique areas of risk along with more standard concerns of all businesses. Outline potential hazards to both guests and staff. You may include a history of past accidents. For each job type or division, describe specific policies and practices for reducing risks from these hazards.

3. *Risk transfer and insurance.* For major risks identified, describe the insurance coverage the company will acquire or has acquired. Discuss limits and key policy requirements.

4. *Inspection and abatement.* Describe the inspection procedures, forms, and responsible persons in this section. When hazardous conditions are identified, discuss abatement (hazard reduction) programs and how repairs and maintenance will be conducted.

5. *Accident reporting and investigation.* Present clear policies and procedures for accident investigation, including responsibilities and time frames. Describe protocols and limitations for release of information to the media and outside parties.

6. *Safety and health committee.* As required by state and federal laws, establish a safety and health committee for every major division. Describe committee responsibilities, makeup of the committee, when the committee will meet with employees, and how and where it will report meeting results. Describe the process where management must respond to significant employee safety concerns.

7. *Training.* Describe the types of employee training programs that will address identified client and staff safety hazards. Provide instructor minimum qualifications and sources of instructors. Specify sources and amounts of funding for training.

8. *Emergency procedures.* Identify standard emergency response protocols, and identify responsible staff members. Describe the emergency response procedures for each division or major program for the treatment of injured or ill guests and staff.

A comprehensive risk management plan is critically important to prevent or minimize losses to guests, employees, and company assets. The plan must cover management policies and responsibilities, identification of hazards and risk factors along with effective mitigation measures, the transfer of risk through insurance coverage, minimizing accidents and losses through inspections and abatement, employee training, proper emergency procedures, accident investigation, and the creation of employee health and safety committees. Synthesis and coordination are critical elements of any risk management plan. See Case Study 10.1 on the online student resource, which shows an outline of what types of information the U.S. National Park Service requires in a Loss Control and Management Plan.

INTEGRATING RISK MANAGEMENT INTO THE BUSINESS PLAN

Much of risk management deals with operational policies and activities, but it is still important to build risk management into your business plan, especially if you are proposing an adventure, event, or tourism business. Government permitting agencies and lending institutions want you to demonstrate that your team is aware of the risks and that you are willing to commit substantial resources to reduce risk and ensure client safety. They will require you to identify the manager primarily responsible for risk management at the company level and show this in your organization chart or key job descriptions. Integration of risk management into the plan could include things such as assigning risk management responsibility to a senior manager in the proposed organizational chart, describing the risk management experience of this manager, and briefly discussing likely risks and how you plan to minimize risk and enhance guest safety in the management section of the plan.

SUMMARY

The purpose of this chapter is to learn how recreation, event, and tourism organizations can prevent injuries, protect their assets, limit liability, and reduce losses through risk management. An entrepreneur or manager must be familiar with relevant laws and regulations in addition to retaining qualified legal council. It is critically important that you be well versed in the legal concepts of liability, negligence, and industry standards of care. This chapter describes the broad types of losses that an RET company should be concerned about, ranging from injuries to clients and employees to financial and asset losses. It is impossible to eliminate all risk, so managers must manage risk. They do this through transferring some risk to insurance companies. There are many types of insurance coverage, but you must purchase the correct type and customize coverage to your specific programs and hazards. Commercial general liability and workers' compensation are the basic types of policies for RET companies, but they do not cover other important risks.

In addition to managing risk through adequate insurance coverage, you must establish clear operational policies, procedures, and guidelines. An important component of managing operational risks is preventing accidents through proper training and its documentation, inspection and maintenance of equipment, warning guests and staff about risks and hazards, providing preprogram safety orientation, learning about and accommodating clients' medical and health conditions before the activity, and developing special policies for particularly risky program elements.

If an accident should occur, a quick and appropriate emergency response is required. This ranges from providing first aid, documenting accident details, and company responses to the proper handling of communications about the accident or incident to relatives, regulatory agencies, and the media. All of these elements are combined into a comprehensive risk management plan. Eight components of a risk management plan are described.

Check out the online student resource for additional material, including case studies, Web links, and more.

IV

Pulling the Plan Together

Chapter 11

Financial Planning and Analysis

Learning Objectives

After reading this chapter you will be able to

- understand methods for estimating revenues and operating expenses;
- prepare pro forma financial statements and conduct a break-even analysis;
- examine techniques for determining return on investment;
- identify start-up costs and potential sources of funding; and
- learn how recreation, event, and tourism businesses maintain financial control.

Key Terms

accounts payable	income statement	pro forma statement
accounts receivable	installment loan	profit centers
balance sheet	line of credit	return on equity
cash flow statement	liquidity ratio	sensitivity analysis
chart of accounts	loans	stockholders equity
cost of goods sold (COGS)	mortgages payable	total assets turnover ratio
debt to equity ratio	net margin	variable costs
fixed costs	owners equity	working capital
home equity loan		

Imagine this scenario:

It has been an exciting two months since you opened your new RET business. You have been working overtime to keep up with sales opportunities, hiring staff, and buying new equipment. You have been too busy to enter your checks and credit card expenses into your accounting system because you think there should be plenty of cash on hand, and there are more pressing matters. Then one afternoon you get a letter in the mail stating that your business checking account is overdrawn. How can this be? You had plenty of money; the bank must have made a mistake. Quickly you go online and check the balance. Yes, you are overdrawn by $4,500. In the last month you made some big purchases that you had not planned for initially, but you thought at the time that you would be able to find the money. Other items cost much more than you had projected. Ouch, this is a big problem because tomorrow you have payroll, and your new staff must be paid on time—you even committed to a large bonus. In two days you are meeting with your advertising consultant, and she expects payment for the promotions related to your grand opening. You could use the extra promotional push because your sales staff hinted the other day that the reservations are not as strong as you had hoped. Unfortunately, you have not compiled the sales totals yet, and just looking at the checking account statement does not tell you what deposits are sales. Then you notice that the check for the park service quarterly permit fee, required in advance of opening, has not cleared yet. If that check bounces you could lose the operating permit in the park where most of your tours are based. So you start scrambling for funds. A call to your banker reveals you've already borrowed the maximum loan amount. You call the credit card company to see if you can get a cash advance. No luck, as you are over the limit there too because you have been using your card for business and personal expenses. Sweat is pouring down your face. Financially speaking, you realize your company is out of control.

This story illustrates that your company may have an exceptional business concept, a great service or product, an experienced management team, and a thorough promotions plan to jump-start sales; but if you do not know how much money it will take to get started and tide you through the initial difficult period, lack a funding plan to raise needed capital, or are not able to maintain control over company spending during operation, it is doomed to failure. An entrepreneur can be so focused on developing the business concept and hiring staff that they may think all they need are the funds to get started and then he will worry about financial planning later. But research by the Small Business Administration (2007) documents that financial issues are one of the top five reasons that new businesses collapse. So it is critically important that you develop a comprehensive and strategic financial plan, set up financial controls before you start the company, be very disciplined with spending, and frequently evaluate financial performance during operations.

The other chapters in this book discuss and demonstrate theories and practices that affect the financial feasibility and profitability of a small- to medium-size RET business. One thing is certain, an RET business must be profitable, and you must get a reasonable return on your investment in order for the company to be successful and financially sustainable. The company is not a welfare agency or an environmental nonprofit that can depend on taxes, grants, and donations to survive. Profits that come from understanding and serving its customers extremely well are its only means of survival. An RET business is not a multinational corporation that has amassed so much capital that it can financially dominate a marketplace. Small RET businesses must view everything they do through a cost-effectiveness lens and keep expenses under control. However, government regulations and, more important, informed citizens will not support or tolerate a shortsighted company that is robbing our children's future through environmental pollution, and directly or indirectly adding to social degeneration through unjust amoral practices, for their own short-term gain. So for relatively little additional cost a company can build into its financial planning and manage the additional expenses associated with environmental stewardship and social responsibility. Many companies highlighted in this book have shown that it is not only possible to be financially, environmentally, and socially successful but also requisite (see the green tip on p. 223).

In this chapter we help you pull all the pieces together to turn your concept into reality by assessing the financial feasibility, undertaking financial planning, and acquiring the funds needed to start your

RET business. You will learn about the four principle components of the financial planning process:

1. Projecting revenues
2. Estimating costs
3. Developing pro forma financial statements
4. Financing your RET business

The chapter concludes with a description of proven management techniques for maintaining financial control during operations. This includes setting up an accounting system, developing a budget, monitoring performance, and exhibiting control of expenditures and receivables. We will provide a case study of RET businesses to illustrate concepts and allow for a more industry-focused perspective. The first step in the financial planning process is projecting revenues.

PROJECTING REVENUES

Your business concept will lead to sales, but how much sales revenue can be expected? Will it be sufficient to grow the company and give you a reasonable return on your investment? Projecting revenue in advance will help you answer these questions. Sales forecasts also allow you to plan sufficient staff levels and supply purchases. Projecting sales before your operation even begins is a challenge, but it becomes much more manageable in your second year. It is time now to paint the financial picture of your company at the start-up, at the end of the first year, and for several years into the future. The projection of revenues is both science and art, exemplified by solid research and best guesstimates. Here are the critical elements of projecting sales and revenue:

- In-depth research
- Transparent estimation method
- Clear identification and documentation of underlying assumptions
- Comparison with similar enterprises

In this section we explore and learn how these elements are used and provide examples of their application.

IN-DEPTH RESEARCH

Objective research is the key to making your projections accurate. You have already gathered a good deal of relevant data. In earlier chapters you investigated the recreation, event, and tourism industry and learned about trends driving growth, market size, growth rates, and external factors influencing consumer demand. Your competitor analysis provided data on the level of competition and the marketplace gaps or opportunities available. This gives you a sense of how rapidly your sales may grow. You discovered that many recreation services are highly seasonal from winter to summer, month to month, and even weekend to weekday. So you know if sales vary a great deal over the year. You also learned that the average price charged may vary by the season, month, or week. The industry analysis you conducted earlier alluded to some of the facilities and major equipment that would be required to provide your services. The capacity of this equipment or facility, such as the number of rooms in your resort or the square footage of your retail store, must also be worked into your projections because it is often the critical limiting factor to sales. Supplement this past research as you see the need by talking with suppliers, making further observations of competitors, and reading from industry journals. Gather all this research and supporting data, and integrate the information into your revenue projections.

TRANSPARENT ESTIMATION METHOD

The sales projection methods used vary from sophisticated econometric models to simple projection tables. For small businesses, a relatively straightforward projection method is often sufficient. Table 11.1 provides a table to use in estimating sales of your service and product types. The initial output is sales volume of the number of units for each service, such as tours, river trips, fishing gear rentals, or corporate events. Later you will add in the average revenues per sale for each service type to calculate monthly sales in dollars. If your business is highly seasonal, then you might want to develop high- and low-season tables, rather than initially by month. In table 11.1 you will identify profit centers, average daily unit sales by profit center, unit sales per week, and then average unit sales per month. You will need to have reasonable estimates of prices that you can charge, such as average daily rate (ADR), average check size (ACS), average trip rate (ATR), and load or use factors, such as average occupancy rates and average number of passengers per

Table 11.1 Sales Projections Table and Related Assumptions

	Season (high or low)				
Profit center	**Avg. sales/ day* (in units)**	**Avg. sales/ week** (daily sales x 7 days) (in units)**	**Avg. sales/ month (weekly sales x 4 weeks) (in units)**	**Avg. price per unit*** (in $)**	**Avg. sales per month (avg. units × avg. price)**
Store sales					
Rentals					
Tours					
Other					
Total					

*Estimate the average sales from each profit center on an average day in that particular season.

**Multiply average daily sales by number of days a week you are open. Then make any adjustments for unusually strong sales on weekends versus weekdays.

***Estimate the average sales (ticket) price you will receive for all services in each profit center, for that particular season. Often the average price per unit declines in the low season because of discounting.

From R. Pfister and P. Tierney, 2008, *Recreation, event, and tourism businesses* (Champaign, IL: Human Kinetics).

trip. You acquire this data from your industry analysis and financial planning research.

Profit centers are distinct areas of your business that generate substantial revenues. If your business is a sport fishing service and store, then you may have profit centers related to fishing gear sales, guided fishing trips, and fishing gear rentals, for example. Think about how many gear sales, fishing trip sales, and rentals you could reasonably expect on an average weekend day in your high season, given your facility and equipment capacities and demand for these services. It is very important to start with a typical day of sales and be comfortable with your daily projections before you move on to other estimates. You can then calculate average weekly sales for each profit center by multiplying daily sales by seven days and adjusting for differences in weekday versus weekend sales (if necessary). Finally, estimate average monthly sales by multiplying adjusted weekly sales by four weeks.

The far right column of table 11.1 is the estimated average sales per month. This amount results from

multiplying average unit sales per month by the average price per unit sold. The average price will normally vary by season. Then average sales per month for all revenue centers is the sum of average month sales for each center. This figure can be used for revenue during each month of that season in a forthcoming pro forma income statement.

DOCUMENTATION OF ASSUMPTIONS

An important component of sales projection is an assumptions table that shows and describes the key assumptions used in determining sales and the sources of these. Do not make it a mystery how you determined sales. Every key number should have backup support and a source and be clearly shown in the assumptions table or sales projection table. This allows a mentor, reviewers, and potential financial backers to see exactly what you have based these all-important revenue projections on. Sales growth for

Carefully estimate costs of purchasing and preparing food for an event.

Associated Press/Toby Talbot

the next three to five years should be projected using conservative estimates.

COMPARISON WITH SIMILAR ORGANIZATIONS

A final check of the accuracy of your sales projections should be made by comparing your projections with data from other similar businesses. This will help ensure you are not overly optimistic, as is often the case with inexperienced owners. Although it is impossible to get potential competitors to give you financial information, you can sometimes acquire this type of data from businesses in other locations, by counting the number of customers going into a similar business

over several days, and from sites on the Internet. Industry average figures may also be available from trade associations. However, it is better to have developed your own projections first because a new owner learns so much in the process, and no two businesses are exactly alike. But it is also important to check the reality of your projections with existing businesses or experienced mentors.

ESTIMATING COSTS

A second part of the financial plan is the estimation of costs. There are two broad types of costs: start-up costs and operating expenses. Start-up costs are expenditures needed to get the business from the decision to start, through the first day it is open, and these will be discussed later in this chapter. The estimation of operating expenses is critical to projecting the financial viability of your business. There are two types of operating expenses: fixed costs and variable costs.

Variable costs vary with the amount of sales. For instance, with an increase in sales a company has additional expenses from carrying more inventory, higher wage expenses, and trip supply costs. As total sales go down, these expenses normally go down proportionally. Labor costs that are considered variable are limited to hourly wages and related taxes and benefits but not salaries. Your variable costs will change each month depending on projected sales volume. When estimating variable costs, use a projection approach similar to that described for sales projections. Consider an average weekend day in the high season when you are projecting a certain level of sales. How many staff persons will be needed to operate facilities and equipment? What will you be paying them? What will their benefits be? What will be the cost of supplies, such as food, shuttle vehicle gasoline, agency per-person user fees, or resort rooms you will use to create the recreation, event, and tourism experience?

Fixed costs, in contrast, do not greatly vary with the amount of sales over a specific activity range or time. They are often referred to as *overhead costs* as they are not proportionately related to sales volume. Examples of these costs include rent, administrative salaries, business licenses, insurance, and depreciation.

Cost of goods sold (COGS), another category of costs, is most frequently related to retail product sales versus the sales of services. Although most recreation, event, and tourism companies are primarily service oriented and COGS may not apply, many also gain significant revenues from product resales in a store. COGS is considered the cost of obtaining *raw materials* that are sold directly, without adding much value, to consumers. In this book we refer to COGS as *merchandise* sold in retail stores, such as books sold in a gift shop, but COGS does not refer to *supplies* purchased to create new products, such as raw food that is modified by staff to create meals.

Cost of goods sold = (beginning merchandise inventory + net purchases of merchandise) – ending merchandise inventory

As you shall see in the next section, COGS is normally considered to reduce revenues, rather than increase expenses, and is shown under the revenues heading of a financial statement.

The methods used to project operating costs are similar to those described for sales projections. You'll need to research the industry and use a transparent estimation method. The "from scratch" (zero-based) approach described for sales projections is recommended. In this method you take your sales projections for an average day for each profit center during the high or low season, and then estimate the variable and fixed costs incurred to operate your services and facilities with this amount of sales. This process is very enlightening, and you learn a great deal about your business. Unfortunately, unless you are experienced in the industry, large estimation errors can be made. Therefore, it is important to compare your figures with those from a comparable business or industry average to either estimate costs or at least cross-check them with your self-generated estimates. Averages are most helpful as a percentage of gross sales, such as the percentage of utilities and communications costs relative to gross sales. However, every business is unique, and relying completely on industry averages without adequately researching your specific environment and opportunity can lead to substantial errors. Now that you have estimated revenues and costs, you can develop pro forma financial statements.

DEVELOPING PRO FORMA FINANCIAL STATEMENTS

Whether you are starting a new recreation, event, and tourism business or you have been operating one for years, financial statements are essential for the success of your firm. This is the third step in the financial planning process. Financial statements provide you, your lending institutions, and the Internal Revenue Service or Revenue Canada with basic information about how your company is performing financially, and they allow you to control the finances of your company. Projections for the next year are referred to as **pro forma statements**. The basic financial statements are

- income statements,
- cash flow statements, and
- balance sheets.

As you will see later, each statement offers a different perspective on the company's financial status.

Financial information about any business, but especially that of a small business, is tightly held and usually kept confidential. To secure financial data for a small RET business in this book, we cooperated with an actual resort and promised not to reveal its identity; in turn the resort shared general financial data that are presented on the following pages as financial statements. So the name Rimstone Resort is fictitious, but the percentages shown in the data are actual information. The resort is found in a scenic rural area of the southwestern United States and has about 125 rooms, a spa, horseback riding, a golf course, an upscale restaurant, children's activities, and extensive tour programs. These data complement financial information found in other case studies throughout the book and provide keen insights into the financial characteristics of RET companies.

INCOME STATEMENT

An **income statement** describes monthly revenues and expenditures and the resultant monthly net profit or loss. Net income illustrates whether you have a profit on paper. As you will see in the section on cash management, "paper profit" is not the same as cash flow. The far right column illustrates the projected year-total amounts and percentages (percentage is based on total net revenue). Table 11.2 shows the format and figures for an income statement, types of expenses, and a list of accounts for Rimstone Resort. It is common for a new business to show a net loss for many initial months and often for the total first year.

It is also important to estimate what your profit and loss picture will look like in five years. Projecting out three to five years is more challenging because of the greater uncertainty with each new year, but it is needed to estimate your financial performance after the initial years where you might be relatively unprofitable. The later years are used in the cash flow statements to show when loans may be paid back. Only year-total estimates, rather than monthly, are determined after the first year. Planners often use a percent increase from the prior year applied to all or some of the accounts the next year. Table 11.3 presents a multiyear income statement for the hypothetical resort.

A key for the income statement is predicting sales, as described earlier. Revenues for each profit center are located at the top. Gross revenues for every month and for the year total are the result of subtracting any cost of goods sold (COGS) from total revenue. You can estimate expenses using the previously described methods. The figures to the far right express a specific account as a percentage of gross revenues. The "bottom line," or net profit or loss before income taxes and depreciation (BTD), is derived by subtracting total expenses from gross profit. Therefore, it is critical to note that there are still substantial cash outflows for capital and tax expenses before a true net profit can be determined, but estimation of true net profit is not needed for this type of analysis.

It is often helpful to conduct a **sensitivity analysis** to see what effects an overestimation of revenues combined with an underestimation of key cost projections might have on the bottom line. In this type of analysis, you develop a low scenario by reducing revenues by 5 to 10 percent and increasing the projections for key expense accounts by, say, 5 to 10 percent and seeing what your net profit becomes. If the financial picture is still positive, then you should proceed, but if you end up with a large negative net profit, then review your projections assumption again and possibly revise your "likely" scenario. This scenario reduces the risk of overestimating your profitability.

A pro forma income statement can be used to develop a company's operating budget for the upcoming year. It is also required during the application process to secure any external funding, as discussed later in this chapter. The revenue and cost figures calculated in the pro forma income statement are next used to estimate cash flow.

CASH FLOW STATEMENT

A **cash flow statement** provides information on inflows and outflows of cash from operations, if you will need additional funding to meet working capital obligations, or if you might be able to place any cash surpluses into new equipment or investments. A cash flow statement is considered the foundation for analyzing financial viability of a new company (Investopedia, 2007). Cash flow is not the same as profit because most businesses sell their services or products without generating cash, through extending payments (credit) to consumers. For example, a tour company may allow guests to pay a down payment then pay off the balance through installments after the trip is complete. Another unique feature of a cash flow statement is it identifies any capital costs (depreciation) and uses that are not shown on an income statement. For example, an RET business may secure a loan at start-up (a cash source) and use that to purchase land and a building (a cash use). Cash flow statements also identify uses of cash besides operations, such as paying off a loan from a line of credit and providing investor payoff or owner draw.

To further complicate the financial situation, many recreation, event, and tourism businesses are highly seasonal. In the off-season this can result in negative cash flow that requires the buildup of cash reserves during the preseason—when deposits come in but programs are not operating yet—or short-term loans. In essence, the cash flow statement is your cash plan, and it will show you when you have negative cash flow periods that might require your company to take from financial reserves or secure carryover financing. In cash-short times, delaying payments to suppliers can result in additional interest expenses and hurt your credit rating, and emergency financing is much more costly than securing a line of credit well in advance to meet short-term needs. To avoid the cash crunch, take in higher company profits, and give

Table 11.2 Pro Forma Income Statement, Year 1: Rimstone Resort

Revenues	Jan	Feb	Mar	Apr	May	June
Room revenues	52,150	61,800	67,500	71,500	102,730	125,430
Food and beverage	36,858	43,678	47,706	50,533	72,605	88,649
Recreation, events, activities	30,454	36,089	39,418	41,753	59,991	73,246
Retail shop	7,189	8,519	9,305	9,856	14,161	17,290
Other	4,052	4,802	5,244	5,555	7,982	9,745
Gross sales	130,702	154,887	169,173	179,198	257,469	314,361
Less COGS	3,451	4,089	4,466	4,731	6,797	8,299
Gross margin	127,251	150,798	164,707	174,467	250,672	306,062
Expenses						
Wages, payroll	78,340	86,960	87,012	88,778	96,665	99,670
Operation materials, supplies	11,457	13,577	14,829	15,708	22,569	27,556
Agent commissions	2,353	2,788	3,045	3,225	4,634	5,658
Repairs and maintenance	1,830	2,169	2,369	2,509	3,605	4,402
Marketing	7,058	8,364	9,136	9,677	13,904	16,976
Utilities and communications	2,755	3,264	3,565	3,777	5,426	6,625
Insurance and fees	5,030	5,030	5,030	5,030	5,030	5,030
Rent/capital expenses	17,851	17,851	17,851	17,851	17,851	17,851
Interest	6,224	6,174	6,124	6,074	6,024	5,974
Property tax	0	0	0	0	0	41,230
Other expenses	2,091	2,478	2,707	2,867	4,119	4,529
Total expenses	134,988	148,655	151,668	155,496	179,828	235,502
Net income BTD ($)	−7,737	2,143	13,039	18,971	70,844	70,560
Net income BTD (%)	−6.1%	1.4%	7.9%	10.9%	28.3%	23.1%

July	Aug	Sep	Oct	Nov	Dec	Total ($)	Total (%)
134,700	136,600	124,540	86,230	62,900	86,730	1,112,810	39.9%
95,201	96,543	88,020	60,944	44,455	61,297	786,490	28.2%
78,660	79,769	72,727	50,355	36,731	50,647	649,840	23.3%
18,568	18,830	17,168	11,887	8,671	11,956	153,400	5.5%
10,466	10,613	9,676	6,700	4,887	6,739	86,460	3.1%
337,594	342,356	312,131	216,115	157,644	217,369	2,789,000	100.0%
8,913	9,038	8,241	5,706	4,491	5,739	73,961	2.7%
328,682	333,318	303,890	210,410	153,153	211,630	2,715,039	97.3%
102,340	102,670	96,667	87,771	86,623	101,779	1,115,275	40.0%
29,593	30,010	27,361	18,944	13,819	19,054	244,480	8.8%
6,076	6,162	5,618	3,890	2,837	3,912	50,200	1.8%
4,727	4,793	4,370	3,026	2,207	3,043	39,050	1.4%
18,231	18,488	16,856	11,671	8,513	11,738	150,610	5.4%
6,715	6,844	6,578	4,555	3,322	4,581	58,009	2.1%
5,030	5,030	5,030	5,030	5,030	5,030	60,360	2.2%
17,851	17,851	17,851	17,851	17,851	17,851	214,212	7.7%
5,924	5,874	5,824	5,774	5,724	5,674	71,388	2.6%
0	0	0	0	0	41,230	82,460	3.0%
4,601	4,877	4,494	3,058	2,522	3,478	41,820	1.5%
201,088	202,600	190,649	161,570	148,449	217,371	2,127,864	76.3%
127,594	130,718	113,241	48,840	4,704	−5,741	587,175	21.1%
38.8%	39.2%	37.3%	23.2%	3.1%	−2.7%		

Table 11.4 Pro Forma Cash Flow Statement, Year 1: Rimstone Resort

	Start-up costs	Jan	Feb	Mar	Apr	May
Cash sources						
Net cash sales		127,251	150,798	164,707	174,467	250,672
Owner contribution	289,652					
Line of credit	240,000					
Bank loan	867,000					
Total cash inflows	1,396,652	127,251	150,798	164,707	174,467	250,672
Cash uses						
To capital costs						
Land and buildings	1,195,770					
Furniture, equipment	99,000					
Vehicles and other	93,290					
To operations						
Wages, payroll		87,264	95,884	95,936	97,702	105,589
Operation materials, supplies		16,319	18,439	19,691	20,570	27,431
Agent commissions		2,353	2,788	3,045	3,225	4,634
Repairs and maintenance		1,830	2,169	2,369	2,509	3,605
Marketing		7,058	8,364	9,136	9,677	13,904
Utilities and communications		2,755	3,264	3,565	3,777	5,426
Insurance and fees		5,030	5,030	5,030	5,030	5,030
Interest		6,224	6,174	6,124	6,074	6,024
Property tax		0	0	0	0	0
Other expenses		2,091	2,478	2,707	2,867	4,119
Other uses						
Pay off credit line						30,000
Pay off loan						
Income taxes					30,000	
Owner draw						
Total cash outflows	1,388,060	130,923	144,590	147,603	181,431	205,763
Net cash flow	8,592	−3,672	6,208	17,104	−6,964	44,909
Beginning cash balance	0	8,592	4,920	11,128	28,232	21,268
Ending cash balance	8,592	4,920	11,128	28,232	21,268	66,176

June	July	Aug	Sep	Oct	Nov	Dec	Total ($)
306,062	328,682	333,318	303,890	210,410	153,153	211,630	2,715,039
							289,652
							240,000
							867,000
306,062	328,682	333,318	303,890	210,410	153,153	211,630	4,111,691
50,000					150,000		1,395,770
		100,000			50,000		249,000
							93,290
108,594	111,264	111,594	105,591	96,695	95,547	110,703	1,222,363
32,418	34,455	34,872	32,223	23,806	18,681	23,916	302,824
5,658	6,076	6,162	5,618	3,890	2,837	3,912	50,200
4,402	4,727	4,793	4,370	3,026	2,207	3,043	39,050
16,976	18,231	18,488	16,856	11,671	8,513	11,738	150,610
6,625	6,715	6,844	6,578	4,555	3,322	4,581	58,009
5,030	5,030	5,030	5,030	5,030	5,030	5,030	60,360
5,974	5,924	5,874	5,824	5,774	5,724	5,674	71,388
41,230	0	0	0	0	0	41,230	82,460
4,529	4,601	4,877	4,494	3,058	2,522	3,478	41,820
30,000	30,000	30,000	30,000	10,000			160,000
							0
	30,000			30,000		30,000	120,000
311,437	257,023	328,535	216,584	197,505	344,384	243,306	4,097,144
−5,375	71,659	4,783	87,306	12,905	−191,231	−31,676	
66,176	60,802	132,460	137,243	224,549	237,454	46,223	14,547
60,802	132,460	137,243	224,549	237,454	46,223	14,547	

Table 11.5 Pro Forma Balance Sheet, Year End: Rimstone Resort

		Year to date
Assets		
Current assets		
Cash		14,547
Receivables		66,936
Inventory		115,677
	Total current assets	197,160
Capital assets		
Buildings, improvements		1,395,770
Furniture, fixtures, equipment		566,550
Vehicles		65,400
Other property		27,890
Less accumulated depreciation		−350,000
	Total capital assets	1,705,610
Total assets		1,902,770
Liabilities		
Accounts payable		98,521
Bank loan		867,000
Line of credit		127,890
	Total liabilities	1,093,411
Equity		
Personal investment		289,652
Retained earnings		519,707
	Total equity	809,359
Total equity and liabilities		1,902,770

Liabilities

There are two general types of liabilities—money owed by the company to others—shown on a balance sheet:

- *Current liabilities.* Debt that a business has to pay back within a one-year period. These could include **accounts payable**, notes payable, and taxes due.
- *Long-term liabilities.* Liabilities that are due more than a year from the current date. Frequently cited examples are mortgages payable, owners equity, and stockholders equity.

Owners equity, or net worth, represents the owner's claim on the assets of the business. It results from cash investments made by the owner and retained earnings from operations put back into the firm. A basic rule of accounting is that assets minus the liabilities must total zero, thus assets and liabilities balance each other. The amount of retained earnings is adjusted to ensure that liabilities equal assets. For a company just starting, current assets are meager because you are cash poor. Fixed assets should be estimated with careful consideration, as often you have the option to get a loan and buy equipment (incurring a long-term liability) or leasing it (an expense that conserves your cash).

Mortgages payable refers to a legal contract where property (real or personal) is used as security for the payment of a debt. A company must pay back the principle (amount borrowed) plus interest, the financial charge for use of the lender's money. Payments are usually made in equal monthly installments, but there are also loans with balloon payments (entire amount is due at one time).

Stockholders equity is considered the owner's residual interest in assets of the company after deducting liabilities. A number of factors could result in an increase in stockholders equity, such as when book value of the company increases because new stock shares are issued, assets increase, liabilities decrease, or profits are earned. Stockholders equity would decrease when outstanding shares of stock are repurchased by the company, liabilities increase, assets decrease, or losses occur.

Green Tip

Increasing Profitability Through Going Green

An RET entrepreneur must take a critical look at all expenses in order to maximize profits and repay debt. Even if you personally have an interest in going green and being more earth friendly, you still have a fiduciary responsibility to maintaining profitability. When managers consider green eco-friendly practices, their first thought might be that being environmentally conscious will significantly increase company expenses, make their products uncompetitive, and ultimately reduce profitability. When viewed narrowly and in the short term, this may appear true. For example, free-trade, shade-grown organic coffee beans can cost 5 to 15 percent more than other similar types of coffee. However, offering this coffee to your clients at an event may have other immediate and more long-term positive financial impacts. And a company certainly needs to minimize labor-cost increases associated with moving toward green practices. But many innovative companies that have implemented green practices and technology have not seen severe cost increases or a drop in competitiveness. In contrast to this view, they are some of the most successful and profitable firms. This green tip illustrates ways instituting green business practices can save money or make an RET business more profit.

Immediate Financial Returns

- Recycling or reusing "waste" can significantly save on garbage collection costs.
- Reusing and minimizing use of raw materials can reduce materials costs.
- Energy conservation practices reduce the cost of electricity and other forms of energy.
- Reducing use of toxic substances minimizes the risk of employee injury.
- Reducing travel through more teleconferencing and electronic communications saves transportation and labor costs.
- Use of innovative green technology and practices is now more often required by resource agencies and event sponsors to win a competitive contract.
- More consumers are demanding green practices and products, and they will select those firms that offer them.

Longer-Term Financial Returns

- Construction of renewable energy sources, such as solar, can recoup initial investment in a two- to five-year period and subsequently provide very low-cost energy.
- Building a reputation for environmental concern develops customer loyalty and gains your company favor among resource and regulatory agencies.
- Installation of carbon-reducing technology may prevent more-expensive retrofits and legal costs down the road, when carbon emissions will likely be regulated, as has been seen with other air pollutants.
- Many employees are willing to assist in making your company more eco-friendly, and this can lead to greater productivity and loyalty toward management and the company.
- Workers' compensation costs can be reduced by eliminating workplace toxic materials and working in healthier buildings.
- An entrepreneur could start up a new division or an entire company based on green services or products.

These are just some examples of how expenditures in green technology and practices will produce short- and long-term financial gains. But you should also consider that the marginal cost of implementing green practices is often a small percentage of the total production costs. Using the coffee example again, an additional 10 percent boost in the cost of beans translates to just a 1 to 2 percent increase in the final retail price. If your staff feels better about working there because of the extra lengths you went to, and the final little push to win a $100,000 contract was the shade-grown coffee, then the return on investment is considerable. It is important for an entrepreneur to view money spent on green technology as an investment and evaluate its return versus seeing it as just another regulatory burden. With this perspective, more-creative solutions can be developed. Since the probable cost of installing similar equipment will be considerably greater in the future, then eco-friendly green technology and practices contribute to profitability and are much more justified right now.

RATIO ANALYSIS

Information provided on the balance sheet and income statement can be used to calculate financial ratios that allow for comparisons with other similar companies, degree of indebtedness, or returns expected in the industry. The range of what is considered "normal" for a financial ratio varies considerably. Financial ratios become valuable only when they are compared with other ratios in the same set of financial statements and when they are compared with the same ratio in previous financial statements. The commonly used ratios and normative values provided here are only general guides; they come from overall industry averages (http://beginnersinvest.about.com/cs/investinglessons). The prudent entrepreneur will investigate further into appropriate financial ratios.

- The **liquidity ratio** shows the ability of a company to meet immediate debts and how much money is available for working capital. A general rule is that the liquidity ratio should be about 2.

liquidity = current assets/current liabilities

- The **total assets turnover ratio** measures how effective the business is in using its resources. In general, the greater a company's total asset turnover, the more efficiently its assets are being utilized.

total assets turnover = net sale/total assets

- A **debt to equity ratio** illustrates how much the owners have invested in the company compared with financial contributions of others. Generally speaking, a company with a debt to equity ratio of more than 50 percent may find it hard to get a typical bank loan.

equity to debt = equity/total liabilities

- A very frequently referenced ratio is **net margin**, which is used to show what percentage of sales is turned into profit. This ratio varies greatly by the type and size of business. Generally, small businesses need to have a greater net margin than do large corporations because their total sales are considerably less. Several RET businesses profiled in this book had net margins between 8 and 20 percent.

net margin = net profit before taxes/net sales

- The **return on equity** allows for a comparison of the financial returns of the company versus other companies and types of investments. What is acceptable varies with your needs but is normally at least what you could earn from a low-risk investment, such as a bond fund (4-10 percent).

return on equity = net profit/total equity (total assets – total liabilities)

Using these ratios with your pro forma data can tell you if you can cover large unforeseen expenses with cash, how effectively you are using your assets, your level of debt, your profit margin, and how the projected returns compare with the returns from other types of investments. These ratios should also be calculated after the first and in subsequent years of operation.

BREAK-EVEN ANALYSIS

If you are considering starting an RET business, you need to know when the company will start making a profit to determine if the venture is worth your time and investment. A banker from whom you are seeking a loan would also want to know what amount of sales would be needed to become profitable before she approves the transaction. Using data from the income statement, you can estimate when the company will break even or make a profit. This recognizes that growth in sales takes time and that the profit from each sale adds to the overall operating profit. A company has broken even at the time when its total sales or revenues equal its total expenses. Figure 11.2 provides an example of where the break-even point is found. When total revenue first exceeds the fixed costs plus variable costs, this is considered the break-even point.

A condensed financial picture of a small RET business is presented in Spotlight On. It shows sources of revenues, major types of expenditures, and how the start-up of Half Moon Bay Kayak Company was financed. Case Study 11.1 in the online student resource provides more details on its history, owner, and financial performance.

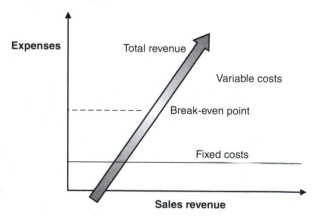

Figure 11.2 Hypothetical break-even point.

Half Moon Bay Kayak Company

Location

Half Moon Bay Kayak Company is a small kayak rental and tour operator located in the town of Half Moon Bay, about 40 miles north of Santa Cruz, California. The company is adjacent to Monterey Bay National Marine Sanctuary with its plentiful wildlife—seals, dolphins, sea lions, sea birds, and occasional sea otters and gray whales. It is inside Pillar Point Harbor near the Mavericks Big Surf Contest site.

Background

The kayak company is headquartered out of an eco-friendly, solar-powered, canvas-covered shop. The Pillar Point Harbor location provides sheltered waters, allowing beginning kayakers a safe place for lessons and for exploring a working fishing port and nearby marine wildlife. One owner, Chris Manchester, was a National Outdoor Leadership School (NOLS) kayak and climbing instructor; the other owner was an Olympic kayaker and manager of another kayaking outfitter. They combined their expertise and passion for kayaking to start the company.

Products and Services

HMB Kayak Company rents sea kayaks to beginning and expert boaters. The durable plastic boats are from top manufacturers. Rental rates are about $50 per day for a one-person kayak and $90 for a two-person kayak, personal flotation device (lifejacket), wetsuit, paddle, and safety orientation. Unguided kayakers are limited to paddling inside the harbor.

Guided tours are an important part of the business. In winter they offer multiday trips in Baja, Mexico, and in Honduras. Guides provide both interpretation and safety so that people of all abilities can enjoy one-hour to four-day tours. Programs are also offered for business staff members to enhance communication and team building.

Chris Manchester and Half Moon Bay Kayak Company.

Another element of their business is instruction in sea kayaking. Classes are geared toward beginners, but programs are also available for intermediate and expert kayakers. Settings include the calm harbor, open ocean, and surf zone waves. An introductory class costs about $100 and includes instructor and equipment.

HMB operates a very small retail shop because their space is limited and the canvas eco-tent does not provide the security of a typical store. So, with the help of a student intern, the owners developed an online store. They do not have secure space for much inventory, but they do carry enough to allow clients to come and demonstrate the gear and kayaking accessories sold on their Web site. Once an order is placed, they work with manufacturers to drop-ship the merchandise as quickly as possible.

The company is a highly seasonal business. Summer is the peak sales period, and August is the top month. January sales are bolstered by trips to Baja, Mexico.

Business Advice and Plans

Half Moon Bay Kayaks just created an online store to substitute for the inability to have a large, secure retail store on the site. But they still would like to have a moderate increase in the shop size and retail space in the future. This would entail acquiring a permit from the harbor district and other regulatory agencies and hiring full-time staff (they currently have only part-time employees). They would need to carefully plan and manage growth to financially support this expansion and allow them to maintain the lifestyle they currently enjoy.

FINANCING YOUR RET BUSINESS

As an entrepreneur, you have done your financial "homework" to this point. You have estimated sales of the proposed company, cash flows, likely expenses, projected profit, and your break-even point. Even if all these figures are positive, you still have a potentially huge hurdle to leap: getting the funding to not only start but also maintain your company until at least your break-even point. Many a great business concept has failed to get off the ground because of the inability to raise start-up funds. Or a business can be undercapitalized at the start and unable to operate at projected levels, ultimately leading to failure.

One advantage of many RET service-only businesses is the relatively low start-up costs needed, compared with an upscale retail store that must buy inventory and lease a facility of substantial size, or a manufacturing firm with expensive specialized equipment. But the low entry funding needed also means your competition may be greater and profit margins smaller because more persons are able to afford to start such a company. Combine this with a service that does not require a high degree of technical skills, and competition can be fierce. This is not an uncommon situation for many types of recreation, event, and tourism businesses, and it emphasizes the need for sound strategic and financial planning. Now is the moment in your planning when you need to do the following:

- Identify the level of funding needed to start.
- Determine the amount of working capital needed to operate for the first year or two.
- Find a mix of funding sources to provide needed capital at a modest cost.

START-UP COSTS

It usually takes more money to get to the opening day of your business, when you are able to start selling services, than an entrepreneur initially considers. If your business is undercapitalized at the beginning, you may not be able to open at all; you may need to delay opening (costing you more money); and you may have to draw from your working capital reserves, which hurts your operations. Therefore, it is important to carefully identify the costs that would likely be incurred to get to the opening day. These may be one-time costs, such as purchase of office equipment, or recurring costs, such as rent for the months prior to the public opening. Figure 11.3 illustrates some typical start-up cost categories and considerations. Start-up costs are built into the first month of the pro forma income and cash flow statements. But they are also identified separately in more detail in a start-up costs table because this increases accuracy and assists in determining the amount of funding needed. Be careful not to double count these costs.

What is the average amount of money required to start up a small RET business? Although individual amounts vary widely, one study found the median

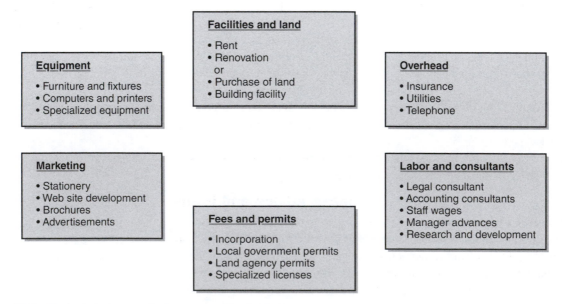

Figure 11.3 Typical start-up costs for a recreation business.

amount of their own money that solo entrepreneurs thought they would need to start their business was $6,000, while it was $20,000 for team ventures (Blade Consulting, 2003). But consider that these are mostly sole proprietorships and very small retail corporations with one location. The amount of capital costs (e.g., buying costly equipment, buying land, and building a facility) will have a large effect on start-up costs. Starting a small nonfranchise health club is estimated to cost between $75,000 and $150,000 (Adams Media Corporation, 2006). Other situations require significantly more funding. For example, opening a new high-end restaurant in San Francisco that involves extensive refurbishing of a prime location costs an average of more than $1,000,000. Franchise fees for well-known franchises alone can exceed $100,000. So there is great variety in start-up costs, but in most cases required funds are more than what the entrepreneur has in personal funds.

WORKING CAPITAL

Working capital is defined as current assets minus current liabilities. But in essence it is the cash or financing needed to optimally operate a business. This includes more than the start-up funds because a new venture is cash poor and needs time to build sales and profitability. So how much working capital will you need after the opening? Your cash flow statement will give you an indication of how much and when you will need additional cash to pay for operations. But even with a cash flow projection, entrepreneurs tend to underestimate working capital needs. Bamford and Bruton (2006) provide a rule of thumb for determining initial equity needs of a new company. First, calculate your cash flow projection without adding in any equity investment. Look for the lowest ending balance in the cash flow projection, and multiply that amount by 150 percent. For example, if the lowest monthly cash flow balance is $9,500, the amount of initial equity needed would be $14,250. This amount is the initial working capital needed. Having this level of funds after start-up allows the cash balance to remain above zero and provides a reserve so the company can meet unexpected expenses or go after unforeseen opportunities.

An indirect source of working capital that is common in seasonal RET businesses is one member of a family who continues to work full time outside the business and uses that outside job to support family financial needs during the initial years. This reduces the need for the other family member to draw as large a salary. Likewise, a start-up solo entrepreneur may initially work another job at the same time. However, this can place severe time and financial strain on family members.

FUNDING SOURCES

Small business entrepreneurs sometimes have a more difficult time than expected attaining adequate funding to start their ventures, especially recreation, event, and tourism companies. Traditional sources of capital lack an understanding of the professionalism and profitability of our industry; they want to fund more customary businesses, and the owners may not have a proven record of performance. So potential funders often see recreation, event, and tourism businesses as too high of a risk from both financial and liability standpoints. Consequently, this means you may need to come up with creative financing that will propel the company forward and not completely drain your personal and family assets.

Many small businesses, some say the majority (Ryan and Hiduke, 2003), are self-financed. But even if that is the case, at some point in the life of a small recreation, event, and tourism business it will need to seek external funding to be able to grow or meet unforeseen financial demands. Growth in the business is frequently tied to having reasonably priced capital, as much as it is to market demand and successful promotion. Buying an undervalued competitor company, moving to a larger facility, or significantly increasing your output capacity usually require outside funds. As the old saying goes, "It takes money to make money."

Self-Financing

When entrepreneurs are able to provide funds to cover all the start-up costs and working capital themselves, this is referred to as self-financing. Acquiring funding for a new small business always starts with the founders. How risk tolerant are you? Are you willing to put up your own money to fund your idea, with the inherent risks, or is it more your style to work for a company where you don't jeopardize your own funds and you get a regular paycheck? What are your personal and family resources? Do you have the support of your family if proposing to use their resources? What is your credit rating? How have you managed your own personal funds and debt in the past five years? What kind of access to capital have you had in the past? Financial returns are generally not large in the first two years, so can you wait two to five years for your business to become very profitable? These are all important questions.

Types of Outside Funding

There are two broad types of funding: nonequity and equity investments. Each has very different sources of money and rights.

Equity Investments

Equity investments are funds contributed to the business in return for a percentage of ownership, and there is no legal requirement to repay the investor. Examples include stock purchased and the cash contribution of a partner. Venture capitalists seek to invest in companies with extremely high growth potential that offer the opportunity to sell and realize large capital gains after a few years. Therefore, they are not very likely to invest in very small businesses. Equity investors can be passive or actively involved in company operations.

A potential challenge of using equity funding from outside sources is it brings a new level of accountability. It may be especially tempting at the start-up stage to seek many small investors, such as social friends, but they often expect preferential treatment, want discounts, and demand time-consuming information and justifications from management on the business operation. The so-called "angel investors" are wealthy individuals who want to actively oversee the operations. They can be helpful if they have very related expertise; if they do not, they can restrict the growth of the firm. A worst-case scenario is where an equity investor owns 51 percent or more of the company stock (i.e., has legal control of the company) and fires the founders who worked 14-hour days and built up the company.

Nonequity Investments

A *nonequity investment* must be paid back over time, but this type of investor does not become owner of a percentage of the business (unless you default). Debt, or funds secured with a promissory agreement, is the most common form of nonequity investment. Some examples of nonequity investments are shown here:

Associated Press/Chitose Suzuki

It is wise to shop around when selecting a bank because some banks solicit small business accounts more actively than others.

Loans are promissory agreements that require payment of a portion of the original amount at specified time periods with interest. Monthly installments are the common form. Loans are secured by collateral, such as your company equipment and real estate, which can be garnered if you fail to make payments. Loans may be hard to get for start-up funds and can be quite costly, depending on the repayment terms. The most common types or sources of loans include the following:

• Friends and relatives: You receive money from parents, relatives, or good friends. This is not a gift, and it requires repayment, but sometimes with a below-market interest rate and extended repayment time. This is a very frequently used source of funding for small businesses. However, there are not only financial but also personal implications if you default on friends or family.

• Banks, credit bureaus, and savings and loan companies are another commonly used source of funding for loans. There are three common types of bank loans:

  • A **line of credit** is a preapproved amount of credit from a bank (with specified terms) that costs you interest only when cash is withdrawn. This is an excellent source of funds for temporary cash flow needs.

  • An **installment loan** for your business is paid back with interest over a period of time by monthly installments. However, as was described previously, banks are often reluctant to provide funding to start up small businesses, frequently recreation, event, and tourism companies. But banks may consider loans to purchase equipment for start-ups with a solid business plan because they can secure the loan with the equipment. Another way to overcome the reticence of banks to make loans to start-ups is by having the loan secured by the federal Small Business Administration (SBA) in the United States or the Business Development Bank of Canada (BDC). The SBA does not provide the loan; rather, it provides planning assistance to the company and guarantees repayment to a bank or financial institution. See figure 11.4 for details on SBA loan alternatives and qualification criteria. SBA-secured loans are very common for start-ups.

Features of Small Business Administration Section 7(a) Loans

• This is the most frequently used SBA loan type.
• Loans are made and administered by lending partners (banks).
• SBA guarantees a portion of the loan against default, thus expanding availability.
• Businesses apply to lender.
• There are eligibility requirements:
  • Repayment ability from cash flow is a primary consideration.
  • Principals of applicant must have good record of debt repayment.
• Terms of loan are negotiated with lender. Following are some general loan terms:
  • Maximum loan amount: $2 million
  • Repayment period: 25 years for real estate and equipment; 7 years for working capital
  • Maximum rate: prime + 2.25% if less than 7 years; prime + 2.75% if maturity is 7+ years
• Several documents are required:
  • Income statements for 3 years
  • Balance sheets for 3 fiscal year-ends
  • Cash flow projections indicating cash generated to repay the loan
  • Personal tax returns for past 3 years and personal financial statements from business partners listing all personal assets, liabilities, and monthly payments

Figure 11.4 Small Business Administration loan types and qualifications.

- To secure a **home equity loan**, a founder takes out a second mortgage on their primary residence and uses the accrued equity for the business. This is often a substantial and easily arranged loan. The risk with this loan, of course, is that if the business fails the founder could also lose her home to creditors.

Credit Cards

Most people have several credit cards, which offer revolving credit that is not secured by an asset and does not have a regular repayment plan. Credit cards can be an excellent source of funds for short-term cash flow management if paid off each month, but they are very dangerous to use for longer-term financing. The downside of a credit card is the high interest rates, sometimes in excess of 21 percent per year. A start-up business owner may be tempted to use credit cards for financing, paying off the debt of one with a cash advance from another one, because they are relatively easy to get. However, if one payment is missed, it is twice as hard to make the next payment, and interest and penalties can accrue very quickly. Since these cards are secured to the owners, default may result in personal bankruptcy. Credit cards must be used carefully and not be substituted for other forms of long-term debt.

Trade Credit

Trade credit is credit extended by vendors or suppliers, usually interest free for 30 to 90 days with increasing interest after that. Suppliers do this to encourage sales of their products. This is an excellent way to conserve cash. However, you must have a reasonable credit rating for vendors to offer this option.

Equipment Leasing

There are a number of options besides outright purchase of equipment that can conserve cash and even be a form of credit. This is very important to some recreation, event, and tourism businesses because of high equipment purchase costs (e.g., more than $100,000 for a new deluxe motor coach) and the cash-short situation of a start-up company. Instead of outright purchase you can get a loan from the supplier, acquire equipment with a franchise, or lease the equipment. Leases can be advantageous because you pay monthly payments for a fixed period of time,

often at competitive interest rates. These payments are tax deductible and more affordable. However, at the end of the lease period, you must return the item and have no equity in it. You should seriously consider leasing versus buying equipment if you plan to turn it over in two to five years and if the technology is changing rapidly.

MOST FREQUENT SOURCES OF FUNDING FOR NEW RET BUSINESSES

The sources of funding for small businesses are very different from those used by the large multinational companies highlighted in the business media. Studies (Ward, 2006; National Federation of Independent Businesses, 2007) have identified a consistently used set of funding sources for microsize and small businesses. The number one source is the personal savings of the owners. This must make up a substantial percentage of the start-up funds in order to get support from other providers, such as friends and relatives or SBA-secured loans. Funders want to be sure the entrepreneur also has a substantial amount of personal money to potentially lose as a motive to drive for success. If only others provide funds, the owner could "walk away" from a poorly functioning start-up with little loss of personal funds. The sources shown here also tend to be most accessible and keep financing costs to a minimum. So start saving now.

Most Frequent Sources of Funds to Start a Small Business

1. Personal savings
2. Friends and relatives
3. Angel investors
4. Line of credit
5. Home equity loan
6. Government agency–secured bank loan

As a small business owner, you have a number of sources of funding for start-up costs and working capital. Personal savings has got to be a starting point, and friends and relatives have long been utilized, but today more and more entrepreneurs are using credit cards and home equity loans and finding angel investors via the Internet. You will need to weigh your risk tolerance and personal resources in deciding which sources to use.

MAINTAINING FINANCIAL CONTROL DURING OPERATIONS

Much of the discussion so far in this chapter centers on developing pro forma statements and identifying funds for start-up. But after start-up, maintaining financial control during operations of a new business is critically important. Small businesses are the most likely to fall into the trap of "shoebox accounting" where receipts and invoices are kept in a "shoebox," and there is little understanding of where and when these funds come and go. This approach eventually leads to disaster (Zahorsky, 2007). This section does not provide a discussion of all elements of financial control, since that is beyond the scope of this text and there are many other excellent texts on the subject, but it does cover some basic actions that should be taken during operations of recreation, event, and tourism businesses, including the following:

- Set up an accounting system.
- Develop a budget.
- Monitor the budget versus actual performance.
- Establish controls for expenditures and receivables.

SET UP AN ACCOUNTING SYSTEM

Every small business must have a **chart of accounts**, the expense and revenue categories for recording business activity. The chart allows you to analyze the business and its financial performance in fine detail. Small businesses now employ accounting software, such as Microsoft Office Accounting (see http://office. microsoft.com/en-us/accounting/default.aspx) and Peachtree Accounting, to help them record and track financial activity. These software packages have integrated modules for the general ledger (to record cash inflows and outflows), inventory, payroll, accounts payable, and accounts receivable, and the user can choose to use one or more of the modules, depending on organization needs. See tech application for a detailed look at the popular QuickBooks software for an example of what contemporary accounting software can provide.

DEVELOP AN OPERATIONS BUDGET

An operations budget that you prepare for the upcoming year shows your projected revenues, expenditures, and profit. If you are preparing an operations budget for a new business, then you can use your pro forma

Tech Application

QuickBooks Accounting Software

QuickBooks by Intuit (www.quickbooks.intuit.com) is a very popular accounting software package with more features than a very small business generally can use. There are various editions, ranging from the free Simple Start to the full-featured Premier. The software has the basic components of most accounting software: general ledger, accounts receivable, payroll, accounts payable, time billing, job costing, inventory, and fixed assets management. But it goes well beyond these basic features, and the Premier edition has many enhancements, such as multiple user access; tools to create estimates, customized invoices and reports; downloading of bank and credit card transactions; management of payroll and direct deposit; tracking inventory and setting reorder times; forecasting; and accounts receivable billing. It also has many online features that allow a person to manage her finances at home, on the road, or from the office, such as online time sheets, online product sales, and remote inventory management. QuickBooks also interfaces with Word, Excel, Outlook, and TurboTax to make data exchange easy and accurate. There are data conversion tools, interactive tutorials, and live support, which makes the software easy to set up and learn, and there are so many users that it is usually easy to find someone locally to ask for advice. It is even possible to have your accountant remotely access your files during tax preparation. QuickBooks has won numerous awards including the CNET Editors' Choice award and Product of the Year from *Small Business Technology Magazine* in 2006. All this for a cost of about $179.

cash flow statement or pro forma income statement from the business plan. The cash flow statement, with some modification, can become the first-year budget. You may need to add more detail to the cash flow statement, such as more line items to break down revenues and expenses into finer specificity. A capital budget is different from an operations budget because it identifies only major capital costs (land, buildings, and equipment) and when and how the company will buy and pay for them over a period of years. We do not discuss a capital budget here, as it is beyond the scope of this book.

Every year your company develops a new operations budget based on the previous year's performance, likely future conditions, and sales goals for the next year. It is important not to determine the next year's budget based only on a percentage increase that is equal across all accounts; some parts of your business may need more funding than others because of growth potential.

MONITOR BUDGETED VERSUS ACTUAL FINANCIAL PERFORMANCE

Once an operations budget has been accepted, compare actual revenues and expenses against projected amounts each month. Identifying variance between budgeted and actual revenues, expenditures, and profits is critical for detecting problems or opportunities early so that the management can modify future spending and investments in order to maintain profitability. Without carefully preparing a budget before the next fiscal year begins, frequently identifying large variance from it, and making needed adjustments, your company is like a ship without a compass and radar in the fog: The captain (you) does not know where it is going or what it might hit and is very unlikely to get where he hopes to go.

ESTABLISH CONTROLS FOR EXPENDITURES AND RECEIVABLES

Purchasing control is done through a combination of purchase restrictions and purchase orders, which require management approval for purchases above a specified amount; limited check signature authority;

expense reports; and the recording of expenditures in the accounting software's general ledger. The accounting software produces a variety of reports that reflect other financial controls by management. These include a petty cash register, inventory, accounts payable, accounts receivable, and payroll.

- Petty cash register: Many items a business must buy are too small to warrant a check or purchase order. A small lockbox is used to store a small amount of cash, and a register is used to record disbursement of this petty cash.

- Inventory accounts: The current inventory and records of purchases and replacement orders are crucial not only for retail stores (see chapter 4) but also for the supplies necessary to produce company services.

- Accounts payable: This is a record of funds due to each creditor. Invoices from vendors and creditors and their payment are recorded.

- Accounts receivable: Money due from purchasers, including payments, balances, and automated billing, must be easy to identify and recorded accurately. It is easy but deadly for a business to lose track of accounts receivable.

- Payroll: Labor costs are usually the largest expense for an RET business, and accurate development of payroll materials can take considerable staff time. Therefore, it is very important to securely, quickly, and accurately maintain payroll records. Some companies prefer specialized payroll programs, while many today have payroll as part of their general accounting software.

SUMMARY

In this chapter we explore methods to project potential revenues, expenses, cash flow, and profit. These processes employ pro forma statements, ratio analysis, and break-even analysis. Another part of the chapter identifies the needs and sources of funds to start the venture and methods to maintain financial control during operation of the recreation, event, and tourism company. These elements fit into the financial component of your business plan. You will use the financial plan to determine if it is profitable enough to go forward with starting the business, the amount of funds needed, and sources of funding. Financial institutions will rely on pro forma statements before they commit to providing a loan or other financing.

Government agencies, such as the Internal Revenue Service or Revenue Canada, will require the company to adhere to strict financial management procedures in preparation of financial statements and in operations. You cannot focus just on operations planning; you must also give very careful consideration and a good deal of time to financial planning before and during operations.

 Check out the online student resource for additional material, including case studies, Web links, and more.

Chapter 12

Completing and Implementing the Business Plan

Learning Objectives

After reading this chapter you will be able to

- identify how you can organize the business plan now that you have made a series of decisions and have written down your ideas in regard to the previous chapters;
- describe the focus, format, and content of a superior business plan proposal;
- formulate the actions to be taken in the first three months after the launch of the business plan; and
- define mileposts by which to judge progress in the implementation of the plan.

Key Terms

business description

business plan template

cover letter

executive summary

financial plan

PERT chart

sensitivity analysis

Imagine this scenario:

You have unexpectedly come upon a large sum of money and you have decided to either create or buy a tourism business. Upon looking at existing businesses more closely, you choose to create a business as you are a creative individual and prefer to have the latitude to implement several ideas you feel strongly about. Over a period of a month, you creatively write down your ideas as they come to you and put them into a three-ring binder. You feel confident the details important to you are now on paper and after finishing a profit–loss statement you conclude it will be helpful if you could get a loan to buy the property, as your cash on-hand will be committed to operational plans and start-up. So you make an appointment with the local bank manager and present him with your notebook. Shortly after beginning the discussion, the bank manager looks at your notebook and asks, "How did you choose to organize your ideas in this fashion?" You truthfully reply that it was spontaneous and, as you found the time, you just made notes of key elements that you understand to be important. He compliments you for the thoughtful work and creative aspects contained in the notebook. He pauses and says, "I am sure you have what the bank needs to see when considering a property loan, but it needs to be organized differently in order for me to evaluate the merits of the proposal. There are some customary formats or templates we recommend when applying for a business loan. I don't think it will take a great deal of time for you to reorganize the notebook, bind it as a more formal submission, and it may very well permit you to identify some gaps in the current information you have pulled together to date." You are provided with a suggested format and head back home to present your ideas in a more formal business submission.

This chapter sets out a template for organizing the material you have prepared to date and provides some examples of where components of a plan fit together using a hypothetical business. You should be the primary author of your plan, but there are alternatives for assistance in writing it, such as Web sites (e.g., Small Business Administration, www.sba.gov), trusted colleagues, banks and financial institutions, small business assistance programs at universities, small business incubators, industry associations, and paid consultants. These choices can assist in advising on how thoroughly you have covered key elements, the links between the sections, and the effectiveness of your executive summary in representing what you have included in the business plan.

Although the precise format may vary from one type of business to another, the objectives for preparing every plan are simple. See figure 12.1 for a **business plan template**. Your objectives are to

- ensure the opening remarks and introductory sections of your plan create a favorable first impression;
- communicate in a captivating and persuasive manner the decisions you have made concerning products and services, other profit centers, target markets, and marketing strategies;
- present the operational decisions about how the business will be managed, which may include

the start-up team, service quality standards, environmental management practices, and risk and liability; and

- lay out your financial strategy in terms of financial statements, the analysis of your financial data, and the funding needed to get your proposal ready to implement.

On the following pages, each of these objectives will be realized in one or more of the sections you present in each part of your business plan.

PART ONE: INTRODUCTION TO THE DOCUMENT

The business plan has a dual purpose. On the one hand it is designed to display the decisions and actions you will follow in launching your business; on the other hand, the plan is a solid promotional document because it can serve as an invitation to someone you would like to actively support and be involved with your ideas. The **cover letter** is a customized invitation that you address to a person you would like to read the plan with a purpose in mind; often it is someone you wish to help finance your business. The **executive summary** is a succinct summary of the plan, and it functions like the preface to this book in the context that it introduces the reader to what follows. Both of these components fit into part one, and each

Part 1 **Introduction**	**Part 2** **Business description**	**Part 3** **Financial strategy**
Cover letter Executive summary	Business concept • Products and services • Experiences, mission statement, and industry profile Market and competitor analysis Marketing and promotion plan Management practices • Organizational chart • Service standards • Environmental management • Risk management	Financial analysis Funding plan Key action steps

Figure 12.1 A business plan template.

is designed to create a positive first impression with the reader and to introduce the reader to the contents of your document.

COVER LETTER

In terms of content, the cover letter contains contact information (name, address, and phone number) and identifies who has prepared the plan (see figure 12.2). Since you may write letters to more than one lender, it is common to note the copy number of the business plan that is being circulated to the addressee. You may wish to add a confidentiality statement concerning the contents of the plan.

Your cover letter is addressed to a specific person whom you believe can help with the business. It could be a mentor, potential team member, or potential investor such as a banker, venture capitalist, or credit manager. The best-prepared letter will seek to be persuasive and informative and to convey excitement about the plan. It is best to identify the interest you believe the addressee may have in either the business concept or its prospect for profitability. Consider, for example, a letter you might address to your banker, which is presented in the online student resource.

The sample letter has several positive elements that can be replicated in almost any such letter:

- Mr. Jones communicates a passion for the business concept and the customers to be served.

- He communicates the purpose of the letter (i.e., purchasing tangible assets) and yet leaves open

the financial options by asking about sources of capital and not a specific type of business loan.

- He provides details of a previous financial relationship with the bank in securing a home mortgage and having several personal accounts for a period of time.

EXECUTIVE SUMMARY

The executive summary is written at the conclusion of the final business plan document. When writing your plan, your ideas will change, you will discover new possibilities, and you will rethink parts of the plan you have written previously. Thus, it makes sense to formulate your executive summary after all the changes have been made and the plan has been edited. Your summary may highlight the origin of the business project, the mission statement guiding the business plan, and the more immediate objectives of the venture. It will identify and condense key aspects of the general business environment, the strength of the proposal, and the market, as well as reveal the future financial prospects for the business. If the proposal has unique or innovative qualities, then those qualities should be highlighted. The numbers supporting the financial statements should be conservative, credible, and promising.

What follows the introductory part of the plan are the two core areas of the document: (1) the business concept and (2) the financial plan. The concept part

Orange Torpedo Trips
P.O. Box 435
Merlin, OR
October 31, 2008

Mr. Bill Rae
Manager, Oregon Bank
600 Multnomah Blvd.
Portland, OR

Dear Mr. Rae:

Your observations and suggestions for strengthening our business plan for Orange Torpedo Trips are very much appreciated. We have updated the enclosed document based on your input, which has certainly improved the financial section as well as other areas. Those of us who prepared the original draft are most grateful for the time and effort you devoted to helping us. This is a very special business for me because my parents raised me on the free-flowing rivers of Idaho as they shared their love for wild places.

We are now exploring our options for a loan of $45,000 to be used in capital expenditures—new Tahiti kayaks, two support rafts, camping equipment, and a double-axle trailer to transport the equipment. This investment will allow us to expand our trip offerings to other river segments and will establish a new line of revenue for the business. At this time we are operating at capacity and see the need to increase our equipment inventory in response to growing demand.

In view of the revenue projections associated with our expansion, we expect to repay the loan over a 30-month period. We would appreciate any guidance you can offer in regard to sources of capital for our capital investment. Over the past decade, we are grateful for the assistance that you and the staff of the loan department provided in regards to our home mortgage and the car loan for our son. Thank you again for the advice you have so willingly provided to us to date. I look forward to hearing from you.

Best regards,
John Jones, Owner
Orange Torpedo Trips

Figure 12.2 Sample cover letter.

basically reports all of the planning decisions you have made about the business, given the instructional material covered in chapters 3 to 10, and the last part covers all the financial planning and analysis decisions you have prepared based on what you learned in chapter 11.

PART TWO: BUSINESS DESCRIPTION

The second part of the plan, the **business description**, is the place to demonstrate your knowledge about the business venture, your business concept, its market, and the nature of the competition. It will be equally important to describe your management team, to highlight any management practices that will be central to your operation, and to identify

how and when you will promote the product to your target market. Depending on the business, the management practices may highlight service standards, environmental management policies, and how you will handle risk and liability.

BUSINESS CONCEPT

In chapter 3 you identify the services and products of interest to you and draft a mission statement. The goal of this section is to inform and persuade the reader about the merits of the business initiative. Some readers will need to be informed about the nature of the services involved in commercial recreation, events, and tourism. That can be covered by providing an industry overview section. Others will need to be persuaded about the promising growth trends occurring in particular sectors of the industry and the unfulfilled need to provide a target market with a memorable experience and something to do when reaching travel destinations. That can be addressed by sharing knowledge of the prospective market as well as the nature of the services to be provided.

Products and Services

What will be the legal status of the business? In the case of Orange Torpedo Trips, has the paperwork been completed to operate under an assumed business name, and are there any specific permit or guide licensing requirements? Just what are the essential features of the business concept? How would you describe the types of products, services, or experiences that will be offered? Are there any retail goods to be sold? You will want to identify a geographic region you intend to serve. Are there any consumer trends that are changing the nature of the marketplace? This component will be written to describe the core business activity and also to share with the reader the specific part of the market you consider your customer base. An examination of a company providing river trips can help illustrate this. Chapter 8 also provides insights in describing how you will establish a high

level of service and customer loyalty in your service offerings.

What are the trends in this industry? Is the industry growing, flat, or evolving in new ways? Is demand highly seasonal and weekend oriented, or is it spread out evenly over the year? What factors are driving growth or changes in the industry? Be sure to research and cite objective sources, such as industry journals, articles, conference presentations, and discussions with industry professionals. Do not just rely on your perception of the industry. Should your industry overview give primary attention to entertainment services, retail, or a form of travel and tourism? Is the business activity a community-based set of services, or is it more associated with attractions, events, travel destinations, and heritage assets? Answers to these kinds of questions set the stage for what will follow.

Mission Statement

The question to be addressed here is the purpose of your business. The response is traditionally framed in terms of serving your customers. When you answer this question, you are taking the vital step necessary to prepare your mission statement. Although it may be written with the customer in mind, the mission statement basically reminds everyone involved with the business what the purpose is when the time comes to make key decisions and implement the plan.

Profit Centers

You may wish to refer to chapter 2, where you first examined what entrepreneurs do and the basic elements of a recreation business (e.g., experiences, retail sales, rental of equipment, or even small-scale manufacturing). In chapter 4, there is an expansion of the ideas associated with other profit centers that might be complementary to your core purpose. If you have made some preliminary decisions about the supplemental profit center, identify them here because they could be significant in regard

Good directional and informational signs can be important for recreational vehicle parks when customers may arrive or depart at all times of the day.

Robert Pfister

to profitability. In preparing this section, you can draw on your research on the arts, entertainment, and recreation industry covered in chapters 2, 3, and 4. Your goal is to inform the reader about the nature and characteristics of the industry in which you intend to be involved (see figure 12.3). How does the business fit within the larger picture of the industry? Remember that perception is reality to many individuals not as knowledgeable as you are. Most lenders will be familiar with commercial ventures that provide accommodation or a place to eat, but there will also be lenders who are not aware of business initiatives that create memorable experiences for the leisure vacation market.

Orange Torpedo Trips is an assumed business name for a relatively new nature-oriented adventure company incorporated in the state of Oregon. It offers guided river trips on the Rogue and Illinois Rivers, which flow through the Kalmiopsis Wilderness Area in the coastal range of southern Oregon. The backcountry trips range from one to five days in duration and take place along river corridors protected as part of the National Wild and Scenic Rivers System in the United States. We are one of very few commercial enterprises to hold a permit to operate on these pristine free-flowing river valleys, and these places offer exceptional opportunities for enjoying the natural and cultural heritage of remote natural settings. In addition, with careful planning the trip can be rich in outdoor experiences supporting fellowship and wildlife viewing, enjoying the art of backcountry cooking, practicing environmentally friendly minimum-impact skills, and learning the paddling skills that allow for successful navigation of the rapids. The level of adventure can vary from one client to the other as the trip is hosted by trained guides, and each participant can choose to raft the corridor or paddle it in a personal inflatable kayak.

Each person will have the opportunity to travel the river in a Tahiti "orange torpedo" and will receive instruction on how to handle the inflatable. Each trip is supported by two 10-passenger rafts for younger visitors, and these rafts also carry the food and equipment needed for the trip. The guides have years of experience for the river they are traveling, and each one is trained in swiftwater rescue, wilderness first aid, and CPR. In addition, the guides will tell both natural and cultural history interpretation stories at specific locations during stops for lunch and overnight.

There are special attractions associated with floating down a river in a remote part of the state. The white-water rafting opportunities of southern Oregon offer breathtaking scenery, abundant forests and waterfalls, and a full range of mild to expert trips on free-flowing white-water rivers. Outdoor adventure enthusiasts will be hard pressed to find more excitement and variety in river experiences than available in beautiful southern Oregon. This area is rich with cultural and natural heritage features; old cabins, mines, and wildlife are abundant; and there is a choice of four popular river segments to suit the needs of the target audience.

The Rogue River offers class II to IV rapids, and it is easily accessible from a broad range of locations. The rapids on the Rogue River are not difficult for most outdoor enthusiasts, and it is a classic river experience. The Klamath River offers an exciting white-water rafting adventure on the upper segment, with many full-day rafting trips. It is one of the most exciting class IV trips in Oregon, with more than 30 major class III to class IV stretches. The lower segment of the Klamath is a great option for the less experienced because of the many mild sections situated close to easy access points. The Umpqua River sports more rapids per mile than many runs, as numerous class III and III+ rapids are found in the most commonly run segment. The Illinois River flows through the steep-walled canyons of the Kalmiopsis Wilderness Area and offers the river traveler access to one of the most isolated areas in the coastal range.

Nature-oriented travel to remote places is an emerging major trend in vacation travel today. One component of the vacation travel is characterized by a "soft adventure" trip, which means low risk for the travel market seeking more environmentally friendly, adventuresome, and nature-oriented experiences. People seeking nature-oriented or ecotourism experiences tend to value discovery, adventure, fellowship, and pristine destinations that will expand their environmental knowledge and awareness. The attractive settings and activities are diverse: trekking alpine trails, enjoying wildlife safaris, rafting wild river corridors, all while engaged in nature photography, practicing minimum-impact techniques, making new friends, and learning new skills.

Figure 12.3 Products and services offered by Orange Torpedo Trips.

MARKET AND COMPETITOR ANALYSIS

Chapters 5 and 6 describe how important it is to carefully identify and segment your market. If you can provide geographic information about where your market is likely to come from, then you enhance the potential success of the marketing effort. For some entertainment or retail businesses, it is often said the three most important assets for success are location, location, and location. In most RET businesses not dependent on the amenities of a location, your physical location may well be less important than your Internet presence to your customers.

Since it is very rare to be the only business of your type within your region, you will need to carefully analyze your competition. How close are they to where you will locate? What are the products and services they offer? Can you compare their customer orientation with yours? What is their pricing? Have you identified gaps to be filled? How likely are you to be trying to capture the same market share given your services or products? What competitive advantages do you have? Figure 12.4 provides details on the customer base for the product along with a competitor analysis covering the number of similar operators in the vicinity.

Market Analysis

The target market is described as active, adventuresome, and experienced travelers seeking guided nature-oriented, out-of-doors experiences in unique protected areas that have limited public access. The travelers may be families, groups of friends, and couples that could vary in age from twenty-something to seniors. Seventy percent of the market is from California, Oregon, and Washington, with the remainder from the rest of North America. By 2010, more than 25 percent of the 32 million people living in California will be part of the baby boomer population. About 17 to 20 percent of the population living in the states of Washington and Oregon will be in that target market. The second target audience will be the Gen X population, and research has shown this market seeks adventure and ecotourism experiences.

The growing leisure travel market ranges in age from early 30s to 60s. One of the large market segments driving the environmentally friendly, nature-oriented vacation trend is the baby boomer population—people born between 1946 and 1964. This age cohort has already set noteworthy market trends, from their earliest age in baby food and diapers and later with TV sets and personal computers. Now as adults reaching their peak in earnings and free time, they are establishing themselves as a desirable target market of recreation and tourism businesses with travel products and services that match their interest. The data reveal that among all adults today that have chosen an adventure vacation, more than 56 percent of the clients represent the baby boomer cohort.

Many recreation businesses seek to serve a portion of this large market because the consumer profile reveals this segment tends to place a high value on active health activities, and they have been spending 30 percent more per individual than younger travelers. However, closing the gap in per capita spending for leisure travel is a second age cohort referred to as the Gen X population—those people born between 1965 and 1976. Although the boomer consumers are a larger population and dominate on the basis of total spending, $157 billion in 2004, the Gen X consumers spend nearly the same as the boomers on a per capita basis in terms of leisure travel (De Lollis, 2005).

The baby boomer market continues to be a trendsetter in selecting unique nature-based opportunities because this market segment controls 75 percent of the wealth in the United States and can afford it. Thus, they are willing to pay top dollar for vacations where they can enjoy healthy food, exercise, and outdoor experience. Rafting trips down scenic river corridors is one such opportunity where this market can enjoy and learn about the natural environment, make new friends, acquire outdoor skills, and indulge in the pleasure of being hosted by experienced river guides who know how to prepare memorable backcountry meals. Taken all together, these attributes represent potential features of a river trip in protected areas, and packaging them creates a product well matched for this target market.

(continued)

Figure 12.4 Market analysis and competitor analysis.

Competitor Analysis

Located in Grants Pass, Oregon, Orange Torpedo Trips is in the heartland of the rafting activity, and it is one of 10 rafting companies in the region that commercially raft the segments of the Rogue River. Each of the competitors for the outdoor adventure market can be examined in terms of their location, advertised package, the river segment on which they operate, and whether or not the competitor offers trips using the inflatable Tahiti kayak. Geographically, the competitors are not concentrated in southern Oregon but distributed over a 40-mile (64 kilometer) corridor from Ashland to Merlin; three competitors are located in Ashland, three in the Medford area, two in Grants Pass, and two in Merlin. The table describes the characteristics of each competitor as they appear in their advertising.

Competitors Offering White-Water Outdoor Adventures in the Area

Company and location	Advertised packages	Offers the option of inflatable kayaks?
Kokopelli River Guides, Ashland	Full-service paddle sports destination. Family-friendly white-water rafting trips, kayak instruction, multiday or daily raft and kayak rentals.	No
Momentum River Expeditions, Ashland	White-water rafting in Oregon and Northern California. Some of the finest rivers anywhere, most off the beaten path. Offers incredible white water and scenery.	No
Noah's River Adventures, Ashland	Southern Oregon and northern California's "number one" professional white-water rafting and year-round drift boat fishing guide service since 1974.	No
Get Wett, Shady Grove	Tahiti inflatable kayaks. Entertaining, friendly environment featuring brand new, state-of-the-art rafting equipment and accessories. Note: Closed for 2007.	Yes
River Trips Unlimited, Medford	48 years of boating Oregon's famed Rogue River. 1- or 2-day scenic or fishing trips including steelhead fishing trips. Salmon and steelhead specialist.	Yes
Rogue Klamath River Adventure, Medford	Southern Oregon's premier outfitter for 32 years. 1/2- to multiday guided white-water rafting and fishing trips. Gourmet food, world-class guides.	No
Orange Torpedo Trips, Grants Pass	Unique paddle-yourself inflatable kayaking and rafting adventures throughout the west and the world. Guided trips range from 1/2 day to 12 days. Camping or lodging.	Yes
Echo River Trips, Grants Pass	Rafting on Rogue River and the Middle Fork of the Salmon. Among the most experienced, most respected, and best-run companies; 35 years of running river trips.	No
Rogue River Raft Trips, Merlin	Spectacular white-water rafting down the Rogue River canyon. 3-day lodge trips at remote wilderness lodges, 3-day camp/lodge combination trips, and 4-day camping trips.	No
Rogue Wilderness Adventures, Merlin	Wild and scenic Rogue River. More than 30 years' experience. 1/2- to 4-day white-water rafting and inflatable kayaking trips; camping or lodging. 1- to 4-day salmon and steelhead fishing trips.	No

Currently, there are only two competitors advertising the kind of inflatable kayak equipment offered by Orange Torpedo Trips: one in Medford and the other in Shady Grove, 20 miles (32 kilometers) north of Medford. The Shady Grove business has posted a notice they will not operate in the 2007 season because of a water supply problem. Thus, only one competitor is prepared to offer a white-water adventure trip similar in terms of equipment to the trip package offered by Orange Torpedo Trips. It is a company, however, based in a different community in the region.

Figure 12.4   *(continued)*

MARKETING AND PROMOTION PLAN

With the product, target market, and competition identified, it is time to describe what you believe should be the key marketing elements of the promotion plan. If you need a review, refer to chapter 6. This section of the business plan is where the best promotional tools available to you are matched and integrated in such a manner as to create a synergistic effect. Essentially, the goal is to produce an outcome that is greater than the sum of the parts. Every business has a wide array of promotional choices in the print and electronic media, and the initial step will be deciding how to get the best value. You will need to cite specific promotional actions and their costs.

There are at least three information items that may help you make effective choices when outlining your marketing plan. One item is your target market; how is your market most likely to find out about you?

Do you have information about the decision-making behavior of the market segments of primary interest? What aspects of the product experience that you will deliver are most likely to appeal to your target audience? A second valuable item of information is your careful assessment of the competition for your target market. What does their advertising emphasize, and how can you differentiate your package from theirs? This second item is about positioning yourself relative to your primary competitors. What are your known strengths relative to the other companies, and what opportunities do you have to ensure the market recognizes your distinctive assets? If you are seeking to occupy a market niche, what advertising and public relations tools might give you an advantage in capturing your share of the market? Positioning can be about differentiation of the services and also the price. Figure 12.5 shows a promotion plan and marketing strategies.

The final item is the marketing mix. How will you price your services? What channels of distribution do

---

Given the characteristics of the two primary target markets—boomers and Gen Xers—it is important to employ a diversity of print and electronic media strategies in the promotion plan. Market research suggests both segments are likely to be attracted to the environmental features of a river trip package and definitely value quality time with their spouses (boomers) or their children (Gen Xers). Both are active and sophisticated consumers who have high per capita expenditures on vacation travel. In terms of travel preferences, Gen Xers reveal more interest in outdoor adventure activities than do boomers (51 percent versus 43 percent, respectively) (De Lollis, B. 2005). Images selected for print and electronic media will reflect the general preferences for adventure, sightseeing, and fellowship.

The baby boomers are likely to carefully search many sources for information, write away for printed material, and plan their travel experiences in advance. Gen X consumers are early adopters of technology, are hooked on electronic media, and will be more inclined to make spontaneous decisions in choosing a trip. For the Gen X market, a Web site with an online reservation option will be a priority; of course, an Internet Web site serves all market segments.

Orange Torpedo Trips is committed to a range of marketing strategies to let the target markets know about the company, the products offered, and what makes the river trips memorable and unique. The advertising will include radio spots, newspaper features, and video clips from prior river adventures that can be played on long-haul airline flights coming to Pacific Northwest airports from major metropolitan areas. Most adventure travelers come from major urban areas. Special promotions will include special pricing offers on the Internet for early-season trips, brochures placed in the highway visitor centers in the three-state area, brochures in hotel chains, an Internet newsletter targeting the loyal customers, and a press release telling the story of Orange Torpedo's initiative to sponsor multiday activities to pick up litter along the urbanized section of the Rogue River in Grants Pass. Press kits and sponsorship kits will be prepared to involve as many partners as possible. All newsworthy articles appearing in the newspaper will be posted on the Web site to illustrate the company's concern for a quality environment not only along protected river corridors but in the community as well. Personal selling will involve commissioned salespeople and cooperative tour packages with attractions in the Jacksonville and Ashland areas along with trade show participation in urban centers—Los Angeles, Portland, and Seattle—as well as the annual Adventures in Travel Expo.

Figure 12.5 Promotion plan and marketing strategies.

you plan to utilize, and how will you promote your services? Describe proposed advertising, personal sales, publicity, and sales promotion you plan to undertake and the expected returns from these efforts. You will undoubtedly have a strong Internet marketing presence. What will this effort entail?

MANAGEMENT PRACTICES

There is probably nothing more important than the key people who will make the business operate as planned. Chapter 7 covers what lenders and others seeking information about a business's potential to succeed will look at and carefully read once they understand the description of the business. The questions underlying the examination of this section involve the credentials and prior work experience of those identified to perform specific duties. Who is assigned the financial duties, and does this person have the skills and experience to match the assignment? What about the responsibility for marketing? How many people have prior management experience?

The basic components of this management section are the job descriptions for the key positions and the organizational chart, which reveals the organizational structure and reporting relationships. If in doubt as to

what to include in a job description, refer to chapter 7. Several examples of organizational charts and position descriptions can be found in figures 7.2 through 7.4. In the case of this business, Orange Torpedo Trips will operate as an S corporation as shown in figure 12.6. See figure 12.7 for a sample management profile.

Given the nature of the business, it may be important in this part of the business plan to address qual-

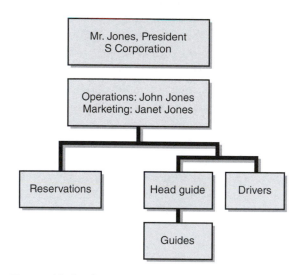

Figure 12.6 Organizational chart for Orange Torpedo Trips.

John Jones is the second generation in a family that chose to earn a living guiding river trips to remote protected areas. His parents operated a guiding service for 20 years. John grew up on the Middle Fork of the Salmon River. He is a certified guide who organized and ran trips when working on the Middle Fork, so he has a good working knowledge. John met Janet in graduate school, where she completed her business degree in marketing and he in natural resource management. They traveled extensively for a year, evaluating options for a business venture that would suit their lifestyle preferences. John and Janet then negotiated to purchase Orange Torpedo Trips in 2004, and the acquisition was jointly funded by them as well as John's parents.

As president and founder, John is responsible for directing daily operations (e.g., purchasing, hiring, training, quality control) and handling supervisory duties of the seasonal staff. He is the liaison person for all contracted services (e.g., insurance, bookkeeping, tax preparation, and legal). He represents the business in meetings with elected officials and in negotiations with government agencies, and he sets financial goals and the standards for financial records and budgets. Janet serves as an office manager and prepares the payroll for seasonal staff. She has sole responsibility for design and implementation of the marketing strategy and represents the company on the committee working with the visitor services center.

After completing their most recent equipment audit, it was apparent the business needs to replace certain items and purchase a range of new equipment to grow the business. Thus, Orange Torpedo Trips is ready to shop around for a loan.

Figure 12.7 Management profile of business owner.

ity of service goals (chapter 8), codes of conduct and environmental management practices (chapter 9), and your approach to risk management (chapter 10).

PART THREE: FINANCIAL PLANNING AND ANALYSIS

The figures prepared to document projected income, expenses, and operating capital are presented in part three, and they represent the **financial plan** for the business.

FINANCIAL STATEMENTS

The types of financial statements that address the financial strategy are described in chapter 11 of the text, and such statements are most commonly prepared in a spreadsheet format using software such as Excel. While part two of the business plan is a narrative description of the enterprise, part three contains the numbers associated with income and expenditure projections, along with the flow of cash on a monthly basis. The three most important statements are your income statement, cash flow statement, and balance sheet. You should have financial projections for the first two years, and most business plans also show the first three to five years. You would be wise to

document assumptions you made in preparing your statements, otherwise lenders and others might question how you came up with these figures and whether you are overly optimistic.

Your income statement showing profit and loss by month is effectively illustrated in chapter 11. Perhaps the most important financial statement is your cash flow since it reveals cash inflow and outflow for the year, so you will be able to identify shortfall in cash flow periods. The final statement is the balance sheet. The preparation of a balance sheet documents the assets and liabilities of the business.

FINANCIAL ANALYSIS

Understanding the financial position of your RET business gives you the best opportunity to assess profitability. You saw in the previous chapter that an owner needs to look at easily attainable numbers such as sales, profits, debts, and total assets. One of the purposes of ratio analysis is to identify and quantify the strengths and growth potential of your company (such as return on investment or return on sales), to consider the nature of any financial risks that exist (e.g., debt to equity ratio), and to assess your capacity to meet current obligations (e.g., liquidity ratio). Every successful business owner is likely to constantly evaluate the performance of his company at different times of the year. As noted, the ratios look at the business from different perspectives and can assist in comparing your current

- financial data with historical figures for the business,
- performance with competitors in the industry,
- financial situation with successful businesses in other industries, and
- financial situation with average indicators in the business sector.

J.S. Pfister

Your bank manager will be a vital partner not only in advising but helping you have access to funds when you need them.

SENSITIVITY ANALYSIS

Once completed, the financial statements provide the opportunity for systematic analysis of the assumptions underlying the financial documents. **Sensitivity analysis** enables the business owner to examine different scenarios based on the original profit and loss forecast. Although the financial ratios are valuable when a business is fully operational, this analysis is valuable for a start-up business. It provides the opportunity to critique whether or not the profitability of the business changes drastically given pessimistic or optimistic financial assumptions.

Once you have done the initial forecasts for income and costs, a sensitivity analysis enables you to test your assumptions for different revenue and expense forecasts. The purpose is to examine what effect, for example, a pessimistic scenario will have on your profit margin in comparison with a "realistic" or "optimistic" forecast. This examination provides an indication of just how "sensitive" your profitability is to changes in the economic conditions or financial assumptions. If your business plan forecasts are highly sensitive to subtle changes in profit and loss figures, then a decision needs to be made about modifying parts of the business plan that most influences the financial bottom line, or simply put the document on the shelf until the uncertainty of profitably no longer exists.

FUNDING PLAN

A part of your business plan that will be highly scrutinized is how you plan to fund the start-up

---

SPOTLIGHT ON

FlexPetz, A Flexible Pet Ownership Company

Location

FlexPetz's corporate headquarters are in Wilmington, Delaware.

Background

Marlena Cervantes, a behavioral therapist working with autistic children and pets, realized the need and came up with the idea for her company. She realized that not everyone who lived in a large city and loved dogs was able to have them. She explored the options and found that no company was providing the opportunity to share a pet on a part-time basis.

Products and Services

Akin to a vacation time-share, FlexPetz is a shared pet ownership company except that instead of a condominium unit, clients get to enjoy the company of a friendly, highly trained dog for a fixed period of time. The service is for dog lovers who know they cannot have a dog of their own full time because of circumstances such as prohibition of pets in their apartments, frequent traveling, or family obligations. It also gives people a chance to "try out" a dog and possibly adopt it in the future.

FlexPetz is a membership organization in which the company provides access to a variety of dogs in the local area where services are available. Each dog has been rescued from an animal shelter or rehomed, evaluated for people-friendly personality, and then fully trained. For an annual membership fee of $100, monthly membership dues of $49.95, a one-time registration fee, and then $40 per day with a dog, a member is entitled to a complete package of services. First the member selects a compatible pooch either in person or online. There is a drop-off and pickup service and introduction to the dog by a company dog trainer at the member's home. Even leashes, bowls, and dog food are provided. Dogs have GPS tracking collars to ensure that a lost dog can be located.

Business Advice and Plans

Services will soon be available in Los Angeles, San Diego, San Francisco, New York, Washington, DC, and London. Cervantes hopes to franchise the concept, allowing the services to be provided in many cities.

costs and first-year working capital. You will need to show significant financial contribution of your personal funds, or else few outside funding sources will be interested. Show if personal funds are to be used from savings and investments. Will you be using debt sources, such as installment loans, credit cards, or a home equity loan? Finally, describe equity funding sources, such as relatives, other partners, angel investors, and silent investors. Eventually you will need to fully document the amount of funds and their commitment (e.g., with personal bank account and mutual fund statements, tax returns, and letters of commitment).

THE FINAL STEPS TO LAUNCH

You have completed a long journey at this point, and it is time to make some decisions. Implementation of a business plan requires coordination of several action-oriented steps, and keeping track of all the scheduled meetings, approvals, and follow-up actions is essential to avoid a false start. To be effective and efficient in plan implementation, there is at least one tool that is helpful. The use of a **program evaluation and review technique (PERT) chart** can be a valuable tool for scheduling and controlling the steps to be taken in the plan. The objective of a PERT chart is to give the author of a business plan improved ability to implement the plan and to allocate the resources needed to accomplish the goals within an overall time frame. An abbreviated example of a PERT chart for the first six weeks is shown in table 12.1.

Do you feel ready for your RET business adventure? You have done your research, reviewed your ideas with potential customers, and shown your pro forma financial statements to mentors. If you decide to postpone now, the opportunity you have identified may slip away. If you need to delay to acquire a

Table 12.1   Sample PERT Chart for Scheduling Key Tasks

Tasks	Wk 1	Wk 2	Wk 3	Wk 4	Wk 5	Wk 6
Register business name; DBA; license	x					
Select the business location; confirm business address for courier services	x					
Befriend a banker	x					
Set up bank account, obtain corporate tax number, and order checks		x				
Establish public utility and phone accounts		x				
Order business stationery and cards			x			
Preview print media promotional strategy			x			
Order printed promotional materials and start on Web site design; find reliable service provider				x		
Launch Internet Web page and Internet reservation system					x	
Meet with lawyer				x		
Meet with accountant				x		
Join networking groups for products					x	
Meet with local state destination marketing officials and distribute brochures						x

From R. Pfister and P. Tierney, 2008, *Recreation, event, and tourism businesses* (Champaign, IL: Human Kinetics).

critical piece of information, get the data as quickly as possible and then make a decision.

If you decide that the proposed RET venture is not financially feasible, can you change the plan to make it better? If a significant improvement just does not seem possible, well, you have learned a great deal in the process that will help you in the future, maybe with another business venture. You can be proud of the fact that you did the research and analysis that prevented you from investing in a venture where you would have lost your financial savings. Maybe you need to advance further in your career before you strike out on your own. Chapter 13 has an extensive discussion on strategies for acquiring the work experience that will advance your career in the RET industry.

If, however, your objective analysis contained in the business plan shows it is feasible and you are still passionate about it, now is the time to act. Proceed with confidence, and start on your commercial recreation, event, and tourism business adventure. Good luck.

SUMMARY

For the sake of having your ideas placed where they best fit, it is very important to adopt a template for your business plan. This chapter provides one such template, and it has sections that closely follow the sequence of each chapter in this text along with the

 material available in the online student resource. While you will need to be the primary author of this document, there are ample choices available to provide assistance in the writing task. The Web sites identified in this chapter and the preceding chapters are excellent starting points for identifying source material that best matches your needs.

Your cover letter and executive summary will be written last even though they will be placed at the front of your business plan when completed. The largest narrative component of the plan, and perhaps the most time-consuming part in terms of writing, will involve part two of the template described in figure 12.1. This part of the plan will draw upon the suggestions, insights, recommendations, and tasks that appear in chapters 3 through 10, together with the support material appearing in the online student resource. Part three is essentially the financial representation of the decisions you have presented in part two. While part two is a narrative commentary, part three must follow the standardized format of numerical notation that is associated with all financial statements as described in chapter 11. Once you have the plan in place, then you are ready to launch the plan. In preparation of your launch, the primary task will be to carefully foresee the sequence of steps that will make it possible to do what needs to be done in the right sequence and in a timely manner.

 Check out the online student resource for additional material, including case studies, Web links, and more.

Chapter 13

Preparing for a Career in Commercial Recreation, Events, and Tourism

Learning Objectives

After reading this chapter you will be able to

- describe two common programs that utilize experiential education to strengthen your work experience;
- apply the objectives of work-integrated learning to a customized set of activities undertaken in a directed studies course;
- compare the differences between acquiring work experience by means of internship versus cooperative education; and
- describe how involvement with professional associations in a directed studies course can help you apply networking practices and advance your work-related interests.

Key Terms

cooperative education

destination marketing organizations

directed studies course

entrepreneurial associations

experiential education

internship

prework placement skills

portfolio

tourism associations

Imagine this scenario: You attend a meeting of the Association of Collegiate Entrepreneurs featuring an inspiring and successful young entrepreneur. The core message of the address is simply two words: Experience counts. The speaker impresses everyone in the room by sharing many success stories that include frequent and clear references to how work experience combined with formal learning is the time-tested road to success. At the end, the speaker solicits questions and is asked, "How do you get experience without a job, and how do you start a business without experience?" The speaker replies that you need to have considerable self-initiative, and you can carefully select a degree program that supports some form of experiential education, such as internship or cooperative education requirements. Both these requirements combine academic course work with specific work terms that give you the opportunity to test your skills and expand your knowledge by means of integrated professional placement in an industry sector of interest to you. The point is that a well-rounded education is a combination of both classroom and workplace experiences, and this is separate and apart from temporary or part-time jobs you might hold from one time to another.

Just like others in the audience, you believe you are at a crossroad in your life in terms of investing in your career. Some are at the point of changing careers, others are expanding into new areas, and you recognize there are several important choices on the immediate horizon. If you take the speaker's advice to heart, then work experience linked to your course of study will be important in order to hit the ground running. You feel certain that being in business for yourself at some point early in your career is your goal, so the speaker's message has struck a chord with you.

This chapter examines options for acquiring valuable work experience before you graduate and having the benefit of linking your classroom education to that work experience. Understanding what postsecondary institutions can offer in terms of experiential education and work-integrated learning activities is central to making education work for you. Upon making a choice about your field of study, there will be required course work to be completed. However, there are instructions that occur outside the classroom that you will want to know about. The choices to be explored cover internship, cooperative education, and elective self-study courses which are customized to offer prework placement skills and knowledge.

EXPERIENTIAL EDUCATION

As you look into details of strategies for having work experiences integrated with your formal learning activities, you will learn that **experiential education**, or what is sometimes referred to as work-integrated learning, has been accomplished in a variety of ways. Generally speaking, experiential education is both a teaching philosophy as well as an instructional practice designed to engage learners' "direct experiences and focused reflection in order to increase knowledge, develop skills and clarify values" (Association for Experiential Education, www.aee.org/customer/pages.php?pageid=47). The experiential learning process for an academic program that values work experiences

means direct engagement with appropriate field professionals in the teaching–learning process. The course work together with the curriculum is arranged in such a way that the employer becomes a partner in the professional preparation of a student as part of the degree program.

Experiential education essentially means the semesters of academic study are integrated with one or more periods of work experience in appropriate fields of business, industry, government, or an RET industry in the context of the academic program. The integrated professional work experience commonly goes by one of two labels: internship or cooperative education. There are other practical activities, however, such as service learning experience or field practicum that may be integrated into the curriculum. Whatever the experience is called, it will be carefully integrated into the degree requirements. The intriguing element of both these terms in the postsecondary environment is that the work experience is linked to your degree program, and the learner is encouraged to take initiative, make decisions, and be accountable for results. See figure 13.1 for your options.

A prework placement course provides you with a variety of workplace skills and professional expectations before the actual work term, and you will have the assistance of faculty or staff during the work term. Thus, you are supported by the people directly involved with your formal education. Often, there is credit for the work experience itself, and you will be

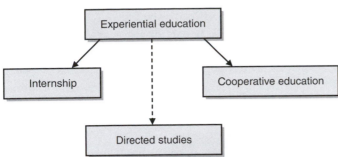

Figure 13.1 Off-campus options for experiential education.

monitored and evaluated and receive feedback on your performance from both faculty and your employer or field professional. These features should begin to paint a picture that a professional field experience is quite different from just having a summer job. It is time now to take a closer look at the choices available and what the benefits are.

PREWORK PLACEMENT COURSE

Before selecting a work experience of interest, you need to know what is out there for consideration. You probably know that the RET industry is diverse, and it is not easy to know what areas are expanding, changing, or growing. The prework placement course you take should cover labor market research, an exercise that specifically targets your field of interest. If you were to take the initiative, it is possible to examine a series of economic census reports prepared by the national census office (e.g., U.S. Bureau of Labor or Statistics Canada) and focused perhaps on the NAICS sector of Arts, Entertainment, and Recreation. In such reports, there is helpful information about growth and change in the industry sections as recorded by census officers who regularly examine the labor force data. See the online student resource for examples of this type of information. However, in the case of your preplacement course, the information will be more local and based on the personal contacts your faculty and academic advisors have with employers in the immediate area. Besides learning about what the workplace has to offer, there is the matter of being personally prepared for making the best of the experiential education opportunity. The course prepares you for such **prework placement skills** as employment research, professional communication, human rights, workplace standards, resume prepara-

tion, interviewing techniques, and background knowledge of the students that have gone before you into the work setting.

INTERNSHIP REQUIREMENT

Internship is commonly a capstone course taken for university credit in the last semester of a four-year degree program. It has several components of the work experience, some of which will be the responsibility of your employment supervisor and some of which will be the responsibility of the faculty member serving as the internship supervisor. The supervisor at your work site will assist in outlining a range of hands-on, progressive job experiences you have available to you as well as individuals you will get to know in the course of observing the duties and skills that have to be performed within the organization. Your supervisor will work with you to select a major project that meets a need of your workplace. Your academic supervisor will be involved with guiding your major project to ensure academic guidelines are met, will identify the support needed to carry it out, and will make one or more site visits to support your internship experiences. An example of guidelines commonly incorporated into an internship manual is found in the online student resource. The content of the manual will vary from one institution to another but generally will try to cover aspects of some common components related to documentation, timelines, evaluation standards, and expectations of all parties involved in the work placement.

The university programs listed in one section of the online student resource lists Web sites which are nationally accredited by the National Recreation and Park Association, and many have RET concentrations or emphasis areas. These degree programs have curriculums that encompass a basic understanding of leisure experiences, consumer behavior, leadership, human relations and organizations, environmental awareness, tourism systems, event planning, integrated communication and marketing, and technology and computer applications. Each school requires an internship, culminating in work experience after completion of four years of academic course work. At Canadian universities there are provincial guidelines to be met for programs that offer a certificate, diploma, or degree related to RET subject areas. Every province has a Tourism Education Council which meets annually to address the framework and guidelines for course content and suggest standards for curriculum. For example, in British Columbia, any university awarding a Bachelor of Tourism Management (BTM) degree will have to offer a set of courses the adhere to the degree framework and eight subject areas with prescribed learning outcomes. A senior capstone course is part of a 4-year degree program in the USA and Canada which is extremely helpful in career development because it is a bridge between the university and professional employment. It should

---

SPOTLIGHT ON

Meetings and Concierges Source, LLC

Location

In Scottsdale, Arizona, Karolyn Kiburz established Meetings and Concierges Source (MCS) in 1999.

Background

Karolyn graduated from Arizona State University with a degree in recreation and tourism. From 2005 to 2007 she was president of and currently serves on the board of ASU's School of Community Resources and Development Alumni Association. In 1998 to '99 she was president of the Arizona Sunbelt Chapter of Meeting Professionals International (MPI). Karolyn was awarded Planner of the Year from the Arizona Sunbelt chapter of MPI in 1996 and serves as a member of the Fiesta Bowl Committee.

Karolyn started her meeting planning career right out of college. She fell into it after working at a resort for her internship. She didn't want to work for the resort, but she wanted to bring the groups to the resort. In 1986, meeting planning was not very well known as a career choice. She landed a job as a convention assistant at the State Bar of Arizona and then worked for National Speakers Association (NSA) planning their national conferences (none were in Arizona). While at NSA and working with entrepreneurs on a daily basis, she decided to start her own planning firm. The company plans conventions and events locally, nationally, and internationally. They also offer a corporate concierge service and manage associations.

Products and Services

MCS, with three professionals on staff, specializes in meeting and event planning as well as managing corporate meetings, special events, conventions, and trade shows. With services including large-scale conferences, corporate incentive programs, annual association meetings, MCS staff provide professional planning and expert detailed execution. Karolyn spearheaded the planning and execution of national conventions for up to 3,000 attendees. The largest local event MCS has planned is the Scottsdale Culinary Festival, a nationally recognized event attracting more than 50,000 people. In 2001, the *Arizona Business Journal* recognized MCS as one of the top 10 meeting and event planning companies in Arizona, and they have been on the list ever since.

Business Plans and Advice

Karolyn offers this advice to those considering working in the event planning field: "You need real passion for the industry and an amazing attention to detail. Because this industry operates 24/7, you should have a flexible schedule and recognize there are many, many details involved in planning. You must enjoy tracking them and making sure everything is in place. The best part is that you get to see all of that hard work come to fruition. It's also a very fun industry. You are able to go places and do things that you might not have an opportunity to do if you were in a different industry."

In terms of client satisfaction, Karolyn realizes that there are many companies that perform this service. Her experiences are built on customer service. "At MCS we are committed to delivering the top value for the money. This means that precise, realistic budget preparation; detailed financial management; and accurate reconciliation are mandatory for every client. We watch every penny of the client's as if it were our own. We are also committed to a partnership with our clients and act as an extension of their staff."

Photo courtesy of Karolyn Kiburz.

provide a broader exposure to the management and operation of an RET business than you get with a normal narrowly defined job, and you have the support of your university professors to help with workplace questions and issues. Canadian institutions and some in the USA often have cooperative education experience which is examined next.

COOPERATIVE EDUCATION REQUIREMENT

Cooperative education is a structured method of combining academic education with practical work experiences. The programs are characterized by many of the same features identified with internships. The primary difference is that cooperative education requires a minimum of three work experiences during your four-year degree program. To obtain a university degree in which a graduate enjoys the distinction of completing a cooperative education program requires that a minimum of 30 percent of the academic program be obtained from on-the-job or professional field work experiences. The first cooperative education program in the United States was established in 1906 in Cincinnati, and the first program in Canada was established at the University of Waterloo in 1957. The cooperative education standard is more common in Canada than in the United States.

Twenty-five years ago, several college and university presidents, educational specialists, and employers from Australia, Canada, Hong Kong, the Nether-

lands, the Philippines, the United States, and the United Kingdom formed the World Council and Assembly on Cooperative Education to foster cooperative education around the world. In 1991, it transformed into the World Association for Cooperative Education (WACE). Today, the association boasts a membership of more than 1,000 people from 43 different countries. A cooperative education experience, commonly known as a "co-op," provides academic credit for structured job experience. The benefits from participation in co-ops have been listed as personal motivation, career clarity, enhanced employability, and vocational maturity. Moreover, studies indicate that employers value the job experience in their newly hired workers as they are more grounded in the profession. Beyond the contextual learning experiences of a co-op, its importance is in preparing the graduate to make a seamless transition from school into the work setting. Working in several industries gives you the opportunity to earn money during your education and a competitive edge when going out into the workforce.

Students attending universities with "certified" co-op programs will often complete three or more placements, and their degrees will indicate the completion of a degree with a cooperative education program. Thus, instead of having a single work experience at the end of an academic program, multiple placements allow you to acquire knowledge of the RET industry at different stages of your academic course of study. The outcomes of the cooperative experience are held

Cooperative education programs benefit from dedicated individuals such as Jim Ketelson and Micki McCarthy, and their efforts bring a smile from successful program graduates such as Shelley-Anne Gajda-Davies (center).

to national standards established by either the Cooperative Education and Internship Association (CEIA), founded in 1963, or the Canadian Association for Co-operative Education (CAFCE), founded in 1973. Their goals are to

- promote cooperative education and internships as premier models of work-integrated learning,
- provide opportunities for professional development, and
- create professional networking opportunities through conferences and Web site links.

The standards adopted for institutions implementing cooperative education ask that

- the cooperative student is engaged in productive work rather than merely observing,
- the cooperative student's performance on the job is supervised and evaluated by the student's cooperative employer,
- the cooperative student receives remuneration for the work performed, and
- the cooperative student's progress on the job is monitored by the cooperative educational institution.

To more closely examine additional details and specific aspects of a cooperative education program, refer to the manual found at www.cafce.ca/pages/manual.php.

DIRECTED STUDIES OPTION

Not all postsecondary programs offer internships or cooperative education, but most offer an option to take a **directed studies course**. This type of course offers an opportunity to accomplish goals associated with a prework placement class, to network with professional associations in a preplanned way, and to acquire valuable experiences by what will be called "prospecting" for a mentor. Historically, prospecting refers to pioneers heading west to strike it rich by finding gold. For a pioneer entrepreneur, the analogy is to head out into the business world and strike it rich by finding a mentor fully engaged in the kind of business that symbolizes a gold nugget for the business concept that you value most. Figure 13.2 shows various options for directed studies.

Since directed studies are defined by the student in consultation with the instructor, there is consider-

Figure 13.2 Options for directed studies.

able latitude as to when you might undertake such an opportunity and how it will be completed. The first step is to take the initiative to find the instructor of record for your directed studies, and second, you must outline a focused and clear study plan. You might want to first take a course that incorporates some of the content of a prework placement course. The objectives may include a systematic examination of industry literature in your area of interest, a preferred career path, and a practicum of skills organized to strengthen your abilities to present yourself professionally.

If you remember nothing else in this chapter, please make a note to yourself that the most important factor in business success is *you*. You are, or will be, the heart and soul of a business venture. Whatever knowledge, skills, and abilities are vital to your professional development, you will need to identify some of them and actively participate in setting priorities. The good news is that a myriad of self-assessment resources are available to mix and match depending on your preferences and needs. The resources range from the commonplace self-help books to a wide range of academic institutions and professional associations that will assist in addressing almost any question you might have. You might begin by examining common traits of entrepreneurs, revealed in a variety of sources, and creating your own checklist to explore your propensity for success based on these attributes. Several sources highlight some common traits of entrepreneurs, such as the following:

- If you are persistent, goal oriented, and willing to make sacrifices in order to succeed, then you are more likely to overcome barriers that arise in business than someone who does not exhibit those qualities.

- If a family member is involved in a business, and you have participated in it, that will assist your own effort in initiating a business.
- If you are creative, innovative, and sensitive to new ideas, then you exhibit a quality associated with an entrepreneur.
- If you communicate effectively, have "people skills," and like to network, you have an attribute associated with an entrepreneur.
- If you are competitive, are not discouraged by setbacks, and have self-confidence, then you possess a trait common to an entrepreneur.

Successful entrepreneurs have a number of other common attributes (see www.smallbiz.ca/2006/07/28/traits-of-successful-entrepreneurs; www.4d.com/startconsulting/gettingstarted/typicaltraits.html), and you should note those applicable to your situation.

Regardless of how applicable one or more of the traits may be, you will need to learn about compatible careers and to expand and grow professionally. Alboher (2007) explored the growing trend of holding multiple careers and suggests that new and expanding technology is making work of this nature more portable and flexible. Added to that trend is a changing attitude about work and life boundaries that encourages multiple careers, both concurrently and sequentially. It may be productive to examine news stories about specific successful individuals in the RET industry.

Periodicals, magazines, journals, workbooks, and guide books will always carry stories of people succeeding in the field. Head to the nearest library and search for articles that shed light on the successes in the recreation, event, and tourism field. If you are interested in assessing your experiences and background in a fascinating manner, you might want to look for a career guide by Richard N. Bolles (2008). For nearly 30 years, *What Color Is Your Parachute?* has been the guiding light for newcomers in pursuit of satisfying and fulfilling employment. The most recent edition has been completely rewritten and is designed to work in conjunction with the book's Web site. This URL is available in the online student resource. At the heart of Bolles' formula for finding the right job are two questions: What do you want to do? Where do you want to do it? As an illustration, one of the exercises he suggests is to list your hobbies and recreation activities. He thinks this can assist with setting priorities for choices in employment, and he has more than 10 exercises to highlight past experiences that you would like to repeat in the future and how the outcome of such a task can help identify things you have done well. There are a variety of equivalent books that fit into the category of general career exploration.

PILOT TESTING START-UP BUSINESS PRACTICES

If you have a modest "sure-fire" business idea together with the necessary funds to do it, then make that part of a directed studies course. When it comes to experiential education, there are lessons to be learned by going through the steps of establishing a business. It is the "learn by doing" method. Even if there are setbacks, many entrepreneurs say they learn a great deal more from their failures in business than the successes. The secret of this approach is to keep it realistic (e.g., follow the procedures for registering a business name, get a license, and create a business card) and have a fixed budget so as not to put more money into your business than you can afford. It helps to have small successes with the various steps, and even failures can be valuable. As the saying goes, nothing ventured, nothing gained.

Since many professional organizations have certification standards, you could use a directed studies course to get certified. For example, find out what is involved in becoming a certified special events professional. Candidates must often meet work experience and educational requirements before they are eligible to take a certification examination. There are frequently different levels of certification, a basic and an advanced form. Besides broad professional certifications, which are the topic of this section, there are also many narrow technically oriented certifications, such as first aid or lifeguarding, that are too numerous to describe here. Professional certification can be valuable because it shows potential employers, clients, or business partners that you are truly committed to the profession and have advanced skills and knowledge. But most professional certifications are still voluntary, and not all employers require a certificate to qualify for certain jobs. However, there has been a recent growing trend toward acquiring certifications in the RET industry. The online student resource contains a list of certifications and their sponsoring organizations. Some examples follow:

Green Tip

Get Involved With the Green Meetings Industry Council

There are many tourism and entrepreneurial associations for young professionals to become involved with while pursuing their educational goals. Associations do not currently present a unified front in setting goals to advance green initiatives, but they could. One common opportunity for all associations to embrace green initiatives practices pertains to annual general meetings (AGMs) and special events. If RET-related associations seek to adopt new green practices and standards that will achieve zero net environmental effects at their meetings, then they need to become involved with the Green Meeting Industry Council (GMIC). The council is partnering with other associations "to support and develop environmentally responsible certification schemes" for a variety of components of meetings, conferences, and exhibitions.

GMIC promotes green practices globally by offering educational programs both online and in on-site training workshops. It is dedicated to improving meeting management practices by encouraging the adoption of environmentally responsible strategies at all stages of the organization, implementation, and closing of meetings, exhibits, and AGMs. In early 2008, the GMIC partnered with a meeting organizer, IMEX, to sponsor the Greening the Hospitality Industry Conference in Vancouver, British Columbia. In preparation for the training program, GMIC also partnered with a nonprofit organization, Offsetters Carbon Neutral Society, to ensure their conference was 100 percent carbon neutral. The carbon-offset program of the GMIC conference funded three projects, one based locally in Vancouver, Canada and two international projects in Honduras and Madagascar. To ensure collaboration among stakeholders, the GMIC program was funded by delegates, exhibitors, speakers, and sponsors.

Student involvement in the GMIC-Vancouver meeting was actively supported by sponsors, and 10 scholarships were awarded to students seeking to expand their knowledge of greening initiatives. One of the aims was to provide the opportunity to apply greening strategies in other associations they may participate in during the course of their professional careers.

- Certified special events professional; International Special Events Society, www.ises.com
- Certified commercial recreation professional; Resort and Commercial Recreation Association, www.r-c-r-a.org
- Certified meeting professional; Convention Industry Council, www.conventionindustry.org

PROSPECTING FOR GOLD

A rewarding and practical experience to try under the umbrella of a directed studies course is to carefully investigate a product or service you would like to have at the core of your business concept and find someone who is doing it. Next proceed to learn how an experienced business owner goes about planning, marketing, and delivering the product. See if that person will become a mentor to you. A mentor is someone who operates an existing business and who will give you advice and the knowledge necessary to build a business around the product you have selected. This person can use his prior experience to teach you

about the industry and can increase your knowledge by letting you observe what he has done to become successful. This opportunity may also become your first initiative at networking in the industry, as your mentor can put you in touch with others who provide goods and services you would like to know more about.

The focus of the prospecting exercise is to contact a specific commercial recreation enterprise that exists in a setting relatively strong in recreation, event, and tourism services. Not all business environments have the type of enterprises and companies you wish to contact, so you may have to adjust your search strategy. Generally, you have several options for starting the process:

- Begin with the local telephone directory to see what is listed. Although the local phone directory will offer some insight into the range of commercial enterprises in your community and surrounding area, not all businesses choose to purchase an advertisement in the Yellow Pages, so you will miss some commercial operations.

- Check with your chamber of commerce or visitors bureau, or on the World Wide Web in the case of tourism-related businesses that might be local in nature.
- Pick up printed advertising material at a nearby visitor center. When in search of clothing, consumers will search the racks. You can do the same at the visitor center to determine the mix of commercial enterprises involved with leisure and tourism products. The brochure rack at a visitor center will have flyers, brochures, guides, and pamphlets with as much detail on local products as the advertiser chooses to reveal. Searching the racks permits you to judge what is available and what does not appear to be offered. Once you have a business name, then you can begin to search for additional details at the location of the business and on the Internet.

Prospecting for a business mentor will yield a different kind of information. Any one of these search strategies may increase your awareness of the diversity of the industry within the geographic area of your search. A more-comprehensive inquiry involves looking at the various business types.

JOINING INDUSTRY AND PROFESSIONAL ASSOCIATIONS

There are many nonprofit industry associations whose mission is to facilitate the exchange of information, develop programs to promote professionalism within the industry, and educate the public. Professional and **tourism associations** have been around for a long time and exist for nearly every sector of the industry. The same can be said for **entrepreneurial associations**.

Tourism industry associations provide great opportunities for both students entering the field and established entrepreneurs to network, attend educational sessions, earn certification, meet other professionals, and possibly find a job or a mentor. Tourism associations also conduct research on the industry. These are some of the greatest benefits for persons starting out in a career. Some groups, such as the Commercial Recreation and Tourism Society, operate under the umbrella of a national organization, as in the case of the National Recreation and Park Association. See table 13.1 for a listing of tourism industry associations.

Numerous professional associations have been created to support young entrepreneurs in general, and a number of the more-common associations for entrepreneurs are presented in the online student resource. Members are challenged to address real-world business and economic issues in their own ventures as well as in their communities. Involvement in one or more of these associations would certainly help the aspiring business-minded person obtain timely information and build a valuable network. Some of the more-common associations for entrepreneurs are presented in table 13.2.

Trade shows and professional conferences offer opportunities for students to network and to expand their professional skills. Here a student team waits for their opportunity to present on a tourism issue to a professional panel in an event hosted by the B.C. Council of Tourism Associations.

Jody Young

Table 13.1 Tourism Industry Associations

Web site	Purpose of the association
www.convention industry.org	**Convention Industry Council** The member organizations of the CIC represent more than 17,300 firms and properties involved in the meetings, conventions, and exhibitions industries. Formed in 1949 to enhance the industry, CIC facilitates the exchange of information, develops programs to promote professionalism within the industry, and educates the public on its profound economic impact.
www.ecotourism.org	**The International Ecotourism Society** TIES promotes responsible travel to natural areas that conserves the environment and improves the well-being of local people by • creating an international network of individuals, institutions, and the tourism industry; • educating tourists and tourism professionals; and • influencing the tourism industry, public institutions, and donors to integrate the principles of ecotourism in their operations and policies.
www.iaapa.org	**International Association of Amusement Parks and Attractions** The IAAPA mission is to serve the membership by promoting the safe operation, global development, professional growth, and commercial success of the amusement park industry. It envisions a professional association regarded as an indispensable resource for its members and an international authority for the industry.
www.ises.com	**International Special Events Society** The society is made up of more than 4,000 professionals in more than 35 countries representing special events producers (from festivals to trade shows), caterers, decorators, florists, destination management companies, rental companies, special effects experts, tent suppliers, audiovisual technicians, party and convention coordinators, balloon artists, educators, journalists, hotel sales managers, specialty entertainers, convention center managers, and many more.
www.mpiweb.org	**Meeting Professionals International** The MPI mission is to help members be their best by building human connections to knowledge, ideas, relationships, and marketplaces. MPI has a membership of 23,000 meeting and event professionals in more than 65 countries.
www.nrpa.org	**National Recreation and Park Association** The NRPA includes the Commercial Recreation and Tourism Section (CRTS) for providing recreation services in commercial recreation settings.
www.r-c-r-a.org	**Resort and Commercial Recreation Association** RCRA is a nonprofit organization established to further the resort and commercial recreation industries through appropriate services to professionals, educators, and students and to increase the profitability of commercial enterprises with a recreation focus.
www.tia.org	**Travel Industry Association of America** Travel Industry Association is the national nonprofit organization representing all components of the $740 billion travel industry. TIA's mission is to promote and facilitate increased travel to and within the United States.
www.tiac-aitc.ca	**Tourism Industry Association of Canada** TIAC is Canada's tourism industry advocacy and lobbying organization on national tourism issues, and it also works to support provincial, territorial, regional, and municipal tourism industry organizations.
www.ttra.com	**Travel and Tourism Research Association** TTRA is an international association of travel, research, and marketing professionals that educates its members on research, marketing, and planning skills through publications, conferences, and networking.

Table 13.2   Professional Associations Serving Young Entrepreneurs

Web site	Purpose of the association
www.acecanada.ca\ http://webs.wichita.edu/ ?u=ace&p=/index/	**Association of Collegiate Entrepreneurs (US) and Advancing Canadian Entrepreneurs (Canada)** ACE is an international organization that enables students to operate small business ventures and interact with other aspiring entrepreneurs. ACE has chapters at universities throughout the United States and Canada.
www.fbla-pbl.org	**Future Business Leaders of America—Phi Beta Lambda** FBLA is a nonprofit 501(c)(3) international educational association of students preparing for careers in business and business-related fields. The association has four divisions: FBLA for high school students; FBLA Middle Level for junior high, middle, and intermediate school students; PBL for postsecondary students; and the Professional Alumni Division for businesspeople, educators, and parents who support the goals of the association.
www.businessownersideacafe. com/genx	**Idea Cafe** The Idea Cafe caters to the business needs of Gen X entrepreneurs with information, advice, and fun to feed their minds and their businesses. The site welcomes biz fans of every age and includes stories of Gen X business successes.
http://www.inc.com/resources/ startup/	**Inc.com** *Inc.* magazine has a Resource Center to assist Young Entrepreneur, Women in Business, Start Up Businesses, tools and kits, etc. Moreover, the magazine has collected profiles of business owners who started their businesses which assist in building a business and provide ideas on networking with peers.
www.sife.org	**Students in Free Enterprise** Through a collaborative effort between business and education, Students in Free Enterprise improves the quality of life and the standard of living around the world by teaching the principles of market economics, entrepreneurship, business ethics, and personal financial success. The program is active on more than 1,000 college and university campuses in more than 25 countries.
www.youngentrepreneur.com	**YoungEntrepreneur.com** Young Entrepreneur Forum is a member-based site that supports online forums and blogs to encourage a community for young entrepreneurs to exchange ideas, find business partners, or get involved with start-up ventures.
http://www.eonetwork.org/	**Young Entrepreneurs' Organization** The Entrepreneurs' Organization (EO) is a membership organization designed to engage leading entrepreneurs to learn and grow. It reports it is a global community of business owners, all of whom run companies that exceed US$1M in revenue. Founded 20 years ago by young, energetic entrepreneurs, EO is now 6,600 members strong with more than 108 chapters in 38 countries around the globe.
http://library.thinkquest.org/ C0114800/about/	Supported by ORACLE Education Foundation, **I Don't Flip Burgers** is The Student's Webguide to Entrepreneurial Success. The purpose of **I Don't Flip Burgers** Web site is promoted as the entrepreneurial success Web site for students seeking help with business ideas. It provides access to downloadable tools helpful in making your new venture an entrepreneurial success. Our goal is to provide you with the experience and resources you need to begin your own business, one which will help you deal with the stress of paying for your post-secondary education. Our primary targets are students will little to no entrepreneurial knowledge who wish to start their own business and become financially secure.

EXPLORING DESTINATION MARKETING ORGANIZATIONS

Destination marketing organizations (DMOs) promote and market places, regions, states, provinces, and even countries as preferred tourism destinations. Their membership can include small and medium businesses, nonprofit organizations, multinational corporations, and incorporated areas and collaborate with visitor service bureaus. It is worthwhile to investigate in a directed studies course how they work, the career options associated with them, and their influence in creating destination images. In the United States and Canada, the states and provinces commit funds to tourism offices, welcome centers, visitor information centers, and their corresponding DMOs. Exploring the Web sites will provide an overview of how destination marketing targets the traveler directly, the nature of the relationships with the tourism partners, and how events and attractions are positioned to build a travel itinerary. Some Web sites will have sections on "how to start a business" within the state or provincial jurisdiction being examined. In addition, many state and provincial DMOs have regular electronic newsletters that keep subscribers up to date on new initiatives, changes in the programs, funding initiatives, and scheduled meetings of professional groups. The Web sites tend to keep up with the latest in Web site technology because the marketing environment is very competitive. It is worth the effort to go online and search the local Web sites for information.

BUILDING A PROFESSIONAL PORTFOLIO

Throughout the process of building your learning experiences, it is wise to create your own portfolio. A **portfolio** refers to a personal collection of information describing and documenting a person's achievements and learning. There are a variety of portfolios ranging from logbooks on learning experiences to extended collections of achievement evidence. Portfolios are also used for many different purposes such as accreditation of prior experience, job searches, continuing professional development, and certification of competence.

Tens of millions of people across the world have already used some kind of portfolio. The recent explosion of knowledge, information, and learning technologies has led to the development of digital portfolios, or electronic portfolios, commonly referred to as e-portfolios. The online student resource identifies strategies and software that will support your effort to create a timely and easy-to-update portfolio.

A mock booth for a trade fair is a practical learning experience.

Courtesy of Tom Delamere

SUMMARY

The underlying premise behind this chapter is the acquisition of work-related experiences concurrent with formal training. The basic choices at many postsecondary institutions are either internships or cooperative education. Each is founded on the philosophy and practices of experiential education. Each will greatly enhance the ability of the student to hit the ground running after graduation. All schools generally offer directed studies, and this is a backup option in the absence of either of the first two choices. In the case of a directed studies course, you may wish to take a business idea and proceed to go through the start-up process as a learning experience. It is very hands-on and practical; just don't commit too much money to it. You can prospect the business world to find a mentor and to cherish the knowledge that comes from working with an experienced person. Professional and destination marketing organizations can provide important practical knowledge as well. Preparing your portfolio is a worthy undertaking because it would be carried out in a prework placement course in any case. Your goal is to find the best opportunities available to you to combine formal classroom knowledge with experiential education options.

 Check out the online student resource for additional material, including case studies, Web links, and more.

Appendix A: NRPA Council on Accreditation Standards for Recreation, Park Resources, and Leisure Services Education

The Council on Accreditation (COA) for Recreation, Park Resources, and Leisure Services Education is sponsored by the National Recreation and Park Association (NRPA) and the Council establishes professional competencies for academic institutions seeking to be accredited. Universities and colleges must document how these standards are met within their curricula so that students gain competence in the identified areas. The authors believe the standards referenced below (i.e., 2004 Edition of the COA standards) have been addressed in part in their chapters and the special features of the text. The chapter numbers for each standard are in parentheses.

CONCEPTUAL FOUNDATIONS

8.04 Understanding of the interrelationship between leisure behavior and the natural environment (chapters 1 and 9)

8.05 Understanding of environmental ethics and its relationship to leisure behavior (chapter 9)

PROFESSION

8.06.02 Professional organizations (chapters 1 and 13)

8.06.03 Current issues and trends in the profession (chapter 1 and each of the profiles of entrepreneurs contained in each chapter)

8.07 Understanding of ethical principles and professionalism (chapters 7 and 9 and the Green Tips)

8.08 Understanding of the importance of maintaining professional competence and the available resources for professional development (chapter 13)

DELIVERY SYSTEMS

8.09 Understanding of the roles, interrelationships, and use of diverse delivery systems addressing recreation, park resources, and leisure (chapter 1)

8.11.01 Operating programs and services (chapter 8)

8.12.02 Understanding of the roles, interrelationships, and use of diverse leisure delivery systems in promoting: Economic development (chapters 1 and 2)

PROGRAM AND EVENT PLANNING

8.13 Understanding of the variety of programs and services to enhance individual, group, and community quality of life (chapters 1, 3, 4, and 8)

8.14.01 Ability to implement the following principles and procedures related to program/event planning for individual, group, and community quality of life: Assessment of needs (chapter 4)

8.14.02 Development of outcome-oriented goals and objectives (chapter 3)

8.14.04 Marketing of programs/events (chapter 5)

8.14.06 Implementation of programs/events (chapter 8)

8.14.07 Evaluation of programs/events (chapters 5 and 8)

8.16 Ability to use various leadership techniques to enhance individual, group, and community experiences (chapters 2 and 7)

ADMINISTRATION/MANAGEMENT

8.17 Ability to apply basic principles of research and data analysis related to recreation, park resources, and leisure services (chapter 5)

8.18 Understanding of the fundamental principles and procedures of management (chapters 7 and 10)

8.19 Understanding of the principles and procedures of human resource management (chapter 7)

8.20 Understanding of the principles and procedures of supervisory leadership (chapter 7)

8.21 Understanding of the principles and procedures of budgeting and financial management (chapter 11)

8.22 Understanding of the principles and procedures related to agency marketing techniques and strategies (chapter 6)

8.24 Ability to apply current technology to professional practice (See Technology Applications)

LEGAL ASPECTS

8.26.02 Contracts and tort law (chapter 10)

8.26.03 Regulatory agents and methods of compliance (chapters 9 and 10)

8.27 Understanding the principles and practices of safety, emergency, and risk management related to recreation, park resources, and leisure services (chapter 10)

8.28 Formal field experience(s) of at least 100 total documented clock hours in appropriate professional recreation organizations/agencies prior to internship (chapter 13)

8.29 Internship, full-time continuing experience in one appropriate professional recreation organization/agency of at least 400 clock hours over an extended period of time, not less than 10 weeks. If an option is accredited, the internship must be directly related to such option (chapter 13)

LEISURE SERVICES MANAGEMENT OPTION

7A.01 Understanding of and ability to apply both traditional and innovative techniques of financial management, including development of budgets for operating and capital budgets, revenue generation and accountability, pricing of services, cost analysis and financial forecasting (chapters 2, 4, and 11)

7A.02 Understanding of the management role, including organizational behavior and relationships, politics of organizations, strategic planning, policy development and implementation, decision-making, cooperative problem solving and managing conflict (chapter 7)

7A.03 Understanding of the relationship of business, society and the economy, including the role of the entrepreneur (chapters 1 and 2)

Adapted with permission of the National Recreation and Park Association.

Appendix B: Resort and Commercial Recreation Association Certified Commercial Recreation Professional Competencies

The following entry level professional competencies areas were included in the Commercial Recreation Professional Certification exam, sponsored by the Resort and Commercial Recreation Association (RCRA). The exam was designed to assess the base knowledge of job-related tasks common to entry-level professionals. The authors believe the competencies referenced below from the 1999 Edition of the RCRA National Exam Information booklet have been addressed in part in their chapters and the special features of the text. The chapter numbers for each competency are shown in parentheses.

Guest Services (chapters 4 and 8)

Communications Skills (chapter 13)

Leadership (chapter 7)

Maintenance (not covered in book)

Programming (chapter 3)

Promotion and Publicity (chapter 6)

Regulations, Rules and Standards (chapters 2, 9, and 10)

Retail Operations (chapter 4)

Supervision (chapter 7)

Adapted, by permission, from Resort and Commercial Recreation Association, 1999, *Commercial Recreation Professional Certification Exam* [information booklet].

Glossary

accident report form—A written document prepared by an employee that describes the basic questions of what, where, when, and who was involved in the accident.

accounts payable—A record of funds due each creditor.

accounts receivable—Money owed to your company.

acknowledgment of risk—A legal document that identifies the risks associated with the activity and goes on to say that the guest is aware of these risks and chooses to participate despite the risks.

added value—Providers give additional benefits through service to someone who has purchased a tangible good or, in other cases, enhances the visitor experience.

advertising—Any form of paid nonpersonal communications placed in the media.

advitorial—A paid advertisement that is designed to look like text written by the media editor. Often has the word *Advertisement* across the top.

balance sheet—A monetary picture of the effects of planned operations on the financial health of the company. These are shown in the assets, liabilities, and owners equity of a small business.

banner ads—An advertisement at the top or side of a specific Web site page, with a short commercial message; when clicked on, it redirects the visitor to another Web site.

behavioral variables—Consumer behaviors that may document previous purchasing decisions, product preference, or preferred mode of travel.

benefits variables—The personal value a customer places on the outcome of the service or experience. Benefits are extensive and may involve acquisition of new skills, relaxation, social status, family bonding, knowledge of place, and so forth.

Blake Mouton Managerial Grid—A behavioral leadership model developed by Robert Blake and Jane Mouton in 1964. It suggests five different leadership styles based on leaders' strength of concern for people and their concern for goal achievement.

blog—A Web site where written entries, commonly displayed in reverse chronological order, provide opinions, commentary, and news on a limited subject area.

bricks and clicks—The use of physical facilities and Internet Web site access via computer to sell a company's services.

business concept—A written description of the basic elements fit within the business description. The concept identifies the purpose of the business, business goal, its products and services, its legal status, and its name.

business description—The second part of a three-part business plan template used in this text. It presents the business concept, its market, and the nature of the competition. It also describes the planned promotion techniques, the management team, the service standards, the environmental management policies, and how risk and liability will be handled.

business interruption insurance—A policy that covers financial losses, up to a stated limit, in case the business cannot continue as before during emergency repairs and recovery.

business plan—A three-part document that contains (1) an introduction, (2) business description, and (3) financial plan.

business plan template—A preformatted way of organizing a business plan. It follows a preset format beginning with a starting point, or section, and then follows a sequence of steps to the preparation of the final section. The underlying assumption of structured format is that there are essential components that need to be identified in some level of detail when writing a plan.

business team—A small number of people, with complementary customer knowledge and technical skills specific to your type of business, who are committed to your business concept, hold themselves mutually accountable to their defined responsibilities, and adhere to your standards of operation.

business typology—A classification system that creates a set of categories of businesses based on characteristics or attributes they share in common.

carbon neutral—Conducting business in such a way that operations do not contribute a net gain in carbon dioxide to the atmosphere.

carbon offsets—Payments made to finance new renewable energy sources and planting of carbon-absorbing trees that counterbalance unavoidable carbon emissions from travel or business activities.

cash flow statement—Provides information on inflows and outflows of cash from operations, whether you will need external funding to meet financial obligations, or whether you might be able to invest any cash surpluses into new equipment or investments.

catchment area—The boundaries of a geographic area from which a business attracts its clients, visitors, or customers.

chart of accounts—The expense and revenue categories for recording business activity.

client safety orientation—A talk given to clients before a recreation experience that reviews participant safety hazards and policies.

code of ethics—A written document that provides guidelines to encourage ethical behavior by company stakeholders.

commercial general liability insurance—Insurance covering injury or loss to the public when they are participating in a recreation program or event with your equipment and staff or on your property.

commercial sector—Composed of for-profit businesses that are distinct because of competitive pricing of the products, services, and experiences they deliver and by the fact that such businesses can be bought, sold, and even franchised.

competitor analysis—A systematic process of gathering, organizing, and evaluating the strengths and weaknesses of a specific business together with its competitors. The purpose of the analysis is to determine if a competitive advantage exists.

consumer experience model—A model consisting of five steps that taken together illustrate the recreation or tourism experience. The steps include anticipation, travel to, on-site experience, travel back, and reflection.

consumer perspective—The examination of the leisure experience from the point of view of the consumer.

contract liability—Lawsuits based on charges of failure to perform as directed by a contract.

conversion studies—Assessments that quantify the gross revenue earned from inquiries generated from a promotion that eventually led to the purchase of a company service.

cooperative education—A structured method of combining classroom-based education with a practical work experience by means of a working partnership between the student, the college, and the employer. Commonly known as a "co-op," cooperative education provides academic credit for structured job experience.

copyright—Legal protection of an original expression of an idea affixed to paper or electronic media that controls the right to reproduce, sell, rent and publicly display it. These include drawings, written text, computer programs, and advertisements. Copyrights cannot be obtained for factual information, short phrases, or words. It is suggested for significant or very important material that a copyright be registered with the Register of Copyrights.

cost of goods sold (COGS)—The cost of beginning inventory, plus purchases, less ending inventory cost.

cost per impression—The media and production costs divided by the number of persons who see or hear your ad.

cover letter—The covering document for a business plan that introduces the reader to the executive summary and plan that follows. In many ways, it is a sales pitch targeted to a specific individual or audience (e.g., investors). It is prepared to answer the question "Why should the business plan enjoy the close attention of the person receiving the material?"

customer loyalty—A feeling or attitude of affection toward a company and willingness to consider only its services in the future.

customer profile—A detailed description of your typical customer.

debt to equity ratio—Illustrates how much the owners have invested in the company compared with the financial contributions of others.

demographic variables—Variables such as age, gender, income, education, occupation, marital status, ethnicity, nationality, and other personal attributes.

destination marketing organizations—A company or non-profit entity involved in the business of increasing tourism to a destination by marketing services and attractions and by improving its public image. See www.destinationmarketing. org/page.asp?pid=20.

directed studies course—Individualized course instruction, often proposed by a student in consultation with an instructor, with the aim of covering specific instructional objectives that are not available as part of regular course scheduling.

distressed business sale—The owner must sell to raise funds and is willing to take less than market value.

distributors—Businesses that buy products from many manufacturers, warehouse this inventory, and then resell it at wholesale prices.

doing business as (DBA)—A registration process with a state or local government that allows a company to operate under a name other than the name of your legal form of business.

domain name—Registered hostnames used to identify a Web site. They are more memorable and stand in for numeric IP addresses. Every domain name ends in a top-level domain code such as com, biz, org, net, travel, or a two-character territory/country code.

e-commerce—The presentation and sale of services and products over the Internet.

ecotourism—The International Ecotourism Society (2006) defines ecotourism as "Responsible travel to natural areas that conserves the environment and sustains the well being of local people."

electronic merchandise surveillance systems—A complete theft prevention system consisting of difficult-to-remove tags placed on merchandise that set off an alarm when passed through a sensor at the door.

employee burnout—Low morale, poor attitude toward customers, and physical exhaustion resulting from working closely with demanding, sometimes rude, service clients for long periods of time.

empowerment—Training, provision of needed tools and materials, and then delegation of responsibility from managers to frontline employees so they will take steps that benefit both the client and the company.

entrepreneur—A person who spots an opportunity; identifies a business idea to capture it; develops a plan to amass the resources to provide the service; and takes the risk by investing his or her time, talent, and funds to start a venture.

entrepreneurial associations—A dozen or more well-established regional, national, and global organizations focused specifically on advancing the interests of their entrepreneurial membership. For additional details, see http://entrepreneurs.about. com/od/associations/Support_Organizations_Associations. htm.

environmental management—The identification and management of the impacts of a company's operations on the environment, with the goal of reducing any adverse effects.

errors and omissions insurance—Covers against claims from customers who suffered losses because of errors you made or things you failed to do but should have done.

ethics—A set of principles of right conduct that causes the greatest good for the greatest number of people.

event industry—Made up of three primary components: client planners, intermediaries acting on their behalf, and suppliers that deliver the basic services that support the planned activities of the event.

executive summary—The section of a business plan, directly after the cover letter, that presents the highlights of the plan. As a summary, it is brief, concise, and focused on the main points of the plan. The purpose of this part of the document is to entice the reader into reading more of the plan. Because it contains information extracted from all other parts of the plan, it is not written until the business plan has been entirely completed.

experience—The process of personally observing, encountering, or undergoing something.

experiential dimension—The emotional or affective part of an experience.

experiential education—A teaching philosophy as well as instructional practice designed to engage learners directly in a set of experiences intended to increase knowledge, skills, and abilities and to assist in the clarification of values.

familiarization (FAM) tour—Specially created low- or no-cost trips only for the travel press, travel agents, and other partnering business representatives.

financial plan—The third part of a three-part business template used in this text. The statements prepared for this part of the plan document projected income, expenses, cash flow, and the required start-up capital.

fixed assets—Items such as company-owned buildings and major equipment.

fixed costs—Expenses that do not greatly vary with the amount of sales over a specific activity range or time.

franchise—A parent company (franchisor) develops a successful business concept and system and then sells the rights to use the franchise name and system to an individual or small company (franchisee) for a fee.

full cost price—Lowest price that can be charged to cover production costs.

general partnership—A legal business form in which all partners manage the business and are personally liable for its debts. Partners share with each other the profits or losses of the business undertaking in which all have invested.

geographic variables—Variables that commonly reflect the origin of the customer. In tourism, the most basic distinction is between domestic travelers—who originate within the country where services are provided—and international travelers whose point of origin is outside the country where services are delivered.

global travel distribution systems (GTDSs)—A global network of interlinked, highly sophisticated computer systems containing the inventory and pricing of travel suppliers and with the capability of selling these services to consumers.

goodwill—The financial value of a company above the market value of equipment and real estate. It is based on the company reputation, size of the customer base, and willingness of past clients to purchase again.

green cuisine—Food supplies that are grown, harvested, processed, packaged, and sold with the goal of minimizing adverse impacts on the environment and local communities.

gross margin—A measure of profitability determined by subtracting total sales from cost of goods sold.

guest experience—An experience goes well beyond a simple product or service, as it becomes a memorable and richly satisfying engagement for which people will pay top dollar.

guest medical insurance—A no-fault policy that covers the costs of any initial medical treatment and emergency transportation related to a guest's injury.

home equity loan—A person takes out a second mortgage on his or her primary residence and uses the accrued equity for business or personal use.

income statement—Describes monthly revenues and expenditures and the resultant monthly net profit or loss.

independent contractor—A person who performs contracted services for a business. Such an individual provides his own tools of the trade (e.g., computers, rafts, climbing gear), sets his own hours, has specific work tasks, and provides his own workers' compensation insurance and federal tax identification number.

installment loan—A loan that is paid back with interest over a period of time by monthly installments.

insurance—Companies transfer or share a portion of the risk of loss with a recreation provider for a fee that is usually based on loss history for that type of service and for the specific business and business practices.

International Organization for Standardization (ISO)—A group of representatives from various nations that develop and maintain established norms, technical criteria, methods, processes, and practices.

internship—Academic study integrated with one or more periods of work experience in appropriate fields of business, industry, government, or the RET industry in the context of the academic program.

intrepreneur—A person who sees an opportunity but prefers to work within and foster change to an existing organization where he or she is employed.

intrinsic price theory—If your price is too much below the competition, then the price alone conveys a message there must be something wrong with the service.

inventory turnover (stock turn)—How frequently inventory sells. Turnover is equal to net sales plus average retail stock.

leadership—The proactive or functional approach advocates the view that leadership is a set of behaviors that help a group perform a task, reach its goal, or perform its function. In the context of business, leaders encourage and reward functional behaviors that advance the mission and vision of the business.

Leave No Trace—A comprehensive system designed to inform both professional guides and individual wild land users on ways to minimize their impacts on the resources and other visitors.

liability—A critically important concept affecting RET owners. It refers to a situation in which a company is subject to a lawsuit because of a failure to carry out certain responsibilities as defined by law, standards of practice, or contractual agreement.

liability waiver—A legal document that includes an acknowledgment of risk and describes how the signer relinquishes the legal right to bring a lawsuit against the service provider.

lifestyle business—A business in which your work requires you to be an expert in exciting or fun activities, such as skiing or rock climbing, that you are passionate about.

limited liability company—A legal form of business that offers limited liability to its owners, and most states do not limit the number of investors. It is similar to a corporation but provides more tax and ownership flexibility than other ownership types.

line of credit—A preapproved amount of credit from a bank, with specified terms, that costs you interest only when cash is withdrawn.

liquidity ratio—Shows the ability of the company to meet immediate debts and how much money it has available for working capital.

loans—Promissory agreements that require payment of a portion of the original amount at specified time periods with interest.

management—Carrying out business activities the right way; the perspective stresses the importance of efficiency and effectiveness. By contrast, leadership stresses doing the right things, such as actions that advance the mission and vision of the company. (See *leadership*.)

managerial duties—A wide range or set of responsibilities performed by managers in the course of planning, developing, and implementing a business plan.

margin—The percentage you earned above the price you paid.

market analysis—Placement of a consumer population into homogeneous groups based on similar interests, product preferences, or individual attributes.

market research—The collection, organization, and interpretation of data important for identifying the characteristics of customers making up your target market.

market segmentation—Refers to the marketing practice of dividing consumers or potential consumers into target markets based upon their behaviors, preferences, physical or psychological attributes, or sets of values they express as important in regard to a product or service.

market share—A measure of how dominant a business is within its service sector.

marketing—The process of identifying consumers' wants; developing products or services to satisfy those wants; and promoting, selling, and distributing the product or service.

marketing mix—The combination of product, price, place, and promotional elements.

mass customization—The concept that service providers offer a range of service alternatives, allowing the consumers to mix, match, and individualize their experience to their desires while keeping the price reasonable.

media kit—A packet about a company that includes relevant and timely press releases, background about the company and its owners, unique features, testimonials, sample articles, a contact person, and photos.

Meeting Professionals International—A national association of professional event planners that provides services primarily to business clients.

mission statement—Tells why the business exists; it is a statement revealing the purpose of the business and how its core values fit into the purpose.

moment of truth—A personal, emotionally charged contact with a client where a timely and appropriate response can make a big difference in customer satisfaction.

mortgages payable—A legal contract in which property is used as security for the repayment of a debt.

Myers-Briggs Type Indicator—An individual self-assessment tool highly suited for team-building activities such as improving communication, enhancing problem-solving skills, valuing diversity of team members, and providing conflict-resolution practices.

naming conventions—The government-established guidelines for registration of a business name; the guidelines often vary for usage of the words *corporation, incorporated, limited, public limited company, proprietary limited company*, and *limited liability partnership*.

negligence—An unintentional act of omission or commission in which a person fails to do something that a "reasonable" person would do under similar circumstances or does something a "reasonable person" would not do.

net margin—Shows what percentage of sales are turned into profit.

neutral third party verification—The checking and accounting of reported data by an independent, neutral organization that does not stand to gain from the outcome of the report.

niche tourism—Characterized by businesses that have established a particular intangible specialty product that garners a reliable market share.

noncompete agreement—A signed legal agreement from the seller that he or she will not compete with the new owner in the same type of business for at least three years.

nonprofit sector—Organizations that often rely on fees and charges obtained from their membership and from foundation grants supporting them.

North American Industry Code—A classification system used by census agencies in Canada, the United States, and Mexico to ensure that the enumeration of businesses is collected and codified in the same way.

on-site experience—Often considered the most important stage of the experience, this is when the consumer is fully engaged in the leisure opportunity and in the setting he or she has anticipated and will later reflect on.

opt-in list—A list of persons who have voluntarily agreed to be placed on the list so they can receive e-mails and other communications.

organic search engine placement—The ranking or placement of a specific Web site in the original search engine results. It is not the result of purchasing keywords or ads.

organizational chart—A diagram that reveals the structure of a business, the positions within it, and the reporting relationships of the team members, if applicable.

owners equity—Also known as net worth, it represents the owner's claim to the assets of the business.

patent—A right granted by the federal government to inventors for the making, selling, or use of an invention. An application must be filed with the U.S. Patent and Trademark Office.

payment dating—Approval for delaying payment to a dealer for wholesale goods to give you extra time to sell the items.

PERT chart—A project management tool that breaks work down into discrete events. It is suitable in situations where it is vital to schedule, organize, and coordinate tasks carefully and in a correct sequence. PERT is an acronym for **P**rogram **E**valu-ation **R**eview **T**echnique and displays tasks to be performed in a network diagram. The diagram consists of events, or tasks, to be completed which are linked by directional arrows indicating the expected sequence for their completion. Another network methodology which accomplishes a similar objective is referred to as the **C**ritical **P**ath **M**ethod. For a comparison of methodologies, see http://studentweb.tulane.edu/~mtruill/dev-pert.html.

point of sale (POS) system—Used to measure and monitor sales, profitability, and inventory levels.

portfolio—An employment strategy for professionals to show their best work, accomplishments, awards, and skills to a po-tential employer or even investor. An *e-portfolio* is an electronic portfolio containing a collection of electronic evidence that has been organized using a portfolio format (see www.eportfolio.org).

position description—A document that provides the employee and supervisor with a common understanding of the work to be performed, the reporting relationships, the level of decision-making authority, and the workplace demands of the position. The description focuses on expected outcomes and may specify how the tasks are to be accomplished in terms of the business culture.

press releases—Professionally formatted press releases are es-sential to get the media's attention and interest and to provide them with the first level of information they may need.

prework placement skills—A set of practical competencies and important abilities associated with resume preparation, inter-viewing techniques, business card preparation, and knowledge for marketing oneself in the work setting.

price point—The price at which consumers are familiar with such products and at which your competitors price similar services.

pro deal—A discount offered by manufacturers and distribu-tors to professionals working in the field and in stores that use or demonstrate their products at work.

product club—A collaborative strategy to support businesses coming together to address issues of common concern in the area of marketing.

product liability insurance—When you purchase this kind of policy, it covers injury to customers from their use or misuse of products you made or sold.

profit centers—Distinct areas of a business that generate sub-stantial revenues.

profit sharing—Allows an employee to receive additional income from one or more incentive options a business offers beyond salary. These options are linked to, and depend on, the company's profitability.

pro forma statement—Projections or estimations for the next year.

promotion mix—A combination or mixture of techniques or tools selected to communicate with a target market. It is the combination of advertising, personal sales, publicity, and sales promotion.

psychographic variables—Characteristics or attributes that relate to attitudes, lifestyle, personality, and preferred travel destinations.

publicist—A professional hired by a company to generate publicity, who specializes in knowing the media and what they are looking for to meet their editorial calendars and writing needs.

publicity—Nonpaid, nonpersonal stimulation of demand by obtaining favorable coverage in the media.

qualifying customers—Choosing from a list of potential customers those who may be interested, authorized, and able to make a purchase.

recruitment—A process of advertising, interviewing, selecting, and hiring to fill staff positions. The process may involve filling vacancies or hiring for new positions.

relationship—Ongoing communications and exchanges be-tween buyer and seller that focus on keeping the customer happy with the seller after the sale.

RET industry model—A complex and integrated model de-scribing the linkages between service providers; the sectors they represent; and the primary role each component provides in transporting, hosting, feeding, and entertaining the consumer engaged in recreation, event, or tourism opportunities.

return on equity—A comparison of the financial returns of the company versus other companies and types of investments. Return on equity equals net profit divided by total equity (total assets minus total liabilities).

return on investment—A frequently used metric of ad effective-ness. ROI equals ad-generated sales divided by total ad media and creation costs.

risk management—The process of doing everything you can to protect your guests, employees, client property, company assets and equipment from losses.

RSS (Really Simple Syndication) feeds—A data format used on the Internet for providing users with frequently updated content. This is done to allow persons to keep up with their favorite Web sites in an automated manner that's easier than checking them manually.

sales promotion—Promotional activities that are not advertis-ing, personal sales, or publicity where the consumer is given short-term incentives to make an immediate purchase.

sensitivity analysis—Enables the author of the business plan to examine different scenarios (e.g., optimistic or pessimistic) based on the original profit and loss forecast. It asks how sensi-tive is profitability if you either decrease income by 10 percent or increase cost by the same amount.

service—The performance of work for another through helpful or professional activity.

service provider—Any organization or business that provides goods or services for consumers of leisure experiences.

service provider model—A model identifying the activities an organization or business typically carries out in order to produce a product or service for the consumer.

severe acute respiratory syndrome (SARS)—A viral disease that compromises the respiratory system, is spread relatively easily by travelers, and can cause death if untreated. SARS arose in Asia in 2000 and 2001 and spread to other continents, but it did not become a widespread epidemic. But the fear of contracting SARS did significantly discourage travel for more than a year.

small and medium enterprises (SMEs)—Businesses that generally employ from 1 to 50 employees are considered small in the service industry, whereas businesses with 50 to 500 employees are considered medium. However, globally there is not a common standard for SMEs.

social media—Web sites that are designed to facilitate social interaction between friends and build online communities of persons with similar interests where opinions and photos are easily exchanged.

sole proprietorship—A business form that is not legally separate from its owner. A sole proprietorship essentially means a person does business in his or her own name, and there is only one owner.

standard of care—(1) Operating requirements set forth in laws and regulations or (2) common practices or standard operating procedures of companies that provide similar services in comparable environments.

stockholders—People who purchase a stock certificate that allows them to receive dividends and have a voice in operation of the firm.

stockholders' equity—The owner's residual interest in assets of the company after deducting liabilities.

subchapter S corporation—A corporation that elects to be taxed under Subchapter S of Chapter 1 of the Internal Revenue Code. An S corporation is normally set up to not pay corporate income taxes on profits; rather, the shareholders pay income taxes on their proportionate shares of the S company's profits. The liability of the corporation is limited to corporate assets, and the personal assets of shareholders and employees are shielded from corporate losses.

sustainability—Living and conducting business in ways that do not compromise the environment or the well-being of future generations.

sustainability report—Presents the company's environmental and social sustainability vision, goals, policies, and performance over a period of years in one comprehensive document.

SWOT analysis—An acronym that refers to the examination of a business in terms of its **S**trengths, **W**eaknesses, **O**pportunities, and **T**hreats.

target market—A preferred group or category of customers to be served by a business in light of the products, services, or experiences it offers to the consumer.

team building—A set of managerial tasks generally focused on the creation and motivation of result-oriented teams. The process requires clarifying the goal, building ownership among team members, removing barriers to cooperation, and collaborating, or at least mitigating the negative effect of barriers on teamwork practices.

tort liability—A wrong committed by an employee or company outside of a contractual agreement that may be grounds for a lawsuit.

total assets turnover ratio—Measures how effective the business is in using its resources. Total assets turnover equals net sales divided by total assets.

total quality management—A management theory characterized by a complete shift in company focus to maximizing customer satisfaction.

tourism associations—Membership- or stakeholder-based organizations engaged in one or more aspects of supporting, enhancing, or advocating the interest of the tourism industry.

tourism-recreation model—A model in which tourism and recreation enterprises may be examined in the context of three basic elements that describe the infrastructure that drives the system (i.e., form), identifies how they operate (i.e., functions), and highlights the outcomes (i.e., consequences).

trade shows—Large-scale, preseason, closed-to-the-public, national or regional events where manufacturers and sales representatives have booths where they show samples available for the upcoming season and take orders.

trademark—A word, phrase, logo, or brand name for your product that is used to identify it and differentiate it from others. An example of a trademarked phrase is "Toyota: Moving Forward." A trade name is the name of your business. You should register these identifying items with the U.S. Patent and Trademark Office.

travel trade—Sales professionals working in the travel industry.

triangulation—The process of confirming the accuracy of an information item by examining it from two or more separate and verifiable sources. It is important in qualitative investigations to ensure that observations about market data are accurately recorded and interpreted.

triple bottom line accounting—A system for measuring and recording the output of a business based on its contributions to financial profit, environmental conservation, and community or society.

uniform resource locator (URL)—The specific network address of the individual computer that is seeking information on the Internet.

up-sell—The tactic of suggesting complementary items to the purchase.

variable costs—Expenses that vary with the amount of sales.

vision statement—A creative, forward-thinking, value-laden, inspiring word picture that reveals where the business is headed.

word of mouth—Informal evaluations of a company's past performance or potential value or of trip experiences through verbal communications to friends or family.

workers' compensation insurance—Provides no-fault coverage for employees injured on the job, including paying for medical expenses and reimbursement for lost wages due to the accident.

working capital—Current assets minus current liabilities. But in essence it is the cash or financing needed to optimally operate the business.

worldwide travel network—Consists of buyers, both individual consumers and businesses; intermediaries (distributors), such as travel counselors and visitors bureaus; and suppliers, such as airlines, local resorts, and recreation and entertainment companies.

yield management systems—Software that identifies and automatically sets the highest price that can be charged for a particular room on a specific night with a high probability that it will be sold.

Bibliography

About.com. 2007. "Theft: Retail's Real Grinch." Available: http://retailindustry.about.com/od/statistics_loss_prevention/l/aa001122a.htm.

Adams Media Corporation. 2006. *Adams Businesses You Can Start Almanac* (2nd ed.). Avon, MA: Adams Media Corporation.

Alboher, M. 2007. *One Person/Multiple Careers*. New York: Warner Books.

American Hospitality Academy. n.d. *AHA Training Manual* (2nd ed.). Hilton Head, SC: American Hospitality Academy.

Asian American Hotel Owners Association. n.d. "About Us." and "History" Available: www.aahoa.com.

Association for Experiential Education. 2008. "What Is Experiential Education?" Available: www.aee.org/customer/pages.php?pageid=47.

B.C. Ministry of Tourism. 1995. *An Analysis of the Ecotourism Market in British Columbia and Alberta*. Victoria, BC: Queens Printer.

Baker, B. 2006. "All Things Internet, or Why 11th Grade Mattered." Presentation at the 2006 California Conference on Tourism, March 28, 2006, Anaheim, CA.

Baldwin, J. 1997. "Failing Concerns: Business Bankruptcy in Canada." Ottawa, ON: Statistics Canada, Micro-Economic Analysis Division.

Bamford, C., and G. Bruton. 2006. *A Framework for Success: Small Business Management*. Mason, OH: Thompson Southwest.

Barnes, M. 2005. "Connecting Californians to the Outdoors." Presentation at the Connecting Californians to the Outdoors Conference, May 2005, Los Angeles.

Barnett, W. 2007. "Stanford Offers Business Program on Environmental Sustainability." *Silicon Valley Business Journal* [Online], May 1. Available: www.bizjournals.com/sanjose/stories/2007/04/30/daily22.html?from_rss=1.

Barrett, R. 2003. *Vocational Business: Training, Developing and Motivating People*. Cheltenham, UK: Nelson Thornes Ltd.

Bartkus, K.R. 2001. "Social Skills Training and Cooperative Education: An Empirical Investigation of Performance Outcomes." *Journal of Cooperative Education and Internships*, 36(1): 48-60.

Beauregard, M., and M. Fitzgerald. 2000. *Hiring, Managing and Keeping the Best*. Toronto: McGraw-Hill.

Bell, C.R., and R. Zemke. 2007. *Managing Knock Your Socks Off Service* (2nd ed.). New York: American Management Association.

Besterfield, D.H. 2002. *Total Quality Management* (3rd ed.). New York: Prentice Hall.

Blade Consulting. 2003. *Expected Costs of Startup Businesses*. SBA contract no. SBAHQ-02-M-0510. Vienna, VA: Blade Consulting.

Blanchard, K. and J. Stoner. 2004. *Full Steam Ahead–Unleash the Power of Vision in Your Work and Your Life*. (San Francisco, CA: Berrett-Koehler Publishers).

Bly, R. 2002. *Fool-Proof Marketing: 15 Winning Methods for Selling Any Product or Service in Any Economy*. New York: Wiley.

Bolles, R.N. 2008. *What Color Is Your Parachute?* New York: Ten Speed Press.

Branson, R. 2004. *Losing My Virginity: How I've Survived, Had Fun, and Made a Fortune Doing Business My Way*. New York: Three Rivers Press.

Brown, M., and C. Orsbom. 2006. *Marketing to the Ultimate Power Consumer: The Baby Boomer Woman*. New York: American Management Association.

Buckingham, M., and C. Coffman. 1999. *First, Break All the Rules: What the World's Greatest Managers Do Differently*. New York: Simon and Schuster.

Buckley, R. 2003. "Environmental Inputs and Outputs in Ecotourism: Geotourism With a Positive Triple Bottom Line?" *Journal of Ecotourism*, 2:1, page 76.

Bullaro, J.J., and C.R. Edginton. 1986. *Commercial Leisure Services: Managing for Profit, Service and Personal Satisfaction*. New York: Macmillan.

BusinessWeek. 1994. "Entertainment Economy." March 14.

Canadian Institute for Research and Innovation in Sustainability. 2008. "What Is Sustainability?" Available: www.sustreport.org.

Cannizzaro, M. 2007. "Online Travel Bookings Will Surpass Offline Bookings for the First Time in 2007." U.S. Online Travel Overview, PhoCusWright Research.

Clarke, N.F. 1990. *The Recreation and Entertainment Industries: A Sourcebook*. Jefferson, NC: McFarland.

Clawson, M., and J.L. Knetch. 1966. *Economics of Outdoor Recreation*. Baltimore: Johns Hopkins University Press.

Cohen, E. 2004. *Contemporary Tourism: Diversity and Change*. The Netherlands: Elsevier.

Colenutt, C. 2000. "The Effect of a Queue-Type Delay on Recreationists' Mood and Satisfaction Levels With a Leisure Provider." *Journal of Park and Recreation Administration*, Summer: 1.

Conley, Chip. 2007. *Peak: How Great Companies Get Their Mojo from Maslow*. San Francisco: Jossey-Bass, p. 229.

Covey, S.R. 1990. *The Seven Habits of Highly Effective People*. New York: Simon and Schuster.

Covey, S.R. 1992. *Principle-Centered Leadership*. New York: Simon and Schuster.

Crossley, J.C., and L. Jamieson. 2001. *Introduction to Commercial Recreation and Tourism: An Entrepreneurial Approach*. Champaign, IL: Sagamore.

Crow, C. 1997. *Cooperative Education in the New Millennium*. Columbia, MD: Cooperative Education Association.

Csikszentmihalyi, M. 1996. *Creativity: Flow and the Psychology of Discovery and Invention*. New York: HarperCollins Publishers, Inc.

Csikszentmihalyi, M. 2003. *Good Business: Flow, Leadership and the Making of Meaning*. New York: Viking Press.

Davidson, A. 2007. "Greening the Super Bowl." Available: www.forbes.com/2007/01/19/super-bowl-green-sports-biz-cz_ad_0119green.html.

De Lollis, B. 2005. "Travel World Tries Catering to Gen X Splurgers." *USA Today*, February 9.

Dean, J.W. 2006. *Conservatives Without Conscience*. New York: Viking Penguin.

Decker, J.M., and J.L. Crompton. 1993. "Attracting Footloose Companies: An Investigation of the Business Location Decision Process." *Journal of Professional Services Marketing*, 9:1.

Drucker, P.F. 1966. *The Effective Executive*. New York: HarperCollins.

Edwards, A. 2005. *The Sustainability Revolution: Portrait of a Paradigm Shift*. Gabriola Island, BC: New Society.

Ellis, T., and R. Norton. 1988. *Commercial Recreation*. St. Louis: Times Mirror/Mosby.

Environmental Protection Agency. 2008. *Enviro Facts Data Warehouse*. [Online]. Available: www.epa.gov/enviro/html/ef_overview.html.

Finklestein, R. 2005. *Celebrating Success: Fourteen Ways to a Successful Company*. New York: Morgan James.

Fjellman, S.M. 1992. *Vinyl Leaves: Walt Disney World and America*. Boulder, CO: Westview Press.

Forester Research. 2006. "The Internet Versus Traditional Media: The Battle Continues." Available: www.forrester.com/Research/Document/Excerpt/0,7211,40632,00.html.

Frangialli, Francesco. 2005. Address on World Tourism Day by the WTO Secretary-General, www.world-tourism.org/wtd/eng/doc/message_sg.pdf.

Fuld, L.M. 1994. *New Competitor Intelligence: The Complete Resource for Finding, Analyzing, and Using Information About Your Competitors*. New York: Wiley.

Gale, D. 2005. "From Data to Dollars: Using Guest Information to Do Targeted E-mail Marketing Is a Road to Additional Revenue for Hoteliers." *Hotels*, October: 61-63.

Godin, S., and G. Kawasaki. 2006. *How Smart Companies Get People Talking*. Chicago: Kaplan.

Grensing-Pophal, L. 1987. *The Small Business Guide to Employee Selection*. Vancouver, BC: International Self-Counsel Press.

Grensing-Pophal, L. 2004. *Motivating Today's Employees*. Vancouver, BC: International Self-Counsel Press.

Gross, S. 2004. *Positively Outrageous Service: How to Delight and Astound Your Customers and Win Them for Life*. Chicago: Kaplan.

Gunn, C.A., and T. Var. 2002. *Tourism Planning: Basics, Concepts, Cases* (4th ed.). Washington, DC: Routledge/Taylor and Francis.

Hawken, P. 1993. *The Ecology of Commerce: A Declaration of Sustainability*. New York: HarperCollins.

Henderson, H. 1991. *Paradigms in Progress: Life Beyond Economics*. New York: Knowledge Systems.

Higgins, M. 2006. "Buzzword of the Year: Ecotourism." *New York Times*, January 20.

Higgins, T., and T. Duane. 2007. "Incorporating Complex Adaptive Systems Theory Into Strategic Planning: The Sierra Nevada Conservancy." *Journal of Environmental Planning and Management*, 51:1.

Hronek, B., and J. Spengler. 2002. *Legal Liability in Recreation and Sport*. Champaign, IL: Sagamore.

Hultsman, J., and W. Harper. 1993. "The Problem of Leisure Reconsidered." *Journal of American Culture*, 16(1): 47-54.

International Association of Professional Brochure Distributors. 2005. Available: www.apbd.org/index.php.

International Ecotourism Society. 2006. Available: www.ecotourism.org/webmodules/webarticlesnet/templates/eco_template.aspx?articleid=95&zoneid=2.

International Ecotourism Society. 2007. "Definitions of Ecotourism." Available: http://206.161.82.194/WebModules/WebArticlesNet/articlefiles/15-NEW%20US%20Factsheet%20Sept%2005.pdf.

International Ecotourism Society. 2007. "Fact Sheet: Global Ecotourism." Available: www.ecotourism.org/webmodules/webarticlesnet/templates/eco_template.aspx?articleid=15&zoneid=2.

Investopedia. 2007. "What Is a Cash Flow Statement?" Available: www.investopedia.com/articles/04/033104.asp.

Jacksack, S. 2006. *Start, Run, and Grow a Successful Small Business* (5th ed.). Chicago: CCH Publishers.

Janes, P. 2006. *Marketing in Leisure and Tourism: Reaching New Heights*. State College, PA: Venture.

Kandampully, J., C. Mok, and B. Sparks. 2001. *Service Quality Management in Hospitality, Tourism and Leisure*. New York: Haworth Hospitality Press.

Kelly, J.R. 1985. *Recreation Business*. New York: Wiley.

Kelly, J.R. 1987. *Recreation Trends Towards the Year 2000*. Champaign, IL: Sagamore.

Kelly, J.R., and R.B. Warnick. 1999. *Recreation Trends and Markets: The 21st Century*. Champaign, IL: Sagamore.

Kiyosaki, R.T., and S.L. Lechter. 2005. *Before You Quit Your Job: Ten Real-Life Lessons Every Entrepreneur Should Know About Building a Multimillion-Dollar Business*. New York: Warner Business Books.

Kotler, P., G. Armstrong, and P.H. Cunningham. 2005. *Principles of Marketing* (Sixth Canadian Edition). Upper Saddle River, NJ: Prentice-Hall, Inc.

Kotter, J.P. 2002. *The Heart of Change*. Boston: Harvard Business School Press.

Kraus, R. 2000. *Leisure in a Changing America: Trends and Issues for the 21st Century*. Boston: Allyn and Bacon.

Kraus, R., and J. Curtis. 2000. *Creative Management in Recreation, Parks and Leisure Services* (6th ed.). Boston: McGraw-Hill.

Leemon, D., and T. Schimelpfenig. 2006. *Risk Management for Outdoor Leaders*. Lander, WY: National Outdoor Leadership School.

Levinson, J. 2007. *Guerrilla Marketing*. New York: Houghton Mifflin.

Levitt, T. 1991. "Levitt on Marketing." *Harvard Business Review*, Special Edition, September 1.

Lindner, J.R. 1995. "Writing Job Descriptions for Small Businesses." Misc. Pub 93-9. Piketon Research and Extension Center. Piketon, Ohio: Ohio State University.

Long, Y. 2007. "Trends in China Tourism and Tourism Education." Presentation at the First International Forum on Tourism Education, December 13, 2007, Guilin, China.

Lorsch, J., L. Berlowitz, and A. Zelleke. 2005. *Restoring Trust in American Business: A Report of the Project on Corporate Responsibility*. New York: American Academy of Arts and Sciences.

Mansfield, Y., and A. Pizam. 2005. *Tourism, Security and Safety: From Theory to Practice*. Oxford, UK: Elsevier, Butterworth-Heinemann.

McCarville, R. 2002. *Improving Leisure Services Through Marketing Action*. Champaign, IL: Sagamore.

Meeting Planners International. 2007. "Future Watch 2007." Available: www.mpiweb.org/CMS/uploadedFiles/Research_and_Whitepapers/2007%20FutureWatch%20Small.pdf.

Meeting Professionals International. 2006. "Meetings Industry to Grow in 2006 with Increase in Meetings, Attendees, Budgets, Lead Times and Demand Outpacing Supply." Available: www.mpiweb.org/CMS/mpiweb/mpicontent.aspx?id=4339.

Mintzberg, H. 2004. *Managers, not MBA's: A Hard Look at the Soft Practices of Managing and Management Development*. San Francisco: Berrett-Koehler.

Mission Expert and Kinetic Wisdom, Inc. 2006. *Mission Statement Impact Assessment: Study to Explore the Correlation Between a Company's Business Success and the Presence of a Company Mission Statement*. (August 15).

Morais, D., T. Zillifro, and G. Nyaupane. 2004. "Resolving Barriers to Participation in Outfitted Trips." Technical Report, School of Hotel, Restaurant and Recreation Management, Penn State University.

Morrison, A. 2002. *Hospitality and Travel Marketing* (3rd ed.). Albany, NY: Delmar.

Murphy, J. 2003. "Restoring Trust in Business: Models for Action." PR Coalition. Available: www.awpagesociety.com/images/uploads/PRCoalitionPaperFinal.pdf.

Naisbitt, J. 1982. *Megatrends: Ten New Directions Transforming Our Lives*. New York: Warner Books Inc.

Nam, S., P. Manchanda, and P. Chintagunta. 2007. "The Effects of Service Quality and Word of Mouth on Customer Acquisition, Retention and Usage." *Social Science Research Network* [Online]. Available: http://papers.ssrn.com/sol3/papers.cfm?abstract_id=969770.

National Federation of Independent Businesses. 2007. "Financing Alternatives When Starting a Business." Available: www.nfib.com/object/IO_17326.html.

Nickerson, N.P., and P. Kerr. 2001. *Snapshots: An Introduction to Tourism*. Toronto: Prentice Hall.

Nicolazzo, P. 2005. "The Components of an Effective Staff Development System." Outdoor Ed [Online]. Available: www.outdoored.com/articles/Article.aspx?ArticleID=203.

Nicolazzo, P. 2007. "Instructor Skills and Competency Versus Program Design: A Delicate Balance." Outdoor Ed [Online]. Available: www.outdoored.com/articles/Article.aspx?ArticleID=200.

Novelli, M. 2005. *Niche Tourism: Contemporary Issues, Trends and Cases*. Burlington, MA: Elsevier Butterworth-Heinemann.

O'Neal, M. 2001. *Service Quality Management in Hospitality, Tourism and Leisure: Measuring Service Quality and Customer Satisfaction*. New York: Haworth Hospitality Press.

O'Sullivan, M., and K.J. Spangler. 1998. *Experience Marketing: Strategies for the New Millennium*. State College, PA: Venture.

Ogilvie, F.W. 1932. "Tourist Traffic." In *Encyclopedia of the Social Sciences*. New York: Macmillan.

Ogilvie, F.W. 1933. *The Tourist Movement*. London: Staples Press.

Outdoor Foundation. 2005. "Active Outdoor Recreation Participation Study." Available, www.outdoorfoundation.org/research.participation.2005.html.

Outdoor Industry Association. 2007a. "Merchandising Know-How: What Do Your Customers Think of Your Store?" *SNews*, May 1.

Outdoor Industry Association. 2007b. "State of the Industry Report 2006."

Parasuraman, A., L. Berry, and V. Zeithaml. 1991. "Understanding Customer Expectations of Services." *Sloan Management Review*, 32:39-49.

Parker, S. 1999. *Leisure in Contemporary Society*. Wallingford: CAB International.

Peters, T. 1987. *Thriving on Chaos: A Handbook for a Management Revolution*. New York: Knopf.

Pfister, Robert E. 2001. "Mountain Culture as a Tourism Resouce: Aboriginal Views on the Privileges of Storytelling." In Godde, Price, Simmermann, (Eds.). *Tourism and Development Mountain Regions*. Wallingford, UK: CABI Publishing.

PhoCusWright. 2007. "The PhoCusWright Consumer Travel Trends Survey, Ninth Edition." Available: www.phocuswright.com/research_publications_buy_a_report/294.

Pinchot, G. 1985. *Why You Don't Have to Leave the Corporation to Become an Entrepreneur*. New York: Harper and Row.

Pine, B.J., and J.H. Gilmore. 1999. *The Experience Economy: Work Is Theatre and Every Business a Stage*. Boston: Harvard Business School Press.

Porter, M.E. 1998. *Competitive Strategy: Techniques for Analyzing Industries and Competitors*. New York: Free Press.

Powell, T. 1992. *Analyzing Your Competition: Its Management, Products, Industry and Markets*. New York: SVP Information Clearinghouse.

Price, L., E. Arnold, and P. Tierney. 1995. "Going to Extremes: Managing Service Encounters and Assessing Provider Performance." *Journal of Marketing*, April: 83-97.

Research and Markets. 2006. "Outbound Travel in the United States." Available: www.researchandmarkets.com/reports/356489.

Retail Owners Institute. 2007. "Sporting Goods Stores: Key Financial Benchmarks and Metrics for Store Owners." Available: www.retailowner.com/56RetailSegments/SportingGoodsStores/tabid/193/Default.aspx.

Ricks, F. 1996. "Principles for Structuring Cooperative Education Programs." *Journal of Cooperative Education and Internships*, 31(2): 8-22.

Roberts, K. 2004. *The Leisure Industries*. New York: Palgrave Macmillan.

Roscoe, T. 1841. "Thoughts on Various Subjects." In *The Works of Jonathan Swift* (Vol. I), p. 835. London: Clowes.

Rosenblum, D. 2008. "British Columbia Introduces Revenue-Neutral Carbon Tax." Available: www.carbontax.org/blogarchives/2008/02/20/british-columbia-introduces-revenue-neutral-carbon-tax.

Ryan, D.J., and G. Hiduke. 2003. *Small Business: An Entrepreneur's Business Plan*. Florence, KY: Cengage, Thompson Learning.

Sawyer, T., and O. Smith. 1999. *The Management of Clubs, Recreation and Sport: Concepts and Applications*. Champaign, IL: Sagamore.

Scott, J.T. 1998. *Fundamentals of Leisure Business Success*. New York: Haworth Press.

Segal, M. 2002. "How to Really Get Started in Business" [Video]. *Inc.* Magazine.

Semenik, R.J. 2002. *Promotion and Integrated Marketing Communications*. Cincinnati: South-Western.

Shinmachi, J. 2004. "Welcome Speech: JATA World Tourism Conference 2004." Available: www.jata-net.or.jp/english/news/2004/pdf/eng_Shinmachi.pdf.

Silverpop. 2006. "Email Marketing Strategy from Silverpop CEO Bill Nussey." Available: http://emailmarketing.silverpop.com.

Slater, R. 2003. *Jack Welch and the GE Way*. New York: McGraw-Hill.

Small Business Administration. 2005. "Are You Ready for Entrepreneurship?" Available: www.sba.gov//starting_business/planning.

Small Business Administration. 2005. "Business Plan Basics." Available: www.sba.gov//starting_business/planning.

Small Business Administration. 2006. "Common Mistakes of New Businesses." Available: www.sba.gov//starting_business/planning.

Small Business Administration. 2007. "Get Ready: Is Entrepreneurship for You?" Available: www.sba.gov/smallbusinessplanner/plan/getready/SERV_SBPLANNER_ISENTFORU.html.

Small Business Administration. 2007. "Small Businesses, Big Burdens: The Nature and Incidence of Crime Within and Against Small Business and Its Customers and Employees, Their Causes, Their Effects, and Their Prevention." Available: http://www.sba.gov/advo/research/rs176.pdf.

Spengler, J., D. Connaughton, and A. Pittman. 2006. *Risk Management in Sport and Recreation*. Champaign, IL: Human Kinetics.

Stankus, J. 2004. *How to Open and Operate a Bed and Breakfast*. Guilford, CT: Globe Pequot Press.

State of California, Department of Aging. 2007. "Aging in California: Impact of Baby Boomers." Available: www.aging.ca.gov/stats/impact_baby_boomers.asp.

Statistics Canada. 1997. "Failing Concerns: Business Bankruptcy in Canada." November. See http://www.statcan.ca/bsolc/english/bsolc?catno=61-525-XPE.

Sullivan, R., and A. Gouldson. 2007. "Pollutant Release and Transfer Registers: Examining the Value of Government-Led Reporting on Corporate Environmental Performance." *Journal of Corporate Responsibility and Environmental Management*, 14:263.

Taylor, M., and R. Taylor. 2004. *Start and Run a Bed and Breakfast* (3rd ed.). Bellingham, WA: International Self-Counsel Press.

Tierney, P., L. Price, and E. Arnold. 1994. "The Relationship of Interpretation to Ecotourism Trip Satisfaction and Attainment of National Park Service Objectives." Paper presented at Rivers Without Boundaries Symposium, May 1994, Grand Junction, CO.

Tierney, P.T. 1997. "California Division of Tourism: An Exploratory Study of the Users and Effectiveness of the CalTour World Wide Website." Unpublished report prepared for California Division of Tourism.

Tierney, P.T. 2000. "Internet-Based Evaluation of Tourism Web Site Effectiveness: Methodological Issues and Survey Results." *Journal of Travel Research*, 39:212-219.

Tierney, P.T. 2003. "Brochure Distribution Industry Characterization, Issues and Threats"; "Comparison of Effectiveness of Brochures Relative to Other Media." Presentations at the 2003 Association of Professional Brochure Distributors Conference, October 14, 2003, Limerick, Ireland.

Tofler, A. 1984. *Future Shock*. New York: Bantam.

Townley, J. 2007. "Outdoor Specialty Retailer Operational Report." Prepared for the Outdoor Industry Association. Available: www.outdoorindustry.org/research.php?action=detail&research_id=50.

Travel Industry Association of America. 2004. "TIA's Travel Forecast." Available: www.tia.org/ivis/MSISummary.asp.

U.S. Bureau of Labor Statistics. 2007. "Occupational Outlook: Arts, Entertainment and Recreation." Available: www.bls.gov/oco/cg/cgs031.htm.

U.S. Bureau of Labor Statistics. 2007. "Occupational Outlook: Meeting and Convention Planners." Available: www.bls.gov/oco/ocos298.htm#outlook.

U.S. Department of Commerce. Census Bureau. 2005. North Carolina, Economic Census for 2002: Arts, Entertainment, and Recreation. Report EC02-71A-NC.

Van Gorder, C. 2007. "Kids and Liability Risks: How Much of a Problem Does This Really Present?" Available: www.vglaw.com/html/or_kids_liability.shtml.

Van Gyn, G.H. 1996. "Reflective Practice: The Needs of Professions and the Promise of Cooperative Education." *Journal of Cooperative Education and Internships*, 31(2): 103-131.

Varma, H. 2007. "Welcome Message." Presentation at the First International Forum on Tourism Education in China, December 13, 2007, Guilin, China.

Walker, J.R. 2006. *Introduction to Hospitality* (4th ed.). Upper Saddle River, NJ: Pearson Prentice Hall.

Ward, S. 2006. "8 Sources of Business Start Up Money." Available: http://sbinfocanada.about.com/od/financing/a/startupmoney.htm.

Waters, S. 2007. "Open-to-Buy." Available: http://retail.about.com/od/glossary/g/opentobuy.htm.

Welch, J.F., with J.A. Byrne. 2001. *Jack: Straight From the Gut*. New York: Warner Books.

Western Economic Diversification Canada. 2005. "Growth Industries and Specially Defined Sectors." Available: www.wd.gc.ca/8218_ENG_ASP.asp.

Weston, S.A. 1996. *Commercial Recreation and Tourism: An Introduction to Business Oriented Recreation*. Dubuque, IA: Brown and Benchmark.

World Tourism Organization. 2003. "War in Iraq and SARS May Postpone Tourism Growth but Will Not Cause Collapse." *WTO News* [Online], 2nd qt, issue 2. Available: www.world-tourism.org.

World Travel and Tourism Council. 2007. "World Travel and Tourism Climbs to US $ 7 Trillion in 2007," Available: www.wttc.travel/eng/News_and_Events/Press/Press_Releases_2007/Global_TSA_2007_launch.

www.missionexpert.com/resources/Mission%20Statement%20Research%20Study.pdf.

Yate, M.J. 1987. *Hiring the Best: A Manager's Guide to Effective Interviewing*. Boston: Peregrine McCoy.

Zahorsky, D. 2007. "8 Reasons to Ditch Your Shoebox Accounting System." Available: http://sbinformation.about.com/od/accounting/a/accountingsys.htm.

Zemke, R., and K. Albrecht. 1990. *Service America*. Los Angeles: Warner.

Index

About the Authors

Robert E. Pfister, PhD, is a professor in the department of recreation and tourism management at Vancouver Island University in Nanaimo, British Columbia, Canada. For over 20 years, Pfister has instructed courses in entrepreneurial recreation and tourism to university students in the United States and Canada.

In 1979, Pfister created and managed a consulting business dedicated to recreation services and tourism, which served public agencies and private companies in Oregon, Washington, and British Columbia for 25 years.

Pfister is a member of the Association of American Geographers and served as chairperson of the Recreation, Tourism, and Sports specialty group from 2005 until 2007. He is a member of the Society of Park and Recreation Educators and the Canadian Council for Small Business and Entrepreneurship. He serves on the editorial board of *Tourism Geographies* and is a member of the board of directors for Tourism Vancouver Island, a regional tourism destination marketing organization.

In his free time, Pfister enjoys whitewater rafting, kayaking, recreational boating, mountaineering, and alpine photography.

Patrick T. Tierney, PhD, is a professor in the department of recreation, parks, and tourism at San Francisco State University. As a business owner, instructor, and researcher, Tierney has more than 30 years of experience in theories and applications of the recreation, event, and tourism industry.

For 25 years, Tierney was co-owner and operator of Adrift Adventures, Inc., a successful adventure recreation business nominated for the Condé Nast International Ecotourism Award. Tierney is past chairperson of the Colorado River Outfitters Association and a member of the board of directors of the California Tourism Industry Association. He is a licensed whitewater guide instructor and former U.S. Forest Service and National Park Service ranger.

In 1997, Tierney was co-recipient of the Best Tourism Research Award from the California Division of Tourism. He was also the recipient of the 1991 Excellence in Research Award from the Resort and Commercial Recreation Association.

Tierney resides in Half Moon Bay, California, and enjoys ocean and river kayaking, Telemark skiing, and mountain biking.

*You'll find
other outstanding
recreation resources at*

www.HumanKinetics.com

In the U.S. call

1-800-747-4457

Australia..08 8372 0999
Canada 1-800-465-7301
Europe..+44 (0) 113 255 5665
New Zealand......................................0064 9 448 1207

HUMAN KINETICS
The Information Leader in Physical Activity
P.O. Box 5076 • Champaign, IL 61825-5076 USA